Investigating Play in the 21st Century

Edited by
Dorothy Justus Sluss
Olga S. Jarrett

PLAY & CULTURE STUDIES, Volume 7

UNIVERSITY PRESS OF AMERICA,® INC.
Lanham • Boulder • New York • Toronto • Plymouth, UK

4501 Forbes Boulevard
Suite 200
Lanham, Maryland 20706
UPA Acquisitions Department (301) 459-3366

Estover Road
Plymouth PL6 7PY
United Kingdom

Printed in the United States of America
British Library Cataloging in Publication Information Available

Library of Congress Control Number: 2007923060
ISBN-13: 978-0-7618-3640-7 (paperback : alk. ppr.)
ISBN-10: 0-7618-3640-3 (paperback : alk. ppr.)

∞™ The paper used in this publication meets the minimum requirements of American National Standard for Information Sciences—Permanence of Paper for Printed Library Materials, ANSI Z39.48—1984

Recent Titles in Play & Culture Studies

Stuart Reifel, Jaipaul L. Roopnarine, and James Johnson, Series Editors

Volume 1: Diversions and Divergences in Fields of Play
Margaret Carlisle Duncan, Garry Chick, and Alan Aycock, editors

Volume 2: Play Contexts Revisited
Stuart Reifel, editor

Volume 3: Theory in Context and Out
Stuart Reifel, editor

Volume 4: Conceptual, Social-Cognitive, and Contextual Issues in the Fields of Play
Jaipaul L. Roopnarine, editor

Volume 5: Play and Educational Theory and Practice
Donald E. Lytle, editor

Volume 6: Play: An Interdisciplinary Synthesis
F.F. McMahon, Donald E. Lytle, and Brian Sutton-Smith, editors

Special thanks to two families who were instrumental
in supporting this endeavor.

Husbands,

Roger and Bob

Children and grandchildren:

Jim, Amy, and Madeline

and

Andy, Chris, and Erik

And for patience throughout the process,

Special thanks to all TASP members.

Contents

Foreword xi

Introduction xiii

Acknowledgements xvii

I. CONCEPTUALIZING PLAY

1 Genesis and Evolution of American Play and Playgrounds 3
Joe L. Frost

2 The Promise of Sociology for Play Studies 32
Thomas Henricks

3 Children's Play in the Journal, Young Children: An Analysis of How it is Portrayed and Why it is Valued 55
David Kuschner

II. COMPARATIVE AND CROSS-CULTURAL RESEARCH

4 Playful Companions for Motherless Monkeys 73
Peggy O'Neill-Wagner

5 What Young Children Say About Play at School: United States and Australian Comparisons 88
Sue Dockett and Alice Meckley

6 Teachers' and Parents' Attitudes About Play and Learning in Taiwanese Kindergartens 114
James E. Johnson and Pei-Yu Chang

7 Playfulness Among Swedish and Japanese Children: A Comparative Study 135
Satomi Taylor, Cosby Steele Rogers, Tetsuya Ogawa, Ingrid Promling Samuelsson, Anita VanBrackle and Arleen Dodd

8 Playgrounds and Children's Play Supply in 14 Districts of Northeastern Portugal 147
Beatriz Pereira, Paula Malta, and Hugo Laranjerio

9 Playground Safety in Brazil 162
Francis Wardle

III. PLAYFULNESS, CREATIVITY, AND SCIENCE

10 Play and Creativity: The Role of the Intersubjective Adult 175
Deborah W. Tegano and James D. Moran III

11 The Role of Fun, Playfulness, and Creativity in Science: Lessons from Geoscientists 188
Olga S. Jarrett and Pamela Burnley

IV PLAY, COMMUNICATION, AND LITERACY

12 Storybook Time and Free Play: Playing with Books 205
Laurelle Phillips

13 Effects of Environmental Print Games and Play Props on Young Children's Print Recognition 220
James Christie, Billie Enz, Myae Han, Jennifer Pryor, Maureen Gerard

14 Communicative Actions and Language Narratives in Preschoolers' Play with "Talking" and "Non-talking" Rescue Heroes 229
Doris Bergen

V. PLAY ACROSS SPACE AND TIME

15 Toy Libraries, Play, and Play Materials 249
Margie I. Mayfield

16 "Hey, no fair:" Young Children's Perceptions of Cheating During Play 259
Robyn M. Holmes, Jennifer M. Valentino-McCarthy, Susan L. Schmidt

17 Clinical Approaches to Achieving Positive Environments with Suicidal Aboriginal Adolescents: Play and Culturally Sensitive Considerations 277
Melanie S. MacNeil

18 Role-Play on Parade: Child, Costume, and Ceremonial Exchange at Halloween 289
Cindy Dell Clark

Epilogue 307

Index 315

About the Contributors 319

Foreword

James Johnson
Series Editor

With this seventh volume of *Play & Culture Studies* I am privileged to begin my stint as series editor and am pleased to serve The Association for the Study of Play in this capacity. *Play & Cultural Studies* as a publication mirrors The Association for the Study of Play as a professional organization—each seeks to advance play theory and research to a higher level, appreciating the richness and complexities of play for its own sake, as well as for its importance in the study of culture and human development and welfare. Turning to the pages that follow in the present volume, I salute the co-editors and the contributing authors for their fine work in making *Investigating Play in the 21st Century* possible, and I hope that you enjoy and benefit from reading the volume as much as I did.

Introduction

Dorothy Sluss and Olga Jarrett

The seventh volume of the *Play & Culture Studies* series follows the tradition of the previous six volumes to promote the mission of The Association for the Study of Play (TASP), a professional group of researchers who study play, to advance knowledge about play and culture. This book adds to this body of knowledge in that it considers the intersection of play and culture at the cusp of the twentieth-first century from a variety of different perspectives that include anthropology, biology, psychology, history, education, sociology, and leisure studies. The contents are at once significant and varied across time and space. As in past volumes, this book includes many papers that were presented at the annual conference of The Association for the Study of Play, as well as additional papers submitted independently of the conference. This compilation of peer-reviewed papers provides a volume that will extend our knowledge of play and culture.

OVERVIEW OF BOOK

The book is divided into five sections plus an epilogue. The first section, Conceptualizing Play, includes three papers that examine different perspectives on play in the twentieth and twenty-first century. In the first chapter, "Genesis and Evolution of American Play and Playgrounds," Joe L. Frost, who is considered the father of the contemporary playground movement, examines the changes in play and play scholarship during the twentieth century and beginning of the twenty-first century. Starting with the beginning of the playground movement and culminating in current challenges, this chapter identifies many changes and issues discussed in later chapters. The next chapter, "The Promise of Sociology for Play Studies" by Tom Henricks, examines how play is interpreted through the lens of four theoretical perspectives in sociology. David Kuschner's paper, "Children's Play in the Journal, *Young Children*: An Analysis of How it is Portrayed and Why it is Valued," moves the reader from theoretical considerations to a scholarly study. His investigation into the depiction of play in a leading early childhood journal gives insights into changes in play concerns and practice from 1973 to 2005.

The second section, Comparative and Cross-Cultural Research, includes a variety of studies. Peggy O'Neill-Wagner's study, "Playful Companions for Motherless Monkeys," begins the section with a study of monkey play with other species, including dogs, horses, and sheep, in a therapeutic environment. The next three chapters examine children's play in various cultural settings. Sue Dockett and Alice Meckley share their research in "What Young Children Say About Play at School: United States and Australian Comparisons." Drawing from kindergarteners' conversations in focus groups, they identified areas of similarities and differences in children's views of school play in the two countries. Next, in "Teachers' and Parents' Attitudes About Play and Learning in Taiwanese Kindergartens," Jim Johnson and Pei-Yu Chang surveyed teachers on their beliefs about play and also examined the beliefs of parents of children in two different types of kindergartens. They found variation between views of teachers and parents and between parents in the two kindergartens. In a cross-cultural study, "Playfulness Among Swedish and Japanese children: A Comparative Study," Satomi Taylor, Cosby Rogers, and their research team analyzed preschool and kindergarten teacher ratings on child playfulness in the two cultures. The last two chapters in this section concern playground availability and playground safety. In "Playgrounds and Children's Play Supply in 14 Districts in the Northeast of Portugal," Beatriz Pereira and her colleagues studied the numbers, types, and maintenance of playgrounds in specific districts of Portugal. "Playground Safety in Brazil" by Francis Wardle examines the safety of playgrounds in three Brazilian states as well as the Federal District of Brasilia. Although these two chapters study very specific regions, they have implications for studying playgrounds and safety needs around the world.

The third section considers the interface among Playfulness, Creativity, and Science with two papers. In "Play and Creativity: The Role of the Intersubjective Adult," Deb Tegano and Jim Moran discuss how adult playfulness and creativity can help teachers share the meaning of play with children. Studying a very different population in "The Role of Fun, Playfulness, and Creativity: Lessons from Geoscientists," Olga Jarrett and Pamela Burnley examine childhood play and exploration experiences of geologists and investigate how the geologists see play in the process of scientific investigation.

The fourth theme of the book considers the popular topic of Play, Communication, and Literacy with three papers considering different ways that early childhood play helps prepare children for reading. Laurelle Phillips' study of "Storybook Time and Free Play: Playing with Books," investigates how two-year-olds play with books in early childcare centers. The study of play and literacy is extended to preschool, pre-kindergarten, and kindergarten children in "Effects of Environmental Print Games and Play Props on Young Children's Print Recognition." In this study, James Christie and his research team examine the effect of incorporating play experiences, puzzles, and games with environmental print (from advertisements and logos) on children's print recognition. Examining another aspect of emerging literacy, the final chapter of the section, "Communicative Actions and Language Narratives in Preschoolers' Play with 'Talking' and 'Non-talking' Rescue Heroes" by Doris Bergen studies communicative actions and language narratives used by preschoolers while playing with technology-enhanced toy figures.

The final theme of the book reflects the diversity of play research that occurs in the organization. Entitled Play Across Space and Time, this section begins with a study by Margie Mayfield, "Toy Libraries, Play, and Play Materials," in which she considers the evolution, role, and services involved in toy lending libraries in a variety of countries. From toys and materials, the topic moves to the development of morality among kindergarteners in a study, " 'Hey, no fair:' Young Children's Perceptions of Cheating During Play." Observations of children playing games and informal interviews with children and teachers are used to explore issues of honesty and fairness. Looking at playfulness in a different way, Melanie MacNeil examines the use of storytelling, playful conversations, and culturally relevant experiences in counseling situations in "Clinical Approaches for Achieving Positive Environments with Suicidal Aboriginal Adolescents: Culturally Sensitive Considerations." Finally, the chapter by Cindy Dell Clark, "Role Play on Parade: Child, Costume, and Ceremonial Exchange at Halloween," examines the ritual role-play that is part of trick-or-treat as a way in which children explore power and issues of who they are becoming.

In the Epilogue, "Contextualizing Play Investigations in the 21st Century," one of the editors considers all the chapters in terms of Sutton-Smith's rhetorics of play and then discusses the dominant themes. Altogether, the papers in this book add to the knowledge base by both answering questions and providing additional questions for study.

Acknowledgments

This book maintains and extends the tradition of excellence found in the other volumes and would not have been possible without the assistance of many dedicated individuals. First, we wish to acknowledge the work of the series editor, Jim Johnson, without whom this volume would not have been possible. Second, special thanks to the contributors who dealt with the delays experienced in bringing this book to publication. Third, we wish to express our sincere thanks to reviewers who provided thoughtful and timely reviews:

Doris Bergen	Miami University of Ohio
Sarah Bexell	Georgia State University
Jim Christie	Arizona State University
Rhonda Clements	Manhattanville College
Margaret Clyde	Consultant in Melbourne, Australia
Sue Dockett	University of Western Sydney
Arleen Dodd	K.W. Post, Long Island, NY
Margaret Carlisle Duncan	University of Wisconsin-Milwaukee
David Kushner	University of Cincinnati
Sue Knox	Therapy in Action, Tarzana, CA
Alice Meckley	Millersville University
Laurelle Phillips	East Tennessee State University
Cosby Steele Rogers	Virginia Tech
John Sutterby	University of Texas at Brownsville
Deborah Teganno	University of Tennessee, Knoxville

Also thanks to the following students in a doctoral seminar at Georgia State University, who wrote additional reviews that were thoughtful and helpful: Frances LeAnna Bryant, Mizrap Bulunuz, Nermin Bulunuz, Andrea Johnson,

Andrea Kiel, Brian Lack, Armandina Macias-Brown, Jill Mainzer, and Gwen Stanley.

Finally, the editors give special thanks to Olga's husband, Bob Jarrett, who painstakingly did a time-consuming first edit of all the chapters. With an eye for clarity as well as typos and extra spaces in the text, his editing saved us considerable time and effort.

Part I

CONCEPTUALIZING PLAY

Chapter One

Genesis and Evolution of American Play and Playgrounds

Joe L. Frost

In the beginning there was play, and its evolution can be traced through the history of civilizations. The existence of play and play materials are found in excavations of ancient ruins throughout the world, notably in ancient Babylonia, Egypt, and many locations in Asia and South America. Traces of play in toys, tops, dolls, sculpture and artistic creations speak to the existence and nature of play and reveal occupations and pastimes such as hunting, fishing, war, festivals and general merriment.

European thinkers produced the richest history and most elaborate action for understanding and facilitating play. Beginning in ancient Greece with Plato and Aristotle and continuing during the Reformation, noted philosophers and educators extolled the value of play, physical exercise, festivals, gymnastics, sports, and games but produced only limited understanding of play's meaning and functions (Mitchell & Mason, 1941). During the fifteenth through the eighteenth centuries, a number of visionary thinkers recognized the educational value of children's play and games, and some expanded thought into action for understanding and providing for children's play activities. Among the noted thinkers credited for such attention are Luther, Rabelias, Comenius, Locke, Rousseau, Basedow, Pestalozzi, and Froebel.

EARLY AMERICAN PLAY AND PLAYGROUNDS

Stoyan Vasil Tsanoff (1897) claims to have written the first book on American playgrounds. In his book, *Educational value of the children's playgrounds*, he wrote:

> . . . the literature devoted to the playgrounds idea, consisting almost exclusively of some articles in the periodical reviews and the daily papers, has treated them

> from a rather one-sided point of view . . . No books seem to have been written on playgrounds, no organized efforts made to regulate them, even words proper to discuss them are lacking . . . Not only playgrounds in particular, but the children's plays in general, seem to have been quite neglected (Tsanoff 1897, p. 1).

Tsanoff (1897) followed the pattern of European educational reformers who rebelled against rote "disciplinary practices" of the school when he called for the inclusion of play in the educative process and for the education of the whole child:

> It does seem to be like instead of giving fresh air to a fainting person, we give him lectures on fresh air; or instead of giving food to the hungry, we give him lectures or instruction on what food is, and how much good it can do him . . . Unless they turn attention . . . out of the library, out of the workshop, out of the book, chalk, pen and ink; unless they turn attention toward the impressions, lessons, examples, amusements, influences, enjoyments, play, and all-around environment of the child . . . they will be doing but half educational work. (p. 115)

Provisions for organized play and playgrounds followed two separate but related paths in the United States. One path drew from the physical fitness traditions of Germany and the German system of gymnastics founded in Berlin by Friedrich Ludwig Jahn in 1810 (Weir, 1937), and the other, to be discussed later, was rooted in the philosophy and practices of noted educational reformers and philosophers such as Rousseau, Pestallozi, and Froebel (Frost, 1992).

In Germany, Jahn established physical activities in the countryside including a wide range of athletics—running, jumping, and climbing—and set up exercise apparatus for gymnastics including parallel bars, vaulting bucks, jumping ditches, running tracks, balance beams, and horizontal bars. Jahn's program was heavily imbued with political, health-related, and moral objectives (Weir, 1937). His American disciples founded a number of gymnasiums in Massachusetts during the 1820s and 1830s (Cavallo, 1881). Guts Muth, a contemporary of Jahn's, objected to Jahn's system because many of his exercises were too heavy for school children, there was little provision for girls, and the prescribed activities did not allow for free exercises. Muth's work influenced the earliest playgrounds in both Europe and the United States (Bowen & Mitchell, 1930).

The introduction of the German-inspired "sandgardens" in Boston in 1887 is generally considered to be the beginning of early nineteenth century play movement in the United States, but the "outdoor gymnasia" were introduced in America more than a half-century before the sandgardens. Muths authored the first manual of physical education, *Gymnastics for youth*, which became the basis of future methodological approaches to educational gymnastics and physical education (Muths, 1793). He introduced outdoor play and exercise training in Schnepfenthal during the first decade of the nineteenth century (Bowen & Mitchell, 1930). The earliest equipment on these German "outdoor gymnasia" was gymnastics equipment transported to the out-of-doors. Muths was an avid reader of Greek and Latin writers who dealt with bodily activities of exercise, games, and sports and he followed in the footsteps of Rousseau and Basedow in promoting natural or harmonious physical and mental education. His classic book, *Gymnastics for youth,* focused on gymnastic exercises and sports, but his practical applications coordinated various aspects of human development: physical development, development of the senses, health education, moral development, nature study, and music and art appreciation.

Muths' concerns about the educational focus of his period on intellectualizing youth at the expense of promoting their physical health through outdoor exercise play, games, proper diet and harmonizing all aspects of human development is disquietingly similar to present-day concerns about the effects of academic regimentation, standardization, high-stakes testing, excessive sedentary activity, and childhood obesity. He looked to other prominent philosophers such as Rousseau for support, quoting Rousseau's dictum on the importance of the effects of physical activity on the development of mental powers (Muths, 1793, English translation 1803, p. 22). However, Muths' emphasis on physical education through gymnastics-type activities proved to be his enduring legacy, and free or spontaneous play and play for girls and young children continued to be largely ignored until the twentieth century. The outdoor gymnasia, credited in part to him, tended to fix the pattern for outdoor playgrounds until the introduction of the sandgardens and the rise of early kindergartens and child development research centers.

The earliest records available show that a crude outdoor gymnasium was started in 1821 at the Latin School in Salem, Massachusetts without supervisor or instructor (Mero, 1908). Two events indicate that this outdoor gymnasium had German roots: first, the chronological proximity of the development of the German and the American sites, and second, the establishment of an outdoor site at the Round Hill School in Northampton, Massachusetts in 1825 using German-type apparatus and supervised by Dr. Charles Beck, a former student of Jahn in Germany (Mero, 1908; Frost, 1992). The developing gymnastics system in America was later influenced by the Swedish system of gymnastics (Sapora & Mitchell, 1948).

Although the first formal American playgrounds were influenced by German practices, the games, sports, and social activities of England and other European countries influenced the formation of various interest groups that were eventually responsible for the growth of the early nineteenth century play movement in America (Sapora & Mitchell, 1948). These forces would not only stimulate participation in a wide range of recreational activities, but they would also influence the development of playgrounds, the training of play leaders, and establish public and private groups to develop and operate recreational programs. Despite Rousseau's teaching about the value of play for mental, physical, and moral development, the early outdoor gymnasia emphasized only physical play and training. The physical fitness tradition of European countries has influenced American playgrounds, particularly public park and school playgrounds, to the present time.

THE SANDGARDENS

During a visit to Berlin, Dr. Marie Zakrzewska was impressed by seeing little children playing in piles of sand placed in city parks. Her letter about the "sandgardens" to the chairman of the Massachusetts Emergency and Hygiene Association led to the placing of three piles of sand in the yards of the Children's Mission on Parmenter Street in 1886. Their success led to the establishment of sandgardens in several other cities. The establishment of the sandgardens is considered by many to be the beginning of the early nineteenth century play movement in America, but in reality, this only marked the beginning of the play movement for young children, many older children having had access to outdoor playgrounds equipped with exercise apparatus for more than a half century.

Interest in sand play was enhanced by the testimonials and studies of noted professionals such as G. Stanley Hall who wrote a delightful little book called *The sand pile* (Hall, 1897). This book told the story of Harry and Jack playing in a sand pile dumped in their back yard by their parents. As Froebel would have expected, this sand pile at once became a major focus of play for the boys, such that "all other boyish interests gradually paled" (p. 3). The developing sand community of hills, roads, bridges, ponds, tunnels, and wells was the subject of intense representational play, which Hall described as industrial training, mercantile pursuits, law enforcement, topological imagination, and valuable civic training. The sand pile drew other boys from the community who were quite alive in fictitious activity up until age 15 when interest began to pale. The parents were of the opinion that the benefits of the sand pile were "about of much yearly value to the boys as eight months of school" (p. 18).

Following the introduction of sandgardens in Boston and other cities, sand was gradually incorporated into public playgrounds throughout the United States. Initially the existing "physical fitness" playgrounds or "outdoor gymnasia" were reserved for older boys, leaving limited provisions for young children and girls. With the establishment of sandgardens, play providers saw older children wistfully observing the play of little children in the sand piles. Eventually sand would become a common fixture on playgrounds. Sand play has endured to the present time in early childhood centers as one of the most developmentally valuable forms of children's activity.

THE AMERICAN PLAY MOVEMENT: 1880–1920

During the late 1800s and early 1900s, there was much concern about children playing in hazardous streets and the need to reduce juvenile crime and delinquency. The passage of child labor laws and reduced working hours of adults increased the frequency of vacations and influenced the call for more public provision for play and recreation (Sapora & Mitchell, 1948; Cavallo, 1981). A number of educational reformers—Henry Curtis (1913, 1925) Luther Gulick (1920), Joseph Lee (1915), Jane Addams (1911)—were leading reformers in the early play movement, calling for organized playgrounds to keep children off the streets and provide wholesome environments.

The first free playground with physical development equipment and supervision for both "men and boys" (older and younger boys) was opened in Charlesbank, Massachusetts in 1889, and the Columbus Avenue playground for both younger and older children was opened in Boston in 1900. By 1909, Massachusetts law required towns of 10,000 to establish public playgrounds (Playground and Recreation Association of America, 1909:10; Mero, 1908:242), and cities around the country had established municipal playgrounds. By the turn of the twentieth century, the American play and playground movement was vibrant and expanding. By 1906 there were fewer than 20 cities with playgrounds, some unsupervised, but by 1923 more than 240 cities had playgrounds with paid workers (Curtis, 1925).

As cities rapidly joined the movement to establish playgrounds, a fledging manufacturing industry emerged to meet the growing need for playground equipment. Advertising their products in *The Playground* and other publications, manufacturers provided an ever-growing array of jungle-gyms, see-saws, slides, merry-go-rounds, giant strides, swings and other massive steel structures. These structures were designed for physical activity with little attention devoted to mental, social, and emotional benefits of play. Many of these early structures remained on playgrounds until the publication of playground safety guidelines by the Consumer Product Safety Commission and playground safety standards by the American Society for Testing and Materials. By 1913 play reformers such as Henry Curtis were warning that most playgrounds were hopelessly inadequate for play and extremely hazardous (Curtis, 1913:26–27).

THE PLAY MOVEMENT AND PROFESSIONAL ORGANIZATIONS

The Playground Association of America (PAA) was formed in 1907 with Luther Gulick as president and Joseph Lee, Jane Addams, Henry Curtis, and Seth Stewart as officers. Stewart was responsible for publishing the PAA monthly periodical *The Playground.* The PAA became perhaps the most influential factor in raising the consciousness of the American public about the need and value of organized playgrounds for children of all ages. By this time, many active play proponents had expanded the functions of play and playgrounds well beyond the physical fitness motive to include idealistic views of cleanliness, politeness, formation of friendships, obedience to law, loyalty, justice, honesty, truthfulness, and determination.

By 1910 as many as 50 letters a day were arriving at the Play Association of America offices requesting assistance in developing playgrounds. Its leaders decided that the term "playground," connoting children's play, was too narrow to represent broader recreational needs. Consequently, the PAA constitution was changed, the title was changed to the Playground and Recreation Association of America (PRAA) and the journal was re-titled *Recreation.* The aims and functions of the association were changed to include a wide range of social work, recreation, and civic affairs. The field of play would not begin to regain its momentum in the organization for almost a century. Despite war, depression, and declining revenues, the PRAA managed to shift the focus in America from informal "play" to public "recreation." By 1930, even by PRAA definitions, less than one fifth of American school age children had access to playgrounds (Knapp & Hartsoe, 1979).

During the Great Depression, the PRAA took steps toward an even broader conception of recreation, removing the "restrictive" name "playground" from the title of the association and making its title, the National Recreation Association (NRA). The association's programs were further expanded to include performing arts, training institutes, consulting, research, site visits, the ill and handicapped, public information, and publications. Despite this expanded scope of services and interests, some still thought the focus was too narrow. The editor of *Youth Digest,* for example, claimed that the NRA was still a playground association! "Thus, another nail was driven into the coffin of children's play" (Frost, 1992).

Limited resources and a broadening focus on services led the NRA and several other organizations to merge as the National Recreation and Park Association in 1966. Since its founding, the NRPA has made substantial contributions to the broad field of recreation, but their emphasis on the broad developmental needs and benefits of children's play has been negligible. The notable exception is their focus on playground safety beginning in the 1970s when they contracted with the U.S. consumer Product Safety Commission (CPSC) to develop the first draft of a playground safety standard and later sponsored playground safety publications, workshops, and the National Playground Safety Institute certification program. The NRPA is now directing attention to the developmental play needs of children. For example, the organization joined other organizations in commissioning a Stanford University Prevention Research Center report (Stanford, 2007) citing extensive evidence that science has sufficiently demonstrated the positive effects of physical activity in preventing obesity and promoting health.

A number of major professional organizations, some devoted exclusively to play and others valuing play as fundamental to children's development and education, promoted children's spontaneous play from their beginnings to the present time. The oldest of these organizations, the Association for Childhood Education International, with roots in the American Froebel Union, was established in 1878 by Elizabeth Peabody and reorganized in 1882 as the Froebel Institute of North America. In 1884, this group organized the Kindergarten Department of the National Education Association and in 1885 the Froebel Institute was formally merged with the new Kindergarten Department to form the International Kindergarten Union (IKU) (Weber, 1969). By 1918 the IKU had 132 branches with 18,000 members and was the third largest educational body in the world. By 1930 the IKU and the National Council of Primary Education had merged to form the Association for Childhood Education, later the Association for Childhood Education International (ACEI), which continues to the present time.

There were heated debates in the national IKU meetings about the use of symbolism, free play, teacher direction, and creative activity. The major dissension was between those supporting the kindergarten gifts and occupations of Friedrich Froebel focusing on his "conservative" imitative play and those supporting the "progressive" or "liberal" self-active play of John Dewey. On the Froebel side were such educational giants as Susan Blow and Elizabeth Harrison and on the Dewey side were Patty Smith Hill and Alice Putnam. A Committee of Nineteen was charged with preparing a clear statement to the IKU to stem the tide of dissension. Their report was published in book form (Committee of Nineteen, 1913, 1924). Although disagreements remained, the progressive approach of aligning kindergarten practices with "scientific thinking" of Dewey, Thorndike and other prominent educators found its way into kindergarten practice. The overall result was a curriculum for America's young children stressing creative activities, spontaneity, self-expression, individual initiative, and constructive and imaginative play and the creative arts. This rich tradition has been upheld to the present time in most American kindergartens and preschools and has been influential in preserving free play and other creative values and activities in child development centers, nursery schools, preschools, and kindergartens to the present time.

In 1925, Patty Smith Hill invited 25 selected professionals to Columbia University. This group formed the National Committee on Nursery Schools in 1926, which in 1929 became the National Association for Nursery Education and was later renamed the National Association for the Education of Young Children (NAEYC). From its inception, this organization has been a champion of children's play, focusing on its broad physical, mental, social, and emotional values and its values for the educative process. Both ACEI and NAEYC continue to champion the broad developmental value of children's play and to resist philosophies and practices that militate against its central role in the development and education of young children.

In 1961, the International Association for the Child's Right to Play, now the International Play Association: Promoting the Child's Right to Play (IPA) was formed in Denmark. More than forty nations, including the United States, became affiliates. The IPA and the American Association of IPA have the primary aim of advocating and protecting the child's right to play. The American IPA produces a quarterly newsletter, disseminates information, supports a national play day, holds seminars, hosts a national conference every three years and supports the IPA triennial world conference.

The Association for the Anthropological Study of Play, which became The Association for the Study of Play (TASP) in 1987, was visualized at a meeting of play scholars in Minneapolis, Minnesota in 1973 and held its first meeting in London, Ontario in 1974. TASP is a multidisciplinary organization whose purpose is to promote the study of play, to cooperate with other organizations, and to organize meetings and publications that facilitate the study of play. The broad scholarly interests of members, including anthropology, education, psychology, sociology, recreation and leisure studies, history, folklore, dance, communication, the arts, kinesiology, philosophy, cultural studies, and musicology make this the premier organization for play researchers and those seeking research on multiple aspects of play. As we will discuss later, such broad interests and expertise are sorely needed to bring logic and reason to bear on factors currently interfering with children's play, e.g., deletion of recess, childhood obesity, disappearance of traditional play, high-stakes testing, and standardization of playgrounds.

THE DEVELOPMENTAL PLAYGROUND: KINDERGARTENS AND NURSERY SCHOOLS

In addition to the influence of professional organizations, a powerful scientific movement focusing on the child development point of view emerged and spread during the 1920s and 1930s. This movement exerted significant influence on the educational philosophy and practice of early childhood educators. Much of the university-based research during this period was centered in child research centers supported by the Laura Spelman Rockefeller Memorial Fund, which was administered by Lawrence Frank. Frank argued that the tendency of professionals to standardize and substitute academic training for study and insight into children and their needs must be reexamined (Frank, 1938; 1962). During this intense period of scientific child study, many periodicals and books emerged to support the child development point of view that substituted developmentally relevant views and practices over standardized, regimented prescriptions. The research contributions of university child research centers, seen in such periodicals at *Child Development* and the *Merrill-Palmer Quarterly,* coupled with the work and publications of the early childhood and child development professional organizations, have preserved play, nature study, and the creative arts in programs for young children. Unfortunately, current policies established and enforced by politicians and law have placed these fundamental developmental needs at risk for children of school age.

During this same period, some were following the ideals of such giants as Rousseau, Pestallozi, and Froebel and expanding the functions of play to include developmental and educational ends. Luella Palmer, assistant director of kindergartens in New York City, wrote that play develops bodily organs, develops keen and quick thoughts, widens mental horizons, and promotes social development (Palmer, 1916). Attitudes toward play were changing as religious convictions against play dating back to colonial days and ignorance of child development gave way to a growing conviction that play was essential for child development (Lehman & Witty1926; Lee 1927; Lloyd 1931; Frost, 1992). However, such progressive thinking was essentially restricted to play and playgrounds for very young children in nursery schools and kindergartens, while municipal parks and public schools continued to focus primarily on the physical benefits of play. Thus, two patterns of practice emerged that continue in large degree to the present time: a broad developmental emphasis on preschool playgrounds rooted in Frobelian principles, child development research, IKU, ACEI, and NAEYC, and a physical fitness emphasis for school and public park playgrounds rooted in the German fitness tradition and the work of the PAA, PRAA, NRA, and NRPA.

RURAL AND URBAN PLAY AND PLAYGROUNDS

The state of play during the first half of the twentieth century was a study in contrasts. Orphan, delinquent, immigrant and abused children roamed the streets of America's large cities and were shipped by train loads to adoptive homes throughout the West to start new lives in rural areas (Fry, 1994; Warren, 1996). Others endured slave-labor conditions, working long hours in dangerous factories and coal mines (Bartoletti, 1996). Children of the Great Depression (Wormser, 1994), two world wars (Tuttle, 1993), and migrants moving to work in the crops (Coles, 1970) managed to play despite circumstances. They found ways to play at work, during brief breaks, at night and during brief holidays and weekends. Children in factories would deliberately jam machines so they would have relief from work to play. They would play tricks on adult supervisors to keep them out of sight while they played, and some would manage to bring joy to their work. The children caring for the mules and other animals used in coal mining and farming would "adopt" them, heap lavish attention on them, share their food treats, and form strong bonds.

Depression-era children, orphan train children and others fortunate enough to be in supportive, intact families and make meaningful contributions to their livelihood took pride in their work and later spoke of the contributions of work to their later success. Having few purchased toys, children of this era were ingenious in creating playthings from scrap or natural materials and in seizing on traditional games and creating games for pleasure and socialization with friends. Even those children living under brutal circumstances who managed to survive kept the play spirit alive and reaped its social and therapeutic benefits. Ironically, the paucity of leisure time and the absence of technological playthings that are so common to today's children appear to have yielded benefits for health, character, and work ethic.

The compelling story of the Weedpatch School for children of migrant workers in California reveals how meaningful work coupled with adult and community support can take on the joyful, rewarding qualities of play. Starting with ten acres of land and two condemned buildings leased for ten dollars, two men, one a friend of John Steinbeck (*Grapes of Wrath),* scrounged, donated, and begged for building materials and supplies. The teachers they recruited and children from the "Okie Camp" pitched in to make the school reality. School and work became one as the children learned carpentry, gardening, and animal care skills to create their own facilities, food and income—all while many continued to spend long hours in the field. The children attended classes, did homework, took tests and engaged in practical training in mechanics, plumbing, carpentry, sewing, cooking, cobbling, animal care, and canning fruits and vegetables. They also built their own outdoor play areas and a pool for swimming, went fishing, and took field trips to fairs and other events.

Such a mix of productive activity could not have taken place without strong adult leadership and community support. One child later said this about Weedpatch School: "The teachers make us feel important and like someone really cared. The school gave us pride and dignity and honor when we didn't have those things. It was our school. It did a great deal to cause us to believe we were special" (Stanley, 1992, p. 69). When these same children had gone to regular schools, most of the teachers ignored them, believing that "Okie kids" were too stupid to learn the alphabet, too dumb to master math, and too "retarded" to learn much of anything. Such stories as these, repeated many times over in the history of distressing eras, give first-hand, historical support for the views of such intellectual giants as Rousseau, Pestallozi, Froebel, Hall, Dewey and countless later specialists in child development regarding the need for an integrated view of education and development that focuses not merely on structured academics, but also involves children in nature, the practical arts, real-life problem solving, and play.

The more fortunate children in cities attended schools and enjoyed the benefits of the play and playgrounds movement resulting in the development of thousands of municipal park and school recreational and play opportunities and equipment. Children in rural areas were hardly affected by the playground movement, but they had ample opportunities to play and work on farms, in gardens, natural wilderness areas and with farm animals. Schools during that period provided ample recess time. The author of this paper, growing up during the depression years in the Ouachita Mountains of Arkansas, played outdoors at school in the early morning while the school bus made a second run to another community, then played during morning, noon, and afternoon recesses, and again after school while the school bus made a run before returning to school to take the children from his community home.

The playgrounds at rural schools were typically areas cleared of trees and brush, often with forests and creeks nearby, and sometimes with hand-made swings, see-saws and other apparatus, but frequently with no equipment at all except that created by the children. Children of all ages played together. Boys favored traditional games of marbles, tops, chase, and kick-the-can, while girls chose Annie over, hop scotch, jacks, and jump rope. Girls and boys played some games together for relatively brief periods. Children created an endless array of improvised games of war, cowboys and Indians, wrestling, building forts, and sand, dirt and water play, and games with knives that most every boy carried for both work and play. They made their baseballs from string and tape wrapped around a jacks ball and played shinney (similar to hockey) with tree limbs and tin cans. The tree-covered hillsides and creeks near the school became the venues for games and for building dams, catching tadpoles, and securing material for forts. Teachers generally remained indoors during recess, only venturing out when a child was injured and to observe or stop fights. Virtually all the country children had before—and after-school farm chores and work during the summer. Many missed days of school to work on the farm. The author does not recall seeing an obese child in his elementary school.

Although playgrounds during the early 1900s were expanding at a rapid rate in major American cities, the children or the neighborhoods in which they were located did not always accept them. Oral histories of that period are perhaps the best source for objective insight into their acceptance and usefulness. Paul Hogan (1995), a national leader in community-built playgrounds and a friend of the present author, wrote a compelling account of his boyhood play experiences in *Philadelphia boyhood: Growing up in the 1930s.* During the first half of the thirties, there was a large lot in Paul's neighborhood. The lot had hills and valleys and was kept clean—no one dumped trash there. It was used by adults for cookouts and picnics and by children for whatever sports were in season. The children dug tunnels, built forts, made fire pits for cooking, and would slide down the hills on cardboard boxes in summer and on their sleds in winter. They careened down the hills on bicycles, wagons, and anything else on wheels. But Doomsday was not far off. The Philadelphia Department of Recreation put up barricades, moved in construction equipment, leveled the hills and filled the valleys. They fenced the area and brought in truckloads of dirty, sharp cinders and covered the playground surface with the "filthy stuff." The cinders became so embedded in children's knees that mothers declared the playground off limits. They then built a "half baked gym" that closed about as soon as it opened. The people in the community stayed away in droves. Many years later, as an adult, Paul visited the site to find a large, clean, well-managed swimming pool.

THE POST-WAR PERIOD

During the war years of 1941–1945 there was relatively little movement in playground development, and the "manufactured appliance era" (Frost, 1992) was winding down. Most of the commercial equipment was manufactured from steel, which was diverted to weapons, and the adults available for playground work were involved in the war effort. Consequently, children's play and playgrounds tended to follow the patterns already established. Following the war, manufacturers resumed their efforts to equip the nation's playgrounds with a wide range of steel structures, but a growing number of designers, architects, handymen and playground manufacturers engaged in new approaches to design.

The 1950s and 1960s was designated the "novelty era" and the "age of fantasy" (Frost, 1992) because of the changes in playground design. Manufacturers continued to emphasize physical fitness, aesthetic quality, and manufacturability motives over broad child development concerns despite an avalanche of imaginative designs by inventors, handymen, and manufacturers (Musselman 1950, 1956; Shaw & Davenport 1956). A nationwide competition was held for play sculptures designed to exercise the imagination of children (National Recreation Association, 1954). Four basic criteria guided the competition: aesthetic quality, play value, safety, and manufacturability. Designs for play sculptures of molded, concrete forms featuring tunnels and labyrinths of spaces and shapes were submitted and many were later built. Most were lifeless, fixed, abstract, and resistant to change, movement, or action by children. Although the motives of the designers were to compensate for the standard municipal playground with its paved surfaces, fences, and traditional swings, jungle gyms and slides, the sculptures were frequently more appealing to adults than to children.

During this period, a number of cities engaged in imaginative playground development, some tailoring it to the perceived needs of the neighborhood (Crawford, 1956; National Recreation Association 1959), and others featuring component parts of concrete sewer pipes, railroad ties, slide chutes, corrugated iron pipe, balance beams, and horizontal ladders. Many playgrounds took on bright colors and other features that would reflect children's "dream world thoughts" (Shaw & Davenport, 1956). In Monterey, California, a "Dennis the Menace" playground was constructed (National Recreation Association, 1957); East Orange, New Jersey created a "nautical playground" from two cabin cruisers, a concrete block lighthouse, and a concrete pole jetty and dock (National Recreation Association 1958); Los Angeles built Western-theme villages, novel slides, multiple purpose exercise equipment, and theme equipment such as sharks and octopus rockers (Frederickson 1959); following Sputnik, rocket play sculptures sprang up around the country (National Recreation Association 1960).

National play equipment manufacturers joined the trend, adding plastic components and vivid colors to their steel structures and designing equipment with different age groups in mind (National Recreation Association 1962). By this time, climbing structures, slides, swings, and seesaws resembled rockets, stagecoaches, ponies, turtles and other fanciful objects and creatures (Frost, 1992). A glaring shortcoming of such thought and activity was to become obvious. Creating novel or fantasy play structures for children obviated the need or opportunity for children to reap the full play benefits of creating and imagining for themselves as they would do if they had access to natural or scrap building materials and with a wide array of portable materials or loose parts.

ADVENTURE PLAY AND PLAYGROUNDS

In 1943, C. Th. Sorensen, a Danish landscape architect, observed that children seemed to enjoy playing with the scrap material left over on construction sites more than with the finished products. This inspired the first junk playground, later named adventure playground, in Endrup, Denmark. The first play leader was John Bertelsen, a nursery school teacher and ex-seaman. Endrup proved to be a great success and the adventure playground concept spread throughout the Scandinavian countries, several other European countries and, in very limited numbers, to American playgrounds.

Lady Allen of Hurtwood, an English landscape architect, organized adventure playgrounds in London in spaces where buildings had been bombed out (Allen, 1968; 1974). The London Adventure Playground Association and the London Handicapped Adventure Playground Associations were formed in London to promote the values of adventure playgrounds and to assist in their development (Jago, 1971). In adventure playgrounds, children are supported (not directed) in building dens, houses, and climbing structures with waste materials. They cook with open fires, dig in the ground, build with real tools, and play with water, sand, and dirt. They also care for animals, plant and tend gardens, and enjoy their indoor social centers during inclement weather (Bengtsson, 1974; Frost & Klein, 1979).

The present author believes that adventure playgrounds are among the most exciting and developmentally appropriate types of outdoor playgrounds, but from a slow beginning in the United States, they have virtually disappeared from the American scene. The American Adventure Playground Association (AAPA) was formed in 1976 by a group of park and recreation professionals, educators, and commissioners in Southern California. In May 1977, the ASAPA identified 16 adventure playgrounds in the United States. These did not include the dozens of playgrounds built by parent and community groups throughout the country using scrap, scrounged material but lacking such features as full-time play leaders and designation as adventure playgrounds. With the demise of the Houston, Texas Adventure Playground Association in about 2002, only a few remain, notably in California. Adventure playgrounds never gained popular support from American adults, apparently because of their "junk" appearance, the misconception that they are more hazardous than typical playgrounds, and the widespread disregard of their developmental value for children.

The demise of American "adventure playgrounds" does not mean that the qualities of such playgrounds disappeared from the scene. Although the dominant pattern in American playground design and development in America is essentially "cookie-cutter" as previously described, a number of playground proponents and professionals have worked since the end of World War II to incorporate many features of adventure playgrounds. Some, including the present author, urged school, community park, and child care center professionals to complement their "standardized" or "cookie-cutter" playgrounds with loose or portable components, sand and water, building tools, and gardens and nature areas. Such features have been most apparent at child development centers for preschool age children, which were influenced by training in child development common for professionals who work at such centers.

THE MODULAR ERA

During the 1970s and 1980s the playground equipment industry switched to modular play equipment featuring multiple decks attached by bridges, tunnels and ramps with multiple play options or events for entry and exit. Support systems for these superstructures or composite units were made available in pressure-treated wood, natural redwood, steel, and aluminum. Eventually, the manufacturing industry began using powder-coated metals and space age plastics to lend color, resiliency, and resistance to heat build-up.

By this time, the playgrounds of America featured diverse types of playground equipment with half-century old equipment still common but with a growing number of newer designs. Three national surveys of American playgrounds (Bruya & Langerdorfer, 1988; Thompson & Bowers, 1989; Wortham & Frost, 1990) concluded that American playgrounds were a national disgrace, hazardous and ill-suited to the developmental needs of children. Ranking in order of safety and developmental appropriateness were child development center playgrounds (best), public parks (middle) and public schools (worst).

Public schools and public parks were following essentially the same pattern pursued for decades—playgrounds equipped with hazardous monolithic structures, designed essentially for physical play and motor development and ill-suited to the broad developmental needs of children. Although generally deficient, preschool and child development centers grounded in the principles and practices of Froebel, Dewey, and child development research were also continuing to follow the same paths they established during the early twentieth century. The training books and manuals for early childhood programs in the early twentieth century and those in use during the latter twentieth century were similar in their broad developmental focus. Consider the following description from a book published in 1916.

Louella Palmer, a student of Patty Smith Hill (an early 20th century early childhood educator and director of the experimental kindergarten in the Speyer School), organized her book, *Play life during the first eight years (Palmer, 1916),* around "the spirit of play" rather than the development of mere games and apparatus. She included sections on sensory play, movement play, language play, song play, manual play, ball play, dramatic play and finger play, stressing that play should be considered in the school but also at home, in nature, on the playground, and in institutions. She followed the International Kindergarten Union in promoting the social ends of play as well as the mental and physical benefits, stressing that the playground for city children should provide as near an approach to healthful country conditions as can be supplied to children in cramped quarters. She believed that playground apparatus could provide some of the natural benefits of the countryside (e.g., climbing trees and playing in streams) and that materials could be provided for urban children to make some of the playthings that country children make for themselves. The playground was seen as a place for country children to develop social skills that might be lacking due to isolation from other children.

THE EVOLUTION OF PLAYGROUND SAFETY STANDARDS AND REGULATIONS

During the 1970s, a series of studies and petitions resulted in the U.S. Consumer Product Safety Commission (CPSC) awarding a contract to the National Recreation and Park Commission to develop proposed safety standards for American playgrounds (Butwinick, 1974, p. 10) NRPA, 1976; Frost & Klein, 1979, Chap. 3).

Following a Federal Register call for citizen input, the CPSC published two *Handbooks for Public Playground Safety* in 1981. These were later integrated into a single handbook and revisions were published in 1991, 1994, and 1997. These handbooks, together with the American Society for Testing and Materials (ASTM) playground equipment standards published in 1993 (revised in 1998, and 2001, 2005), became the principal safety references for playground designers, manufacturers, installers, and consumers. The CPSC and the ASTM standards were commonly recognized in litigation as the "national standard of care." This status resulted essentially from their nationwide adoption by the playground industry, their passage into law by some states, and the influence they wield in litigation. Manufacturers regularly modified their equipment. Child injury lawsuits, having increasingly specific, yet complex standards for evidence, mushroomed, and large awards to plaintiffs were common.

Despite all this activity, the number of children reportedly treated at emergency rooms since the mid-1970s increased from about 117,000 to more than 200,000 annually (Tinsworth & Kramer (1990). The reasons for this are not clear. Some believe that reporting is more accurate now than earlier. Others believe that there are more playgrounds and that more children are playing on them. However, a growing number of public schools are deleting recess, meaning that children will not play on play equipment at schools, and parents are keeping children away from public playgrounds because of the threat of injury and violence. Further, by the turn of the twenty-first century, indoor technology games were replacing outdoor play at a rapid rate. The writer believes, although no conclusive data exists, that increased sedentary activity, fewer opportunities for active play, obesity, and declining fitness levels make children less able to play safely on challenging equipment and may contribute to injuries (Freedman, Dietz, Sathanur, & Berenson, 1999; Ross & Gilbert, 1985).

A number of problems have emerged over the years in developing, interpreting and applying CPSC guidelines and ASTM standards. These problems have now become so complex that some play specialists believe it is time to re-evaluate the scope, nature, and implementation of playground safety standards at all levels—state and national.

THE IMPACT OF PLAYGROUND SAFETY STANDARDS

The ASTM committee membership responsible for creating and revising the safety standards for public playground equipment numbers more than 150, with the large majority representing playground manufacturers and consulting and sales companies. Only a small minority of the membership represents scholars who study children's play and researchers who conduct research into children's play and play environments. Playground safety standards are in a constant state of flux, growing in length, inconsistency, and complexity, and playground equipment may fall into non-compliance within months or a few years of purchase and installation. The following examples illustrate the scope and nature of problems.

A city school system installed 130 major superstructures on 65 playgrounds in January and the ASTM standards were revised in December of that same year. The school system considered several options: expending two to three million dollars to replace the equipment, deleting recess, or risking child injury and litigation by continuing to use the structures. A growing number of schools are now removing playground equipment and/or deleting recess.

Inconsistencies between national playground safety standards and state regulations further illustrate the growing problems. In a study of state playground regulations in 50 states, Wallach (1990) found that none of the states had adopted CPSC guidelines or ASTM standards for their child care centers. The state's playground regulations were brief and general in nature, lacking specific information for identifying potential hazards. During child injury litigation, center owners often unwittingly declare that they meet their state playground safety regulations; yet they frequently lose their cases, not realizing that CPSC and ASTM standards tend to prevail in litigation over state regulations. One state revised its regulations in 2003, prohibiting equipment acceptable by national standards and resulting in public school playgrounds used throughout the day being declared out-of-compliance for use by the same children in after-school programs.

Both national standards and state regulations result in removal of preschool equipment that, with creative design, could be beneficial and reasonably safe (Frost, 2005; 2006). For example, cable walks, free standing climbers, overhead rings, parallel bars, track rides and vertical slide poles are ". . . not recommended for preschool-age children, 2 through 5 years" (CPSC, 1997, p.8, sec. 6.3). Prohibiting types of equipment instead of specific hazards limits creativity of designers and reduces developmentally appropriate play opportunities for children. The University of Texas Play and Playgrounds Research Program (Frost, et al, 2004; Frost, et al, 2005), operational at several sites for more than a quarter century, concluded consistently that using upper-body equipment, certain types of sliding poles and parallel bars, and many types of climbers on playgrounds is developmentally beneficial for most three- to five-year-old children and should be included in recess and free play periods. This conclusion was supported by observational research, interviews with medical, kinesiology, and child development experts, and extensive reviews of research literature. Excessively obese children were generally the only three to five-year-old-children experiencing extended difficulties in mastery of overhead apparatus and climbers designed specifically for preschool age children (3-5 years). A variety of relatively new molded plastic climbers and climbers with flexible components, installed at low heights and protected with resilient surfacing, are developmentally appropriate and reasonably safe for young children.

One hazard not addressed in state or national standards is the growing likelihood of obese children becoming entrapped in crawl-through spaces of equipment openings (Frost, et al, 2004). Obese children are at risk on playgrounds because of their inability to support and control their bodies and because of the possibility of entrapping their bodies in openings commonly used by their peers. Creation of a regulation leading to retooling of equipment could easily result in yet another basis for litigation, retooling by manufacturers, and expensive replacement of existing equipment. This illustrates the complexity resulting from continuous expansion of regulations.

Safety standards are applied in unintended ways in litigation, leading to denial of important play environments for children. Consider one brief CPSC statement (CPSC, 1997, p. 42). "Look out for tripping hazards, like exposed concrete footings, *tree stumps*, and rocks." The CPSC is charged with safety for "consumer products," yet the inclusion of such guidelines leads to claims involving natural materials, such as stumps, tree roots, and rocks, anywhere they are found on playgrounds. A major state university system was sued because a child fell on a stump in a small redwood forest adjacent to the organized games area of a laboratory school playground, resulting in a legal judgment against the university system (Frost, et al, 2004)!

A number of sources of information about playground safety are readily available on the Internet. The National Playground Safety Institute (NPSI), sponsored by the National Recreation and Park Association (NRPA), conducts training for playground safety inspectors in cities throughout the United States, leading to NPSI (www.als.uiuc.edu/nrpa) certification. This service is used primarily by playground designers, play equipment manufacturers, consultants, public park personnel, and school personnel. A growing number of organizations purchasing playground equipment require CPSC (www.cpsc.gov), ASTM (www.astm.org), and American Disabilities Act (ADA) compliance and look for International Playground Manufacturer's Association (IPEMA) compliance by manufacturers and International Playground Contractors Association (NPCA) compliance by installers of equipment. (See *Today's Playground* www.todaysplayground.com), and the National Recreation and Park Association (www.nrpa.org) journal *Recreation,* for on-going information.) The National Program for Playground Safety (NPPS, www.uni.edu/coe/playgrnd) provides a wide range of safety information. The National Electronic Injury Surveillance System (NEISS), operated by CPSC, provides current data on hospital emergency room visits for treatment of playground injuries.

These organizations focus much of their attention on the CPSC guidelines and the ASTM standards rather than on the huge body of research and theory on child development, play, and play environments available from such organizations as ACEI, NAEYC, IPA, TASP, and major research journals such as the *Journal for Research in Child Development* (SRCD). National and state playground safety guidelines, standards, and regulations need thought and revision to ensure that they are based on current research, simplified and pertinent only to major hazards, and consistent across geographical and political boundaries. Developers of safety standards need the ongoing contributions of specialists and researchers representing child development, medicine, kinesiology, and physical education as well as engineers, landscape architects, and manufacturers.

THE STANDARDIZED ERA AND THE DEMISE OF SPONTANEOUS OUTDOOR PLAY

As early as 1976, Devereux (1976) noted that the increase in youth sports and passion for television were possibly resulting in a decline in children's spontaneous play. He also pointed to the resulting loss of learning opportunities offered by spontaneous play. This alert was followed by warnings by Postman

(1982) in his popular book, *The Disappearance of Childhood,* that competitive sports formed on an adult model were displacing such play as street games. Since the time of these publications, other factors have emerged to compete with spontaneous play.

During the latter quarter of the twentieth century, space age plastics, metals, and recycled products were used extensively in the manufacture of playground equipment, and mammoth, expensive superstructures were dominating the playground industry and American playgrounds. Public park and school playgrounds developed an aura of sameness with a typical site featuring a superstructure, a set of swings, and a bench for the adult supervisors. Another form of "standardization," or the illusion that one test can measure the abilities of all children and that all children should succeed on the same test, also began to dominate the classroom during the late twentieth century. This growing focus on high-stakes testing came complete with punishing consequences for children, teachers, and school administrators and resulted in deletion of recess, physical education and the arts in many American schools. "More than 40 per cent of school districts across the country . . . have done away with recess or are considering it" (Mulrine, 2000, p. 50).

Availability of computers and computer games at home, parental fear about child molesters and other criminals, emphasis on high-stakes testing and homework, and parental absence due to work schedules conspired to keep children indoors at home and further reduced time or inclination for outdoor play. Weekend play became essentially sports (pee-wee and youth leagues) and visits to pay-for-play entertainment centers focusing on indoor technology play. By the turn of the twenty-first century, sedentary activity, junk food, and lack of physical activity were leading to an epidemic of childhood obesity and growing early indicators of serious health problems (Gabbard, 2000; Sutterby & Frost, 2002).

A "perfect storm" of safety standards, law suits, high-stakes testing, techno-play or entertainment, children's sports, and "pay-for-play" venues merged to replace free, spontaneous outdoor play (Frost, 2004). A fundamental factor influencing this rapid transition was the lack of understanding of the value of child-directed, unfettered, creative, spontaneous play. Fortunately, the dawning of the new century saw a slow, but heartening interest among professionals in reconsidering and countering such impediments to children's spontaneous outdoor play.

PLAY RECONSIDERED: THE TWENTY-FIRST CENTURY

The first three-quarters of the twentieth century, characterized by creative play and traditional games played out in wild places in the country and streets and vacant lots in cities, witnessed only marginal changes in the play and play environments of children. Beginning with the technological revolution of the last quarter of that century, remarkable transformations were seen. Now, in 2007, both country and city children are turning from spontaneous outdoor play to indoor entertainment featuring cell phones, computers, computer games, chat rooms, music devices, and, among the well-to-do, professionally designed game rooms in the home. A growing number of children are carrying in one small unitary device the ability to tap all these forms of technology play or techno-tainment at any time and in any place. Spontaneous play of the traditional sort, where children create playthings from raw materials and simultaneously engage in strenuous physical activity in the outdoors, is being replaced by the sedentary activity of techno-tainment. To expect that such "entertainment" provides equivalent mental, social, emotional, and physical benefits as traditional spontaneous play is indeed a stretch.

An article in the local *Austin American-Statesman* (May 15, 2005, A-1–A-5) announced the opening of a 75,000 square foot entertainment center catering to almost every play/entertainment interest including bowling, billiards, rock climbing, laser tag, glow-in-the-dark miniature golf, and electronic and other game-playing. Customers can dine at the restaurant and drink at two bars. This "bigger is better" concept is touted as "the wave of the future" and the trend of the entertainment industry. Such venues are spreading and flourishing across the country, now numbering between 10,000 and 12,000. They attract people of all ages, but the target audience is children younger than 12 with an average per-person spending $15 per trip. These "pay-for-play" centers are intended to compete with such entertainment options as theme parks and movie theatres.

Outdoor spaces for children's play are being lost and children are consequently deprived of the richest forms of play, that is, play that transcends, that is very intense, that is characterized by physical, social, and intellectual risk, obsession, complete absorption, ecstasy, and heightened mental states—*transcendental play* (Frost, 2003, 2005). During transcendental play, children lose contact with the outside world, place themselves in mental oneness with the play, revel in physical risk and mental challenge, and create miniature worlds of magic and intrigue. In such intense play, children rise above or transcend ordinary limits of play and become one with the social and environmental milieu (Frost, 2005, p. 9). Transcendental play is likely to be observed when children are building a fort in the woods, building dams in a stream of water, belly-flopping in mud holes, or creating new forms of physically challenging games on the playground. There are striking differences in the forms of children's play and in the places where they play.

> There is good (enabling or constructive) play and bad (disabling or destructive) play. Good play promotes healthy development; bad play or deprivation of play

> may restrict or damage development . . . children are being deprived of rich, healthy play opportunities and contexts (through) substitution of pay-for-play entertainment and other pseudo play forms for traditional, spontaneous play. (Frost, et al, 2005, p. 58)

What happens to children—to all of us—when direct contact with the outdoors is lost? Among the effects are diminished use of the senses, physical and emotional illnesses, attention difficulties, and a lost sense of connection with the world. As people draw deeper into their entertainment cocoons, they disconnect from nature and the future of the environment is placed at risk (Louv, 2005). Growing numbers of children are disconnected from nature. "Never having extensive experience in the woodlands or other wild places, they seemingly never bond with nature" (Frost, 2005, p. 11). People who grow up playing in and interacting in creeks, trees, tree houses, private and special places in the bush, gardens, animals and vacant lots speak with passion of the joy derived from such experiences. Children who have limited experience in wild places reflect about ticks, chiggers, snakes, scorpions and lack of modern conveniences. Lacking experiences coping with the risks of natural contexts, and deprived of recess at school, children may never develop the intellectual, intuitive, and motor skills needed to be safe on modern playgrounds equipped with challenging apparatus.

The benefits of children's spontaneous nature play extend into the health dimension. An intriguing "hygiene hypothesis" (http://goanimal.com/newsletters/2005/dir/dirt_hypo.html) holds that children's exposure to harmless microbes, as in dirt play, may teach the immune system how to regulate itself. Such exposure leads to formation of antibodies and cellular memory that can last for decades. Earlier generations had exposure to dirt though work and play almost every day. Modern isolation from dirt and animals, unique in human history, has been replaced with hygienic insulation and hyper-cleanliness bordering on hygienic pathology for many Western people. Obviously, history and experience have taught that humans must be protected against certain disease-producing organisms.

Children need natural, private, wild places for carrying out their play fantasies. During this decade, a quarter of the children born in the United States and more than half of the children in developing countries will grow up in urban slums. Most of these will never experience the wonders of wild places and farms (Nabhan & Trimble, 1994). Countless others will find their places for play dominated by manufactured equipment, regimented games and paved surfaces. Such places are usually devoid of special places for dens, shelters, elevated "lookout" areas, insects, fish, birds, pets, ponds, streams, trees, hills, dense vegetation, flowering shrubs, raw building materials, and gardens.

Fortunately, a growing number of professionals are charting the course for reinvigorating children's outdoor play and play spaces though transformations of sterile, steel and concrete dominated spaces to spaces that are profoundly alive with the riches of nature. Robin Moore and Herb Wong (1997) conducted a decade-long action research project at a Berkeley, California elementary school to redevelop an asphalt-covered schoolyard into an educational resource and community open space. The original site, biologically sealed by asphalt, was almost completely devoid of plant and animal life. The bored children were constantly bickering because the traditional equipment provided little opportunity for healthy, developmentally appropriate activity. The environment was recreated by the children and the community and became a resource for the school curriculum.

The University of Texas play and play environments research program, located at Redeemer Lutheran School in Austin, Texas and operational since 1976, features three constantly changing playgrounds. These are integrated with nature areas, flower, herb, butterfly, and vegetable gardens, greenhouses, and natural habitats for working, studying, and playing. The "Land Down Under", named by a third grade child, is a "wildscape" for rolling down grassy, flower covered hillsides, playing in water, building dens and forts, tending plants, and capturing insects for study in the indoor laboratory. The natural area has been certified as a Schoolyard Habitat by the National Wildlife Association. The Houston School District, have committed to earning such certification for every elementary school in the city. Such action is rapidly increasing across the country, offering a very positive alternative to common sterile, outdoor schoolyards.

Much thought and work will be needed to reverse the early twenty-first century trends that mark the demise of children's spontaneous play and of natural play spaces. A number of resources are available to guide those who wish to preserve outdoor play, recess, nature play or wild play, and to make play and playgrounds once again developmentally productive and magical (Burriss & Boyd, 2005; Frost, et al, 2004; Frost, et al, 2005; Goodenough, 2003; Greenman, 1998; Louv, 2005; Moore, 1990; Moore & Wong, 1997; Nabhan & Trimble, 1994; Rivkin, 1995; Stine, 1997; Talbot & Frost, 1989; *Young Children* special issue, May, 2005).

Children need outdoor play at home and at school and they need natural or wild places as well as designed playgrounds as their stages for play. Spontaneous outdoor play does not steal from reading, writing, and arithmetic, but rather enhances the social, emotional, physical and cognitive bases for such skills. To deprive children of free, outdoor play is consistent with typical definitions of child abuse—deliberate mental or physical injury. In the American workplace, laborers, including performing animals, are given breaks from work. Play is the inherent right of children, protected by the United Nations Charter for Children, and must be preserved.

HIGH-STAKES TESTING AND THE DEMISE OF SPONTANEOUS PLAY

On May 8, 2005, CNN aired a special program, "High Stakes: CNN Presents," about the "No Child Left Behind" program now operational in American schools. First widely implemented in Texas, the program initially promised to be the "Texas Miracle" as schools showed dramatic increases in test scores later shown by CNN as resulting from cheating. Now the testing program intended to end social promotion and to improve the achievement of all children is fraught with cheating, disappointing results, growing rejection by educators and parents, and daily "teaching to the test" becoming the norm. Administrators, teachers, and children, threatened with pressures to perform, are spending long hours teaching and practicing for the tests. Principals facing possible demotion or firing pass the pressures down to teachers, and teachers pass them on the students. Some students are retained for three years in the same grade to prevent their test scores from being entered in school records. Recess, physical education, and the arts, considered frills, are abandoned. Children take prescription drugs, sometimes illegally, to cope with the stress. Others cry, throw up, and lose sleep. Some score As and Bs on their report cards but fail the tests. All this in the misplaced expectation that, somehow, all children, even children with disabilities, should perform the same and that the essence of education is measurable by a single test—no matter the life experiences, the income level, the cultural background, or the native abilities of the child. Such fallacious thinking and practices are fundamental factors in the demise of recess and spontaneous play.

The problems with high-stakes testing have now become so onerous that pre-teenage children are overdosing on drugs the day of exams. In April 2005, the Associated Press (*Austin American-Statesman*, 4-21-05) reported that the National Education Association and school districts in Texas, Michigan and Vermont, plus NEA chapters in Connecticut, Illinois, Indiana, New Hampshire, Ohio, Pennsylvania, and Utah are suing the Bush administration for failing to support the No Child Left Behind Act. In her comprehensive book on the perils of high-stakes testing, Ohanian (2002) reported on the decision of the Atlanta school system to build schools with no playgrounds to prove they are devoted to high standards.

"From California to Chicago to Virginia, school districts have abolished recess, and even in districts where recess is still on the books, increasingly, children who score poorly on standardized tests are forced to forego the play break" (Ohanian 2002, p. 2). The position of the International Play Association (IPA/USA) is that "recess is vital to the child's overall healthy development," maintaining that recess responds to the children's social and emotional needs and gives them opportunities to exercise a sense of wonder, which leads to exploration and creativity. Recess and play also contribute to cultural exchange and to intellectual development.

In historical context, the high-stakes testing myth is seen as ironic and misguided. The American playground movement of the early twentieth century was deeply influenced by major social reformers who wished to protect children wandering the streets from health hazards, crime, and traffic and to help them develop social and intellectual skills to succeed in school. Many schools and playgrounds were influenced by earlier reformers and the early twentieth century Child Study Movement in America to utilize play and play environments as the basis for developing skills needed for academic success. Now, almost a century later, high-stakes testing is overpowering such educational wisdom and tradition and depending upon an industrial model of standardized product testing and academic drill rather than a developmental model valuing the uniqueness of learners, the power of intellectual diversity, the training and motivation of teachers and parents, and the need for a balanced life of work and play both indoors and outdoors.

Children need to taste the fullness of the educative process—the great children's books, the intense activity of engaging with children from different cultures, interacting with skillful, devoted teachers, learning to make decisions and plan for oneself, creating poetry, creating and appreciating art and music, distinguishing right from wrong, solving real problems in the out-of doors, enjoying other children, developing physical and linguistic skills on the playground and balancing seriousness with fun. Assessment of the appropriate sort is, and should remain, a part of every classroom in America, but the misguided notion of politicians and administrators that one single test and the prohibition of play can change the futures of children positively is false and damaging. At the turn of the twenty-first century, the "perfect storm" threatening children's play and health was gaining force. By 2007, as this book was going to press, legislators at both state and national levels were beginning to raise serious reservations about the benefits of high stakes testing, the reduction of recess and outdoor play, and the effects of excessive sedentary activity and poor diets on children's health. In addition, organizations such as the National Wildlife Federation and other organizations concerned about children's growing absence from nature, are leading to a wave of activities for developing habitats and nature study at schools and in communities.

Hopefully, the tide is turning and children will be reintroduced to the benefits and joys of outdoor play and nature.

REFERENCES

Addams, J. (1911). *The spirit of youth and the city streets.* New York: Macmillan.

Allen, L. (1974). *Adventure playgrounds for handicapped children.* London: James Galt.

Allen, L. (1968). *Planning for play.* Cambridge, MS: MIT Press.

American Society for Testing and Materials (2001). *Standard consumer safety performance specification for playground equipment for public use.* West Conshohocken, PA: The Society.

Bartoletti, S. C. (1996). *Growing up in coal country.* Boston: Houghton Mifflin.

Bengtsson, A. (1974). *Adventure playgrounds.* New York: Praeger.

Bowen, W. P., & Mitchell, E. D. (1930). *The theory of organized play: Its nature and significance.* New York: A. S. Barnes.

Bruya, L. D., & Langerdorfer, S. J. (eds.). (1988). *Where our children play: Elementary school playground equipment.* Reston, VA: American Alliance for Health, Physical Education, Recreation, and Dance.

Burriss, K. G., & Boyd, B. F. (Eds.) (2005). *Outdoor learning and play: Ages 8–12.* Olney, MD: Association for Childhood Education International.

Butwinick, E. (1974). *Petition requesting the issuance of a consumer product safety standard for public playground slides, swinging apparatus and climbing equipment.* Washington, DC: CPSC.

Cavallo, D. (1981). *Muscles and morals: Organized playgrounds and urban reform, 1880–1920.* Philadelphia: University of Pennsylvania Press.

Coles, R. (1970). *Uprooted children.* Pittsburgh, PA: University of Pittsburgh Press.

Committee of Nineteen (1924). Pioneers of the kindergarten in America. New York: Century Co.

Committee of Nineteen. (1913). *The kindergarten.* Boston: Houghton Mifflin.

Consumer Product Safety Commission. (1997). *Handbook for public playground safety.* Washington, D.C: The Commission.

Crawford, R. W. (1956). A new look for Philadelphia. *Recreation. 49*(9), 322–323.

Curtis, H. S. (1925). *The practical conduct of play.* New York: Macmillan.

Curtis, H. S. (1913). *The reorganized school playground.* Washington, D. C: U. S. Bureau of Education, No. 40.

Devereux. E. (1976). Backyard versus little league baseball: The impoverishment of children's games. In Landers, D. (Ed.). *Social problems in athletics.* Urbana: University of Illinois Press.

Frank, L. K. (1962). The beginnings of child development and family life education in the twentieth century. *Merrill-Palmer Quarterly, 8*(4), 207-227.

Frank, L. K. (1938). The fundamental needs of the child. *Mental Hygiene,* July.

Frederickson, W., Jr. (1959). Planning play equipment. *Recreation,* (52), 186–189.

Freedman, D. S., Dietz, W. H., Sathanur, R. S., & Berenson, G. S. (June, 1999). The relation of overweight to cardiovascular risk factors among children and adolescents: The Bogalusa heart study. *Pediatrics, 103*, 6, 1175–1182.

Frost, J. L. (2003). Bridging the gaps: Children in a changing society. *Childhood Education, 80*, 29–34.

Frost, J. L. (2005). Introduction. In K. G. Burriss & B. F. Boyd (Eds.), *Outdoor learning and play: Ages 8–13.* Olney, MD: Association for Childhood Education International.

Frost, J. L. (1992). *Play and playscapes.* Albany, NY: Delmar.

Frost, J. L, & Klein, B. L. (1979). *Children's play and playgrounds.* Boston: Allyn & Bacon.

Frost, J. L., Brown, P. S., Sutterby, J. A. & Thornton, C. D. (2004). *The developmental benefits of playgrounds.* Olney, MD: Association for Childhood Education International.

Frost, J. L. Wortham, S. C., & Reifel, S. (2001, 2005, second edition). *Play and child development.* Columbus, OH: Merrill Prentice Hall.

Frost, J. L. (Jan. 2004). How adults enhance or mess up children's play. *Archives of Pediatrics and Adolescent Medicine*. 158, 16.

Fry, A. R. (1994). *The orphan trains.* New York: Macmillan.

Gabbard, C. (2000). Physical education: Should it be part of the core curriculum? *Principal, 79*(3), 29–31.

Goodenough, E. (Ed.) (2003). *Secret spaces of childhood.* Ann Arbor: The University of Michigan Press.

Greenman, J. (1998). *Places for childhood: Making quality happen in the real world.* Bellevue, WA: Exchange Press.

Gulick, L. (1920). *A philosophy of play.* New York: Scribner.

Hall, G. S. (1897). *The story of a sand pile.* New York: E. L. Kellogg.

Hogan, P. (1995). *Philadelphia boyhood: Growing up in the 1930's.* Vienna, VA: Holbrook & Kellogg.

Jago, L. *Learning through experience.* London: London Adventure Playground Association, 1971.

Knapp, R. F., & Hartsoe, C. E. (1979). *Play for America: The National Recreation Association 1906–1965.* Arlington, VA: National Recreation and Park Association.

Lee, J. (1915). *Play in education.* New York: Macmillan.

Lee, J. (1927). Play, the architect of man. *The playground, 21*(9), 460–463.

Lehman, H. C., & Witty, P. A. (1926). Changing attitudes toward play. *The playground, (20)*8, 436–438.

Louv, R. (2005). *Last child in the woods: Saving our children from nature-deficit disorder.* New York: Algonquin.

Lloyd, F. S. (1931). Play as a means of character education for the individual. *Recreation, 24*(11), 587-592.

Mero, E. B. (1908). *American playgrounds: Their construction, equipment, maintenance and utility.* Boston: American Gymnasia Co.

Mitchell, E. D., & Mason, B. S. (1941). *The theory of play.* New York: A. S. Barnes.

Moore, R. C. (1990). *Childhood's domain.* Berkeley, CA: MIG Communications.

Moore, R. C., & Wong, H. H. (1997). *Natural learning: Creating environments for rediscovering nature's way of teaching.* Berkeley, CA: MIG Communications.

Mulrine, A. What's your favorite class? *U. S. News and World Report.* May 1, 2000.

Musselman, C. (1950). What about our playgrounds? *Recreation, 44*(4), 5.

Muths, G. (1793; English translation, 1803). *Gymnastics for youth.* Dubuque, IA: William C. Brown Reprint.

Nabhan, G. P., & Trimble, S. (1994). *The geography of childhood: Why children need wild places.* Boston: Beacon Press.

National Program for Playground Safety. Retrieved October 23, 2003 from http://www.uni/edu/playground/home/html.

National Recreation Association. (1957). Dennis the Menace playground. *Recreation, 50*, 136–137,151.

National Recreation Association. (1959). Designs for play. *Recreation, 52*(4), 130–131.

National Recreation Association. (1958). Imagination visits the playground. *Recreation, 51*, 106–108.

National Recreation Association (1962). Playground equipment: Today and tomorrow. *Recreation, 52,* 186–187.

National Recreation Association (1960). Playgrounds in action. *Recreation, 53*, 154–156.

National Recreation Association (1954). Play structures for playgrounds. *Recreation, 47*, 500–501.

National Recreation and Park Association. (1976). *Proposed safety standard for public playground equipment.* Arlington, VA: U. S. Consumer Product Safety Commission.

Ohanian, S. (2002). *What happened to recess and why are our children struggling in kindergarten?* New York: McGraw Hill.

Palmer, L. A. (1916). *Play in the first eight years.* New York: Ginn.

Postman, N. (1982). *The disappearance of childhood.* New York: Delacorte Press.

Playground and Recreation Association of America. (1909). *Proceedings of the Third Annual Congress of the Association, 3*, 2–24.

Rivkin, M. S. (1995). *The great outdoors: Restoring children's right to play outside.* Washington, D.C: National Association for the Education of Young Children.

Ross, J., & Gilbert, G. (1985). The national youth and fitness study. *Journal of Health, Physical Education, Recreation and Dance, 56*, 45–50.

Sapora, A. V., & Mitchell, E. D. (1948). *The theory of play and recreation.* New York: The Ronald Press.

Shaw, R. H., & Davenport, E. C. (1956). A playground that pleases children. *Recreation, 49*(11), 445.

Stanford Prevention Research Center, Stanford University School of Medicine. (Feb. 2007*). Building "Generation Play"; Addressing the Crisis of inactivity among America's Children*. A Report by Stanford University, commissioned by the Young Men's Christian Association, the National Recreation and Park Association, and the National Association for Sport and Physical Education.

Stanley, J. (1992). *Children of the dust bowl: The true story of the school at Weedpatch Camp.* New York: Scholastic.

Stine, S. (1997). *Landscapes for learning: Creating outdoor environments for children.* New York: John Wiley.

Sutterby, J. A., & Frost, J. L. (2002). Making playgrounds fit for children and children fit on playgrounds. *Young Children,* 57(3), 36–42.

Talbot, J., & Frost, J. L. (1989). Magical playscapes. *Childhood Education, 66*(1), 11–19.

Texas Department of Protective and Regulatory Services. (2003). *Minimum standard rules for licensed child-care centers.* Austin, TX: The Department.

Thompson, D., & Bowers, L. (eds.). (1989). *Where our children play: Community Park Playground Equipment.* Reston, VA: American Alliance for Health, Physical Education, Recreation, and Dance.

Tinsworth, D. K., & Kramer, J. T. (1990). *Playground equipment-related injuries and deaths.* Washington, D.C: U.S. Consumer Product Safety Commission.

Tsanoff, S. V. (1897). *Educational value of the children's playgrounds.* Philadelphia, PA: Published for the author.

Tuttle, W. M., Jr. (1993). *Daddy's gone to war: The second world war in the lives of America's children.* New York: Oxford University Press.

Wallach, F. (1990). *An analysis of the state codes for licensed day care centers focused on playgrounds and supervision.* New York: Total Recreation Management Services.

Warren, A. (1996). *Orphan train rider: One boy's true story.* Boston: Houghton Mifflin.

Weber, E. (1969). *The kindergarten: Its encounter with educational thought in America.* New York: Teachers College Press.

Weir, L. H. (1937). *Europe at play: A study of recreation and leisure time activities.* Washington, D. C: Reprinted by National Recreation and Park Association and McGrath Publishing Co.

Wormser, R. (1994). *Growing up in the Great Depression.* New York: Atheneum.

Wortham, S. C., & Frost, J. L. (eds.). (1990). *Playgrounds for young children: American survey and perspectives.* Reston, VA: American Alliance for Health, Physical Education, Recreation, and Dance.

Chapter Two

The Promise of Sociology for Play Studies

Thomas S. Henricks

Among the guiding ideas of the new field of "cultural studies" is the belief that scholars cannot understand the culture of a community unless they consult the views of subordinate and marginalized categories of people (see Curran and Gurevitch, 1992; Dickens and Fontana, 1994; Ferguson and Golding, 1997). In that light, special attention is paid to the understandings of women, racial and ethnic minorities, poor people, and the young. As history is written by the powerful, so the more official or public visions of societies tend to be sponsored and sustained by dominant groups. Listening to the views of excluded people may seem to be merely a process of righting the scales, of gathering information that deepens and makes more credible the descriptions of those societies. However, the new generation of cultural scholars has emphasized that this process of social exclusion—the setting apart and labeling of people with different vantage points—stands at the very center of public culture. For such scholars, understanding a set of ideas means confronting alternative and opposing visions.

When alternative ideas and customs threaten the dominant culture, those rival viewpoints (and their proponents) may be captured and displayed as spectacles of wrongdoing. Like criminals or foreign enemies, alternative viewpoints may be held up as reminders of what people must not do or become. Somewhat differently, subcultures may be isolated and maintained as public curiosities. In that light, the neighborhoods of ethnic groups and the poor have long functioned as "cultural zoos," sources of amazement or illicit pleasure for the socially established (see Gans, 1971). Differently again, subcultural expressions may be banished to the margins of society, to live and die beyond the boundaries of public concern. Finally, these rival perspectives may grow quietly beneath the officially recognized patterns. Like species of plants invading a garden, the new practices flourish in the very conditions that sustain the dominant culture. What to make of these new patterns is the historic responsibility of social scientists and public policy experts.

As repositories of belief and value, academic disciplines display many of these same tensions and processes. Students in graduate schools become committed to distinctive intellectual perspectives that stress the importance of certain theories, methodologies, and research topics. As professors, they influence the understandings of their students. By such processes academia becomes "colonized" by dominant ideas and populated by their professional spokespersons. Certain perspectives become established as important traditions; others are shouted down, skewered, or otherwise consigned to the lower echelons of the intellectual world.

For its part, the interdisciplinary field of play studies has been remarkably free of such animosity. When play scholars gather, they typically welcome a wide variety of academic disciplines and theoretical approaches. Moreover, those conferences tend to embrace quite expansive definitions of their subject matter, so that research on all types of competition, amusement, creativity, fantasy, role performance, collective festivity, and developmental practice is presented and discussed. Analyses focus on animals as well humans, children as well as adults, and range from the most abstract conceptualizations to careful applications in school or community. Such topics, it should be emphasized, are approached in a generally non-judgmental and integrative spirit. Conference participants seek to understand a complicated and elusive subject in all of its dimensions and, somewhat evangelically, promote its importance within the wider society.

Nevertheless, play studies has its own dominant traditions and perspectives that reflect the disciplinary specialization, educational training, and professional commitment of its practitioners. In his towering work, *The Ambiguity of Play,* Sutton-Smtih (1997) describes these traditions in terms of seven ideologies or rhetorics. The first, and perhaps most pervasive, of these is the rhetoric of *progress*. For more than one hundred years, proponents of this view have argued that youthful play contributes to the moral, social, and cognitive development of the players themselves. In that regard, play is celebrated as one of the great engines of personal and public improvement, a chance to refashion skills and understandings. Quite different is Sutton-Smith's second perspective, the rhetoric of *fate.* Associated especially with gambling and magical practices, fateful play addresses existential conditions that seem confusing or even chaotic. Such forces cannot be controlled in systematic ways but only seduced, tricked, or charmed. This vision of a rivalrous and unpredictable world is set forward as well in the third rhetoric, *power.* Focusing on the role of contests in history, proponents of this view have stressed the struggles and achievements of heroic performers and the implications of hierarchy as a negotiated enterprise.

The fourth rhetoric is termed *identity.* This view of play focuses less on the antagonism of the participants and more on their shared public identity and forms of cooperation. So understood, festivities and celebrations of many types are said to dramatize and affirm social connection. Different again is the rhetoric of the *imaginary.* Many interpreters have stressed play as creative expression in art and literature. However, fantasy and improvisation are fundamental aspects of human experience that are especially prominent in childhood storytelling and role-play. The sixth rhetoric is the *self*, the argument that play commonly focuses on the physical and psychological dimensions of the person. By such lights, the typical object of play is less the world than it is ourselves. The final rhetoric is the view of play as *frivolous.* As expressed in traditional societies, play is frequently an exercise in foolery, status inversion, and trickery. By such lights, play is a teasing and dissembling of exalted forms and persons, an opening in the cracks of social structure.

Considering as it does literally hundreds of studies and understandings of play, Sutton-Smith's approach seems truly encyclopedic in scope. Some of the rhetorics—frivolity, fate, community identity, and power—are presented as being particularly important in ancient and traditional societies. Others—progress, imagination, and the self—are emphasized by interpreters of modern societies. However, all the rhetorics explain in some fashion how play expands the contexts of human (and animal) participation (Sutton-Smith, 1997, pp. 214–231). Play promotes variability or flexibility, and this helps creatures adapt—physically and mentally—to the ever-changing conditions of their lives.

As wide-ranging as *The Ambiguity of Play* is in its vision and arguments, it should be noted that the research that informs that work comes predominantly from five disciplines in the social and behavioral sciences: psychology, education, animal behavior studies, folklore, and anthropology. Contributing also, although in lesser ways, is scholarship from literature, philosophy, and history. Much less conspicuous are studies from a distinctly sociological perspective.

It should also be noted that sociological commentaries have not been emphasized in the other important syntheses of play theory (see Ellis, 1973; Levy, 1978; Spariosu, 1989). To some degree, this neglect is appropriate and reflects the commitment of modern sociologists to this subject. Other disciplines besides sociology have in fact dominated scholarly understandings of play. Sociologists, for their part, have been drawn to the more formally organized versions of expressive activity located in such institutional spheres as sport, art, or religion. Nevertheless, I argue in the following that sociology has much to contribute to the study of play, if only to balance the theoretical emphases of some of the other disciplines.

Among these theoretical emphases is the individualistic, often idealized view of play found in much psychological and educational research. Subscribing to Sutton-Smith's play-as-progress rhetoric, such researchers stress the role of play in skills development and self-awareness. Play is functional rather than dysfunctional, creative rather than destructive, a fascinating activity that draws its participants toward increasingly complicated challenges (see, e.g., Sponseller, 1974; Klugman and Smilansky, 1990; Rogers and Sawyers, 1988). Moreover, play—as a psychologically generated behavior—exhibits degrees of freedom and spontaneity found less frequently in other portions of life. Typically, such studies focus on children. When adults appear in this tradition, they are often presented as helpful guides. Carefully organized and rationally controlled play allows people to become their better selves, or so it seems.

This tradition is paralleled by research in animal behavior studies (see Fagen, 1981). For the scholars of animal life, play is associated especially with the activities of the young and with the need to become fully functioning adults (see Chick, 2001). Moreover, a sense of orderliness and control prevails. Like wrestlers preparing for "real" matches in a not-so-distant future, players practice move and countermove and learn the meanings of cooperation and competition, dominance and subordination.

Such a viewpoint is profoundly important. The young (of all species) surely develop skills through intrinsically satisfying exercises in object and self mastery; and adults can help direct those activities in socially beneficial ways. However, play can also be a largely non-rational, mean-spirited, and even antisocial affair. These latter themes have been well-developed in folklore studies (see Sutton-Smith, Mechling, Johnson, and McMahon, 1995). By such accounts, the playworld of children is marked by rebellious, aggressive, and even sexual preoccupations. Like graffiti artists, players make their marks upon the walls of social order. The purpose of play, it seems, is to disturb and defile, to learn just how far people can go before the world opposes and stops them.

All of these traditions, however, emphasize the relatively self-directed and intrinsically satisfying qualities of play. Play is a primarily an informally organized, personal affair that people pursue for their own reasons. Although folklore scholars speak clearly of the social worlds of childhood, an even stronger correction to this individualistic, idealistic view of play is found in cultural anthropology (see Lancy and Tindall, 1976; Roopnarine, Johnson, and Hooper, 1994; Lancy, 2002). For anthropologists, play is an important activity of adults that partakes of all the complexities and commitments of that status (see Handelman, 1998; Turner, 1969). Moreovoer, play is frequently a public rather than personal matter, something that people do before others in elaborately configured ceremonies or festivities. More clearly than other disciplines then, anthropology has comprehended play as a carefully protected and quite pointed commentary on community power structures and values. In such ways, play is embedded deeply in ritual and freedom is harnessed to obligation.

Despite the fundamental contributions of all these disciplines, there are still some pieces missing from the interdisciplinary study of play. Chief among these is an explicitly sociological perspective. As developed below, sociology emphasizes the degree to which most human behaviors—including play—either feature human interaction directly or are touched intimately by that theme. Thus, play for the sociologist is less a pattern of personal expression than an interplay, a quality of action and reaction between "actors" committed to a clearly understood line of activity. Furthermore, sociologists argue that behaviors of every type are "framed" by well-established social institutions (see Goffman, 1961; 1974). In general ways, these institutions channel and reward specific kinds of action; however, they may also feature distinctive social organizations with special commitments to promote such behavior. To this degree, private expression is nested in socially recognized and supported patterns that include norms, roles, relationships, and organizational forms.

An interest in the social aspects of play is, of course, not new. Many of the great writers on play, including some sociologists (see Erikson, 1950; Piaget, 1962; Denzin, 1977; Fine, 1983) have stressed play's social contexts and meanings. However, it is argued here that the sociological perspective itself, and the range of research questions that it raises, has not been appreciated fully in the play studies literature. Furthermore, it is claimed that sociology's major theoretical traditions have not been addressed in a systematic or explicit way. In what follows then, the author addresses these themes and advocates further sociological enquiries into the nature and contexts of play.

CENTRAL ELEMENTS OF THE SOCIOLOGICAL PERSPECTIVE

Studies in the social sciences tend to be united by a common question: What kinds of people (or other social subjects) engage in what kinds of activities in what ways under what conditions and for what reasons? Within the terms of this broad approach, sociology distinguishes itself from other disciplines by the way in which it understands certain fundamental concepts and by the more specific range of questions it chooses to address.

Certainly the most obvious difference between sociology and other disciplines is sociology's emphasis on *social* rather than *psychological* or *cultural* phenomena. That is, sociology focuses on the patterning of human relationship, including all the ways in which people communicate, interact and organize one another. Such a level of analysis is quite different from that patterning of individual disposition and behavior tendency that serves as the core subject matter of psychology. Furthermore, social phenomena are related to but significantly different from culture, the patterning of humanly created resources (both informational and artifactual) that provide directives for human thought and action. In contradistinction to sociology, anthropology focuses on the role of culture—especially culture as this has been "institutionalized" by societies and groups—in guiding human affairs. While keenly interested in both psychological and cultural phenomena (as conditions for social life), sociology tends to emphasize the disjunctions or tensions between such matters and social phenomena. Indeed, some of the most profound issues in the social sciences concern relationships between the personal and the social (reflecting all the ways in which people resist, comply, and assert themselves in groups) and between the cultural and the social (as groups and organizations create, resist, and modify public ideas).

For modern sociologists then, the experience of individuals in social or cultural contexts is routinely problematic (see e.g., Giddens, 1991; Hurst, 2000). That is, participation by individuals (categorized by gender, age, ethnicity, social class, etc.) and by collectivities (i.e., groups, organizations, communities, nation-states, etc.) with one another is marked by political or "resource-allocation" issues. Put differently again, the interests and value-commitments of one social unit are always potentially at odds with those of other social units. The "miracle of social order" then is the way in which complicated human arrangements—featuring all manner of coercion, compliance, and compromise—are created and sustained. Continuities (and discontinuities) in such arrangements are sociology's subject matter.

Issues of Concern to Sociologists

This preoccupation with the social is of course pertinent to other disciplines in the social sciences as well. However, in contradistinction to sociology, most of the other social sciences focus on relationships within a single social institution or set of societal issues. Thus, political science focuses on governmental and legal matters; economics, the production and distribution of goods and services; geography, the physical resources of the earth; education, matters related to socialization and learning, etc. Sociology transcends—and attempts to unite—such approaches by focusing on human relationships and organizational issues of every type.

The typical activity of sociologists then is the description and evaluation of organizational characteristics and processes. A list of these matters commonly includes the following:

1) *Organizational Composition*: Descriptions of the membership (size, density, and social characteristics) of groups and organizations.
2) *Culture*: Descriptions of ideas, values, norms, and artifacts employed by groups in various ways.
3) *Recruitment/Socialization*: Descriptions of the processes by which individuals are brought into groups and "trained" for membership.
4) *Interaction/Communication*: Descriptions of the "networks" or patterns of interconnection between members. Who talks, eats, recreates, works, etc. with one another?
5) *Leadership/Admininistration*: Descriptions of the organization of authority and processes of decision-making.
6) *Social Stratification*. Descriptions of patterns of access to valued social resources, including power, prestige, wealth, and knowledge.
7) *Deviance and social control*. Descriptions of both the processes by which groups control others and the processes by which individuals evade that control.

Play groups and activities then represent interesting sets of phenomena for this type of analysis. For example, in the sociological vision the player is as much a role as a person. That role—which in various ways is distinctive from other roles like worker or worshipper—carries with it certain obligations. Indeed, play activities display a host of roles (leaders, followers, sponsors, observers, etc.) that are interrelated in the wider group. For such events to be successful, each of these roles must be played at the appropriate time in the appropriate way and individuals may shift roles as the occasion demands. To repeat, sociological analysis emphasizes the interaction of cultural frameworks for action as much as the interaction of the individuals who occupy those roles.

Similarly, groups and organizations are constituent elements of the event. As Durkheim (1964) argued, the social body is a reality of its own sort. Participants recognize that their identity derives to some degree from membership in that body and commonly commit themselves to its integrity. In the case of groups, individuals informally may enforce norms that keep individuals from disrupting play or otherwise serving as spoilsports. In the case of organizations, specialized norms and officials may be in place to guarantee the proceedings. More generally, players typically acknowledge a set of procedures that allow them to enter the playground, pursue their activities, and exit gracefully at the conclusion.

Further questions may be asked. How are the boundaries of the play world created and enforced? Who is allowed to participate? Who occupies positions of leadership and what kinds of leadership do they provide? How do external organizations or authority figures exercise their influences on the activity? What other varieties of roles exist in the play world and how do these roles interact with one another? Are there hierarchies of prestige within the group and how are these maintained? How are dissatisfied players, observers, etc. kept in control? How do they express their dissatisfaction? What subgroups form within the broader group and how do these influence the wider activity? How does the sheer size and density of the group affect the nature of the interaction? Such questions could be extended at length but the implications of this general approach seem clear enough. Play—and the experience of players—is no unitary phenomenon. Rather play events must be understood as a set of distinctive social arrangements that players create, inhabit, and sustain.

FOUR THEORETICAL PERSPECTIVES IN SOCIOLOGY

Within the social sciences, theoretical perspectives function in a double sense. On the one hand, they offer metaphors of social life that sensitize observers to certain kinds of variables. On the other, they provide explanations of how these variables may be linked. In sociology, the four most prominent perspectives are structural-functionalism, conflict theory, exchange theory, and symbolic interactionism (see Collins, 1994). Each offers its own distinctive picture of the machinery of society. Not surprisingly, play activities appear quite differently under the terms of each perspective.

Structural-Functionalism

The first set of approaches owes its beginnings in sociology to various organismic models made popular in social anthropology and biology during the latter part of the nineteenth century (see Turner, 1978; Martindale, 1981). If the human body could be seen as a system of interrelated elements in a state of dynamic equilibrium, then perhaps these ideas could be applied to the "social body" as well. Just as people are composed of constituent organs dependent on one another, by extension society is composed of various "institutions," including the family, economy, polity, and religion. To the degree that individual organs like the heart or kidneys perform certain functions necessary to the health of the entire body, so the family, economy, etc. provide needed services for society. Such a viewpoint seemed particularly well suited to the traditional societies studied by anthropologists (see Radcliffe-Brown,

1952). These societies were typically small, tightly integrated, slow-to-change, and guided by overarching value systems. A sudden change in one part (such as the introduction of Western commodities) could produce ripple effects throughout the entire system.

However, as Durkheim (1933) argued, modern society tends to feature a carefully articulated division of labor among its various institutions. Indeed, contemporary society is held together by the network of services that these institutions (replete with their own specialized organizations) perform for one another. He termed this type of integration "organic solidarity," in deference to the social body's composition of tightly interrelated parts.

Whether this organism is entirely self-regulating was a matter of much disagreement among the early social scientists. Some like Spencer or the early Scottish economists argued that social health was the result of unregulated competition; others like Mill, Saint-Simon, and Durkheim himself saw a clear role for government as the self-conscious head of the body (see Turner, 1978, pp. 19–30). All this notwithstanding, the metaphor of body or machine did not seem to capture adequately the capacities of social units for self-consciousness and reflexive action. Unlike organisms or machines, societies were composed of thinking members who could comprehend the character of their societies and bring about changes, even revolutionary ones. Furthermore, the idea of "needs" for bodies or machines was not quite equivalent to the idea of social needs.

In deference to these concerns, structural-functionalism attempts to explain social patterns by focusing on the consequences of certain practices for patterns at broader levels of social structure (including society itself). For functionalists, the previously noted "miracle of social life" is its relative continuity and orderliness. Typically then, functionalists seek the possible contributions of a persistent practice—even potentially destabilizing activities like poverty or crime—for the continuity of society itself. Pointedly also, practices that seem unpleasant or dangerous for the individuals involved (e.g., a military draft) nevertheless may be held to be functional for the group as a whole.

In response to critics who claim that this approach overemphasizes both the stability of society and the beneficent effects of dubious practices (see, e.g., Wilson, 1983, pp. 63–78; Turner, 1978, pp. 93–117), modern functionalism has become more subtle and flexible. Consequences are not made equivalent to purposes; that is, there is no imputation that individuals or groups recognize or intend the stipulated social effects that their actions produce. Indeed, consequences may be completely hidden (i.e., have "latent" meanings) from both participants and analysts (see Merton, 1968, pp. 19–84). Furthermore, it is recognized that practices may have not only a mixture of beneficial (eufunctional) and harmful (dysfunctional) effects but also somewhat different effects for different parts of society. Nevertheless, functionalism retains its view that small actions are explicable in terms of their effects on larger patterns and that form itself is ultimately a response to functional requirements.

In a well-known argument, the sociologist Talcott Parsons (1951) claimed that these requirements of social units as "systems" could be reduced to four basic types: adaptation (adjustment to environmental forms and demands), goal-attainment (the coordinated achievement of group ambitions), integration (the requirement for social cooperation and harmony) and pattern-maintenance (including processes to clarify group goals and reduce social tensions). Typically, however, scholars working in this tradition create somewhat looser inventories of the possible social effects of persistent patterns.

For a structural-functionalist then, why does play—as a distinctive pattern of human relating—occur? In education, psychology or biology, the inventory of play's effects is normally traced to the individual or species (see, e.g., Barnett, 1998). In sociology, it is traced to the social collectivity. In this latter view, play exists in society because ultimately it strengthens rather than weakens social order. By providing a relatively safe environment for the exploration of social and cultural themes, play makes society more conscious of itself. Play displays characteristic tensions in society and provides pathways (including times and places) for working these out. Play offers alternative statuses to actors in ways that deepen public knowledge of social order and social hierarchy. Play acquaints actors with the vicissitudes of social success and failure and with the public consequences of certain kinds of action. Play provides opportunities for leadership roles and for statuses expressing social subordination. Play illustrates cherished values in simplified settings. Play allows opportunities for emotional release and publicly accepted deviance.

The development of these skills and sensitivities in actors is held to be important, not for the individuals themselves, but for the continuity of the group. Frequently, play brings members of the community together to participate and to observe. To that degree, it makes communities more aware of their membership patterns and their common commitments. It identifies rival communities and social categories and hence gives shape to the meaning of shared social identity. It provides opportunities for successful players to receive public esteem thereby thickening and diversifying the social stratification system. Play frequently offers strong or even spectacular action that can be used as metaphors of character or accomplishment in society at large. It constitutes a significant portion of a society's economic activity and fills the calendar of daily activities for both youth and adults.

In such ways, play is deemed useful to a society's churches, schools, businesses, and families. In play, students are trained, soldiers hardened, children civilized. Ministers, moralists, and politicians find material for a thousand invocations. As Huizinga (1955, pp. 173–213) argued, a society or epoch that is "played" is more creative and vibrant than its plodding rivals.

How is such an approach to be judged? As Wilson (1983, p. 73) has argued, functionalism is perhaps better understood as a perspective or "way of building theories" than an actual theory itself. In other words, functionalism is a viewpoint based on a number of assumptions about how social life occurs. These assumptions include the ideas that social structures have identifiable requirements that must be satisfied to ensure their continuity and that the fulfillment of these needs in larger structures is the force behind the creation of patterns in smaller structures. Although there is no claim that the pattern being studied is the "best practice" for maintaining society, there is a sense that groups or organizations find the practice to be a socially acceptable way of meeting these requirements. To the extent that society works at all, stability and continuity are held to be valuable.

As might be imagined, critics dispute the validity of these assumptions. Can one really identify specific needs of social structures? Can it be shown that a pattern or practice actually meets these needs? Why aren't more effective practices substituted instead? Is it true that the needs of larger social structures drive the activities of smaller units or is the reverse equally true? And why is there so much emphasis on the value of stability and continuity? Doesn't this approach neglect the extent to which society is a living, ever-changing form?

Finally, the functionalist analysis of play tends to be a litany of possible benefits more than a documentation of effects. To state the matter bluntly: does play actually produce the social consequences described above? Does it accomplish these activities more effectively than alternative practices, such as work or ritual? Is play driven more by the requirements of groups and organizations or by the needs and desires of individuals? Structural-functionalism remains important in the social sciences because it suggests a fascinating range of possible social effects and even a direction of explanation—i.e., that processes within larger social units somehow determine processes within smaller, constituent ones. However, the actual direction and impact of these connections is a matter for empirical demonstration.

Conflict Theory

Conflict theorists dispute most of the arguments made above. As functionalism celebrates the social whole, so conflict theory emphasizes the interests of constituent parts (see Collins, 1975; Turner, 1978; Collins, 1994). Functionalism emphasizes social coordination and social sharing (e.g., common values, goals, and identities). In contrast, conflict theory emphasizes competition and the division of society over scarce resources. The former prizes stability and continuity, the latter disorder and change. Functionalism looks at the world from the outside in; conflict theory sees things from the inside out.

In sociology, the outstanding example of conflict theory has been the dialectical materialism of Karl Marx (see Marx, 1964; Lefebvre, 1969). For Marx, as for other conflict theorists, social life is organized ultimately around the ownership and control of scarce resources. In that light, the history of society itself is understood to be a history of inter-group struggle. Groups fortunate enough to win control attempt to consolidate their positions by exploiting or otherwise marginalizing those less successful. Far from accepting their lot, dispossessed people ponder ways to gather their forces against the controlling groups. However slow to materialize or painful in consequence, conflict between the powerful and powerless leads ultimately to new syntheses and alignments. Although Marx argued famously that communism might end such disputes over property and thus history itself, conflict theorists tend to see social life for the most part as a ceaseless plotting for advantage. What the functionalist sees as stability and order is for the conflict theorist merely a veneer for rampant forms of coercion, compliance, and uneasy compromise.

A clearer idea of the contrast between conflict theory and structural-functionalism can be gained by comparing quickly their respective explanations of wealth inequality. One well-known functionalist account (Davis and Moore, 1945) claims that wealth inequality is ultimately beneficial for society. As these authors explain, societies have various jobs that must be performed. Some of these jobs are more difficult and important than others. The question thus arises: How can society motivate people to perform difficult or stressful jobs that may require years of training? The answer, for Davis and Moore at least, is monetary reward. Ultimately, then, wealth differences are a way of motivating people to fulfill the complicated tasks of society. By such devices, talented people are encouraged to locate themselves in positions of leadership and control. Despite the unpleasant statuses granted to the less successful, society as a whole is said to benefit.

Again, conflict theory opposes this explanation (see Abrahamson, 1981, pp. 107–125). Functionalism, the conflict theorists claim, ignores such basic causes of wealth as inheritance, cronyism, artificial scarcities in the job market, and other forms of protectionism. To the Marxist, stratification is synonymous with exploitation and control. Wealth inequality is an expression of cumulative advantage and disadvantage perpetuated through the class position of families. Social mobility, the movement of individuals up and down the class structure, may occur, but that movement is systematically restricted by educational institutions and other "filtering" devices. Furthermore, those who do climb upward are frequently co-opted by the value systems of the dominant groups. In the "elitist" version of conflict theory, controlling groups intermarry and otherwise huddle together in special schools, clubs, resorts, and boards of directors. Thus, even as the faces of the powerful change, the values and sensibilities of the group do not.

For the conflict theorist then, social stratification may have "functions," but these should be understood as effects contributing to the stability and continuity of the controlling groups alone. Indeed, the concept of "society" itself may be something of a sham, a pretense that people are united in a common enterprise. The success of this illusion requires the cooperation of an array of institutions that keep less fortunate people intentionally misinformed about their true interests or otherwise stupefied.

Is the glass half empty or half full? For its part, conflict theory is a powerful commentary on human discontent. To understand the world is to acquaint oneself with expropriation and deceit. Only if people sever their false connections, ideas, and allegiances can a better society be attained.

When the conflict theorist looks at play, games, and sport, then what he or she sees is a fancy party made possible by the labor of the uninvited (see, e.g., Roszak, 1972; Cantelon and Gruneau, 1982; Hargreaves, 1986). These excluded others frequently prepare the food, erect the tents and tables, launder the clothing, craft the gifts and favors, and clean up after the event. Sometimes, they work as maids and servants; more typically, their faraway labor makes possible the wealth of the hosts and guests. This relationship between guests and servants is seen as particularly damaging when the uninvited are made to applaud the spectacle or otherwise admire a world they can never inhabit.

In more general terms, conflict theory reminds us of the political and economic dimensions of play (see MacAloon, 1981; Spariosu, 1989; Sutton-Smith, 1997, pp. 74–90). For the players themselves, play is frequently a spectacle of festivity and cooperation. People find pleasure in one another's presence and in the overall sense of belonging. Yet this sense of pleasure is tinged by the fact of social exclusion. Places at the dinner table or the guest list are, like other spots in society, scarce.

This emphasis on devices and criteria for social exclusion represents a useful correction to prevailing traditions in play studies (see Duncan, Chick, and Aycock, 1998). Potential players are excluded for reasons of wealth, prestige, knowledge and power. Some are excluded from the playground entirely. Others are made to watch, nurse, cajole, and reward participants. Social factors like race, class, age, gender, religion, region, etc., affect the play world as they affect other locales in society. To the degree that these excluded others are truly disadvantaged, exploited, or blocked from legitimate forms of expression, the arguments of the conflict theorists become compelling.

These ideas about exploitation can be used to characterize the event itself. Do players really suspend all their "material" interests and concerns when they enter the playground? Are they as intent on gathering and spending "social capital" as on fun and games? Is the play world rife with internecine struggles for advantage and control that spill over into relationships in the other parts of life?

As might be imagined, conflict theory can be criticized as a willful looking-for-trouble (see Turner, 1978, pp. 179–200). To be sure, players are sometimes Machiavellian and sometimes not. And events may be more or less competitive in character. Furthermore, the existence of paid workers at an event is not prima facie evidence of exclusion or exploitation. As noted above, conflict theory tends to see society as dominated by a relatively unified social elite who conspire against others. However, such a claim suggests the importance of evidence regarding processes of exclusion, treatment of outsiders, social composition of insiders, and the character of prevailing values. Not unlike structural-functionalism, conflict theory is largely a set of intellectual directions, a collection of concerns and sensibilities. Although the theory reminds us of matters we must never forget, it describes only certain cases well.

Exchange Theory

In the early 1960s the sociologist George Homans delivered a presidential address to the American Sociological Association entitled "Bringing Men Back In." Homans (1964) argued that macro-sociological approaches like conflict theory and structural-functionalism were missing the ways in which society truly operated—that is, they tended to disregard the energy and commitment of individuals in specific social situations. The approach Homans advocated is known as exchange theory, an emphasis on the calculations of individuals as they plan strategies to meet their own private goals (see Blau, 1964; Turner, 1978, pp. 201–305). From such a vantage point, social structure, to the extent that this term can be applied at all, is merely a set of temporary relationships reflecting the choices of these actors.

Of course, the idea that society is largely the aggregate of numerous acts of private decision-making can be traced back much further, at least to the utilitarian philosophers of the nineteenth century (see Collins, 1994, pp. 121–180). This latter viewpoint, it will be recalled, focused on the relative rationality of individuals, in particular on their desires to maximize individual happiness or pleasure while minimizing discomfort. As developed most fully by the early economists, utilitarianism provided both a theoretical explanation of society and a moral philosophy for its administration. As society itself was the product of all these attempts to pursue self-interest in the most efficient way, so social policy should not interfere with earnest private endeavor. Taken together, the comings and goings of a population would reveal natural laws of competition and collaboration. On its own, the good society would emerge.

The idea that social life might be seen as exchange was developed at the turn of the twentieth century by the German sociologist George Simmel (1971, pp. 43–69). The early economists had stressed the ways in which people sought goods and services of roughly agreed-upon monetary value. Simmel, by contrast, discussed how people pursued statuses or opportunities that have only personal or vague social value. In these purely social exchanges no goods or products change hands. Activities like a conversation or a kiss are valuable only to the extent that they create an expanded feeling of pleasure or self-worth in the participants. And of course, such gestures are not scarce resources in the manner of material goods. One can offer gracious comments or give kisses in virtually endless supply. However, even these gestures may be cheapened if they are traded indiscriminately. For a gesture to be socially valuable, other people must not only impute a certain amount of prestige to the producer but also recognize that some sacrifice or cost was involved in the giving. For each social act is performed with the knowledge that actors could be pursuing other satisfying courses of action instead. To that degree a favor—of more or less value—has been performed.

To illustrate this theory, let us consider the romantic date as a form of exchange (see Waller, 1937). Both parties are presumably interested in similar things—having a good time, experiencing the boost in self-esteem that comes from having another person care for you, attaining public recognition that one is socially attractive or marketable, creating opportunities for a deeper relationship, or even obtaining certain physical pleasures. For such reasons, the date may be seen as superior to other ways of spending an evening. However, the event entails considerable costs. Such matters include money, time, energy, psychological anxiety, and significantly the knowledge that one could be spending time, money, etc. in other ways. What the date reveals then is a kind of compromise between two people; both have decided to endure certain costs so as to obtain certain benefits. In that light, the event unfolds as a complicated game of persiflage, flattery, and wit; each player boosts the esteem of the other and receives similar rewards in return.

In the view of the exchange theorists, all social life exhibits similar patterns of bargaining and compromise. People give up so that they may get. We choose between alternative strategies on the basis of how closely they can take us to our goals and how much they cost. And, as Homans (1974) argues, we build in subjective estimates of the probability that these costs and benefits will be realized. Asking someone out for a date involves some calculation about the prospect of that offer's being refused (see also Blalock and Wilken, 1979). To operate in the social world then, we make mental estimates of the value of others and of the likelihood of their responding in certain ways to our gestures. Such matters become very complicated when several people are involved. In certain cases, we act so that we may receive responses from an observer or other type of third party. Or we may hope only to boost our general status within the group as a whole.

It should be emphasized that exchange theory differs from conflict theory in that the former tends to emphasize non-coercive situations. Although there are frequently "imbalanced exchanges" and problems of "equity," for the most part relationships reveal some degree of compliance or acceptance by the parties involved. Put differently, conflict theory typically explores zero-sum relationships; exchange theory characteristically describes relationships where both parties win in some degree. Furthermore, actors in exchange theory tend to be satisfied with less than the best (or most ideally rational) solutions (see Simon, 1957). Instead, workable strategies are routinely adopted. Indeed, in a clearly recognized parallel to behaviorist psychology, initial decisions about rewards and punishments may become fixed later as social habits.

This broad theme of exchange theory—that collective behavior is ultimately the expression of aggregated self-interest—has a natural appeal in individualistic and psychologically preoccupied societies like the United States. And because play is commonly considered to be a distinctive locale for individual pleasure seeking, this theory has a clear affinity for work in play studies as well. However, as in the cases of the previous two theories, only certain kinds of questions and sensitivities are brought forward in this model.

What exchange theory highlights explicitly are incentives for individual participation in play. Two particular aspects of this are the decision to enter the play setting in the first place and then later to quit and move on to other endeavors. Rather than accepting the entry of players as some "natural" or uncomplicated desire for challenge or fun, exchange theory invites inquiry into other, more specifically social motives. Will playing maintain or enhance my relationship with the other? Will I have an acceptable level of success? Will others notice me in a positive light? Will accepting an offer to play allow me to ask for similar or other kinds of favors in the future? Will there be other social pleasures (e.g., joking, gossip, new social contacts, etc.) associated with the event?

Against these potential enhancements to social identity are a set of nagging concerns. Will playing with this group actually deflate my prospects with others? Will I be over-matched or undermatched in terms of skill levels? Might

I spend my time more profitably—and pleasurably—pursuing other activities? Even more generally, will what I bring to the event be incongruous with the capabilities and status of the others? Will I be like the older child who refuses to play with younger ones because she brings too much to the event or will I find myself out of my league, frustrated and rejected? Exchange theory argues that individuals typically seek some level of perceived equity. Just as Cskizentmihalyi (1977) argued that players are most involved in activities when their physical skills match the challenges of their environment, so exchange theory emphasizes the matching of social skills. People are attracted by the prospect of a good match; at some point during the event, the benefits people give each other exhibit what the economists call "declining marginal utility." Typically, by mutual assent we quit and go on to other endeavors.

If exchange theory sensitizes us to the dynamics of "time-to-play" and "time-to-quit" issues, it also invites us to think somewhat differently about the dynamics of the event itself. In cases where roles are not clearly assigned, what causes some players to move into leadership roles and others into more subservient postures? How do people rationalize the fairness of these statuses? Similarly, attention is drawn to interaction patterns. On what basis are "teams" or social cliques formed? How do these formations reflect perceived social desirability and patterns of interaction in the world beyond the playground? Even social control patterns are looked at from the viewpoint of the individuals involved. By the terms of exchange theory, controlling others or allowing oneself to be controlled reflects a set of calculations regarding potential rewards and punishments as well as an estimation of the likelihood that these sanctions will be imposed. In these ways, the interactions of the playground feature attempt to enhance or protect social status. Our desires for success and competence in the moments of play are modified by our need to preserve the group's good opinion in more general terms. Said differently, the play is "on" at many different levels.

Like the previously described positions, exchange theory can be criticized (see Wilson, 1983, pp. 30–39). Any position that traces all human motivation to a single factor (such as self-interest) tends to have little explanatory power. This is particularly the case when explanations are offered after an action has occurred. For example, a person may be considered selfish if he gives all his money to charity (so that he will be thought well of) or, oppositely, keeps it all to himself. Stronger theories are those that specify a range of variation on some factor (e.g., some activities being more selfish than others) and discover (independently of the event) ways of measuring how people estimate the importance of certain benefits and costs. Furthermore, exchange theory seems to be less effective in describing macro-social processes (such as large social changes) or in acknowledging the extent to which social structures restrict or channel private desires. Nevertheless, exchange theory invites researchers to inquire deeply into the dynamics of actual play events. To that degree, it moves analysis beyond the generalizing or philosophizing tone of the previous approaches.

Symbolic Interactionism

The last approach to be considered places the sociologist even more deeply into the dynamics of human interaction (see Stryker, 1980; Collins, 1994, pp. 242–290). Indeed, describing the ways in which people develop and sustain various "lines of action" in their relationships with one another is almost the entire focus of symbolic interactionism (see Blumer, 1969). While other approaches point to a range of external or preexisting causes to account for group behavior, symbolic interactionism is largely content to describe the "hows" rather than the "whys" of such conduct.

To be sure, this turning away from general explanations of behavior is based on a distinctive view of social life. As developed by such scholars as G.H. Mead, Charles Horton Cooley, and W. I. Thomas in the first decades of the twentieth century, symbolic interactionism takes quite seriously the idea that social life can be seen as a kind of play in which actors perform roles (see Turner, 1978, pp.347–365). Of course, in the play of life there is no formal script; the actors move back and forth between many different roles, including those of performer and audience. What results then is something much more akin to improvisational theater. Action must be pushed forward by individual participants as they try to "read" the intentions behind others' actions and then interpret how their own actions are being perceived by those same people. As Cooley (1964) stated in his famous "looking glass" theory of the self, we form judgments about the effectiveness of our behaviors and about our own social characteristics by scrutinizing the responses of others to us. Because we can never know what others really think, we must gather our conclusions from a world of fleeting behaviors and appearances.

As Mead (1964, pp. 199–246) explained then, social behavior is much more complicated for humans than for other animals because humans have an unusual ability for "reflexive consciousness". In fact, human social life is the result of people's being able to "move outside themselves" to create abstract mental images of their own qualities or traits. Just as a baby comes to see his body as an object among other objects in the world, so people use increasingly complicated and abstract perspectives (e.g., the vantage point of another role or a group or the community in general) from which to assess their own lives.

All this surmising about one's place in the social world would have little utility were it not for the presence of "symbols". Humans effectively nail down phenomena by assigning arbitrary, collectively-shared meanings to it. Such human behaviors as spoken or written words, facial expressions, gestures, ways of touching, style of dress, maintenance of physical distance from others, etc. all have culturally-defined meanings. People share these understandings and then use them so others may read their intentions correctly. Similarly, collective understandings about social or personal traits may be attributed to whole categories of people. Thus, race, religion, gender, age, etc. are social constructions with broadly elaborated meanings. This "labeling process" commonly has profound consequences for the opportunities of those who are characterized in these ways.

While symbolic interactionism could have developed as a kind of culturalist approach that emphasizes the ways in which thought and behavior are narrowed by social convention, it has, for the most part, developed in the opposite direction. That is, theorists of this type typically focus on the ways in which people actively construct and manipulate shared meanings. In other words, public understandings about roles, community norms, social class status, etc. are understood as guidelines rather than confinements. As Erving Goffman (1959) argued, people manipulate the impressions that others get by revealing, concealing, or shading the ways in which verbal information and gestures are presented. Furthermore, as audiences of such behavior, we must decide whether actors are really committed to the roles that they are enacting or whether they are merely playing at them. So understood, social life is an incredibly complicated information game, a never-ending process of public (and private) discovery. For such reasons, one can see why symbolic interactionists typically disavow the scientifically-based search for general laws regarding human behavior. Social life is not something that exists beforehand but rather something that is created. Each social moment is different than the next—a response to the opportunities available in specific situations, to social roles, and the to inventiveness of the actors themselves.

As might be imagined, play activities are phenomena especially congenial to the symbolic interactionist approach (see. e.g., Stone, 1955; Denney, 1964; Fine, 1983). After all, symbolic interactionism focuses on the creation and maintenance of shared meanings in social situations; this theme is also central to most forms of play. A researcher of this type will wish to know how the norms of the playground become established. That is, who suggests them and what processes do they use to get agreement from others? Once norms have been established (as is the case in games with clearly established rules), symbolic interactionists are concerned with the social control procedures used to maintain these norms. In this light, shared ideas about various categories of actors (e.g., younger versus older children, girls rather than boys, etc.) will influence their abilities to participate fully. In general, symbolic interactionists ask how these meaning systems are erected and maintained.

A closely related theme concerns the social consequences for those who fail to meet the prevailing "definition of the situation"—either because of their personal qualities or because of their behavior. As noted above, symbolic interactionism focuses upon processes of social labeling. What opportunities have been diminished for those now identified as spoilsports, losers, crybabies, bullies, sissies, etc.? Will such now marginalized people be able to shed those labels or will they enter what symbolic interactionists describe as a "deviant career," a shift in both their network of associations and their sense of self (see Lemert, 1951; Becker, 1963)?

This broader theme—how people are defined by others and by themselves—is critical to the study of play. As I have argued in other contexts (Henricks, 1991), play activities commonly function as "identity ceremonies". That is, they are more or less public occasions in which people get to display their personal and social qualities before others. In more formal settings, the terms of that display—i.e., the nature of the game itself and the procedures for playing it—have already been established. In more informal play, individuals have a wider latitude to define themselves. Indeed, the ability to conceive the game and then get others to play it may be the most valued form of personal skill. As the symbolic interactionists emphasize, we act before others and then judge ourselves by the reactions that we produce.

In even more general terms, play seems amenable to symbolic interactionist descriptions. In play, people create, maintain, and dissemble social meanings. Players commonly take elements from outside the play setting itself (e.g., shared ideas, norms, stereotypes, etc.) and then twist them about for public amusement. In symbolic interactionism, actors are similarly manipulative. We take as much or as little of an idea as we desire and turn it to our purposes. We skirt about the edges of propriety seeking to cultivate images of ourselves as competent, rebellious, or clever. The specific shape those actions will take cannot be predicted by social scientists. Like social life more generally, play is a dance that can only be appreciated in the moments of its making.

It should not be surprising that symbolic interactionism is subject to the range of criticisms that can be applied to all micro-social theories. That is, individuals seem to have too much power to shape their own destinies while collectivities have too little. Said differently, symbolic interactionists recognize social roles and culture as significant elements of social structure but give too little prominence to other levels (i.e., groups, communities, society, etc.). Furthermore, the management of identity issues, while important, hardly exhausts the scope of public and private concerns. Even more problematic is the reticence to offer general propositions about social behavior. After all, sociology historically has been a generalizing science. Inquiries about the kinds of social groups performing certain kinds of behavior in various ways in distinctive circumstances have been central to the development of the discipline.

Clearly, each theoretical perspective has its strengths and its limitations. Taken together, however, the four approaches do seem to highlight a great range of issues that are commonly overlooked in the study of play. Characteristically, people play with other people. The resulting patterns of communication and confrontation are arguably more important to the quality of the experience than the mechanics of the game itself. In that sense, the social stands beside the personal and the cultural as fundamental contexts for the examination of expressive life.

REFERENCES

Abrahamson, M. (1981). *Sociological theory: An introduction to concepts, issues, and research.* Englewood Cliffs, NJ: Prentice-Hall.

Barnett, L. (1998). The adaptive powers of being playful. In M. Duncan, G. Chick, and A. Aycock, eds. *Diversions and divergences in fields of play: Play and culture studies,* vol. 1. (Pp. 97–120). Greenwich, CT: Ablex.

Becker, H. (1963). *Outsiders: Studies in the sociology of deviance.* New York: Free Press.

Berlyne, D. (1960). *Conflict, arousal, and curiosity*. New York: McGraw-Hill.

Blau, P. (1964) *Exchange and power in social life.* New York: Wiley.

Blalock, H., and Wilken, P. (1979). *Intergroup processes: A micro-macro perspective.* New York: Free Press.

Blumer, H. (1969). *Symbolic interactionism.* Englewood Cliffs, NJ: Prentice-Hall.

Cantelon, H. and Gruneau, R., eds. (1982). *Sport, culture, and the modern state.* Toronto: University of Toronto Press.

Chick, G. (2001). What is play for? Sexual selection and the evolution of play. In S. Reifel. ed. *Theory: In context and out: Play and culture studies*, vol. 3 (Pp. 3–25). Westport, CT: Ablex.

Collins, R. (1975). *Conflict sociology.* New York: Academic Press.

Collins, R. (1994). *Four sociological traditions.* New York: Oxford University Press.

Cooley, C. (1964). *Human nature and social order*. New York: Shocken Books.

Curran, J. and Gurevitch, M., ed. (1992). *Mass media and society.* New York: Edward Arnold.

Csikszentmihalyi, M. (1977). *Beyond boredom and anxiety.* San Francisco: Jossey-Bass.

Davis, K. and Moore, W. (1945). Some principles of stratification. *American sociological review* 10.

Denney, R. (1964). *The astonished muse.* New York: Grosset and Dunlop.

Denzin, N. (1977). *Childhood socialization.* San Francisco: Jossey-Bass.

Dickens, D. and Fontana, A., ed. (1994) *Postmodernism and social inquiry.* New York: Guilford.

Duncan, M., Chick, G., and Aycock, A., eds. (1998). *Diversions and divergences in fields of play: Play and culture studies*, Vol. 1. Greenwich, CT.: Ablex .
Durkheim, E. (1933). *The division of labor in society.* New York: Macmillan.
Durkheim, E. (1964). *The rules of the sociological method.* New York: Free Press.
Ellis, M. (1973). *Why people play.* Englewood Cliffs, NJ: Prentice-Hall.
Erikson, E. (1950). *Childhood and society*. New York: Norton.
Fagen, R. (1981). *Animal play behavior*. New York: Oxford University Press.
Ferguson, M. and Golding, P., eds. *Cultural studies in question.* Thousand Oaks, CA: Sage.
Fine, G. (1983). *Shared fantasy: Role-playing games as social worlds.* Chicago: University if Chicago Press.
Gans, H. (1971). The uses of poverty: The poor pay all. *Social Policy.* July–August: 21–24.
Giddens, A. (1991). *Modernity and self-identity: Self and society in the late modern age.* Stanford, CA: Stanford University Press.
Goffman, E. (1959). *The presentation of self in everyday life.* New York: Doubleday and Co.
Goffman, E. (1961). *Encounters*. Indianapolis: Bobbs-Merrill.
Goffman, E. (1974). *Frame analysis: An essay on the organization of experience.* New York: Harper and Row.
Handelman, D. (1998). *Models and mirrors: Toward an anthropology of public events*. New York: Berghahn Books.
Hargreaves, J. (1986). *Sport, power, and culture.* Oxford, England: Polity Press.
Henricks, T. (1991). *Disputed pleasures: Sport and society in preindustrial England.* New York: Greenwood Press.
Homans, G. (1964). Bringing men back in. *American sociological review* 21: 809–818.
Homans, G. (1974). *Social behavior: Elementary forms,* rev. ed. New York:Harcourt, Brace, Jovanovich.
Huizinga, J. (1955). *Homo ludens: A study of the play-element in culture.* Boston; Beacon.
Hurst, C. (2000). *Living Theory: The applications of classical social theory to contemporary life.* New York: Allyn and Bacon.
Klugman, E., and Smilansky, S, eds. (1990). *Children's play and learning: Perspectives and policy implications*. New York: Teacher's College Press.
Lancy, D. (2002). Cultural constraints on children's play. In J. Roopnarine, ed., *Conceptual, social-cognitive, and contextual issues in the fields of play. Play and culture studies,* vol. 4 (pp. 151–176) Westport, CT: Ablex.
Lancy, D. and Tindall, B, eds. (1976). *The anthropological study of play: Problems and prospects*. Cornwall, NY: Leisure Press.
Lefebvre, H. (1969). *The sociology of Marx.* New York: Vintage.
Lemert, E. (1951). *Social pathology.* New York: McGraw-Hill.
Levy, J. (1978). *Play behavior.* New York: Wiley.
MacAloon, J. (1981). *The great symbol: Pierre de Coubertin and the origins of the modern Olympic Games.* Chicago: University of Chicago Press.

Martindale, D. (1981). *The nature and types of sociological theory.* Boston: Houghton Mifflin.

Marx, K. (1964). *Karl Marx: Selected writings in sociology and social philosophy.* T. Bottomore, ed. New York: McGraw-Hill.

Mead, G. (1964). *On social psychology.* A. Strauss, ed. Chicago: University of Chicago Press.

Mergen, B. (ed). (1986). *Cultural dimensions of play, games, and sports.* Champaign. IL; Human Kinetics.

Merton, R. (1968). *Social theory and social structure.* New York: Free Press.

Parsons, T. (1951). *The social system.* New York: Free Press.

Piaget, J. (1962). *Play, dreams, and imitation in childhood.* New York: Norton.

Radcliffe-Brown, A. (1952). *Structure and function in primitive society.* Glencoe, IL: Free Press.

Roopnarine, J., Johnson, J., and Hooper, F. (1994). *Children's play in diverse cultures.* Albany, State University of New York Press.

Roszak, T. (1972). Forbidden Games. In M. Hart, Ed. *Sport in the socio-cultural process.* Dubuque, IA: W. C. Brown.

Rubin, K., ed. (1980). *Children's play.* San Francisco: Jossey-Bass.

Simmel, G. (1971). *On individuality and social forms.* D. Levine, ed. Chicago: University of Chicago Press.

Simon, H. (1957). *Models of Man.* New York: Wiley.

Stone, G. (1955). American sports: Play and display. *Chicago review* 9: 83–100.

Spariosu. M. (1989). *Dionysus reborn: play and the aesthetic dimension in modern philosophical and scientific discourse.* Ithaca, NY: Cornell University Press.

Sponseller, D. 1974. *Play as a learning medium.* Washington, D.C.: National Association for the Education of Young Children.

Stryker, S. (1980). *Symbolic interactionism: A social structural version.* Menlo Park, CA.: Cummings.

Sutton-Smith, B., Mechling, J., Johnson, T, and McMahon, F. (1995). *Children's folklore: a sourcebook.* New York: Garland.

Sutton-Smith, B. (1997). *The ambiguity of play.* Cambridge: Harvard University Press.

Turner, J. (1978). *The structure of social theory.* Homewood, IL: Dorsey Press.

Turner, V. (1969). *The ritual process.* Chicago: Aldine.

Waller, W. (1937). The rating and dating complex. *American sociological review* 2: 727–734.

Wilson, J. (1983). *Social theory.* Englewood Cliffs, NJ: Prentice-Hall.

Chapter Three

Children's Play in the Journal, *Young Children*: An Analysis of How it is Portrayed and Why it is Valued[1]

David Kuschner

I have been a member of the National Association for the Education of Young Children (NAEYC) since 1973. As a member, I have received six issues of the organization's journal, *Young Children*, each year since my membership started. In 1987 I had an article published in the journal titled, "Put your name on your painting . . . but the blocks go back on the shelves" (Kuschner, 1987) which had as its focus the unintended messages about play that teachers and the curriculum may send to children and parents. This present article takes that question a step further and examines the messages about play that might be sent by the journal itself.

The journal, *Young Children*, is arguably the most widely disseminated professional publication in the field of early childhood education. As a membership benefit of NAEYC, each of the six issues per year currently has a circulation of over 100,000 copies. With a circulation of that size, the journal has the potential for influencing the ways in which professionals in the field think about a wide range of issues related to the education of young children. In addition, since NAEYC membership is comprised of a cross-section of professionals in the field, including college and university faculty members, child-care workers, preschool through primary grade teachers, and policy advocates, the potential audience for the information presented in the journal is also quite diverse.

One of the topics discussed with some frequency in the issues of the journal is children's play. Given the long history and tradition in the field of early childhood education of emphasizing the importance of children's play this is not surprising. The purpose of the present article is to examine the ways in which play is portrayed in the pages of *Young Children.* My interest, however, was not simply the specific topics addressed by the individual articles. I was curious as to what the articles *taken as a whole* might be communicating—explicitly as well as implicitly—about young children's play. If the journal is viewed as a tool of a particular 'culture' (in this case the profession of early childhood education), my interest was in how this tool might be potentially shaping the thinking and views of the members of that culture.

I chose the journal, *Young Children*, as the focus of this study because of the extent of its potential readership and the possible influence the journal's content has on its audience. In terms of a data set, I reviewed all of the issues that were published from 1973 (my first year of membership) through 2002. To keep the task at a reasonably manageable level, I considered for review only those parts of each issue that would be classified as an *article*. This included the "Research in Review" reports that regularly appear in the journal but excluded other regular features of the journal such as the President's Message, public policy updates, and book reviews. The decision to review only articles also excluded descriptions of curriculum activities as well as the occasional photomontage and poem.

Once I identified all of the articles that were published between 1973 and 2002, I then identified those articles that specifically focused on the topic of play. In some cases the focus was on the topic of play itself and in other cases the focus was on a material typically provided for children's play, for example, blocks or puzzles. These were the articles I chose to review for the present study. I did not include, once again for reasons of manageability, articles that may have mentioned or discussed play within the context of another topic. For example, an article about literacy development in which the author briefly discusses how play fosters the development of reading and writing would not be included for review. I reviewed only those articles that by title and/or primary content were specifically about some aspect of children's play.

Based on these criteria, I was able to identify a total 1408 articles published in 184 issues of the journal between 1973 and 2002. Of these 1408 articles, 108 were "Research in Review" articles. Out of the 1408 articles, I identified a total of 101 articles as focusing specifically on children's play; five of these articles were "Research in Review" reports.

As might be expected, there was a range of topics discussed in the 101 articles that focused on children's play and a number of the topics were the subjects of multiple articles over the years. Role-play in its various forms was the subject of sixteen articles; of these sixteen, six were about sociodramatic play, five about superhero play, and five about symbolic play specifically. There were thirteen articles about playground or outdoor play including six articles in a special section that appeared in 2002. The play of infants and toddlers was the subject of ten articles while play during the primary grade years was the topic of seven articles. In terms of the usual materials provided for children in early childhood settings, six articles were about blocks, five about water play, and there were two articles each about sand play and puzzle play. There were also four articles about the relationship of play to language and literacy development.

As noted above, there were five Research in Review articles that focused on play and the subjects of these reviews were: pretend play (Fein, 1979); play and learning in infancy (Caruso, 1988); symbolic play in preschool and primary settings (Nourot and Van Hoorn, 1991); the importance of make-believe play within Vygotsky's theory (Berk, 1994); and the early development of symbolic play (Gowen, 1995).

My main interest in reviewing the articles, however, was not in quantifying the topics covered. I was more interested in any underlying themes or images of play that were being communicated in these articles—intentionally or otherwise. My curiosity focused on what the articles *taken as a whole* were communicating about the play of young children and on how these messages might be shaping the thinking and views of the readers. The remainder of this article discusses three themes that emerged as I read through those 101 articles about children's play.

WHY PLAY SHOULD BE INCLUDED IN THE CURRICULUM

As mentioned earlier, given the long history and tradition in early childhood education for valuing children's play, it was not surprising to find that all of the 101 articles extolled the benefits of emphasizing play within the early childhood curriculum. It was also not surprising to find that the majority of articles emphasized the value of play for the purpose of fostering intellectual and academic development. The intellectual, cognitive, and academic benefits of play discussed in the articles included fostering the development of:

- language and literacy skills (Barbour, Webster, and Drosdeck, 1987; Christie, 1982; Fayden, 1997; Kostelnik, Whiren, and Stein, 1986; Nourot and Van Hoorn, 1991; Reifel, 1984; Roskos and Christie, 2001; Stalmack, 1981);
- problem solving skills (Cain and Bohrer, 1997; Christie, 1982; Christie and Wardle, 1992; Fayden, 1997; Kostelnik, Whiren, and Stein, 1986; Nourot and Van Hoorn, 1991; Stalmack, 1981);
- planning skills (Barbour, Webster, and Drosdeck, 1987; Casey and Lippman, 1991; Christie and Wardle, 1992; Feeney and Magarick, 1984; Fein, 1979);
- creativity and imagination (Cain and Bohrer, 1997; Christie, 1982; Fayden, 1997; Kostelnik, Whiren, and Stein, 1986; Nourot and Van Hoorn, 1991; Stalmack, 1981);

- math understanding and skills (Cooper and Dever, 2001; Fayden, 1997;
- Nourot and Van Hoorn, 1991; Stalmack, 1981);
- science concepts (Cooper and Dever, 2001; Fayden, 1997);
- spatial relationships (Reifel, 1984);
- Piagetian conservation abilities (Fein, 1979);
- political science concepts (Greenberg, 1989); and
- IQ (Fein, 1979).

Although I was not surprised to find the emphasis on intellectual and cognitive development, I was somewhat surprised at how little attention was paid to the relationship of play to children's emotional development. There were, in fact, only two articles specifically about the relationship of play and emotional issues. One was Klein's article on the use of play with hospitalized children (Klein, 1979) and the second was Curry and Arnaud's (1995) discussion of how play may reveal children's emotional and personality difficulties. In addition to these two articles, there were a few articles that discussed the relationship of play to emotional development within the context of other topics. For example, Eggleston and Weir (1975) noted the relaxing effect of water play and Barbour, Webster, and Drosdeck (1987) discussed the soothing qualities of sand play.

My belief is that the relative lack of emphasis on the relationship of play to children's emotional development runs counter to what we know and understand about young children's lives in early childhood settings. Vivian Paley (1996), for example, suggests that a concern for the emotional life of young children isn't just restricted to those children who might have a label of being 'emotionally disturbed.' She writes that all children experience some important emotional issues when they enter the preschool or any other classroom environment.

> Is there a preschool anywhere that does not include those who at times feel sad, angry, and helpless? Young as children are when they enter school, few can escape the sudden fear of abandonment and the inability to make their feelings known. There is the frightened or aggressive child we are unable to calm, the isolate who refuses to emerge from hiding, the child too worried to play: We see them in all our classrooms. (Paley, 1996, p. vii)

From this perspective, Paley believes that teachers need to see themselves as "actors in the theater of affective communication" (vii). She also believes that there is a crucial relationship between children's emotional development and their cognitive and academic development: "For, by now, we must all realize that when we acknowledge and learn to deal with children's emotional needs, *in the classroom*, we directly influence their social and cognitive development" (p. viii).

Koplow (1996b) makes the case that there is a danger to the overemphasis of the intellectual and cognitive at the expense of the emotional. She relates the story of a four-year-old boy who had been referred to her therapeutic preschool program. He came to her after two years in a preschool program for learning disabled children where he had not uttered a spoken word, offered no responses when given standardized tests, and provided no evidence that he knew the names of colors or could recognize numbers. His teacher had concluded that he was mentally retarded and wanted to transfer him to a lower group. It was during the transfer process that the boy was referred to Koplow's program.

For the first three weeks, the boy continued his pattern of not speaking and was relatively inactive. Then one day he was overhead speaking into a play telephone and yelling, "You crackhead, you stink!" (p. x). It turns out that he was neither nonverbal nor retarded; he had come from an environment that included regular drug-related violence and he himself had experienced abuse during infancy. Koplow's conclusion was, "Tragically, he had not been able to find a way to fit his emotional agenda into his academically oriented preschool. Therefore, his actual potential remained hidden" (p. x). Koplow (1996a) believes that healthy emotional development serves as a necessary foundation for the intellectual and academic tasks facing children in preschool.

> In order for the preschool child to build a solid developmental basis for learning, he must have new experiences that support the acquisition of essential developmental precursors. Preschools that heal will provide children with an opportunity to finish this important developmental work before insisting that they devote their energies to the mastery of abstract pre-academic tasks. (p. 14–15)

Play has long been viewed as a medium through which children can express their emotional needs and achieve some mastery and control over experiences and circumstances that might be emotionally troubling. Anna Freud, for example, pointed out, "when adults go over their experiences in conscious thought and speech, children do the same in play" (Freud and Burlingham, 1943, p. 67). As an example, she described how nursery school children in London during World War II expressed their wartime experiences in their block play.

> War games play a part in our nursery as they do in others. Houses which are built are not simply thrown over as in former times, they are bombed from above, bricks being used as bombs. Playing train has given way to playing aeroplanes . . . Games like these will come more into the foreground after air attacks, and give way to peace time games when things are again normal. (p. 67–68)

As far back as 1948, Kanner suggested that play was a powerful therapeutic tool because "It's self-expressive nature suggests its use for the combined purpose of revealing children's feelings and allowing the child to approach reality via the quasi-reality of his own creation" (Kanner, 1948, p. 230). Virginia Axline (1947), one of the originators of non-directive play therapy, wrote that play can have a powerful effect on emotional development because,

> the *child* is the most important person . . . is in command of the situation and of himself . . . he suddenly feels that . . . he can look squarely at himself . . . for this is his world, and he no longer has to compete with other forces such as adult authority or . . . situations where he is not an individual in his own right. (p. 16)

Guerny (1984) contrasted the focus of the play therapist with that of the classroom teacher and this contrast captures the tension between seeing play as a vehicle for emotional development as opposed to emphasizing play primarily for cognitive and academic development.

> The classroom teacher, interested in cognitive development, may introduce play aspects to stimulate, reduce threat, or in other ways utilize the powers of play to enhance learning. However, she/he is interested ultimately in a product . . . The play therapist rarely is concerned with a specific product but rather is concerned with the meaning of the acts and words in relation to the child's emotional and interpersonal psychological life. (p. 296–297)

The fact that most of the 101 articles saw the value of play primarily in intellectual and academic terms was actually foreshadowed by Eggleston and Weir who, as far back as 1975, wrote in the pages of *Young Children*, "In recent years most of the experiences offered to young children have had to be rationalized for the intellectual content even though we feel the social and emotional reasons for activities are equally important" (Eggleston and Weir, 1975, p. 6). Their statement seems to have held true for the twenty-five years that followed.

AN EMPHASIS ON THE UNIVERSAL CHILD

A second theme that emerged during my review had to do with play and cultural differences. Although there were a number of the 1408 articles that focused on issues related to cultural differences, multicultural education, and diversity, there were very few articles that addressed the relationship of cultural differences to children's play.

The only article to directly address the issue of cultural differences and play was published in 1996 and promoted the use of multicultural (and non-sexist) prop boxes for children's sociodramatic play (Boutte, Van Scoy, and Hendley, 1996). The authors suggested in this article that teachers should provide props and artifacts from many cultures as a way of promoting multicultural awareness and an appreciation for diversity.

There were a few articles that mentioned the topic of cultural differences within the context of a larger discussion about play. Nourot and Van Hoorn (1991), for example, wrote that teachers need to understand and respect the differences they may observe in children's play and that one of the sources of these differences might be culture. This point is also acknowledged by Fayden (1997) in an article about sociodramatic play and by Griffing (1983) who suggested that the ways in which a teacher facilitates play must take into consideration a number of variables, including cultural background.

Most of the articles, however, appeared to have been written from what Lubeck (1996) terms the perspective of the *universal child.* This perspective suggests that there are some general principles of child development that apply to all children, regardless of their particular backgrounds and experiences. Lubeck argues that a more appropriate perspective is one that sees each individual child as what might be termed a *culturally constituted* child. In other words, each individual child is the product of her own personal history that took place within a particular culture. As Nourot (1995) writes,

> Children come to school as products of their backgrounds—not only their own family's heritage, traditions, and language but also their broader cultural heritage. Self-concept, styles of communication, and relationships with peers and authority are but a few of the variables that are culturally conditioned and affect children's behavior, development, and approaches to learning at school. (p. 6)

Nourot goes on to specifically discuss the cultural implications for children's play and suggests that children play at and express what they know, that they "express the 'event scripts' of their lives" (p. 11). She provides an example of a Laotian child in a preschool classroom who had only been in the United States for two weeks. Nourot describes how this child would come to the preschool everyday and put on a cloth baby carrier into which she placed a doll that had Asian features. The little girl would then carry the doll around with her for most of the day, emulating the way in which her mother carried around her baby sister at home.

A number of problems have been identified that emerge when play is considered separate and apart from cultural context. One concern relates to the assessment of children's play. Roopnarine and Johnson (2001) cite research conducted by Farver and Shinn (1997) that compared the play of Korean-American preschool-aged children with that of Anglo-American children. Data was gathered from direct observations of the children in their respective preschools and from parental reports of home play. The researchers found that the Korean-American children engaged in significantly less social pretend play than the Anglo-American children and were observed to participate in unoccupied play and parallel play significantly more. Farver and Shinn suggested that one of the reasons for these differences is that according to the parental reports, the parents of the Anglo-American children believed in the importance of pretend play for intellectual development, language development, and school readiness. The parents of the Anglo-American children also reported that their children engaged in pretend play quite a bit at home. The Korean-American parents, on the other hand, did not share this belief in the importance of pretend play. Without considering the cultural context, the play of the Korean-American children in the study might be considered deficient relative to some of the scales used to categorize and evaluate play. In this case, however, the Korean-American children might have been manifesting the levels of play valued by their culture because as King (1992) points out, "cultural context exerts an indirect influence on play because the family acts as a 'mediating link' between the transmission of culture and the emergent patterns of play" (p. 53). It may not be the case that the Korean-American children weren't able to produce the more social levels of play but that those levels weren't valued in their family culture. Göncü, Tuermer, Jain, and Johnson (1999) support this point when they write,

> the development of play characterized in Western theories is only one of many possible cultural models of children's play. Social class and cultural differences may be due to varying cultural norms of development rather than children's deficit. Thus, adequate examination of children's play in a given community can be accomplished only by taking into account the unique cultural milieu in which play is embedded. (p. 152)

The second (and related) problem raised by a "culture-free" approach to looking at children's play concerns the development and implementation of play interventions. It is not uncommon in the field of early childhood education for interventions to be designed to remediate the perceived deficiencies in children's play. Göncü, et al. (1999) argue that a cultural context perspective suggests a cautious approach to the implementation of play interventions.

> For us, the immediate issue is that interventions prohibited the emergence of efforts to understand the play of children in low-income or non-Western commu-

> nities, which may not be deficient but may simply be different from the play described in the dominant literature. (p. 152)

This point is echoed by Roopnarine, Lasker, Sacks, and Stores (1998) who write,

> Play intervention strategies developed in the United States and Europe may not be relevant for some children because quite often the early childhood curricula reflect play materials and activities relevant to white families, disregarding the diverse environments within which children live. (p. 210)

The finding that there was little specific attention in the *Young Children* articles on cultural differences in play supports King's (1992) position that there is a general lack of focus on context in the study of children's play, with culture being one aspect of context. For King, context is important because it is

> the source of the meaning of all human behavior, and context variables must be investigated if we hope to achieve an understanding of any human interaction. This is very true in the area of play, where the very definition requires attention to aspects of context. (p. 44)

The results of my review also relate to the suggestion made by Roopnarine et al. (1998) that there is a bias to the literature on play because it is based for the most part on North American and European children and "may be limited in its generalizability when considering culture, gender, and social class issues" (p. 194). The authors go on to claim, "Most textbooks and articles on play have failed to provide a comprehensive theory of play that seriously incorporates the vast properties of culture" (p. 197). And Roopnarine and Johnson (2001) might have been talking about the *Young Children* articles when they write, "existing play theories may be inadequate in guiding research on diverse groups of children because they appear insensitive to considerations of factors within the ecocultural system that may influence growth and development" (p. 301).

PLAY WITHIN THE CONTEXT OF SCHOOL

The final theme that emerged during the review of the *Young Children* articles suggests that although play may naturally emerge from the experiences and interests of the children, when this natural play enters the classroom there is often an attempt by teachers and/curriculum to modify, shape, and change the play in some way. Teachers may value play but they do so within the context of the behaviors and activities that are acceptable and valued in the classroom. A number of the *Young Children* articles suggested ways in which teachers could transform the play behaviors of children to make them more acceptable within the school context. Kinsman and Berk (1979), for example, suggested, "early childhood teachers plan the arrangement of the classroom activity centers to promote desirable behaviors in children" (p. 66). In writing about the use of sand play for fostering language development, Barbour, Webster, and Drosdeck (1987) made the point, "Productive sand play does not just happen by simply putting sand and children together" (p. 24). Similarly, in terms of what occurs on the elementary school playground, Pellegrini and Perlmutter (1988) wrote, "Based on social skill coaching, the adults engineer the child's social experience" (p. 17). And for teachers dealing with "undesirable" block play behaviors, Cartwright (1988) offered the following guidance.

> Except for special controlled situations, there should be no crashing of buildings . . . no hording, swinging, throwing, dropping. No stepping, sitting, lying, or rolling on unit blocks. While conveying your love to the child, gently disengage him from the blocks and say with complete assurance in your heart, "I can't allow that." (Cartwright, 1988, p. 47)

This tension between naturally emerging play behaviors and what may be considered productive or desirable behaviors was very apparent in the articles that addressed the issue of superhero play. In an article titled, "Living with He-Man: Managing superhero fantasy play" (Kostelnik, Whiren, and Stein, 1986), the authors acknowledged that superhero play is natural to childhood and that this type of play "gives children access to power and prestige unavailable to them in daily experience" (p. 5). At the same time, however, the authors noted that teachers are often less than enthusiastic about this type of play; they are not comfortable with its somewhat rowdy nature and they can be bothered when children carry over the superhero character into other activities. As a solution to this problem, the authors provided a number of suggestions for how teachers can shape the naturally emerging superhero play into forms more acceptable in the classroom. They suggested, for example, that various superhero themes can be used to explore related academic concepts such as Batman play leading to the study of bats and caves, and Spiderman play leading to the study of spiders and webs. (Here again are examples of the emphasis on using play to promote intellectual and academic development.)

In an article titled, "Battling Jurassic Park: From a fascination with violence toward constructive knowledge," Cain and Bohrer (1997) addressed this same tension when they looked at the play and behavior issues that arose in classrooms at the time the first "Jurassic Park" movie was released. Their basic premise was, "To move forward we needed to examine the developmental benefits of make-believe play so that the children's interests could be guided toward constructive knowledge" (p. 71). Although the authors acknowledged that the dinosaur play that emerged might be helping the children work through feelings generated by the movie, they believed that the children's play still needed to be shaped in a particular direction because even though, "the children were using dinosaurs as a means of empowerment through aggression and violence . . . [we] argue that there are other, more constructive, ways to empower children" (p. 72).

CONCLUSION

All of the 101 articles reviewed extolled the virtues of children's play and many of the articles were proposing that opportunities for play should be incorporated into the early childhood curriculum. The perhaps unintended message of the articles, however, was that certain kinds of play are valued over others: play that fosters intellectual and academic development is valued over play that benefits emotional development; play that is viewed as 'universal' in nature is valued over play that may be more culturally determined; and play that conforms to the behavioral and academic expectations of school is valued over the sometimes unruly, messy, and aggressive play that often emerges naturally from children's interests and experiences. As Brown and Freeman (2001) write, there is a "conviction [among early childhood educators] that play appears chaotic and undisciplined, undermining the school's primary purpose which is to bring order and control to children's lives" (p. 263).

My review of the *Young Children* articles seems to support Brown and Freeman's (2001) claim, "even though early childhood educators say they support play, their behavior indicates that their supporters doubt its worth and developmental value" (p. 263). The authors of the articles reviewed certainly support the importance of play; none of the 101 articles calls for the elimination of play in the early childhood curriculum. All of the articles suggest that there is developmental value to children's play.

The value attributed to children's play in the articles, however, tends to be defined and circumscribed by some intrinsic characteristics of schooling: an emphasis on the intellectual and academic sides of children's development, a focus on what is perceived to be universal aspects of children's development, and constraints on the types of behaviors that are seen as acceptable in the classroom context. A number of the authors of the *Young Children* articles themselves recognized that a tension exists between what may be the nature of children's play and the socially determined context of school. As noted earlier,

Eggleston and Weir (1975), in an article about the value of water play wrote, "In recent years most of the experiences offered to young children have had to be rationalized for the intellectual content even though we feel the social and emotional reasons for activities are equally important" (p. 6). Roskos and Christie (2001), although writing specifically about the use of play to foster literacy development, suggest a concern that might generalize to the use of play in school when they write: "But play's easygoing ways also makes it susceptible to all sorts of pressure and inappropriate expectations from adults who, with the best of intentions, wish to use play as a context for promoting literacy" (p. 65).

Finally, I think Nourot and Van Hoorn (1991) capture the tension between emphasizing what is natural to play and the constraints and demands of the school setting when they write, "One of the major issues teachers and researchers struggle with is the precise relationship of play to the concepts and skills valued by our educational system . . . Can we understand it [play] and support it without destroying its very nature?" (p. 40).

EPILOGUE

One of the reviewers of this present article suggested that I update my findings to include articles published in *Young Children* through 2005. (I had ended my original review with the issues published through 2002.) Using the criteria that I described earlier, I was able to identify a total of 197 articles in the sixteen issues published between 2002 and the most recent issue of July 2005. There were also five "Research in Review" articles published. Of these 202 articles, seventeen focused on the topics related to children's play. Three of the these seventeen articles focused on some form of symbolic play and two addressed issues related to outdoor play. The remaining articles covered such topics as the play of babies, music play, the modification of play opportunities for children with disabilities, play policy, and how play fosters the development of mathematical abilities.

Ten of the seventeen articles on play appeared in a special section entitled, "Play for All Children," that appeared in the May 2003 issue of the journal. I suspect that the catalyst for this special section on play was the emphasis in early childhood education on academic standards and assessment that has been increasing since the passage of the No Child Left Behind Act in 2001. In fact, there were at least four articles during the 2003 volume year that specifically addressed the issue of learning standards in early childhood education.

In terms of the three themes I identified earlier in this paper—an emphasis on play for the fostering of academic and intellectual development, a lack of attention paid to cultural differences and play, and the issue of play within the context of school—the seventeen articles generally fell into the same pattern. The general focus of the articles was on how play relates to academic and intellectual development, although a couple of articles did note a link between play and socio-emotional development. Levin (2003), in particular, discussed the difficult issue of superhero and war play from the perspective of how this type of play may help some children deal with troubling emotional issues. She writes, for example, "children now more than ever need to find ways to work out the violence they see. For many, play helps them do so" (p. 62).

In regards to the topic of play and cultural differences, one article did note the importance of equipping the classroom with culturally relevant materials (Jones, 2003) and one article discussed the use of resources for play in Malaysia (Tee, 2004), but there were no articles specifically focused on the issue of cultural differences in play.

Finally, in terms of play in the context of classrooms, my reading of the articles again suggests that there are aspects of children's play that are somewhat difficult to accommodate within the classroom and that one of the tasks for the teacher is to shape and modify play to meet the goals of the classroom. Levin (2003), in writing about superhero and war play in the early childhood classroom captures this tension when she writes, "Play, viewed for decades as an essential part of the early childhood years, has become a problem in many classrooms, even something to avoid" (p. 60).

NOTE

1. An earlier version of this article was presented at the annual conference of The Association for the Study of Play, Santa Fe, NM, February 21, 2002.

REFERENCES

Axline, V. (1947). *Play Therapy*. NY: Houghton Mifflin.

Barbour, N., Webster, T. D., and Drosdeck, S. (1987). Sand: Resource for the language arts. *Young Children, 42*(2), 20–25.

Berk, L. E. (1994). Research in review. Vygotsky's theory: The importance of make-believe play. *Young Children, 50*(1), 30–39.

Boutte, G. S., Van Scoy, I, and Hendley, S. (1996). Multicultural and nonsexist prop boxes. *Young Children, 52*(1), 34–39.

Brown, M. H. and Freeman, N. (2001). "We don't play that way at preschool": The moral and ethical dimensions of controlling children's play. In S. Reifel and M. H. Brown (Eds.), *Early education and care, and reconceptualizing play* (pp. 259–274). NY: JAI.

Cain, B. and Bohrer, C. (1997). Battling Jurassic Park: From fascination with violence toward constructive knowledge. *Young Children*, *52*(7), 71–73.

Cartwright, S. (1988). Play can be the building blocks of learning. *Young Children*, *43*(5), 44–47.

Caruso, D. A. (1988). Research in review. Play and learning in infancy: Research and implications. *Young Children*, *43*(5), 63–70.

Casey, M. B., and Lippman, M. (1991). Learning to plan through play. *Young Children*, *46*(4), 52–58.

Christie, J. F. (1982). Sociodramatic play training. *Young Children*, *37*(4), 25–32.

Christie, J. F., and Wardle, F. (1992). How much time is needed for play? *Young Children*, *47*(3), 28–32.

Cooper, J. L., and Dever, M. T. (2001). Sociodramatic play as a vehicle for curriculum integration in first grade. *Young Children*, *56*(3), 58–63.

Curry, N. E., and Arnaud, S. H. (1995). Personality difficulties in preschool children as revealed through play themes and styles. *Young Children*, *50*(4), 4–9.

Eggleston, P. J., and Weir, M. K. (1975). Water play for preschoolers. *Young Children*, *31*(1), 5–11.

Farver, J. A. M., and Shinn, Y. L. (1997). Social pretend play in Korean- and Anglo-American preschoolers. *Child Development*, *68*, 544–556.

Fayden, T. (1997). Children's choice: Planting seeds for creating a thematic sociodramatic center. *Young Children*, *52*(3), 15–20.

Feeney, S., and Magarick, M. (1984). Choosing good toys for young children. *Young Children, 40*(1), 21–25.

Fein, G. G. (1979). Research in review. Pretend play: New perspectives. *Young Children, 34*(5), 61–66.

Freud, A., and Burlingham, D. T. (1943). *War and children.* NY: Medical War Books.

Göncü, A., Tuermer, U., Jain, J., and Johnson, D. (1999). Children's play as cultural activity. In A. Göncü (Ed.), *Children's engagement in the world: Sociocultural perspectives.* (pp. 148–170). NY: Cambridge University Press.

Gowen, J. W. (1995). Research in review. The early development of symbolic play. *Young Children*, *50*(3), 75–84.

Greenberg, J. (1995). Viewpoint #3—Making friends with the Power Rangers. *Young Children*, *50*(5), 60–61.

Griffing, P. (1983). Encouraging dramatic play in early childhood. *Young Children*, *38*(2), 13–22.

Guerney, L. F. (1984). Play therapy in counseling settings. In T. D. Yawkey and A. D. Pellegrini (Eds.), *Child's play: Developmental and applied* (pp. 291–321). Hillsdale, NJ: Lawrence Erlbaum.

Jones, E. (2003). Viewpoint: "Playing to get smart". *Young Children*, *58*(3), 32–36.

Kanner, L. (1948). *Child Psychiatry*. Springfield, IL: Charles C. Thomas.

King, N. R. (1992). The impact of context on the play of young children. In S. Kessler and B. B. Swadener (Eds.), *Reconceptualizing the early childhood curriculum: Beginning the dialogue* (pp. 43–61). NY: Teachers College Press.

Kinsman, C. A., and Berk, L. E. (1979). Joining the block and housekeeping areas: Changes in play and social behavior. *Young Children*, *35*(1), 66–75.

Klein, D. (1979). Rx for pediatric patients: Play while you wait. *Young Children, 34*(1), 13–19.

Koplow, L. (1996a). Developmental reality and the reality of experience. In L. Koplow (Ed.), *Unsmiling Faces: How preschools can heal* (pp. 3–15). NY: Teachers College Press.

Koplow, L. (1996b). Preface. In L. Koplow (Ed.), *Unsmiling Faces: How preschools can heal* (pp. ix-xi). NY: Teachers College Press.

Kostelnik, M. J., Whiren, A., and Stein, L. C. (1986). Living with He-Man: Managing superhero fantasy play. *Young Children, 41*(4), 3–9.

Kuschner, D. (1989). Put your name on your painting, but . . . the blocks go back on the shelves. *Young Children, 45*(1), 49–56.

Levin, D. (2003). Beyond banning war and superhero play: Meeting children's needs in violent times. *Young Children, 58*(3), 60–64.

Lubeck, S. (1996). Deconstructing "child development knowledge" and "teacher preparation. *Early childhood research quarterly, 11*(2), 147–167.

Nourot, P. M. (1995). Playing across the curriculum and culture: Strengthening early primary education in California. In E. Klugman (Ed.), *Play, policy & practice* (pp. 3–20). St. Paul, MN: Redleaf Press.

Nourot, P. M., and Van Hoorn, J. L. (1991). Research in review. Symbolic play in preschool and primary settings. *Young Children, 46*(6), 40–50.

Paley, V. G. (1996). Foreword. In L. Koplow (Ed.), *Unsmiling Faces: How preschools can heal* (pp. vii-viii). NY: Teachers College Press.

Pellegrini, A. D., and Perlmutter, J. C. (1988). Rough-and-tumble play on the elementary school playground. *Young Children, 43*(2), 14–17.

Reifel, S. (1984). Block construction: Children's developmental landmarks in representation of space. *Young Children, 40*(1), 61–67.

Roopnarine, J., and Johnson, J. E. (2001). Play and diverse cultures: Implications for early childhood education. In S. Reifel and M. H. Brown (Eds.), *Early education and care, and reconceptualizing play* (pp. 295–319). NY: JAI.

Roopnarine, J., Lasker, J., Sacks, M., and Stores, M. (1998). The cultural contexts of children's play. In O. N. Saracho and B. Spodek (Eds.), *Multiple perspectives on play in early childhood education* (pp. 194–219). Albany, NY: State University of New York Press.

Roskos, K., and Christie, J. (2001). On not pushing too hard: A few cautionary remarks about linking literacy and play. *Young Children, 56*(3), 46–54.

Stalmack, J. E. (1981). S. W. A. P.—Strategies which affect programs: A framework for staff development. *Young Children, 36*(6), 16–24.

Tee, O. P. (2004). Innovative use of local resources for children's play: A case in Malaysia. *Young Children, 59*(5), 14–18.

Part II

COMPARATIVE AND CROSS-CULTURAL RESEARCH

Chapter Four

Playful Companions for Motherless Monkeys

Peggy O'Neill-Wagner

Research communities have become increasingly creative in their efforts to enrich the lives of captive nonhuman primates. One of the reasons for this comes from the knowledge that early experience is critical to the development of normative behaviors required for breeding and for nurturing young. In the case of captive nonhuman primate populations it is not always possible for young monkeys to experience rearing by their birth mothers. When nurturing mothers are not available, alternatives for positive socialization are necessary. One successful alternative for infant monkeys and apes has been the use of companion animals.

Social attachments have developed between dogs and infant rhesus monkeys (Mason & Kenney, 1974) as well as dogs and infant chimpanzees, (Thompson, Bloomsmith, & Taylor, 1991). Social attachment was also reported between a male rhesus monkey and a kitten (Collazo, 1989) and between infant baboons and billie goats (Henzi & MacDonald, 1986). After observing an orphaned infant baboon that had bonded and traveled with a herd of goats, for well over a year, Henzi concluded that primates have a capacity and capability for sociality that extends beyond conspecifics. Similarly, a 1990 study (Struthers et. al.) concluded, "Primates seem to demonstrate a natural affiliative curiosity toward other animals".

Research studies introducing motherless infant rhesus to female mongrel dogs for social contact and stimulation demonstrated positive outcomes. When infant monkeys were introduced to mature mongrels as infants, the attachments were found to endure throughout the term of the five-year study (Mason & Capitanio, 1988). Fritz and Fritz (1985) reported that with infant chimps, as with rhesus monkeys, dogs acted as playmates, grooming partners, and disciplinarians. In fact, Mason (1983) concluded that "there is a profound importance to primates of a close and ongoing relationship with another social being . . . and results show that the companion need not be a member of the same species".

Mastery of social and physical surroundings begins early for young rhesus monkeys (Fairbanks, 1993; Hinde & Spencer-Booth, 1967; Lee, 1983). However, when this project began the state of laboratory caging and restrictive socialization were no substitute for the complex and challenging natural habitat of the rhesus monkey. As a result, eight juvenile rhesus monkeys, motherless since birth, had not reached species-typical levels of independence, confidence, and fitness. In fact, at 22 months of age they appeared as defenseless newborns when faced with new challenges in a stimulating habitat designed for them (see Figure 4.1).

Since play behavior is instrumental in the development of social and physical competence and is characterized by strong social and physical components (Dolhinow & Bishop, 1970; O'Neill-Wagner, Bolig & Price, 2002), a well-designed habitat was provided for the young monkeys with sufficient space and complexity to stimulate play behavior. The habitat also provided security for the animals to safely experience the physical environment and to seek an expanded social enrichment in diverse ways. There was a corncrib enclosure with playground equipment in the form of a large hanging mobile. The research habitat was secluded and was home to a number of domestic and companion animals, as one might find in a petting zoo. (Bringing these animals into the laboratory was not possible at the time due to regulations and lack of appropriate facilities.) Trees and a pasture surrounded the enclosure. This environment was deemed appropriate for social and environmental stimulation (O'Neill, 1989). Thus, eight inexperienced laboratory-reared young monkeys, exhibiting extensive anxiety in the form of aberrant behavior (O'Neill, Novak, & Suomi, 1991), were given the opportunity to develop new skills and confidence via play and exploration in this stimulating and safe habitat (see Figure 4.2).

What would be the impact of introducing a group of eight naive juvenile laboratory rhesus monkeys to well-adjusted companion animals for playful and sophisticated social interaction? If positive interactions were to develop between these animals and the monkeys, would they be short-term or would they provide more lasting benefit as was observed in studies of bonding between infant monkeys and companion animals? Would the socially "at risk" juvenile monkeys mature into successful breeders and parents? Descriptions of the initial interactions and the long-term outcomes are presented here.

Figure 4.1. Naïve Monkeys Express Fear of Novel Enriched Environment as They Cling to Their Lab Transport Cage Interior.

Figure 4.2. The Enclosure Designed for Monkeys to Play.

METHODS

Subjects

Subjects included eight juvenile rhesus monkeys, all 22 months of age. There were four males and four females. All were laboratory-reared using cloth-covered surrogates. All subjects had only five hours per week social contact experience from two months until one year of age. At one year of age the surrogates were removed and the monkeys were then placed together as a social group. This group was released into the outdoor study site after ten months of adaptation to the group living experience.

Initially, the study area residents included five mature dogs, between two and ten years of age. Breeds included one female Pekinese terrier mix, one female Shepherd-Collie mix, one male German Shepherd, one female German Shepherd, and one female Black Labrador Retriever. Later, in addition to this there were two litters of puppies, and a young female Beagle joined the companion animal collection.

Other study area residents included four riding horses. Two were geldings, including a Morgan, and an Arabian-Appaloosa. Two were mares, including a Quarter horse and a Thoroughbred. There were also two yearling ram sheep and three mature female housecats.

Diet

The monkeys were fed monkey chow diet in a corncrib away from other animal feeding areas. Their diet was supplemented with seasonal fruits and vegetables.

Research Area

The habitat included five-acres of secluded countryside with open pasture and mature stands of elm and oak trees. A small cabin was for the research staff. Underground wells provided fresh potable water. Seasonal temperature fluctuations restricted the use of the outdoor habitat to seven months per year.

Procedure

Monkeys were first released to a corncrib at the outdoor site for three months where they could only view the other animals (see Figure 4.3). The following spring, when monkeys returned to the habitat, they were allowed outside the corncrib during the day to interact directly with the domestic

Figure 4.3. Introduction to the Companion Animals Through a Protective Mesh.

animals. Each evening the monkeys were fed and locked inside the corn-crib for the night.

Data Collection

Film footage and photographic documentation was collected throughout the term of the project.

OBSERVATIONS

Puppies and Juvenile Monkeys

From the start the most frequent and positive interactions took place between the monkeys and the puppies (see Figure 4.4). Observations were made which included mutual chasing as well as rough and tumble play, grooming and embracing of puppies by monkeys, and resting or sleep contact. The nature of activity appeared to be relative to the age of the puppies, as well as the gender of the monkeys. Very young puppies were groomed and embraced, exclusively by the female monkeys. Once male monkeys were disciplined by the bitch for their roughness, they seemed to lose interest in playing with the puppies. Not so for the female monkeys.

Labrador, Shepherd, and Beagle pups communicated without hesitation that ear, tail, and hair pulling were not acceptable by nipping back and crying in response. The persistent female monkeys also learned exploratory limitations when the targets of their anatomical manipulations ran away. All puppies were capable of unconditional affection, however, as they typically returned playfully to the source of their temporary discomfort (Figure 4.5). Through trial and error then, contact between female monkeys and puppies continued until all the puppies were given away to adoptive homes. The one exception will be described later.

Growing Puppies and Adolescent Monkeys: Estrous

Once the female monkeys experienced a first estrous cycle their behavior toward puppies changed. They began cuffing the pups, as if to control and relax the play bouts. This controlling behavior was also concurrent with a noticeable size increase in the pups, as they matured. However, since there was only one litter of Shepherd pups at the time, it is difficult to discern if this would have been the case with a different breed of puppy. Shepherd puppies attempted to herd the monkeys playfully with chasing activity. As juveniles,

Figure 4.4. Monkeys Greet the Puppies.

Figure 4.5. Rough and Tumble Play with Wrestling and Biting.

and later as adolescents, male monkeys engaged in long-lasting mutual chase episodes and seemingly endless bouts of rough and tumble play with the pups. Female monkeys, on the other hand, were not observed in rough or chase play with the pups at any age.

When the female monkeys started showing signs of estrous the adolescent male monkeys engaged in threat barking and dominance posturing toward the puppies. Puppies sniffed and barked as the monkeys engaged in breeding behavior. Although the developmental stages of the monkeys and the puppies appeared to be in awkward conflict at this point, there were no injuries associated with this increase in disciplinary activity by the monkeys. The monkeys sometimes responded to the overly exuberant puppies with ear and hair pulling techniques previously outlawed when they were young and defenseless. Some female monkeys, as juveniles (1–3 years old) and later as adolescents (4–5 years old), huddled and slept with the maturing puppies, as well as dogs of both genders. Male monkeys were not observed doing the same.

Mature Dogs and Juvenile Monkeys

Mature Shepherd and Labrador dogs and the small female mixed terrier were tolerant of the monkeys and observed them with keen interest, but were not as welcoming of playful advances. The female terrier did play regularly with other dogs of various breeds, but was never observed as receptive to play with the monkeys. In fact she typically responded by snapping at them. She was the only dog that successfully controlled the location and behavior of the monkeys. She was tenacious about having her way and earned the respect of the monkeys from the start. She never retreated from them. She held her ground and scolded them during their attempts to engage her in play. By contrast, mature Shepherd and Labrador dogs typically retreated quickly when they objected to an invasion of their space by the playful juvenile monkeys.

Mature Dogs and Adolescent Monkeys

As adolescents (4–5 year of age), the monkeys showed reduced interest in having active interactions with the dogs. Dogs watched the monkeys but also showed little interest in shared activity. They accepted female monkeys as sleeping partners without complaint, and seemed agreeable to grooming and proximity from the monkeys for long periods of time. During the eight years of observation one male puppy reached maturity and was subsequently ganged up on by a group of hostile adult male monkeys. His sexual maturation was observable. Once he was neutered and returned to the farm, he was no longer a target of their serious aggression.

Firstborn Infant Rhesus and Puppy

The only female rhesus that maintained regular companionship with a dog after puberty was introduced to the puppy as an infant. She was first-born to the original group of monkeys, and she had no conspecific peers. She and a solitary male Shepherd puppy became playmates. They appeared to be inseparable. She rode on his back (Figure 4.6), and she clung to his ventral side. She groomed him but was never observed reciprocating his attempts for chase play or rough and tumble play. He also played with some of the adult male monkeys. Years later, after puberty, she entered into consort with an adult male monkey. Where the Shepherd dog went, she and her consort followed. Following the birth of her first infant time spent with "her" dog decreased.

Monkeys and Horses

The interactions between monkeys and horses were not spontaneous as with monkeys and puppies. In fact, not until the monkeys had tackled other aspects of their outdoor habitat did they initiate contact with the horses. As a four-year old, one of the females was the first monkey to drop out of a tree onto a mare's back. The result was a bucking bronco rodeo ride that sent her flying

Figure 4.6. Inseparable Monkey and Dog Were Reared Together.

through the air. She appeared to enjoy it, as she repeated the experience again and again. Since all the horses were regularly ridden, it was probably the unexpected nature of the mounting technique that sent the horses into bucking and spinning. Only female monkeys showed considerable interest in riding on the horse's backs. Once adapted to their lightweight riders, the horses would accept multiple rhesus riders at a time, without complaint. Both mares and geldings allowed the monkeys to mount them from the trees, and from the ground, climbing, and leaping up their legs and tails. The female monkeys engaged in grooming the backs of the grazing horses and sat proximal to them in the pasture for extended periods.

Monkeys and Sheep

Even yearling ram sheep were tolerant and gentle when infant monkeys explored their woolly coats. Primates and sheep grazed together with little interaction except for an occasional charge display toward a ram, by a male monkey. Sometimes this resulted in a playful head butt from the young ram, which hurled the monkey into the air. The monkeys appeared to be humbled by the experience, as they were never observed repeating the challenge. The sheep simply went back to grazing, as if nothing of consequence had happened. There was no observable injury resulting from the butting except perhaps injured pride.

Monkeys and Cats

Contact was never witnessed between the monkeys and the adult cats. The cats kept a distance from approaching and curious monkeys, except through the window glass. There were no kittens, as all cats were neutered.

Interspecific Reunion Following Period of Separation

After a five-year separation the monkeys were reunited with a quarter-horse mare that had been a favorite companion. The result was immediate and prolonged contact. Contact was initiated simultaneously by the female monkeys and the mare (Figure 4.7). When the maturing monkeys seemed to have difficulty mounting the horse from the ground, the mare reclined, allowing them easier access to groom her. These monkeys, now mothers, left their offspring nearby when they approached the mare. The naive, hesitant, but curious offspring followed their mothers toward the horse, but did not contact her.

Figure 4.7. Reunion Between Monkeys and Horse.

CONCLUSIONS AND DISCUSSION

In spite of the fact that these monkeys were not helpless infants like those in the referenced studies, the interspecific interactions were similarly positive. As juveniles, the monkeys were observed initiating nurturing behavior with younger animals and also receiving it from mature non-conspecifics. There was also contingent dyadic behavior, sometimes disciplinary in nature, but with no resulting physical injury. The initially naïve juvenile monkeys were able to modify their behavior, when rejected by the other species, with approaches and responses that were more positively received. This was likely a contributing factor to eventual long-term relationship formation. In large part, the successes were also due to the high degree of interest and tolerance from the domestic animals. The same qualities and characteristics in their breeding which make them desirable for service to man probably contributed to necessary levels of patience for positive results with the nonhuman primates. Other contributing factors included a safe environment with non-competitive access to space, to mate selection, and to acquisition of food resources.

In at least two cases, that of the Quarter-horse mare, and that of a puppy raised as sole peer playmate with an infant monkey, the attractiveness and strength of the interspecific social relationship was mutual and lasting (Figure 4.8.). The dogs raised with monkeys were more receptive, tolerant, and

Figure 4.8. Long-Term Companions.

responsive to monkeys of all ages. The breed and disposition of the dogs were likely factors, as Labrador and Shepherd breeds are rated highly for their desirability as family pets. Although these observations were not based on formal quantitative measures of behavior, they may offer valid detailed descriptive information for interspecies rearing alternatives using domestic animals. It is of particular interest that these observations of juvenile monkeys with dogs confirm socialization outcomes found in studies using dogs to help socialize infant primates.

Except for the mature cats, other animals allowed the young monkeys contact comfort, safe social stimulation, and a chance to develop lasting relationships. It is not surprising that the bonding that developed between an adult male monkey and a small kitten in the Collazo paper were not observed between female mature cats and juvenile monkeys. The circumstances with the cats and monkeys in this project were the reverse of the Collazo observations. Not only were the monkeys not small, helpless, and needy as a kitten, but the mature cats were not housed in solitary cages lacking social contact and enrichment. These cats had free range of the house and the habitat.

Because there was not a control group of motherless monkeys back at the lab, it is impossible to conclude for certain that the domestic animals provided a therapeutic benefit, or that they made up for the lack of normative experience during the first year of lab living for these eight monkeys. Likewise, it is impossible to conclude with certainty that monkeys' experiences with the farm animals resulted in learning from social modeling during interactions involving disciplinary expression of aggression, retaliation, social control, and social limitations. However, during the initial phase of these observations one quantitative study did provide findings for significant reduction in the young monkeys' aberrant behaviors following their introduction to this outdoor habitat (O'Neill, 1989). With such an extreme contrast between the laboratory and the outdoor site, it is perhaps impossible to sort out what role the actual interactions with other animals played in this behavioral change. But, when the monkeys subsequently raised their first-born offspring without incident, one cannot help but wonder if this was in some way accomplished by the positive learning experiences they had with a variety of social animals.

What can be concluded with certainty is that for some of the monkeys bonding took place with non-conspecifics that developed into lasting positive relationships. These relationships resembled children and their pets. They were initially endless bouts of chasing, wrestling and slumber parties, but as the animals matured they became long periods of just hanging out together, as favorite companions tend to do.

REFERENCES

Collazo, V.E. (1989). Male rhesus monkey's unusual behavior: Interspecies adoption. *Laboratory Primate Newsletter*, 28: 1, 23.

Capitanio, J.P. (1984). Early experience and social processes in rhesus macaques (*Macaca mulatta*) I. Dyadic social interaction. Journal of Comparative Psychology, 98, 35–44.

Dolhinow P.J. & Bishop, N. (1970). The development of motor skills and social relationships among primates through play. *Minnesota Symposia on Child Psychology*, 4, 141–199.

Fritz, J., Fritz, P. (1985). The hand-rearing unit: Management decisions that may effect chimpanzee development. In Graham & J.A. Bowe (Eds.*), Clinical Management of Infant Great Apes* (pp 1–34). C.E. New York: Alan R. Liss.

Fairbanks, L.A. (1993). Juvenile vervet monkeys: establishing relationships and practicing skills. In M.E. Pereira & L.A. Fairbanks (Eds.), *Juvenile Primates: life history, development, and behavior* (pp. 211–227). New York: Oxford University Press.

Henzi, S.P., & MacDonald, A. (1986). A baboon among goats. *African Wildlife*, 40, 177.

Hinde, R.A. & Spencer-Booth, Y. (1967). The behaviour of socially living rhesus monkeys in the first two and a half years. *Animal Behaviour*, 15, 169–196.

Lee, P.C. (1983). Play as a means for developing relationships. In. R.A. Hinde (Ed.) Primate Social relationships: an integrated approach (pp. 82–89). Oxford: Blackwell Scientific Publishing.

Martinez, H.S., & Kessler, M.T. (1979). Report of an unusual interspecies adoption by a rhesus monkey. *Laboratory Primate Newsletter*, 18, 3:6.

Mason, W.A., & Kenney, M.D. (1974). Redirection of filial attachments in rhesus monkeys: Dogs as mother surrogates. Science, 183, 1209–1211.

Mason, W.A. (1983). Dogs as monkey companions. In A.H. Katcher & A.M. Beck (Eds.), *New Perspectives on our Lives with Companion Animals* (pp 17–25). University of Pennsylvania Press.

Mason, W.A. & Capitanio, J.P. (1988). Formation and expression of filial attachment in rhesus monkeys raised with living and inanimate mother substitutes. Developmental Psychobiology, 21, 401–430.

O'Neill, P.L., Novak, M.A.& Suomi, S.J. (1991). Normalizing Laboratory-reared rhesus macaque (*Macaca mulatta*) behavior with exposure to complex outdoor habitats. *Zoo Biology*, 10, 237–245.

O'Neill-Wagner, P.L., Bolig, R. & Price, C.S. (2002). Developmental aspects of play partner selection in young rhesus monkeys. In J.L. Roopnarine (Ed.*) Conceptual, Social-Cognitive, and Contextual Issues in the Fields of Play* (pp.111–124) Ablex Publishing.

O'Neill, P.L. A room with a view for captive primates: issues, goals, related research and strategies. (1989). In E.F. Segal (Ed), *Housing, Care, and Psychological Well-being of Captive and Laboratory Primates* (pp 135–160) Noyes Publications.

Struthers, E.J., Rodriguez, P., Cooper, P. & Rowell, J. (1990). Xenospecific enrichment at the Primate Research Institute. *Laboratory Primate Newsletter*, 29: 2, 14–15.

Thompson, M.A., Bloomsmith, M.A. & Taylor, L.L. (1991). A canine companion for a nursery-reared infant chimpanzee. *Laboratory Primate Newsletter*, 30:2, 1–5.

ACKNOWLEDGMENTS:

This research was supported in part by USPHS Grant MH-11870 from the National Institute of Mental Health and funds from the University of Wisconsin Graduate School. Thanks are extended to the Town Council of Leeds Township, Wisconsin, for the outdoor site approval and their valued support throughout the project.

Chapter Five

What Young Children Say About Play at School: United States and Australian Comparisons

Sue Dockett and Alice M. Meckley

Play has long been regarded a crucial element of early childhood curricula (Dockett & Fleer, 1999). The importance of play as a context in which school-aged children can acquire social and language competence as well as cognitive and physical skills has been highlighted by numerous researchers (Cooper & Dever, 2001; Johnson, 1998; Trawick-Smith, 1998). In recent times, descriptions of an 'overcrowded' curriculum have led to the perception–certainly among educators–that there is little room for play within an elementary school curriculum (Anning, 1994; Dockett & Fleer, 1999). In Australia, there is some evidence to suggest that teachers in elementary schools feel pressured to implement an academic curriculum at the expense of play (Jones, Dockett, Perry, & Westcott, 2002; Olsen & Sumsion, 2002). This is despite the promotion of play as an appropriate teaching and learning strategy in recent curriculum documents produced in New South Wales (Dockett & Lambert 1996; Board of Studies, NSW, 1998, 1999; NSW Department of Education & Training, 1999) and other states (Department of Education, Training and Employment, South Australia, 2001), and in discussions of the National Statements and Profiles (Fleer, 1996). With the adoption of outcomes-based approaches in Australian schools, the potential for play to provide a context for integrating areas of learning and, within that, to provide information about children's understandings, skills and attitudes has been recognised (Dockett & Lambert, 1996; Fleer, 1996). However, there is not a great deal of evidence to indicate that play has a strong place in school classrooms, or that teachers and parents place a high value on play in schools.

Similar trends are reported in U.S. classrooms (Trawick-Smith, 2001). This is despite research showing a strong connection between play–as an approach to teaching and learning–and academic subjects, such as literacy (Davidson, 1998; Roskos & Neuman, 1998) and numeracy (Baroody, 2000; Ginsburg, Inoue, & Seo, 1999). It is clear that there are many approaches to developing play-based curricula, and that these vary according to–among other things–the theoretical perspectives of the teacher, the philosophy and aims of the school and expectations of the parents and community. It is also clear that the organisation of play-based programs varies, as does the nature of what constitutes play in the classroom (Trawick-Smith, 2001). In many instances, the role and place of play is questioned, as greater focus is placed on academic learning within schools (Jones & Reynolds, 1995).

One indication of the lack of perceived value for play comes from calls to reassess the place of recess in some schools. This has some significant implications for children's play in schools (Blatchford, 1994; Pellegrini & Blatchford, 2000). Typically, Australian schools schedule a recess break of about 30 minutes each day, as well as a lunch break of about 60 minutes. Evans (1996, 1997, 1998, 1999; Evans & Pellegrini, 1997) reports trends to reduce the time available for both recess and lunch breaks, for the following reasons:

- academic pressure to spend more time 'learning,' that is, time in class;
- recess and lunch regarded as a 'break' from the real work of school;
- safety issues, especially related to playground accidents, incidents involving violence and bullying, and issues of supervision;
- teachers' general dislike for playground duty means that they do not oppose the changes.

The concern about bullying is reported from parents and teachers, as adults seem to be aware of the potential dangers in playgrounds and in children's interactions with others. The recognition that bullying is of concern to educators is reflected in the adoption of anti-bullying policies in several Australian school systems, as well as in research reports (Linke, 1998; Slee & Rigby, 1994).

Evans and Pellegrini (1997) report a belief among teachers that recess is for children to 'let off steam,' rather than to engage in worthwhile play. This view is reflected in the time, space and resources made available to children at recess and lunch times in many schools. Children's comments echo the concern that there is often nothing worthwhile doing in the break times at school:

> Terry (age 8) reports: "We can't play football, 'cause there's no grass. And we can't play on the asphalt 'cause it's hard and we might fall over. We can't play marbles 'cause there's nowhere flat . . . (Dockett & Fleer, 1999, p 276)

Traditionally in the United States, recess time in elementary schools encompasses a morning and afternoon break each of approximately 10 minutes and a lunch break of about 20 minutes. However, academic pressures and a current movement to 'teach to the standards' and increase 'instructional time' has caused a recent return to direct instruction in early childhood classrooms. With this perceived need for more teacher-guided time has come the elimination of child-chosen activities, such as play and recess time. In many school systems across America, recess has been eliminated from the school day to provide more 'learning time' toward the belief that the school's academic curriculum is the primary mission (Pellegrini & Bjorklund, 1996). In discussing both play and nonplay early childhood curricular approaches, Trawick-Smith (2001) notes that there is a growing number of nonplay models in the public schools: "Two assumptions underlie nonplay approaches: (a) Play and learning are distinct and mutually exclusive, and (b) learning is more important than play and should be the ultimate goal of education" (pp. 305–306). In fact, an examination of theories about learning and theories about play shows significant similarities between the characteristics of learning and the characteristics of play connecting play and learning as mutually inclusive activities (Meckley, 2000).

Where play is implemented in schools, it is often described by adults as 'structured' or 'developmental' play. Teachers have reported using this term as a means of 'legitimising' inclusion of play in a school curriculum (Jones, et al., 2002). Heaslip (1994) notes that this terminology need not be interpreted as a desire for adults to dominate play by enforcing a structured focus. Rather, it can be regarded as adults taking responsibility for the provision and support of play. However, it also raises issues about definitions of play: is such activity regarded as play by the children involved? The work of Wing (1995) suggests that young children are quite adept at distinguishing play from other, teacher-directed experiences, even when these are presented in the guise of games or play.

WHAT DO CHILDREN IN SCHOOL SAY ABOUT PLAY?

There have been relatively few Australian studies focussing on what children in Kindergarten say about play at school. Such studies have focussed on specific playground games (Marsh, 2001), views of recess (Evans, 1996) or have included children's conversations about play as parts of broader studies (Clyde, 2001; Perry, Dockett, & Howard, 2000).

These studies indicate that children have clear perceptions of what constitutes play for them, as well as recognition of what is play for others. This supports other reports–including several from the U.S.–which indicate that even quite young children have a clear perception of what constitutes play, as opposed to other activities (eg, Fivush, 1984; Garza, Briley, & Reifel, 1985;

Romero, 1989). One description of children's perceptions of play draws upon script theory (Fivush, 1984). Evidence of script use is drawn from children's listing of play as one of the many activities that occurs at school. By reference to a mental script, children are able to recite the daily events of a school day, including play, where appropriate (Fein & Wiltz, 1998). In listing the sequence of events in a school day, children indicate that play occurs, but not how they feel about, understand or respond to it. Hence, script theory is useful in identifying the presence of play at school, but other approaches need to be used in order to access children's interpretations and experiences of play. As may be expected, children's reports of play vary according to their development and stage of schooling. Wiltz and Klein (1994) report that most of the three-year-olds interviewed in their study indicated that they played at school (preschool); four and five-year-olds reported playing and were able to describe their play experiences; and six-year-olds described play as occurring only at recess.

DEFINING PLAY

The definition of play underpinning this paper includes the following characteristics, which, when combined, contribute to the disposition of play (Fromberg, 1992, p. 43):

- symbolic;
- meaningful;
- active;
- pleasurable;
- voluntary;
- rule-governed; and
- episodic.

On their own, each of these characteristics is typical of a range of experiences. For example, not all activity is play, and not all meaningful experiences involve play. However, in combination, each of these elements contributes to the attitude of play (Dockett & Fleer, 1999; Dockett & Perry, 1996).

While other definitions of play–such as those of Bateson (1972), and Neumann (1971)–also inform the bases for this paper, perhaps the most salient definition of play comes from players, such as Brendan (age 9):

> Play is having fun. Not doing school work. When you're having fun, you're sort of doing it the way you want to do it yourself . . . Play is fun and when no one makes

> you do it. You can do it alone, but sometimes with friends. You don't always need your imagination for play, but it's not play if you get told what to do, only if it's what you want to do. (Harrison, 1993 cited in Dockett & Fleer, 1999, p. 20)

This view of play is similar to that reported by King (1987, 1990) and Paley (1984). King's (1987) interviews with children in school led her to conclude that, in children's eyes, what happened in the classroom was rarely considered play. As indicated by Brendan, anything required by an adult, or directed by an adult, was not considered play:

> If a teacher requires the children's participation in an activity, that activity is labelled work. Kindergarteners do not label assigned tasks play no matter how much they may enjoy participating. Activities are labelled play only when the children believe that their participation is voluntary and free of direct supervision by the teacher. (King, 1987, p. 145)

WORK AND PLAY

As indicated above, and in other studies, children clearly distinguish between work and play (Clyde, 2001; King, 1990; Reifel, 1988). When interviewed about their perceptions of starting school, children have indicated that school is a place to learn as well as a place to play. They expect to play, and they expect to have and make friends as they play (Dockett & Perry, 1999). They also expect to learn, and indicate that *learning is work*. What distinguishes work from play tends to be clear in the minds of young children (King, 1982; LeCompte, 1980). The children in Wing's (1995) study distinguished play and work on the basis of:

> the obligatory or voluntary nature of the activity; its evaluation; the child's effort, cognitive and physical activity; the level of teacher involvement; whether the activity had to be finished or could be abandoned at will; the types of materials used; the academic content; and to a lesser degree, fun. (p. 242)

This distinction is reflected clearly in Brendan's comment. Wing also notes that children do not consider all work to be drudgery, and, on occasions, concede that some activities can be play and work, or at least somewhere in between. Fein and Wiltz (1998) conclude that preschool-aged children readily distinguish play from work by its voluntary nature. By the time children enter elementary school, an activity is considered play not only if it is voluntary, but also if it has no teacher direction or involvement. Older children attribute play to activities that are considered fun, rather than boring.

PLAY AT SCHOOL

From her investigations, King (1987) listed three different types of play within a school context:

- play that occurs within the objectives of the school. This is called *instructional play* because it is used to facilitate learning. Play as a means of promoting learning legitimises the role of play in school as it ties it to the perceived purpose of school–instruction. In this way, play is included in the curriculum of schools because it is a way of promoting children's learning. Sometimes this type of play is called developmental play, with the expectation that play is legitimised by being related to development. Games in the classroom, or even sporting games, fall into this category of play.
- playing with the objectives of the school. This is referred to as *illicit play*, as it involves children playing in ways that challenge the established power structure of schools. Examples would be passing notes to others in class, or whispering to each other when this has been forbidden. Other examples would be playing games that have been banned (such as gun games, superhero play, tag) or playing in places that have been prohibited (such as places not easily supervised).
- play outside the objectives of the school. This is termed *recreational play* because it resides outside the aims of the school. Examples include play that occurs at recess or after school, in the playground rather than in class.

Classification of play in these ways enables a consideration of different perspectives of play. For example, one study of teachers' perspectives of play reflected a focus on instructional play, whereas children considered recreational play important within a school context (Dockett, 2001).

In keeping with the view that play is an important part of children's experiences and that play at school has the potential to be a worthwhile and valuable part of the school day for both children and teachers, this paper:

- reports young children's views of play in school;
- compares the views of children in U.S. and Australia; and
- considers implications of these views for early childhood education.

METHOD

To investigate these issues, children in Kindergarten (the first year of school) in Australia and the United States were invited to take part in research conversations. Conversations were preferred to formal interviews, in order to "hand over the agenda to children, so that they can control the pace and direction of the conversation, raising and exploring topics" (Mayall, 2000, p. 133) of relevance and interest to them. Conversations were conducted in small focus groups (up to four children) or individually, depending on the preference of the children and the practicality within the particular school setting. The questions asked in each conversation were similar, though in an informal setting, children were encouraged to discuss issues that mattered to them, rather than being pressured to answer every question. All interviews were conducted in school settings at a time when children had attended school for several months.

With the permission of the children and their parents/guardians, conversations were audio-recorded and transcribed for analysis. Transcripts were coded using the principles of grounded theory (Corbin & Strauss, 1990) to establish categories of response to each of the questions. In addition to 11 common questions, the Australian and American groups were asked some different questions. Two of these are reported in this paper as a means of sharing the insights that young children have, and are willing to share, about their involvement in play at school.

Fifty-two children attending school in NSW, Australia were interviewed. These children were all in their first year of school, and were aged between four-and-a-half and six years of age. They attended schools in both rural and urban areas. The children interviewed represented a range of cultural and language, as well as socio-economic, backgrounds.

Thirty-two children aged between five and six years from rural and suburban areas of Pennsylvania constitute the American sample. These children attended three different schools. A range of cultural backgrounds is represented in this sample.

The data reported in this paper are not claimed to be representative. Rather, they provide some insight into the views of these children and to the issues that are relevant to their consideration of play in schools.

RESULTS AND DISCUSSION

A series of common questions was asked in each conversation. The results, and comparison of these across the two groups, are reported below. Numbers of responses, as well as percentages of total responses, are listed in each table. The small numbers in each of these groups and the diversity of each context mean that comparisons are made cautiously, and in the interest of gaining insights from these children, rather than to promote generalisations across the

Table 5.1. What Is the Best Thing About School?

	United States		Australia	
Activity	*N (31)*	*% (of 31)*	*N (45)*	*% (of 45)*
Playing	9	29	17	37.8
Recess/lunch	2	6.5	2	4.4
Toys/equipment	4	12.9	2	4.4
Teacher	4	12.9	1	2.2
Friends	4	12.9	7	15.6
Being inside	1	3.2	0	0
Being outside	3	9.7	5	11.1
Learning	1	3.2	1	2.2
Making things/activities	0	0	7	15.6
Other	3	9.7	3	6.7

two countries. In reporting children's comments, (A) is used to denote an Australian child and (U.S.) to denote an American child's response.

What is the Best Thing About School?

Twenty-seven children from the U.S. and 37 from Australia answered this question, generating a total of 31 U.S. and 45 Australian responses.

Data reported in Table 5.1 indicate that children can and do employ script knowledge of the school day. In both contexts, they could list the events of the day, with play featuring strongly as the best thing about school for many, but not all, children. The educational focus of the school day, grouped under the category of *Learning*, did not feature highly as the best thing about school for these children.

In their discussion of the best thing about school, Nicki (A), Gary (A) and Gemma (A) described playing outside on the Kindy tree, an area reserved for Kindergarten children:

> **Nicki:** *One of the good things about school is playing. In the Kindy tree.*
>
> **Gary:** *It's a place only Kindy's can play.*
>
> **Interviewer:** *What do you do?*
>
> **Gemma:** *You climb it.*
>
> **Nicki:** *You can play games in it. It's not like a big tree, it's just like a bush.*
>
> **Interviewer:** *What sorts of games can you play in it?*
>
> **Gary:** *Chasing. Chasing girls.*
>
> *And the next day, you chase me [points to girls].*

And we play cops and robbers.

***Nicki:** I try to play cops and robbers, but it's too hard.*

***Gemma:** We play babies. It's where someone has to be the Mum and the Dad and then we play Sleeping Beauty.*

***Gary:** There are some real fun playing things at school.*

Several of the American children also highlighted the importance of play outside, often using the gym equipment. There were some very detailed descriptions of the equipment, listing monkey bars, jungle gym, swings, and slides. For example, Emma commented:

My playground is bigger than yours, if you have one.
Monkey bars are grey and the jungle gym is black and the swings are black.
We have a big slide, it's not too scary . . . you have to slide off.
I like to grab every single one [monkey bars] and do it again and do it again.

What Is the Worst Thing About School?

Twenty-three children from the U.S. and 26 from Australia proffered one response each to this question.

In keeping with the responses indicating the best thing about school, learning tasks are mentioned by several children as the worst thing about school. Playing itself does not feature in these responses, but play equipment was

Table 5.2. What Is the Worst Thing About School?

	United States		Australia	
Activity	N (23)	% (of 23)	N (26)	% (of 26)
Punishment	4	17.4	6	23.1
Homework	1	4.3	0	0
Naps/sleep/rest time	2	8.7	0	0
Going home	3	13	0	0
Fighting/friends mean/no friends	3	13	6	23.1
Learning tasks	4	17.4	5	19.2
Doing nothing	1	4.3	1	3.8
Weather	1	4.3	0	0
Teachers	2	8.7	2	7.7
Play equipment	2	8.7	0	0
Being there	0	0	1	3.8
Big kids	0	0	2	7.7
Lunch	0	0	1	3.8
Other	0	0	2	7.7

mentioned by two children. In each case, the child did not like one aspect of the climbing equipment (slide or swing) in their playground.

Overall, ten children mentioned punishment as the worst thing about school. In some instances punishment meant not being allowed to play at lunch or recess. For example,

Interviewer: *What is the worst thing about school?*

Graham (A): *Getting into trouble. When you do naughty things, you go to the planning room. Yeah, you have to sit in one chair like this and wait, wait, wait, and wait. And you have to plan to be good.*

Kirk (U.S.): *Having to put our heads down and detention.*

Other things mentioned by children included:

Nadia (A): *You can't play if you haven't got any friends.*

Gemma (A): *The big kids. I like it when the classes are not there [in the playground] and it's just the Kindy kids and you get to do what you want and there's no big kids bossing you.*

Sam (A): *Our hands get so tired! Because they have to work all the time . . . colouring, writing stuff.*

Nate (U.S.): *Doing homework.*

Damien (U.S.): *Sitting around and doing nothing.*

Nate (U.S.): *I wish I could do that in school.*

Anna (U.S.): *Trying to learn stuff. Trying to figure out stuff.*

In identifying the best and worst things about school, children were quite able to develop a list of daily events and activities. Rather than revealing any major differences between the two groups, the items listed are remarkable for their similarity. There are some differences, such as Australian children indicating that *making things* was something they enjoyed at school, and several American children indicating that *going home* was the worst thing about school. Not only did Australian children say that going home was not a problem for them, but one also indicated that *being there* was the worst thing about school. Friends were important to both groups, and *having no friends*, or *friends being mean*, was perceived by some as the worst thing about school.

Do You Play at School?

All children in both groups indicated that they played at school.

Table 5.3. When Do You Play?

Response	United States N (8)	United States % (of 8)	Australia N (10)	Australia % (of 10)
Lunch/recess/playtime	3	37.5	10	100
After finished work	3	37.5	0	0
Before the others get here	1	12.5	0	0
When there is no school	1	12.5	0	0

Table 5.4. Who Do You Play With?

Response	United States N (26)	United States % (of 26)	Australia N (29)	Australia % (of 29)
Friends	25	96.2	21	72.4
Siblings	0	0	4	13.8
Teacher	1	3.8	0	0
Big kids	0	0	2	6.9
Buddies	0	0	2	6.9

When Do You Play?

Ten Australian and eight U.S. children responded to this question (Table 5.3). The Australian children all indicated that they played in the break times, whereas some of the U.S. children (3) indicated that they played after some work had been finished, possibly in the classroom.

Twenty-six U.S. children and 29 Australian children answered this question (Table 5.4).

Children in both groups highlighted the importance of friends:

Interviewer: *Who do you play with?*

Connor (A): *Playing with my friends.*

Interviewer: *Are there some kids who don't have friends?*

Connor: *Yes.*

Interviewer: *What happens to them?*

Heidi (A): *They get really sad.*

Interviewer: *Do you help them?*

Heidi: *Yes. You can't leave anyone alone with no friends.*

Connor: *We play with them. We be their friends and play with them.*

Interviewer: *Who do you play with?*

Karl (U.S.): *Mark, Dane, Nate, Braydon, Allena and Norma.*

Interviewer: *What do you play?*

Karl: *With Allena and Norma, I play club. With Mark, Dane, Nate, Braydon, I play football. Depends on the friends what I play.*

In most cases, children listed the friends with whom they played. One to six children were nominated as friends across both groups. In one interaction, this nomination was challenged:

Interviewer: *Who do you play with?*

Mark (U.S.): *Mike, Bruce, Dane, and Kirk.*

Kirk (U.S.): *I don't think that is true. You don't play with me.*

This exchange illustrates one of the positive aspects of interviewing young children in small groups, with their friends. Oftentimes, the interactions among the children clarify both the questions asked and the responses made. These interactions highlight the importance of discourse between children as a means of determining their stance on issues, such as who plays with whom (Dockett, Perry, Woods & Cusack, 2000).

Where Do You Play?

Nine American and 27 Australian children answered this question (Table 5.5). While the numbers are small, it is interesting to note that most of the Australian children said that they played outside, and most of the American children said they played inside. It may be that weather and climate issues influence this, with at least one American child commenting that they couldn't play outside in the snow, and that she didn't like to play at recess when it was cold. Even in winter, the climate in NSW is temperate. Few areas experience snow, and while summer temperatures can be very hot, schools are required to provide ample shade, and to implement suitable sun-safe policies, such as ensuring that children have sunscreen and sunhats.

Table 5.5. Where Do You Play?

	United States		*Australia*	
Response	*N (9)*	*% (of 9)*	*N (27)*	*% (of 27)*
Outside-playground	3	33	18	67
Inside-classroom	6	67	9	33

This compares to the climate in Pennsylvania, which can be very cold in winter, with playgrounds inaccessible due to snow.

The nature of play indoors and outdoors is detailed in Tables 5.6 and 5.7. One Australian child (Chris) clearly distinguished between what happened inside and outside:

Play outside on the equipment.
Not allowed to play inside.
Inside is for talking quietly, and play maths groups and reading groups.
No yelling in class. It gives people headaches.

What Do You Play Outside?

Twenty-seven American children responded to this question, with a total of 30 responses and some children offering more than one response. Thirty Australian children generated 37 responses.

The outdoor play of children is clearly affected by the equipment available, as well as by the climate. One American child, Jake, described his involvement in football, but also indicated that he played football because there was no baseball equipment:

You get trophies . . . to get a trophy for it you need to hit the target without anything.
I really like to play baseball, but there's nothing here to play it with.

American children mentioned playing on the swings and gym equipment more often than the Australian children did. This is probably because such

Table 5.6. What Do You Play Outside?

	United States		*Australia*	
Response	*N (30)*	*% (of 30)*	*N (37)*	*% (of 37)*
Swings/gym/slide/monkey bars/fort	14	46.7	5	13.5
Soccer	1	3.3	7	18.9
Kindy tree	0	0	11	29.7
Friends	1	3.3	2	5.4
Catching game, (eg., Sharky)	0	0	7	18.9
Football	4	13.3	1	2.7
Marbles	0	0	4	10.8
Cars	6	20	0	0
Hopscotch	2	6.7	0	0
Ball	1	3.3	0	0
Run around	1	3.3	0	0

equipment featured in the playgrounds of the American children more than in the playgrounds available for Australian children. Differences between the frequency of mention of *football* and *soccer* also reflect cultural, as well as seasonal, differences. In one Australian school, children mentioned the Kindy tree as their preferred place for play, and in another there was mention of a game called Sharky:

> **Ike (A):** *Me and James play Sharky. We're friends.*
> *The sharks are under the equipment and the equipment is your ship.*
> *They have to tip you 20 times.*
> *Sometimes they tip us and we just run away.*
> *They can't even get us when we run, can they?*
> *We got this big shark cage.*
>
> **Interviewer:** *Who makes up the rules?*
>
> **Ike:** *Ben. They're the boss of the game, but we're not afraid, are we?*
>
> **James (A):** *[nods]*
>
> **Ike:** *Sometimes we play on the yellow bars.*
> *The ones out here.*
> *Out the back is the big kids and out here is ours.*
> *We're not allowed to play on the big kids' equipment.*
> *Cause the big kids can hurt us.*
> *The big kids can bully us.*
> *They could stick their rude finger up at us.*
> *When you are up at the big, high big kids' equipment in this school, you could get pushed off, like Jarvis did, couldn't you?*
>
> **James:** *Yes.*
>
> **Ike:** *He was like a big dead person, like a starfish falling off the equipment.*
>
> **Interviewer:** *Was he hurt?*
>
> **Ike:** *Yes.*
>
> **Interviewer:** *Where did they take him?*
>
> **James:** *To the teacher.*
>
> **Interviewer:** *And what happened?*
>
> **Ike:** *Gone to the sick bay, I think.*
>
> **James:** *So the teacher said we couldn't play on the big kids' equipment.*

These differences among schools reflect the development of a school culture (Corsaro, 1997) where children have a strong sense of what is valued and accepted within a particular school and the people within that school.

Children quickly become aware of the acceptability of specific types of play, and, in some cases, of how they can push the boundaries associated with that play. One of the boundaries mentioned by Ike, above, is the restriction on which playground can be used by Kindergarten children. As indicated by Ike, the 'big kids' equipment' is regarded as dangerous for younger children, as much for the involvement of the 'big kids' themselves as because of the equipment.

What Do You Play Inside?

Twenty-seven American children responded to this question, generating 58 responses. Thirty Australian children generated 34 responses.

The most common response from both groups was that they played on the computer. This is interesting in the light of Australian research which suggested that many teachers of young children in prior-to-school settings did not regard children's computer use as play, and instead, saw it as taking away from the child's chance to play (Dockett, Perry, & Nanlohy, 1999). It may be that by the time children start school, this view has changed, with the expectation that children will use computers for a range of purposes.

Table 5.7. What Do You Play Inside?

	United States		*Australia*	
Response	*N (58)*	*% (of 58)*	*N (34)*	*% (of 34)*
Computer	10	17.2	10	29.4
Home corner	5	8.6	0	0
Cars	9	15.5	0	0
Blocks	10	17.2	1	2.9
Dinosaurs	5	8.6	0	0
Build	2	3.4	0	0
Sandbox	2	3.4	0	0
Art	7	12.1	0	0
Lego	1	1.7	4	11.8
Maths/reading groups	2	3.4	4	11.8
Beads/puzzles	1	1.7	2	5.9
Dough	0	0	1	2.9
Pretend	1	1.7	0	0
Developmental play	0	0	4	11.8
Toys	1	1.7	4	11.8
Other	2	3.4	4	11.8

In general, American children listed a greater variety of activities as play inside than did the Australian children. In one U.S. classroom, children described a "huge mat" on which they could play with cars:

> ***Nate (U.S.):*** *We play with cars. We pretend the cars are flying.*
> *We have a little car thing and we play with them on.*
> *Sometimes we have them jump off the ramp.*
>
> ***Mark (U.S.):*** *And they fly off in the basket.*
> *They are matchboxes.*

Four Australian children described play inside as developmental play, seemingly assuming the language of their teachers in legitimising play within the curriculum. Comments about developmental play included:

> ***Erina (A):*** *We have developmental play.*
> *Like making caterpillars with paper and toilet rolls.*
>
> ***Meg (A):*** *Developmental play. It means working and having fun.*

These children were well aware of the nature of the activity labelled developmental play. As reported by Wing (1995) they were "not fooled by work activities presented by teachers under the guise of play" (p. 242). This is reinforced by comments from Chris (A) who clearly indicated that "doing maths and reading groups . . . that's not play." This distinction by the children suggests that they recognised different types of play within the school context. On the one hand, they discussed play outside, in the playground, at recess–all play which falls into King's (1987) category of recreational play. This was regarded differently from play that occurred within the classroom, with teacher input or guidance–instructional play.

Do Teachers Play?

Twenty-eight American children and 45 Australian children answered this question (Table 5. 8). All of the Australian, and most of the American children, said that teachers did not play.

Table 5.8. Do Teachers Play?

	United States		*Australia*	
Response	*N (28)*	*% (of 28)*	*N (45)*	*% (of 45)*
Yes	5	17.9	0	0
No	23	82.1	45	100

Table 5.9. What Do Teachers Do?

Response	United States N (28)	United States % (of 28)	Australia N (33)	Australia % (of 33)
Teach	14	50	10	30.3
Paperwork	3	10.7	0	0
Watch us	2	7.1	0	0
Walk around	1	3.6	5	15.2
Sit around	1	3.6	0	0
Talk	1	3.6	0	0
Help us	2	7.1	8	24.2
Punish	2	7.1	4	12.1
Play	1	3.6	0	0
Has her lunch	0	0	6	18.2
Clean up	1	3.6	0	0

What Do Teachers Do?

Twenty-eight American children responded to this question, generating 28 responses. The 20 Australian children who responded generated 33 responses (Table 5.9).

Clearly, for many children, teachers teach. Allied to this is the view that teachers help children, complete written work, walk around, watch children and punish children. Play is not regarded by children as a prominent feature of a teacher's role. Children who mentioned the teacher playing, in response to one or both of the questions above, indicated that it was an exception, rather than a rule:

> ***Chantal (U.S.):*** *At the beginning of the school year–Sometimes, on the first day of school, my teacher, Miss D. played with us.*
>
> ***Interviewer:*** *Do they play with you now?*
>
> ***Chantal:*** *No.*
>
> ***Anna (U.S.):*** Sometimes they do [play] and sometimes they don't. If they have kids they play with their kids.

It is not surprising that children did not regard teachers as players, as very often teachers themselves do not adopt that role. Teachers often espouse the importance of play (Hughes, 1995; Kemple, 1996: Kitson, 1994), but the practice of many reveals a focus on the managerial aspects of play–such as providing time, space and materials–rather than on adopting the role of player (Jones et al., 2002; Jones & Reynolds, 1992; Olsen & Sumsion, 2002). This is despite consistent research which indicates that the complexity and quality

Table 5.10. Are There Times You Are Not Allowed to Play?

	United States		Australia	
Response	*N (37)*	*% (of 37)*	*N (15)*	*% (of 15)*
Punishment	7	18.9	15	100
Work activities	20	54	0	0
When eating	3	8.1	0	0
Cleaning up	2	5.4	0	0
Nap	1	2.7	0	0
Early dismissal	2	5.4	0	0
Other	2	5.4	0	0

of children's play improves with teacher involvement (Jones & Reynolds, 1992; Leseman, Rollenberg, & Rispens, 2001; Smilansky & Shefatya, 1990).

Are There Times When You Are Not Allowed to Play?

Twenty-four American children responded to this question, generating 37 responses. Fifteen Australian children generated 15 responses (Table 5.10).

Most of the American children who responded indicated that they were not allowed to play when they were working. This pattern of response suggests that the children did not regard work and play as something that could be undertaken at the same time:

> ***Interviewer:*** *Are there times you are not allowed to play?*
>
> ***Jack (U.S.):*** *When you are doing homework.*
> *When we are cleaning up we are not allowed to play.*
> *During literacy centres, you have to do what the teacher says.*

The Australian children who responded said that the occasions on which they were not allowed to play all related to punishment. A typical punishment is described by Lance (A):

> *If you are in trouble, you have to go to Mr C's office [principal].*
> *And no play because that's why you have to go to the office.*

Further Questions

In addition to the common questions, each group responded to other questions. Responses to one of these questions from each group are included here because they add depth to the issues raised in some other responses.

How Do You Know When You Are Playing?

Thirty American children responded to this question. Their comments suggest that they have a very clear understanding of what play means for them:

- *We are getting along with our friends*
- *We are having fun, we are using our imaginations, because toys are real things*
- *That it is just pretending. That it is not really true*
- *Because you are doing something, something fun; because we are playing*
- *You just think*
- *We know that we are having fun or not*
- *My brain. I always think in my brain I tell stuff that is happening in my brain*
- *Doing fun stuff*
- *We are pretending and with Barbies at a party or something*
- *We do stories, we pretend*
- *I see that I am playing. I can see what I'm playing and I can see what I'm playing with.*
- *It's just play; I just do.*

These responses suggest that, at least for some children, play was regarded as a mental, as well as a physical, phenomenon. References to using imagination, pretending versus what is real, and thinking as the basis of play all indicate that there is much more to play than enactment: the mental dimension is also recognised. This is in contrast to some of the research reported by Lillard (1993; 1998) suggesting that young children do not necessarily understand the role of mental representation in play, particularly pretend play. Rather, it suggests that play can be a rich opportunity to develop understandings about mental phenomena, as well as to demonstrate these (Dockett, 1998).

At the same time, it is clear that some children just know when they are playing. There is a sense that they have generated a playframe (Bateson, 1972), they know it exists and other children know that it exists, and play proceeds. Children engaged in play know that they are playing.

Do You Work and Play at School?

Twenty-two Australian children responded to this question. Various conversations raised issues of play and work:

Gary: *Paintings are boring.*

Gail: *When I'm drawing pictures that's not boring–you have to draw them inside the lines and that's boring.*

Interviewer: *Gary, do you like painting?*

Gary: *No, because Miss tells us what to paint.*

Interviewer: *So, is that work or play?*

Gary: *Work. Because it's boring . . .*
I would like there to be no teacher.
Because it's fun and you get to draw whatever you like . . .
I like being outside and then we don't have to do what the teacher tells us to do.

Adam: *Work is when you have to do stuff neatly. Not just playing.*
Like write in your sentence book.
You have to work so you will learn.

Sam: *Can't do work and play together.*

Jane: *But maybe work can be fun.*
You do work in school. It can be fun, a little bit.

Meg: *Work is something where you learn.*
When you learn to write.

Jock: *When you build things that is sort of learning things, sort of work.*

Zeth: *You build so you can make money.*
Cause you sell them and you make heaps and heaps of money so that you can buy what you want.

Jock: *I didn't want to come to school because I didn't want to do work.*
I just wanted to play.

Meg: *It's hard work at school, because you have to learn.*

These children made some clear distinctions between work and play, but also suggested that some work things could be a little fun. These comments reflect the view that play is voluntary, and that is does not involve teacher direction. There is also a focus on performance, doing things neatly, and a connection between work and learning. These are similar to the characteristics listed by Wing (1995) as determinants of work. There is a suggestion from Jock that building things could involve learning, but Zeth clearly has a different perspective on building and the importance of it. Jock regards school as a place to learn, and in this conversation, learning is regarded as work, not play.

CONCLUSION

The children's voices reported in this paper cannot be construed as representative of anything but their own perspectives of play within the bounds of their school. However, the comments and responses of these children suggest some similarities in their understandings of the role and place of play within school, as well as their own experiences of play. At the very least, these children all had a clear idea of what they did at school and of what constituted play for them. They used a script to list events that occur at school, but were also able to go beyond this and to describe what play was like for them. They were adamant that they did play at school, though for some children, notably the Australians, play occurred mainly at break times and mainly outside the classroom. The American children indicated that play could occur within the classroom, but not at the same time as work or other routine activities, such as cleaning up.

Overall, many of the children reported that friends were an important element of play at school, and that not having friends, or having friends "be mean," was not conducive to play. Australian children, more than the American children, mentioned the impact of big kids and the perceived dangers of play with big kids, whether it be on the big kids' equipment or in the playground generally. The term bullying was used, suggesting that children, as well as teachers, are talking about these issues as they seek to redress them.

The types of play mentioned by both American and Australian children are remarkably similar. Both groups mention what King (1987) has described as recreational play. The Australian children regard this as a feature of outside activity, whereas the American children report that such play could happen both inside and outside. Instructional play is also mentioned by both groups. It is clear that children understand that this is play under the guidance of teachers and with a specific educational purpose in mind. It can still be play for these children, but they are under no illusions about who controls such activity. Interestingly, none of the children in either group mentioned illicit play. Yet, children who have been in school for only a few years more are explicit in their discussion of illicit play and the ways in which they can adapt the agenda of teachers and schools through such play (Dockett & Fleer, 1999; King, 1987).

There was an overwhelmingly negative response from both groups about teachers' involvement in play. Even where children said that teachers did play, it was regarded as an exception rather than a rule. Clearly, teachers are not regarded by children as players. Teachers often do not regard themselves as players (Dockett & Fleer, 1999; Jones & Reynolds, 1992). Play times within school curricula may be regarded as opportunities for teachers to 'catch up on some work,' to observe or record what children are doing, or to let 'children work things out for themselves' (Jones, et al., 2002). Leseman et al., (2001) report that teachers were more actively involved in children's work than children's play, a finding consistent with U.S. research (Kontos & Keyes, 1999).

There are several concerns from the notion that teachers tend to distance themselves from play. Firstly, if educators regard play as a valuable approach to teaching and learning, this needs to be reflected in a curriculum that provides the time, space and resources for play as well as levels of teacher and child engagement that promote complex play. Secondly, such a move requires a recognition that all play may not be positive and valuable for all children (Dockett & Fleer, 1999). Further, it suggests that it is the responsibility of the teacher to recognise the play that is complex and valuable as well as the play which may cause concern, distress or anxiety for others. Thirdly, the value of play as a means of intervening positively and promoting equity needs to be recognised (Dockett & Lambert, 1996). Leseman et al., (2001), note that "individual and socioeconomic differences between children were more strongly reproduced in free play than in work activities" (p. 381). One implication is that this results in "a risk that free play with low teacher involvement merely reproduces existing socioeconomic and individual differences" (Leseman, et al., 2001, p. 382).

Fourthly, if we believe that play is a disposition, and accept that children are most likely to learn dispositions from being around people who display those dispositions (Katz & Chard, 1989), we need to encourage teachers to demonstrate that playful disposition. This does not imply that teachers should become players, just as the children are players. Nor does it suggest that adults should take an active role in directing or controlling children's play. Rather, it suggests that teachers can demonstrate many aspects of play in their interactions and in their planning–as well as within their approaches to classroom management and organisation–that reflect the value and importance of play (Frost, Wortham, & Reifel, 2001). A range of roles is available for teachers in play (Jones & Reynolds, 1992). Educators need to be confident in using these different roles to support, complicate and extend children's play.

Importantly, the children's responses and comments reported in this paper remind us that seeking to understand children's experiences of play at school requires us to involve children in research, rather than to conduct research 'on' them. Having conversations with children is but one way of seeking to understand children's experiences. It is remarkable that in many of the debates about play and what constitutes play, relatively few studies have sought the views of children. Those that have, have reported a rich array of information, reflecting children's competence and confidence sharing information that is relevant to them and that matters. This paper adds to this corpus.

REFERENCES

Anning, A. (1994). Play and legislated curriculum-back to basics: An alternative view. In J. R. Moyles (Ed.), *The experience of play* (pp. 67–75). Buckingham, UK: Open University Press.

Baroody, A. J. (2000). Does mathematics instruction for three-to-five-year-olds really make sense? *Young Children*, *55*(4), 61–67.

Bateson, G. (1972). *Steps to an ecology of mind*. New York: Ballantine.

Blatchford, P. (1994). Research on children's school playground behaviour in the United Kingdom. In P. Blatchford & S. Sharp (Eds.), *Breaktime and the school: Understanding and changing playground behaviour* (pp. 16–35). London: Routledge.

Board of Studies, NSW. (1998). *Human society and its environment, K-6 syllabus*. Sydney: Author.

Board of Studies, NSW. (1999). *Personal development, health and physical education, K-6 syllabus*. Sydney: Author.

Clyde, M. (2001). Children's responses to starting school: Some Victorian stories. *Journal of Australian Research in Early Childhood Education*, *8*(1), 23–32.

Cooper, J. L., & Dever, M. T. (2001). Sociodramatic play as a vehicle for curriculum integration in first grade. *Young Children*, *56*(3), 58–63.

Corbin, J., & Strauss, A. (1990). Grounded theory research: Procedures, canons, and evaluative criteria. *Qualitative Sociology*, *13*(1), 3–21.

Corsaro, W. (1997). *The sociology of childhood.* Thousand Oaks, CA: Pine Forge Press.

Davidson, J. I. F. (1998). Language and play: Natural partners. D. P. Fromberg & D. Bergen (Eds.), *Play from birth to twelve and beyond: Contexts, perspectives and meanings* (pp. 175–184). New York: Garland.

Department of Education, Training and Employment, South Australia. (2001). *South Australian curriculum, standards and accountability framework.* Adelaide, South Australia: Author.

Dockett, S. (1998). Constructing understandings through play in the early years. *International Journal of Early Years Education*, *6*(1), 105–116.

Dockett, S. (2001, July). *Views of play in the early years of school.* Paper presented at the Dimensions of Play Conference, Sheffield, UK.

Dockett, S., & Fleer, M. (1999). *Play and pedagogy in early childhood: Bending the rules*. Sydney: Harcourt.

Dockett, S., & Lambert, P. (1996). *The importance of play.* Sydney: NSW Board of Studies.

Dockett, S., & Perry, B. (1996, January). *Re: Playing (and) constructivism.* Paper presented at the *Sixth Australia and New Zealand Conference on the First Years of School*, Hobart.

Dockett, S., & Perry, B. (1999). *Starting school: What matters for children, parents and educators? Research in Practice, 6*(3). Canberra: Australian Early Childhood Association.

Dockett, S., Perry, B., & Nanlohy, P. (1999). Computers in early childhood services: A part of the educational program or less time to play? *Journal for Australian Research in Early Childhood Education*, *6*(2), 165–176.

Dockett, S., Woods, L., Cusack, M., & Perry, B. (2000, January). *Young children's views of Australia and Australians*. Paper presented at the *Australian Research in Early Childhood Education Conference*, Canberra.

Evans, J. (1996). Children's attitudes towards recess and the changes taking place in Australian primary schools. *Research in Education*, *56*, 49–61.

Evans, J. (1997). Rethinking recess: Signs of change in Australian primary schools. *Education Research and Perspectives*, *24*(1), 14–27.

Evans, J. (1998). School closures, amalgamations and children's play: Bigger may not be better. *Children Australia*, *23*(1), 12–18.

Evans, J. (1999). Playtime: More than just a break. *Topic*, No.22, 1–4.

Evans, J., & Pellegrini, A. (1997). Surplus energy theory: An enduring but inadequate justification for school breaktime. *Educational Review*, *49*(3), 229–236.

Fein, G., & Wiltz, N. W. (1998). Play as children see it. In D. P. Fromberg & D. Bergen (Eds.), *Play from birth to twelve and beyond: Contexts, perspectives and meanings* (pp. 37–49). New York: Garland.

Fivush, R. (1984). Learning about school: The development of kindergarteners' school scripts. *Child Development*, *55*(5), 1697–1709.

Fleer, M. (Ed.) (1996). *Play through the profiles: Profiles through play*. Canberra: Australian Early Childhood Association.

Fromberg, D. P. (1992). A review of research on play. In C. Seefeldt (Ed.), *The early childhood curriculum: A review of current research* (2nd ed.) (pp. 42–84). New York: Teachers College Press.

Frost, J. L., Wortham, S. C., & Reifel, S. (2001). *Play and child development.* Upper Saddle River, NJ: Merrill/Prentice Hall.

Garza, M., Briley, S., & Reifel, S. (1985). Children's views of play. In J. L. Frost & S. Sunderlin (Eds.), *When children play* (pp. 31–37). Wheaton, MD: Association for Childhood Education International.

Ginsburg, H. P., Inoue, N., & Seo, K-H. (1999). Young children doing mathematics: Observations of everyday activities. In J. V. Copley (Ed.), *Mathematics in the early years* (pp. 48–65) Reston, VA: National Council of Teachers of Mathematics.

Heaslip, P. (1994). Making play work in the classroom. In J. Moyles (Ed.), *The excellence of play* (pp. 99–110). Buckingham: Open University Press.

Hughes, F. P. (1995). *Children, play and development* (2nd ed.). Boston, MA: Allyn & Bacon.

Johnson, J. E. (1998). Play development from ages four to eight. In D. P. Fromberg & D. Bergen (Eds.), *Play from birth to twelve and beyond: Contexts, perspectives and meanings* (pp. 146–153). New York: Garland.

Jones, E., & Reynolds, G. (1992). *The play's the thing . . . Teachers' roles in children's play.* New York: Teachers College Press.

Jones, E., & Reynolds, G. (1995). Enabling children's play–the teacher's role. In E. Klugman (Ed.), *Play, policy and practice* (pp. 37–46). St Paul, MN: Redleaf Press.

Jones, K., Dockett, S., Perry, B., & Westcott, K. (2002). Play in the first years of school. *Journal of Australian Research in Early Childhood Education*, *9*(1), 11–26.

Katz, L. G., & Chard, S. C. (1989). *Engaging children's minds: The project approach*. Norwood NJ: Ablex.

Kemple, K. M. (1996). Teachers' beliefs and reported practices concerning sociodramatic play. *Journal of Early Childhood Teacher Education*, *17*(2), 19–31.

King, N. R. (1982). Children's play as a form of resistance in the classroom. *Journal of Education*, *164*(3), 320–329.

King, N. R. (1987). Elementary school play: Theory and research. In J. Block & N. King, (Eds.), *School play. A source book* (pp. 143–166). New York: Garland.

King, N. R. (1990). Economics and control in everyday school life. In M. W. Apple (Ed.), *Ideology and curriculum* (pp. 43–60). Boston: Routledge and Kegan Paul.

Kitson, N. (1994). "Please Miss Alexander: will you be the robber?" Fantasy play: A case for adult intervention. In J. Moyles (Ed.), *The excellence of play* (pp. 88–98). Buckingham: Open University Press.

Kontos, S., & Keyes, L. (1999). An ecobehavioral analysis of early childhood classrooms. *Early Childhood Research Quarterly*, *14*(1), 35–50.

LeCompte, M. D. (1980). The civilising of children: How children learn to become students. *Journal of Thought*, *15*(3), 105–127.

Leseman, P. P. M., Rollenberg, L., & Rispens, J. (2001). Playing and working in kindergarten: Cognitive co-construction in two educational situations. *Early Childhood Research Quarterly*, *16*, 363–384.

Lillard, A. (1993). Young children's conceptualisation of pretense: Action or mental representational state? *Child Development*, *64*, 372–386.

Lillard, A. S. (1998). Playing with a theory of mind. In O. Saracho & B. Spodek (Eds.), *Multiple perspectives on play in early childhood education* (pp. 11–33). Albany: State University of New York Press.

Linke, P. (1998). *Let's stop bullying*. Canberra, ACT: Australian Early Childhood Association.

Marsh, K. (2001). It's not all black and white: The influence of the media, the classroom and immigrant groups on children's playground singing games. In J. C. Bishop & M. Curtis (Eds.), *Play today in the primary school playground* (pp. 62–79). Buckingham: Open University Press.

Mayall, B. (2000). Conversations with children: Working with generational issues. In P. Christensen & A. James (Eds.), *Research with children: Perspectives and practices* (pp. 120–135). New York: Falmer Press.

Meckley, A. M. (2000, October). *Play and learning connections*. Play research colloquium at the annual conference of the *National Association for the Education of Young Children*, Atlanta, GA.

Neumann, (1971). *The elements of play*. New York: MSS Modular Publications.

NSW Department of Education and Training. (1999). *Foundations for learning: Kindergarten*. Sydney: Author.

Olsen, A. E., & Sumsion, J. (2002). Early childhood teacher practices regarding the use of dramatic play in K-2 classrooms. *Journal of Australian Research in Early Childhood Education*, *9*(1), 37–39.

Paley, V. (1984). *Boys and girls*. Chicago: University of Chicago Press.

Pellegrini, A. D., & Bjorklund, D. (1996). The place of recess in school: Issues in the role of recess in children's education and development. *Journal of Research in Childhood Education International.* 11(1) (Fall/Winter).

Pellegrini, A., & Blatchford, P. (2000). *The child at school: Interactions with peers and teachers*. London: Oxford University Press.

Perry, B., Dockett, S., & Howard, P. (2000). Starting school: Issues for children, parents and teachers. *Journal of Australian Research in Early Childhood Education, 7*(1), 41–53.

Reifel, S. (1988). Children's thinking about their early education experience. *Theory into Practice*, *27*(1), 62–66.

Romero, M. (1989). Work and play in the nursery school. In L. Weis, P. Altback, G. Kelly, & H. Petrie (Eds.), *Childhood education* (pp. 119–138). Albany: SUNY.

Roskos, K., & Neuman, S. (1998). Play as an opportunity for literacy. In O. Saracho & B. Spodek (Eds.), *Multiple perspectives on play in early childhood education* (pp. 100–115). Albany: State University of New York Press.

Slee, P. T., & Rigby, K. (1994). Peer victimisation at school. *Australian Journal of Early Childhood*, *19*(1), 3–10.

Smilansky, S., & Shefatya, L. (1990). *Facilitating play: A medium for promoting cognitive, socioemotional, and academic development in young children*. Gaithersburg, MD: Psychosocial & Educational Publications.

Trawick-Smith, J. (1998). School-based play and social interactions: Opportunities and limitations. In D. P. Fromberg & D. Bergen (Eds.), *Play from birth to twelve and beyond: Contexts, perspectives and meanings* (pp. 241–247). New York: Garland.

Trawick-Smith, J. (2001). Play and the curriculum. In J. L. Frost, S. C. Wortham, & S. Reifel, *Play and child development* (pp. 294–339). Upper Saddle River, NJ: Merrill/Prentice Hall.

Wiltz, N. W., & Klein, E. (1994, April). *What did you do at school today? Activities in child care from the child's point of view.* Paper presented at the annual meeting of the *American Educational Research Association*, New Orleans, LA.

Wing, L. A. (1995). Play is not the work of the child: Young children's perceptions of work and play. *Early Childhood Research Quarterly*, *10*(2), 223–247.

Chapter Six

Teachers' and Parents' Attitudes About Play and Learning in Taiwanese Kindergartens

James E. Johnson and Pei-Yu Chang

> Pretend play serves the child well for self-entertainment and for assimilating the complexities of the world. But it is also the foundation of a long-term incorporation and consolidation of a major human characteristic: our human imagination, our capacity through consciousness to form experiences into stories, to manipulate memory representations of our physical and social worlds into new scenarios. We can travel mentally through time and space, and not only to entertain ourselves to pass the time but also explore a range of possible futures, of alternative courses of action. We can sustain ourselves in periods of stress with the hope generated by such imagined explorations.
>
> Jerome L. Singer, 1999, page 7 from *Imaginative and Adaptive development play* In J. Goldstein *Toys, Play, And Child Development*, 6–26, New York: Cambridge University Press.

CONCEPTUAL FRAMEWORK AND BACKGROUND

Western sensibilities concerning the value of pretending in childhood are reflected in the above Singer quote. Widely appreciated worldwide—but perhaps especially in Europe and North America—is the idea that playing well and developing well go hand-in-hand, even as the nature of the complex relation between playing and developing remains elusive and indeterminate. Of the various metaphorical ways in which scholars have conceptualized play—including play as fantasy, play as power, play as affect, play as cognition (Singer's primary focus)—perhaps none surpass the notion of play as cultural activity and interpretation. Goncu (2002) notes that the meaning and importance of play is an ever-evolving conceptualization and that writing a 'dictionary' on this intriguing and curious activity is an endless task, one which will last forever.

As summarized in Johnson, Christie, and Wardle (2005), Goncu, Tuermer, Jain, and Johnson (1999) posit five precepts for research on play from a sociocultural perspective. First, both *play* and *not play* behaviors should be included in the study because in some cultures perhaps play is not as important in childhood as other behaviors. These behaviors must be examined as activities in social contexts, which themselves are shaped by economic, social, and political factors operating within the larger culture.

The second of Goncu et al.'s precepts is that research needs to shed light on the meaning and significance attributed to play by the adults inside the culture and the third concerns how adult values are communicated to children. In the American middle class, for example, play –and the toys manufactured to support play—are generally thought to be necessary for the stimulation of cognitive and social development, crucial for success in school and later life. Pretend play is particularly valued, and play is an appropriate activity for adults to share with children. Considerable literature, however, documents cultural differences in beliefs, attitudes and practices related to children's play. In many traditional and pre-literate societies, for example, play is seen as a natural but inconsequential aspect of childhood, and manufactured toys and time for play are nonexistent. Furthermore, adults are not part of the participant structure (Roopnarine, Johnson, & Hooper, 1994; Schwartzman, 1978). Cultures differ in how adult beliefs and values are transmitted to children. Do adults explicitly encourage children to play, inform them that it is all right to play? Do they actually engage in play with children? Implicitly or overtly how are their play attitudes communicated to children through toys, play space and time?

Fourth, comprehending children's play requires seeing how children represent their worlds in play. When children play, play represents their cultures. We must study play in relation to non-playful contexts, and not only as an isolated phenomenon. What adult roles do children enact? What types of events are represented? How do they symbolically represent their lives? How is the physical, social and symbolic environment used? What are the different contexts in which play desires are developed? How are play actions and accompanying operations expressed in various environments? How are children transforming meaning and conserving meaning across play media and contexts, and what does this information tell us about the development of imagination and creativity?

Finally, Goncu et al. (1999) point out that investigators must use interdisciplinary thinking and research methods to illuminate children's play in the cultural context. What are play's economic, cultural, educational, and psychological contexts in a given culture? Clearly, it is necessary to employ a diverse array of tools of inquiry to obtain information on multiple levels—from historical and archival analysis to understanding labor relations and economic structures, to understanding how adults think about play, and children represent adult life in their play (e.g., observation, interview, and narrative research techniques).

Figure 6.1 shows our general model for the cultural study of children's play consistent with Goncu et al.'s socio-cultural orientation (Johnson & Chang,

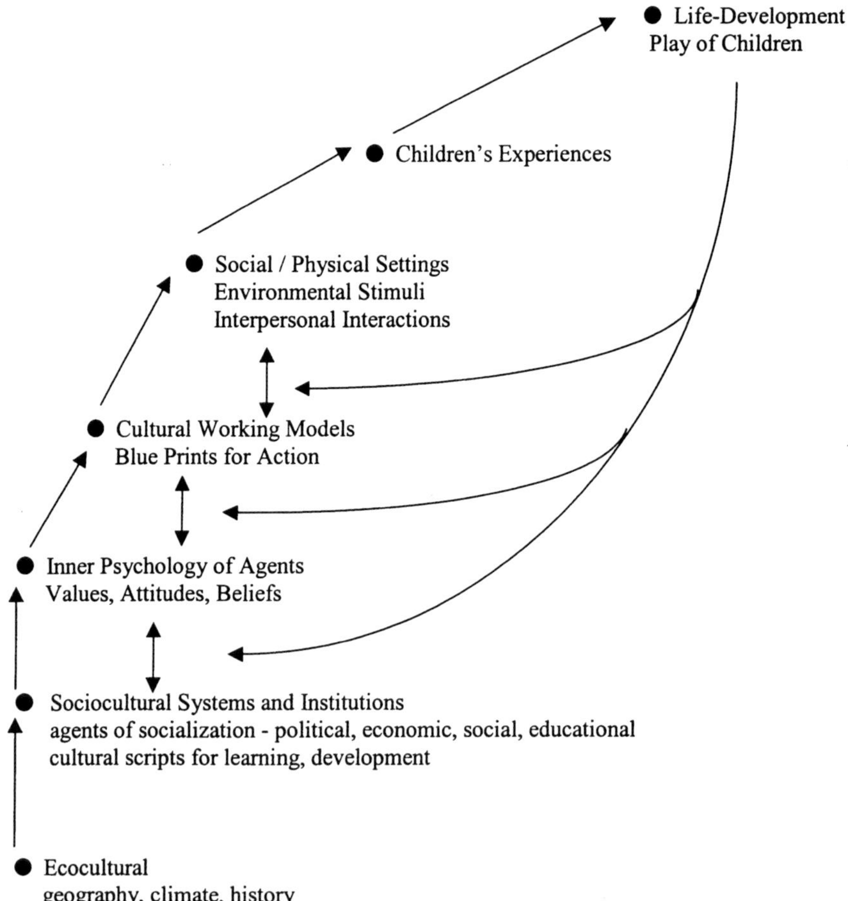

Figure 6.1. Conceptual Framework for Macro-/Micro- Level Analysis of Play-Environment Relations. ***Source:*** **Johnson, Christie and Wardle. *Play, Development and Early Education.* Published by Allyn and Bacon, Boston, MA. Copyright © 2005 by Pearson Education, Reprinted by permission of the publisher.**

2002). This general model represents major categories of factors operating on both macro-and micro-levels about which information is needed to understand play-in-culture. Foundational are ecocultural factors, or the history, climate and geography of a given culture that influence its social systems and institutions. The thoughts and actions of members of a culture are in a process of dynamic reciprocal relation over time with the sociocultural systems on the one hand, and with generation of physical-material, temporal-spatial, and interpersonal activity settings, on the other hand. Activity settings, which require analysis in terms of actors-participants, task-activities (e.g., chores, schooling, care-giving, play, etc.), scripts (i.e., norms for self expression), motives, and goals (related to salient cultural values), are the various contexts for children's play and non-play experiences growing up in a culture that impact ontogenesis. In turn, the life course developmental manifestations of children, including their play behaviors, affect both the transactions occurring between social systems and the thoughts and actions of caregivers and the thoughts and actions of caregivers in relation to the activity settings they influence.

In the present study, data are presented relating to the category *Inner Psychology of Agents: Values, Attitudes, Beliefs*. Our general model, influenced by empirical ethnographic and survey research in Taiwan (Chang, 2001; Chang, 2002; Chang, Johnson & Lin, 2001), was first presented by Johnson and Chang (2002). The general model is related to a more specific conceptual model for understanding kindergarten children's play within the Taiwanese cultural context, originally proposed by Chang (2002) based on her dissertation research (Chang, 2001).

In volume six of *Play & Cultural Studies,* Chang specified a comprehensive model for kindergarten play within the present day Taiwanese cultural context. There she discusses and provides a diagram illustrating the complex pattern of influences linking culture, history, society, parents, and schools with children's play. For example, she notes that in the traditional Chinese culture education is regarded as a most important ladder to the achievement of higher social status and economic advancement. The ancient sages' sayings are well known: "All things are beneath contempt, only education is to be esteemed," "Only if you suffer can you surpass others," "You must study well to rise to be an official"; *The Three-Word Classic* says—"Diligence has its own reward; play has no advantages." Parents judge children's achievement from their performance on academic work using a narrow definition of success. By tradition, children learn by being told and by being shown how to do things. They learn from didactic instruction, a mimetic as opposed to a transformational approach to learning (Gardner, 1989). The Chinese language system biases one towards mimetic instruction since it requires memorization of thousands of Chinese characters and training in stroke sequences. Parents learned this way when they were young. Other factors affecting parents' expectations for their own children include the government's exam-oriented educational system and peer pressure from their social network. Parental choices and decisions for children's learning (i.e., selections of kindergartens, enrollment in out of school programs, and work at home) impact children's play and their right to play (Chang, 2003).

In her dissertation, Chang (2001) found that children's play is affected by the school they attend. She studied classrooms in depth, using ethnographic research methods. Table 6.1 provides a summary of the images of toys created by the classroom contexts in the two Taiwanese kindergartens. A sharp contrast is seen. The metaphors for play in the Efficient Learning Kindergarten are "bait used by the teacher," "oxygen pursued by the children," and "a conditional gift," while in the Exploratory Learning Kindergarten the metaphors are "a chip exchanged among children," "a tool for learning and development," and "a vehicle to realize dreams and fulfill needs." Children in the so-called "Exploratory Learning Kindergarten" played at school and even invited their parents to engage in pretend play at home. But children enrolled in the so-called "Efficient Learning Kindergarten" had no time scheduled for play, and the small number of available toys were almost always "off limits," kept high up on a shelf. Interestingly, some resilient children dared to take risks to play when the teacher was busy correcting worksheets or preparing worksheets. Even though there was a paucity of play material in the classroom, children still made use of objects to play such as transforming the straps of schoolbags into horsewhips and pretending to be horsemen or to drive carriages, or using a string as a phone line to initiate a conversation, or a chalkboard erasure as a cell phone. Classroom structures influence children's play behavior; education in kindergarten is related to children's right to play.

Moreover, Chang found that parents in Taiwan often sent their kindergarten children to after-school programs to practice academic skills or to take lessons in the arts, such as piano, drawing, or dancing. These children had quite a busy week, with little time for play. All parents feeling traditional cultural pressures to help their young sons to become dragons and their young daughters to become phoenixes (*"Wan tsu chen lung"*) were concerned about their readiness for elementary school. Parents often supervised their children's academic work at home. The work at home decreased time for children to play.

In sum, the present research uses a sociocultural approach to the study of play and culture. Basic to questions about education in Taiwan and in other Asian societies is an understanding of traditional cultural values centered on Confucianism. Academic emphasis in Taiwan derives from the combination of Confucianism and contemporary political will and ideology (Yang, 2002).

Table 6.1. Images of Toys Created by Classroom Contexts in Two Taiwanese Kindergartens

The Efficient Learning School (A private academically-oriented kindergarten)	*Context Influence*	*The Exploratory Learning School (A private kindergarten with more open-ended curriculum)*	*Context Influence*
Toys as a Bait used by teachers	1. The curricular context drove teachers' focus on the learning of academic skills and used toys as a bait to draw children's attention to lessons. 2. The physical context that made toys unavailable to children and thus could be used to elicit children's temporary interests in class.	**Toys as a Chip exchanged among children**	The social context allowed social interactions and negotiations among children. Thus children used the toys as chips to exchange and maintain friendship.
Toys as an Oxygen pursued by children or a Lifeboat taken by children	1. The curricular context evoked children's needs to relax after or between structured lessons and long seating work. 2. The restriction of the physical context stimulated children's creative uses of the materials in the surrounding environment (e.g., transformed a string into a phone line).	**Toys as a Tool for learning and development**	1. The physical context allowed children to add to their knowledge by approaching any area of the classroom and accessing all kinds of learning materials. 2. The social context provided opportunities for social interactions which further facilitated the development of creative ideas and constructive competency.

(continued)

Table 6.1. (*continued*)

The Efficient Learning School (A private academically-oriented kindergarten)	*Context Influence*	*The Exploratory Learning School (A private kindergarten with more open-ended curriculum)*	*Context Influence*
Toys as a Conditional Gift given by teachers	1. The interaction between curricular context and physical context caused the ignorance of providing a variety of opportunities for children to play. Children's opportunity to play with toys (blocks were the only ones in the classroom) was given by the teacher when extra time was left from structured lessons or when children behaved well. 2. The social context (the regimented atmosphere constituted with teacher authority and the powerless children) deprived children's right to play with toys.	**Toys as a Vehicle for children to fulfill their needs and realize their dreams**	1. The physical context allowed children to weave their dreams and create imaginative worlds across the classroom. 2. The social context enabled children to be imaginative and pretending with peers or teachers. 3. The curricular context (teachers' positive attitude toward play) supported children's needs to play.

According to Confucian philosophy, the ultimate goal of socialization and education is maintaining natural social harmony, and in order to achieve this, one must first cultivate oneself, and then harmonize one's own family, and then help govern one's state well. The end is to be able to manifest one's bright virtue to all in the world. The traditional educator's responsibilities include being a role model of virtue, helping students to cultivate themselves, and delivering external knowledge.

PURPOSE AND RATIONALE

The purpose of the present study relates to guidelines two and three in Goncu et al.'s scheme noted above; that is, we sought to find out more about what teachers and parents in Taiwan think and feel about kindergarten children's play and related behaviors at school and at home, and about how these sentiments are communicated to children in these important cultural and developmental spaces for growing young children. Preschool (kindergarten: child ages three to six years) teachers (N-117) in Taiwan were asked to indicate on a survey questionnaire their attitudes and opinions concerning play and related behaviors (story-telling, use of multiple symbolic media, imagination, etc.) on a specially devised 58-item instrument that consisted of short descriptions of school and home situations. The specific aims were to evaluate teachers' attitudes about play and related behaviors by young children at school and to compare their responses to parents' responses to the same questionnaire. In this comparison parents came from two groups: (1) Parents who enrolled their children in a working class tradition kindergarten, the Efficient Learning Kindergarten (N=29); and (2) parents who enrolled their children in a progressive kindergarten affiliated with a National Teacher's College in Taiwan, the Exploratory Learning Kindergarten (N=33).

The present survey study was motivated by need to acquire further information about changing teacher and parental beliefs and practices in Taiwan concerning children's play and related behaviors, particularly in connection with kindergarten education. Taiwan is a fast-changing society that has imported many Western ideas about early education and the value of play and toys at school. These new ideas have come into conflict with traditional cultural values, which have segregated play and toys from serious learning in the classroom (Liang, 2001). Given that changing attitudes about play are taking place, a detailed and differentiated description of teachers' and parents' values and opinions about play, creativity, imagination and other related behaviors would be useful to evaluate the extent of variation which exists within and between samples of teachers and parents of young kindergarten-age children in Taiwan. Results also could prove useful for designing interventions aimed to promote in teachers and parents a better understanding about the value of play and play-related behaviors and the use of toys, games, and media in education, and also to help fashion programs for young children that are consistent with the basic tenets of developmentally and culturally appropriate and enhancing educational practices.

METHODS

Participants

A total of 117 teachers participated in this research survey, filling out the Beliefs Questionnaire as part of workshops conducted by the authors and held during Spring 2000 in three cities in Taiwan—Hsin-Chu, Tainan, and Taichung. Demographic characteristics of the sample are summarized in Table 6.2. The typical participant was a female (97%) head teacher (81%) in her twenties (58%) who was not a parent (64%), who had majored in Early Childhood Education (68%) at a University, and who had been working three years or less at her current place of employment (69%) and who had five years or less ECE work experience (56%).

In addition, 62 parents also completed the Beliefs Questionnaire; 29 parents had their children enrolled in the Efficient Learning Kindergarten, and 33 in the Exploratory Learning Kindergarten. The latter kindergarten did not schedule play in the curriculum and usually had no toys available, while the former allowed for play and provided materials for play. Demographic characteristics of parents in these two samples are presented in Table 6.3. Exploratory Learning parents on the average were older, more educated, and had higher annual incomes than Efficient Learning parents.

Survey Instrument: The Beliefs Questionnaire

The Beliefs Questionnaire had a Demographics Information section to obtain knowledge about person characteristics of respondents, such as their gender, age, education, experience (teachers only) and income (parents only). The remainder of the questionnaire consisted of 58 items grouped under three vignettes (1) *Kindergarten Curriculum, Play, and Teacher Role*; (2) *Children's Pretend Play, Role-taking, and Narrative*; and (3) *Children's Imagination, Creativity, Symbolic Languages, and Social Interactions*. The complete questionnaire is available from the first author. Below is a partial summary of the instrument. Participants spend about 20 minutes completing it.

Table 6.2. Demographic Characteristics, School Environment and Education and Professional Backgrounds of Educator Respondents (N=117)

Gender (N=116)	Percent
Male	3.4
Female	96.6
Parent Status (N=117)	
Yes	35.9
No	64.1
Age (N=117)	
<20	0.9
20–29	58.1
30–39	22.2
40–49	15.4
>50	3.4
Position (N=114)	
Director	4.0
Head Teacher	80.7
Assistant Teacher	7.0
Student Teacher	7.9
Education (N=115)	
High School	20
Jr. College	29.6
University	47.0
Graduate	3.5
ECE Education (N=117)	
None	14.5
Taken Classes	17.1
Majored	68.4
ECE Work Experience (N=117)	
1 year	20.5
2–5	35.0
6–10	23.1
11–20	13.7
>20	7.7
Experience in Current Program	
1 year	33.0
2–3	35.7
4–7	19.1
>7	12.2

Table 6.3. Personal and Family Information About Exploratory K Parents and Efficiency K Parents

	Exploratory K Efficiency K	Parent Parents
Gender		
Father	33.3%	31%
Mother	66.7%	39%
Age		
20–29	15.2%	17.2%
30–39	42.4%	79.3%
40–49	39.4%	3.4%
>50	3.0%	0.0%
Educational Background		
Elementary/Jr. High	12.1%	13.8%
Senior High	42.4%	62.1%
College	27.3%	24.1%
University	12.1%	0.0%
Graduate	6.1%	0.0%
Monthly Family Income		
<50k	6.1%	41.4%
50–70k	30.3%	31.0%
70–100k	39.4%	17.2%
100k–150k	15.2%	3.4%
150–200k	3.0%	0.0%
>200k	6.1%	6.9%
Children's Enrollments In and Out-of-School Programs		
None	33.3%	69%
1 Program	9.1%	24.1%
2 Programs	33.3%	0.0%
3 or more Programs	24.2%	6.9%

The first vignette, *Kindergarten Curriculum, Play, and Teacher Role*, portrayed two kindergartens, one taught by Ms. Pan and the other by Ms. Wu. Ms. Pan's kindergarten allowed for play, exploration, imagination, art, stories and expressiveness, while Ms. Wu's kindergarten stressed direct teaching of academic subjects, with the use of drill and practice, worksheets, and homework. Twenty-one items followed grouped under four subsections: (a) *purpose of kindergarten education;* (b) *value of play for learning;* (c) *playful teaching;* and (d) *preparing children for the future*. Five items assessed opinions about (a), six items (b), and five items each for (c) and (d). A five-point scale (1 = strongly agree, 2 = agree, 3 = undecided, 4 = disagree, and 5 = strongly disagree) was employed to evaluate how much the respondent agreed with each item statement (e.g., "*I like Ms. Pan's play-filled classroom because the environment provides rich opportunities and lots of free choices for children*").

The second vignette, *Children's Pretend Play, Role-taking, and Narrative*, can be summarized as follows: "At home, Ting-Wei, a six year-old boy in Taiwan, pretends he is a cook with two children and three dogs. He draws and designs menus for a variety of dishes, cakes, and soups to feed his 'family.' When they are sad, he will sing, dance, tell stories, or draw pictures to cheer them up." Six items followed grouped under *pretend play* (e.g., "It is good when parents encourage children to pretend"), and five items under storytelling (e.g., "Story-telling is one of the most important ways for children to think about problems and practice ways to solve them").

The third vignette, *Children's Imagination, Creativity, Symbolic Languages, and Social Interactions*, can be summarized as follows: "When at school, Ting-Wei will participate in group-dramatic play. One day he pretends to be a member of a ship's crew bound on a treasure hunt. Six children in the play group designed costumes from blankets and towels. The children pass through a sequence of play: 1) casting off, 2) cooking lunch, 3) chasing a mouse, 4) going fishing, 5) catching a shark, and 6) eating the shark." Six items evaluated *creativity* (e.g., "One of the most important goals of kindergarten education is the cultivation of children's creativity"), seven items assessed *imagination* (e.g., "If I were in charge of a kindergarten, my goal is to provide a place where my children can be as imaginative as they wish"), six items measured attitudes about transforming *or connecting story-telling, dramatic play, singing, dancing, gestures, counting actions, and drawing or multi-symbolic, multi-media activities* (e.g., "Every school day, teachers should help children to do activities such as transforming music into dance, into gestures, into art, and into dramatic play, etc."), and seven items estimated *social interaction and learning from each other or the value of social play in learning* (e.g., "It is good when children have many opportunities to play together during school time").

Scores were computed by averaging item scores under each of ten response categories: *Kindergarten Curriculum, Play, Teacher's Role, Preparation for Future, Value of Pretend Play, Value of Story Telling, Importance of Creativity, Value of Imagination, Learning Through Transformation, Learning Through Social Interaction*. Before computing these mean scores, scores on positively worded items were reversed (1 = 5, 2 = 4, . . .) so that higher scores on the response variables indicated greater endorsement of the value of the behavior in question.

Interviews and Workshop Discussions

In addition to the Beliefs Questionnaire, there were two other sources of data that informed the study, although these data are not reported here. The teachers and some parents of the Exploratory Learning Kindergarten and the Efficient Learning Kindergarten were interviewed individually. Also, there were general question-and-answers discussions in the workshops attended by the 117 teacher participants in this study. Information from these interviews and from the workshop session discussions assists in the interpretation and discussion of questionnaire results.

RESULTS AND DISCUSSION

The primary purpose of this study was to describe the beliefs and attitudes of the teachers concerning play and play-related activities. A secondary purpose was to compare teachers' responses to the questionnaire with parents' responses to the questionnaire. A tertiary purpose was to compare the responses of parents who enrolled their children in the Efficient Learning Kindergarten with the questionnaire responses of parents who enrolled their children in the Exploratory Learning Kindergarten.

Table 6.4 summarizes the responses of the teachers to the questionnaire (as well as parents to be discussed later). As can be seen, teachers endorsed seven

Table 6.4. Comparison of Educators' Responses to Questionnaire Sections with Parents Enrolling Their Child in Exploratory or Efficient Kindergarten

	Respondent Group		
Section	*Efficient K Parents (N=29)*	*Exploratory K Parents (N=33)*	*Educators (N=117)*
Open-ended Curriculum	3.07	3.27	3.39
Learning Through Play	3.19	3.45	3.52
Playful Teachers	3.29	3.56	3.5
Learning and Future	3.31	3.43	3.48
Value of Pretend Play	3.67	3.97	3.95
Value of Story Telling	3.71	3.67	3.93
Importance of Creativity	3.81	4.13	4.13
Value of Imagination	3.97	4.14	4.17
Learning Through Transformation	3.86	4.1	4.08
Learning from Social Interactions	2.92	2.94	4.02

Note: Number in table refer to averages for the groups of respondents. 5 = Strongly Endorse, 4 = Endorse, 3 = Uncertain, 2 = Disagree, 1 = Strongly Disagree response categories if you consider any number over mean = 3.5 to be a favorable response (on the five point Likert-type scale 3 = uncertain or neutral and 4 = endorse). Interestingly, the lower scores occurred for the first four categories, which followed the first vignette where the items pertained to the kindergarten curriculum, play and the teacher's role. Teachers felt more positive about the six response categories following the second and third vignette dealing with child behaviors. Children's imagination, pretend play, story telling, creativity, transformations across symbol systems or symbolic media, and social interaction all received mean scores over 4, while the mean scores for pretend play and story telling were 3.95 and 3.93, respectively. Teachers approve these child behaviors, even as they happen in the classroom, but are less favorable about taking an active role in promoting them, and teachers seem unsure about these behaviors being valuable preparation for the children's future.

Table 6.5 presents the correlations among the mean scores on the 10 response categories. The average correlation among the first four response categories was .49, and among the remaining six response categories was .67, but the average correlation between the first four and the last six response categories was only .13 (n.s.). In other words, teachers appeared to be responding in a patterned way to the items following vignette one dealing with teacher behaviors, roles and thoughts relating to play in the kindergarten, and in a consistent way to the questionnaire items following vignettes two and three concerned with child behaviors, but not in a consistent way across these two groups of response categories. For example, while the teachers' responses to the social interaction items (response category no. 10) was positively and significantly correlated with their responses to child expressions of imagination, creativity, pretend play, story telling, and transformations, their responses to social interaction was not significantly related to their responses under vignette number one dealing with the kindergarten curriculum, play and the role of the teacher.

Interestingly, when scores on the ten response categories were correlated with teacher characteristics, it was found that educational background was positively and significantly correlated with the first four response categories (on the average r = .26) and that experience (number of years working in kindergarten) was positively and significantly related with the remaining response categories on the average r = .23. Teachers with more experience have a greater appreciation of child expressions of creativity, imagination, and other similar behaviors. Teachers with more education seemed more positive about the teacher's role in fostering play in the kindergarten. Teachers who were also parents responded more favorably to child expressions of creativity, imagination and other similar behaviors more so than did teachers

Table 6.5. Correlations Among Questionnaire Section Means (N=117)

	1	*2*	*3*	*4*	*5*	*6*	*7*	*8*	*9*	*10*
1. Kindergarten Curriculum	1.0	.49	.34	.60	.17	.22	.23	.12	.15	−.05
2. Play		1.0	.4	.57	.19	.17	.19	.11	.10	0
3. Teacher's Role			1.0	.51	.26	.27	.30	.30	.27	.15
4. Preparation and Future				1.0	.32	.30	.34	.19	.23	.10
5 Pretend Play					1.0	.68	.56	.61	.56	.56
6 Story-telling						1.0	.60	.62	.67	.55
7. Creativity							1.0	.67	.56	.51
8. Imagination								1.0	.69	.54
9. Transformations									1.0	.66
10. Social Interaction										−1.0

Note: Correlation: under r =.19 are not statistically significant
r > .19 but < .26, are significant at the .05 level (2-tailed)
r > .26 are significant at the .01 level (2-tailed)

who were not parents themselves. Perhaps experiences with children in one's own home are like experiences with children in the kindergarten setting in promoting a greater appreciation of these behaviors in children.

As previously mentioned, Table 6.4 also presents the mean scores of the two samples of parents and compares them with the mean scores of the teachers on the ten response variables (see Table 6.4). With only one exception, the mean scores of the Exploratory Learning Kindergarten parents are higher than those of the Efficient Learning Kindergarten. Story telling was the exception (mean score of 3.71 to 3.67, for Efficient Learning and Exploratory Learning parents, respectively). Otherwise, higher mean scores appear for Exploratory Learning parents. This is especially the case for the response categories of pretend play and creativity where the mean score difference was greater than .3. Parent interview data corroborate these findings that play and play-related behaviors are valued more by parents in the Exploratory Learning kindergarten. The beliefs of the Exploratory Learning parents resemble more those of the teachers than do the scores of the Efficient Learning parents.

Most interesting, however, is the questionnaire data result for response category Social Interaction. Teachers approved social interaction (mean score = 4.02), while Efficient Learning parents were generally neutral or disapproved (mean score = 2.92), as were Exploratory Learning parents (mean score = 2.94).

Teachers approve social interaction in child expression of various symbolic behaviors (e.g., story telling, creativity, etc.) at school because of their professional knowledge. Teachers have read the research literature and have taken courses in higher education, which help them perceive the value of social interaction in these child-initiated behaviors. Also, they have inferred the cognitive value of child-child transactions in light of their experiences in the kindergarten classroom. This value is not so deeply perceived by parents. Parents see social interaction among children as instrumental or as potentially effective in learning or practicing social skills, but not as part of cognitive development or knowledge acquisition. Parents hold to the traditional Chinese value of cultivating the child to be a good member of the social group and to be in harmony with the group. Parents see the peer group and informal social commerce at school as important to cultivating social skills, but parents see teachers as important in promoting formal learning through their teaching and providing well-arranged activities. Parents do not seem to integrate the two processes of social interaction and formal learning as they unfold in the school setting. They fail to see how children construct knowledge from social interaction, although they realize that children learn to get along with others from social interactions. Interestingly, parents in Korea were found to demonstrate a similar belief, seeing the value of contemporary playthings for amusement or cognitive stimulation, and the value of traditional Korean toys for instilling social skills and graces (Jin & Johnson, 2002).

Teachers may endorse the integration between social interaction and formal learning and intellectual development more so than they actually put this attitude into practice in their classroom. While the Exploratory Learning but not Efficient Learning parents may have learned from the teachers the importance of learning through exploration and play and the use of the imagination and the like (from seeing the curriculum in operation and seeing teacher-children interactions), Exploratory Learning parents may miss realizing the importance of peer social interaction for knowledge construction or cognitive development because they do not see this more subtle application of Western theory about play and early childhood education going on in the classroom.

The curriculum and teacher behaviors in the Exploratory Learning kindergarten did not emphasize peer social interactions while children spontaneously expressed symbolic playful behaviors. Most of the time the children were given individual choices for activities. Teachers did not intervene in peer interactions to enrich these play experiences for the participants. Teachers emphasized instead whole group activities for social learning, such as the morning ceremony, circle time for teacher-led discussion, group dancing, teacher directed story telling and dramatic play or creative drama. These group activities, however, did not occupy as much curriculum time as did the time allotted for individualized learning. Hence, the parents in Taiwan who were better educated and who had opportunities to observe their children in the Exploratory Learning kindergarten were in a position to recognize the importance of individualized learning based on play, with the nature of the curriculum and kindergarten schedule greatly influenced by Western theory.

CONCLUSION

By tradition training and didactic instruction is valued as effective education. The Chinese word for such education is *tianya*, which means feeding of ducks. Chinese children are believed to be highly malleable, moldable like clay. High academic expectations are placed on children. In the traditional Chinese society, people are classified into four classes, which are scholars, farmers, labors, and merchants. Among these four levels, scholars are regarded as the highest and are most respected compared with the other occupations (Stevens & Lee, 1996). Teachers are revered as "embodiments of truth." They are ranked as one with the "Five Human Relationships," the others being Parents, Monarchs, Heaven, and Earth. Memorization, not an imaginative playful disposition or creative thinking, is the road to excellence in traditional Chinese society. As an old Confucian scholar in the Ming dynasty, Shi-Yi Lu, averred, "anyone who can remember can understand." Recitation without understanding is justified, as in memorizing the classics, in that it is like filling the four stomachs of a cow: "once its stomachs are filled, it can slowly ruminate on what it ate" (Liou, 1996, p. 85).

Taiwan is a fast-changing society still very much influenced by Confucian philosophy, but one that is questioning basic assumptions. As in other developed and developing countries, there has been a strong trend towards diversity and liberalization. Over 44% of Taiwanese graduate from college compared to 25% of the general adult population in the US (Chen & Teng, 1995). A big factor in this success has been the stress on academic achievement. Now, however, there is growing concern on educational reform, and how to help children become smart, happy, and creative all at once. Many children have been stressed out by the traditional system and many parents and educators are concerned and wish to find alternatives to the pressure-cooker model of education, both through and around the existing system. Educational innovations, such as private schools that enroll fewer children and have fewer pupils per classroom with an emphasis on learning by doing an experimental pedagogy, have been on the rise (Chen & Teng, 1995). The results of this study also provide evidence of shifting winds along the educational social landscape in Taiwan.

Yang (2002) has identified several dilemmas or tension points facing parents and teachers in any educational reform effort in Taiwan. On the one side, there are the traditional values of time and energy constraint, and on the other side there is this new interest in children's play and expression at school and at home. By tradition, there is stress on order and control, competition and having products of learning or child outcomes, extrinsic motivation in formal schooling, the priority given to elementary school judged narrowly, and academic expectations. By contrast, there is now also side by side with the above a newfound concern for having a space at home and school for children's freedom and pleasure, cooperation and a more means-over-ends orientation in examining learning and development, intrinsic motivation, kindergarten quality judged broadly, and last but not least, the importance of play, creativity, and imagination to the developing child. The results of this study of teachers and parents point to a greater willingness on the part of many adults in Taiwan to take on the challenges of educational reform.

These findings can be compared to Holloway (2002) who studied the educational and philosophical underpinnings of early childhood education in Japan. Holloway employed observations and interviews in 32 early childhood settings (both preschools and child care centers) in the Kansai area, which includes the major cities of Kobe and Osaka. She reported the extent to which beliefs or cultural models varied (cultural models are mental representations of how things work or should work in a culture). A considerable amount of conflict was revealed between and among teachers and parents concerning how young children should be socialized and educated to relate to the group. Differences existed with respect to how much the values of independence, interdependence, and tradition were stressed. Our research in Taiwan focusing on play likewise yielded evidence of conflicts, contradictions, and contextual variations existing within a culture. People in different situations and social positions have different perspectives on topics of importance, such as the rearing and educating of preschoolers.

Our study provides evidence of within-country variation in Taiwan concerning play and early childhood education in general, and between teachers and parents in particular. Parents were also seen to differ with middle-class parents being more like teachers than were the working-class parents. More importantly, however, our findings suggest that we need to be alert to subtle differences in play beliefs, such as the distinction between teacher roles in play and children's spontaneous expressions in the classroom, and the belief in the importance of social interaction occurring along with expressions of creativity, play, and imagination. Also, we need to be alert to lags in the adoption of actual classroom practices compared with the eagerness to espouse beliefs based on Western theories of child development and early childhood education. Teachers in this study supported the importance of social commerce in the classroom and believed it to be related to positive outcomes in the areas of creativity, imagination, and play, but they may not facilitate peer interaction when children were engaged in dramatic play or other symbolic behaviors such as story telling.

Sharing across cultures of early childhood beliefs and practices requires socio-cultural research seeking to comprehend the importance of eco- and socio-cultural systems in relation to local contextual factors. Early childhood beliefs and practices are borrowed and shared across cultures as well as emanating from within cultures. Early childhood educational practices today in this era of globalization are diasporic, or global in their identification, local in their execution, and altered by processes of diffusion, recontextualization and conventionalization (Wollons, 2000). Assuming that it is worthwhile to have some transplanting of curricular and programmatic elements from one culture to another, this must be done through a process of co-constructivism, with exporter and importer early childhood education experts working together, and with the importer early childhood expert also working closely with other stakeholders in their local situations. One might ask whether in Taiwan early childhood teachers should put into practice better their Western-inspired beliefs concerning the importance of social interaction in the expressions of imagination, creativity and play (as opposed to the value of social interaction for learning social graces and group harmony inspired by traditional Chinese values), or whether early childhood teachers in Taiwan should change their stated beliefs to be more in accord with their actual practices in this specific area of their early childhood curriculum? Who is more important here, Vygotsky or Confucius? Or can we (they) have both?

REFERENCES

Chang, P.-Y. (2001). *Taiwanese kindergartener's play and artistic representations: Differences between two classrooms and relationships to parents' and teachers' beliefs about education.* Unpublished doctoral dissertation, The Pennsylvania State University.

Chang, P.-Y. (2003). Contextual understanding of children's play in Taiwan. In D. Lytle (Ed.), *Play & Cultural Studies, Vol. 6: Play Theory, Children's Playfulness, and Educational Theory and Practice*, pp. 277–297, Westport, CT: *Greenwood Publishers.*

Chang, P.-Y. Johnson, J. & Lin, M-C. (2001, June). *Studies on play and toys in Taiwan: Images of toys created by kindergarten contexts and teacher and parent beliefs about play*. Paper presented at ICCP. Erfurt, Germany.

Chen, H.-M., & Teng, H.F. (1995). No longer just an academic question: Educational alternatives come to Taiwan. *Sinorama,* 20(3), 8–10.

Gardner, H. (1989). The key in the slot: Creativity in a Chinese key. *Journal of Aesthetic Education,* 23(1), 141–155.

Goncu, A. (2002, February). *Children's Play as Interpretation.* Keynote Address. TASP, Santa Fe, NM.

Goncu, A., Tuermer, U., Jain, J., & Johnson, D. (1999). Children's play as cultural activity. In A. Goncu (Ed.) *Children's engagement in the world: Sociocultural perspectives*. p.148–170. New York: Cambridge University Press.

Holloway, S. (2000). *Contested childhood: Diversity and change in Japanese preschools.* New York: Routledge.

Jin, M.-H. & Johnson, J. (2002, February). *Beliefs and attitudes of rural and urban Korean parents regarding play and the significance of modern and traditional toys.* Paper presented at TASP, Santa Fe, NM.

Johnson, J., Christie, J., & Wardle, F. (2005). *Play, development and early education.* Boston : Allyn and Bacon.

Johnson, J. & Chang, P.-Y. (2002, February). *Play, imagination, and creativity and kindergartens in Taiwan*. Paper presented at TASP, Santa Fe, NM.

Liang, C.-H. (2001, April). *Earning the right to play in a working class Taiwanese preschool*. Paper presented at AERA, Seattle, WA.

Liou, Y. F. (1996). Little readers of the classics. *Sinorama*, 21(1), 78–85.

Roopnarine, J., Johnson, J., & Hooper, F. (1994). *Children's play in diverse cultures*. Albany, NY: SUNY Press.

Schwartzman, H. (1978). *Transformations: The anthropology of children's play*. New York: Plenum.

Singer, J. (1999). Imaginative and adaptive development. In J. Goldstein (Ed.), *Toys, play and child development*. New York: Cambridge University Press.

Stevens, H. & Lee, S. (1996). The academic achievement of Chinese students. In M. Bond (Ed.) *The handbook of Chinese psychology* (pp. 124–142). New York: Oxford University Press.

Wollons, R. (2000). *Kindergartens and cultures: The global diffusion of an idea.* New Haven, CT: Yale University Press.

Yang, C-T. (2002, February). *The commonality and difference of Taiwanese parents' and teachers' perception of play*. Paper presented at TASP, Santa Fe, NM.

Chapter Seven

Playfulness Among Swedish and Japanese Children: A Comparative Study

Satomi Taylor, Cosby Steele Rogers, Tetsuya Ogawa, Ingrid Pramling, Anita VanBrackle and Arleen Dodd

Playfulness is a behavioral disposition that shows wide individual differences. It has been operationalized in terms of observable behaviors that can be reliably measured through ratings by adults who have observed the child's dispositions over time (e.g., Barnett, 1990, 1991a; Bundy, 1998; Lieberman, 1965, Rogers, Impara, Frary, Harris, Meeks, Semanic-Lauth, & Reynolds, 1998). Commonly accepted criteria for the dispositional dimension of play include intrinsic motivation, process rather than goal orientation, play rather than exploration, non-literality, freedom from externally imposed rules, and active involvement (Rubin, Fein, & Vandenberg, 1983).

Researchers have been interested in playfulness both as a means and as an outcome. For example, numerous researchers have examined the relationship between playfulness and socially valued abilities such as creativity and intelligence (e.g., Barnett & Kleiber, 1982; Lieberman, 1965, 1967, 1977; Rogers & Taylor, 1999). Others have emphasized the intrinsic value of playfulness as an indicator of quality of life. For example, Erik H. Erikson (1972a, 1972b) emphasized playfulness as an indicator of healthy psychosocial development.

While most of the literature on playfulness is conducted within the paradigm of individual difference studies in personality, it is probably both a trait and state variable. Individuals with a predisposition toward playfulness may have a slight biological tendency to respond in certain ways. Such a hypothesis is congruent with Kagan's (1997,1998) observation that biological factors in temperament predispose one toward stable personality traits such as shyness or fearfulness. Research in child psychology has provided ample evidence of a heritability factor in temperament (see Rothbart & Bates, 1998). Hence, if playfulness can be considered to be a dimension of temperament, then we should expect to find positive correlations between some components of temperament and playfulness. Indeed, Blevins (1987) found significant correlations between

Playfulness ratings mothers gave their children on the Child Behaviors Inventory of Playfulness and two subscales (Persistence and Positive Mood) of the Behavioral Style Questionnaire on temperament (McDevitt & Carey, 1978). When data from fathers' ratings of their children's behavioral tendencies were examined, Playfulness was correlated with temperament scores on Approachability, Adaptability, and Persistence. Externality scores were associated with High Intensity and Negative Mood when rated by mothers, but not when rated by fathers. The shared variance between playfulness and temperament supports the notion that playfulness is determined in part by inherited biological tendencies.

Although playfulness may be, in part, determined by "nature" or inherited biological tendencies, there is a substantial body of research documenting the environmental factors that "nurture" play. Rubin et al. (1983) summarized contextual variables that affect the ability to play and they included (a) familiar peers, toys and other materials that are interesting, (b) choices within limits, (c) minimal adult intrusion, (d) a psychologically warm and accepting environment and freedom from stressors such as hunger and fatigue. In addition to the effect of concurrent situational influences on play, anthropologists have provided voluminous documentation on the role of cultural context in play. In spite of the evidence of contributions by both "nature" and "nurture" to play and playfulness, it is not clear how these two factors interact to produce the results that they do. However, scientists continue to study cultural differences in order to contribute pieces of information that will inform our understandings of the various factors that facilitate and/or deter play.

Anthropological studies have provided widely varying descriptors of culturally embedded play behaviors (see for example, Roopnarine, Johnson, & Hooper, 1994). Yet, few studies have examined cross-cultural differences in the disposition to play. The present study adds to the literature by comparing the dispositional dimension of play, i.e., playfulness, in two countries—Japan and Sweden. These two countries were of special interest to the researchers because they are comparable in having a high literacy rate and in placing a high value on play in the early childhood curriculum. Yet, they differ in at least one major area, i.e., independence is highly valued in Sweden, while interdependence is more highly valued in Japan. In the present study, teachers of young children in Japan and Sweden rated 4- to 6-year-olds on Playfulness and Externality.

METHOD

Subjects

Preschool and kindergarten teachers in Sweden and Japan completed the Child Behaviors Inventory of Playfulness (CBI) for individual children in enrolled in their respective classrooms. The total sample (N = 238) included 104 Swedish (50 females, 54 males) and 134 Japanese (62 females, 72 males) children.

Instruments

The Child Behaviors Inventory of Playfulness (Rogers et al., 1998) was used by teachers in Sweden and Japan to rate behavioral dispositions of preschool and kindergarten children whom they had observed over a period of time in early childhood classrooms. The CBI is comprised of two factors: Playfulness and Externality. The playfulness factor includes 21 items that measure overall playfulness descriptive phrases designed to estimate intrinsic motivation (e.g. "Enjoys doing things with no purpose"), process-over-product orientation (e.g., "Has fun doing things and doesn't worry how well they turn out"), non-literality (e.g., "Pretends a lot."), freedom from externally imposed rules, and active involvement. Cronbach's alphas for items on the Playfulness scale ranged from .81 to .94 (Rogers et al., 1998).

Externality, a 7-item factor, measures the child's dependency on external cues in the environment, e.g., people, rules, or props to guide behavior. While Externality is negatively related to playfulness (Rogers et al., 1998) it is a different construct. It focuses on the behaviors that are likely to reduce the ability to play. Therefore, high scores on Externality indicate the presence of dispositions that are likely to interfere with play. This scale includes items such as "Asks many questions about what to do", "Seeks approval frequently," and "Looks to others to tell him/her what to do." Cronbach's alphas for items on the Externality scale ranged from .62 to .72 in the 1998 study (Rogers et al., 1998).

Analysis

A composite score for playfulness was obtained by summing the scores on items 1, 4, 6, 9,11–17, 19–21, 23, 24, and 26–30. In the present study, Cronbach's alpha for the composite Playfulness scale was .92 when computed for the entire data set (.91 for the Japanese data and .95 for the Swedish data), indicating high reliability. A composite score for Externality was obtained by summing the scores on items 2, 3, 5, 7, 8, 10, and 18. This scale yielded a Cronbach's alpha of .57 for Japanese and Swedish data combined (.63 for the Japanese data and .56 for the Swedish data), indicating that this subscale is somewhat reliable.

A three-way analysis of variance was computed for each of the CBI subscales (Playfulness and Externality) with country, age and gender as factors.

Then, to examine further the age, gender, and cultural differences in specific items within each scale, 3-way ANOVAs were computed for each item. Because multiple comparisons were made for analysis of items, a conservative alpha level of .01 for each test was used. Only individual items that yielded significance are reported.

RESULTS

Playfulness Scale

The analysis of variance for Playfulness yielded a significant country effect ($p < .01$). Playfulness scores ($M = 85.1$) for Swedish children were significantly higher than those of Japanese children ($M = 78.9$). With data for both countries combined, a significant main effect for age ($p < .05$) was also found with mean Playfulness scores as follows: (a) 87.3 for 4-year-olds, (b) 80.0 for 5-year-olds, and (c) 78.4 for 6-year-olds. Playfulness scores showed no significant main effects due to gender.

Playfulness Items

To examine how specific items contributed to the overall results, additional 3-way ANOVAs were computed for individual items on the Playfulness and Externality scales. Significant main effects for country were found for 6 of the 23 Playfulness scale items. Four of the six were similar in that Swedish scores were significantly higher ($p < .01$) than Japanese scores. This pattern occurred in the following items: (a) Item 9, "Uses things his/her own way," (b) Item 15, "Gets so involved, he/she forgets what is going on," (c) Item 19, "Plays eagerly," and (d) Item 30, "Gets so involved in an activity that he/she forgets what is going on in the room" ($p < .0001$). Japanese mean scores were significantly higher ($p < .01$) than Swedish scores on two items: (a) Item 13, "Enjoys doing things even when there is no purpose," and (b) Item 24 "Once the child has been shown how to do something, he/she creates his/her own way.

Gender

Two items on the Playfulness scale showed significant gender differences with females having higher ($p < .01$) scores on both. These were (a) Item 11, "Enjoys learning new skills," and (b) Item 29, "Identifies with many characters instead of playing the same role over again."

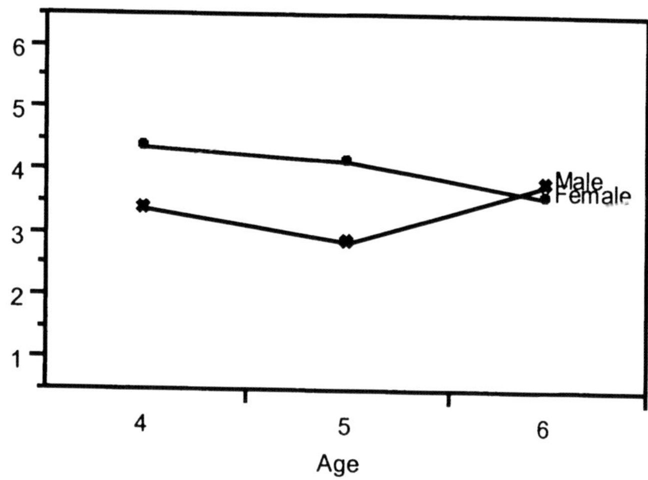

Figure 7.1. Mean Scores for Item 21: "Invents Variations on Stories Such as Different endings or New Characters."

A significant gender by age interaction ($p < .01$) appeared in Item 21, "Invents variations on stories such as different ending or new characters." As seen in Figure 7.1, at ages 4 and 5 females had significantly higher ($p < .01$) scores than did males, but this difference was not found at age 6. A gender by country ($p < .01$) interaction on Item 23, "Rearranges situations to come up

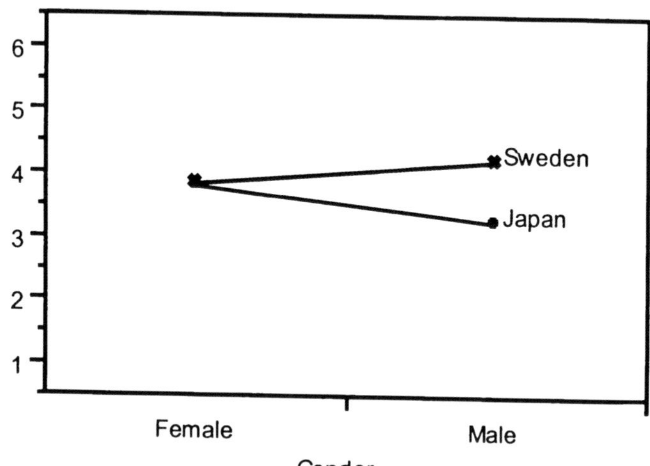

Figure 7.2. Mean Scores for Item 23: "Rearranges Situations to Come Up with Novel Ones."

with novel ones," occurred with Swedish males having a higher mean score ($p < .0001$) (Figure 7.2).

Age

One-third of the items on the Playfulness scale showed significant age effects with 4-year-olds having higher scores than both 5- ($p < .01$) and 6-year-olds ($p < .01$) on most items. Theses included (a) Item 14, "Has fun doing things without worrying how well they turn out," (b) Item 15, "Gets so involved in activity that it is hard to get him/her to quit," (c) Item 19 "Plays eagerly, " (d) Item 16, "Starts activities for his/her enjoyment," (e) Item 20, "Plays intently, " and (f) Item 30, "Gets so involved, he/she forgets what is going on in the room. On Item 22 "Displays exuberance much of the time," 4-year-olds' scores were higher than were 5-year-olds' ($p = .01$), but were not significantly higher than for 6-year-olds.

Country by Age Interactions

Significant country by age interactions were found for five Playfulness scale items. On all five, Swedish scores were higher ($p < .01$) at age 4 but not at age 5 or 6. The five items included (a) Item 6: "Invents new games" (Figure 7.3), (b) Item 12, "Works well on his/her own," (Figure 7.4); (c) Item 17 "Pretends a lot" (Figure 7.5), (d) Item 23, "Rearranges situations to come up with novel ones," (Figure 7.6) and (e) Item 29, "Identifies with many characters instead of playing the same role over again " (Figure 7.7).

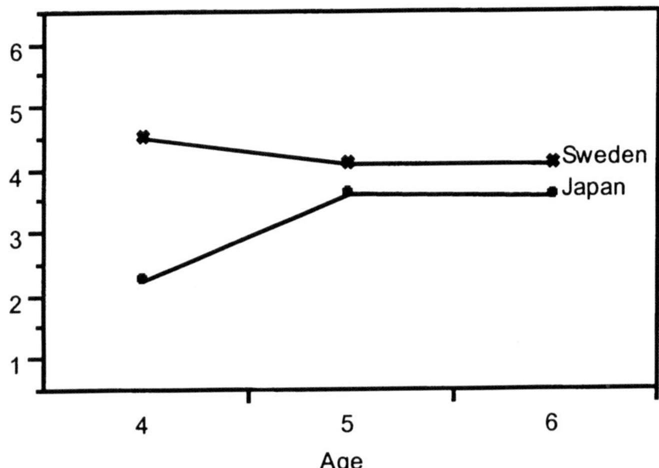

Figure 7.3. Means Scores for Item 6 "Invents New Games."

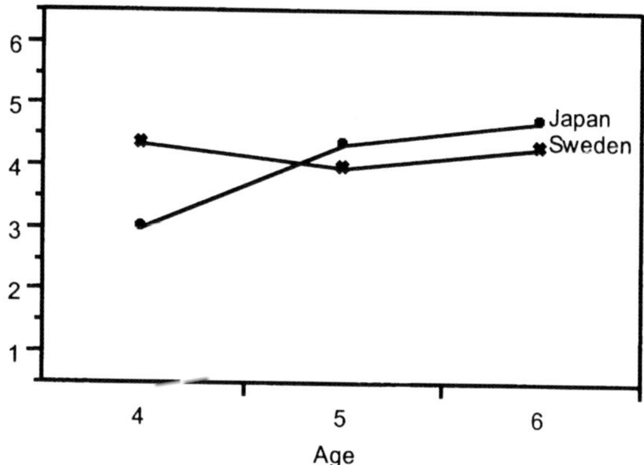

Figure 7.4. Mean Scores for Item 12, "Works Well on His/Her Own."

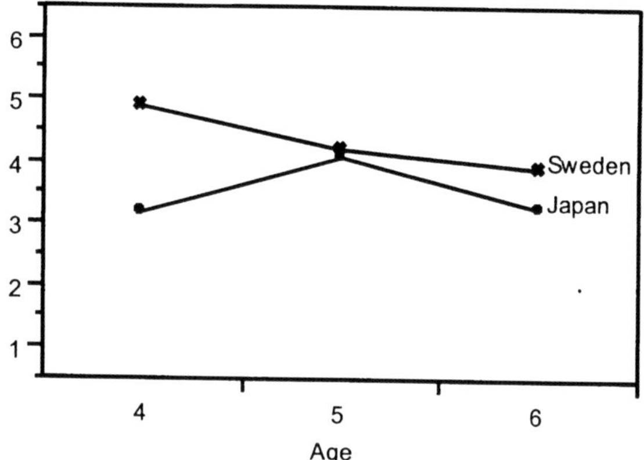

Figure 7.5. Mean Scores for Item 17: "Pretends a Lot."

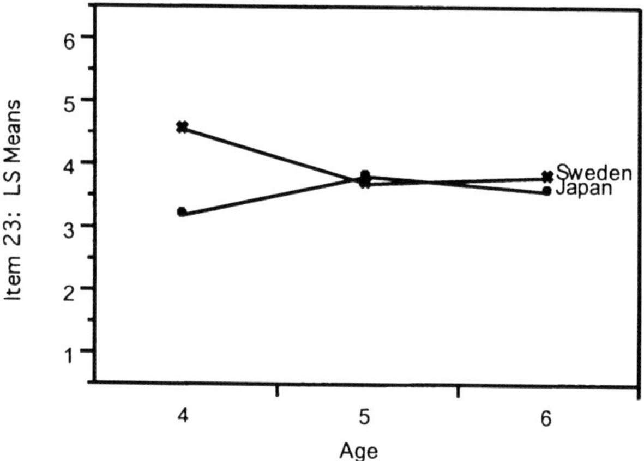

Figure 7.6. Mean Scores for Item 23: "Rearranges Situations to Come Up with Novel Ones."

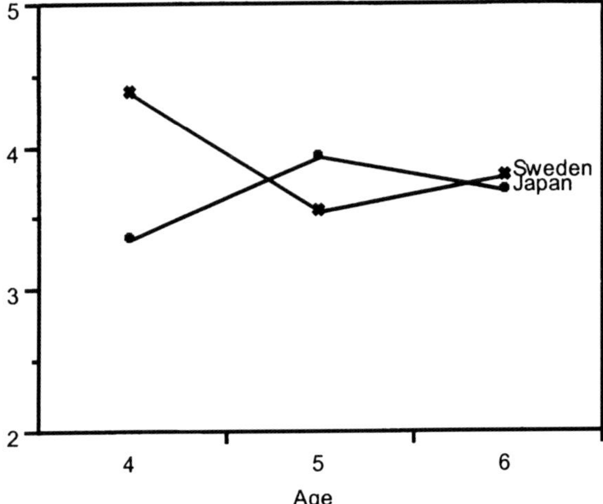

Figure 7. 7. Mean Scores for 29: "Identifies with Many Characters Instead of Playing the Same Role Over Again."

EXTERNALITY

Overall Externality Scale

The analysis of variance for the composite Externality scores yielded a significant country by age interaction (See Figure 7.8). Japanese 4-year-olds had higher mean Externality scores ($p < .0001$), while at age 6, Swedish children had higher mean scores ($p < .01$) and there was no significant difference between composite Externality scores for the two countries at age 5.

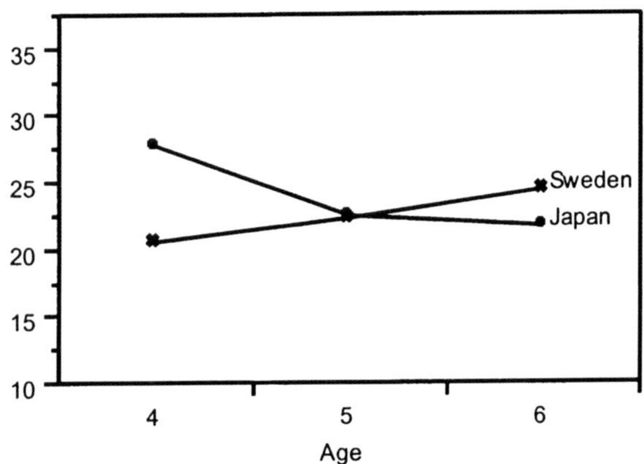

Figure 7.8. Mean Composite Scores on Externality.

Externality Items

Two of the seven items comprising the composite Externality score indicated main effects due to country. Swedish subjects had higher scores ($p < .0001$) for Item 10, "Looks to others to tell him/her what to do." In contrast, Japanese children had higher scores on Item 18, "Uses toys/objects in the way they were designed to be used ($p < .0001$). For both of these items, 4-year-olds were more likely than 5- and 6-year olds to "Look to others to tell him/her what to do," but they were less likely to use toys in the way that they were designed to be used (Item 18), $p < .0001$. No significant effects due to gender were found on any of the Externality items.

Country by Age Interaction

Three items on the Externality scale showed significant country by age interactions. On item 5, "Needs reinforcement to continue activities," (see Figure 7.9) Japanese scores were higher at age 4 ($p < .0001$), Swedish children's mean scores were significantly higher ($p < .001$) at age 6. On Item 7, "Asks many questions about what to do" (p < .001) (Figure 7.10) $p < .0001$) Japanese children had higher scores at age 4 ($p < .01$) but not at 5 or 6 years. Item 8, "Seeks approval frequently" had significant differences ($p < .0001$) in mean scores occur at ages 4 and 6 (Figure 7.11). At 4, Japanese scores were significantly higher ($p < .001$), but at age six, Swedish children's scores were higher ($p < .01$)

Insert-p. 144

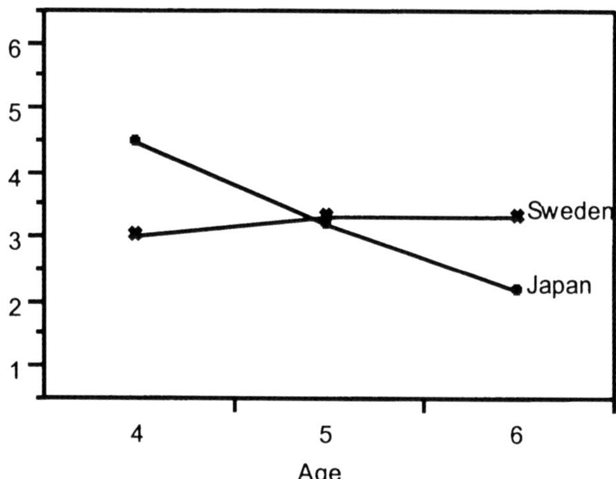

Figure 7.9. Mean Scores on Item 5: "Needs Reinforcement to Continue Activities."

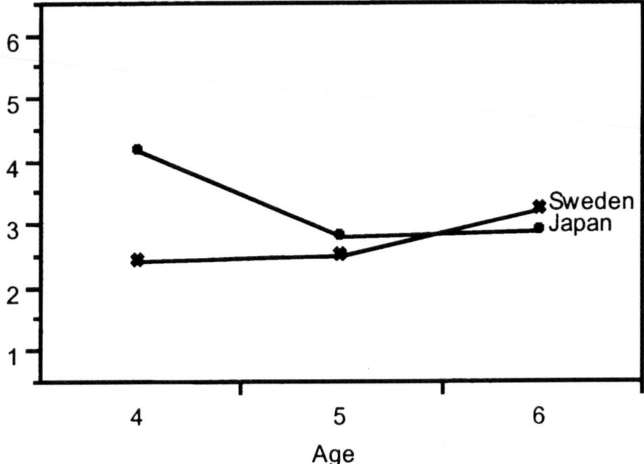

Figure 7.10. Mean Scores on Item 7: "Asks Many Questions About What to Do."

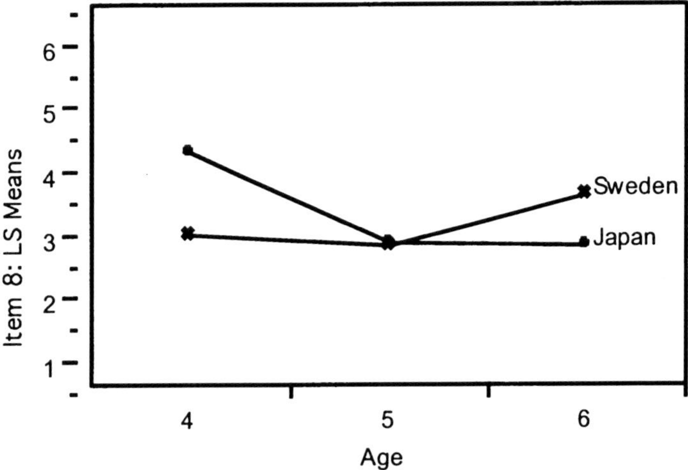

Figure 7.11. Mean Scores on Item 8: "Seeks Approval Frequently."

DISCUSSION

A steady decline in Playfulness scores across the 4- to 6-year age range is congruent with the common view that play declines with age. Swedish children had higher playfulness scores than did Japanese children, an interesting finding in light of an earlier study in which Japanese children had lower playfulness ratings than did American children (Taylor, Rogers, & Kaiser, 1999). Although substantial evidence documents gender differences in play behaviors, results of this study indicate no gender differences in the disposition toward play. Externality, the second factor on the playfulness scale, involves concern with doing things "the right way." The results were mixed, i.e., Japanese children had higher Externality scores at age 4, but Swedish children scored higher at age six. Further study is needed to determine whether differences in socialization set the context for external dispositions in various cultures at different ages.

REFERENCES

Barnett, L. A. (1990). Playfulness: Definition, design, and measurement. *Play and Culture, 3,* 319–336.

Barnett, L. A. (1991a). The playful child: Measurement of the disposition to play. *Play and Culture, 4,* 51–74.

Barnett, L. A. (1991b). Characterizing playfulness: Correlates with individual attributes and personality traits. *Play and Culture, 4,* 371–393.

Barnett, L. A. (1998). The adaptive powers of being playful. In G. Chick, A. Aycock, & M. Duncan (Eds.). *Play & culture studies, Volume 1*, pp. 97–120. Greenwich, CT: Ablex.

Barnett, L. A., & Kleiber, D. A. (1982). Concomitants of playfulness in early childhood: Cognitive abilities and gender. *Journal of Genetic Psychology 141,* 115–127.

Blevins, T. (1987). Dispositions of play: Correlates of temperament. Unpublished manuscript. Virginia Polytechnic Institute and State University, Blacksburg, VA.

Bundy, A. C., & Clifton, J. L. (1998). Construct validity of the Children's Playfulness Scale. In M. C. Duncan, G. Chick, & A. Aycock (Eds.), *Play and culture studies, Vol. 1: Divergesions and divergencies in fields of play* (pp. 37–47). Greenwich, CT: Ablex.

Erikson, E. H. (1972a). Play and actuality. In M. W. Piers (Ed.), *Play and development* (pp. 127–167). New York: Norton.

Erikson, E. H. (1972b). Play and civilization. In J. Jolly, & K. Sylva (Eds.), *Play: Its role in development and evolution* (pp. 690–703). New York: Penguin.

Holmes, R. M. (2001). Parental notions about their children's playfulness and children's notions of play in the United States and Hong Kong. In S. Reifel (Ed.), *Play and culture studies, Vol. 3: Theory in context and out* (pp. 291–314). Westport, CT: Ablex.

Kagan, J. (1997). Temperament and the reactions to unfamiliarity. *Child Development, 68,* 139–143.

Kagan, J. (1998). Biology and the child. In W. Damon (Series Ed.) & N. Eisenberg (Vol. Ed.), *Handbook of child psychology: Vol. 3. Social, emotional, and personality development* (5th ed., pp. 177–235). New York: Wiley.

Lieberman, J. N. (1965). Playfulness and divergent thinking: An investigation of their relationship at the kindergarten level. *Journal of Genetic Psychology, 107,* 219–224.

Lieberman, J. N. (1967). A developmental analysis of playfulness as a clue to cognitive style. *Journal of Creative Behavior, 1,* 391–397.

Lieberman, J. N. (1977). *Playfulness: Its relationship to imagination and creativity.* New York: Academic Press.

McDevitt, S. C., & Carey, W. B. (1978). The measurement of temperament in three- to seven-year-old children. *Journal of Child Psychology and Psychiatry, 19,* 245–253.

Porter, C., & Bundy, A. (2001). Validity of three tests of playfulness with African American children and their parents and relationships among parental beliefs and values and children's observed playfulness. In S. Reifel (Ed.), *Play and culture studies, Vol.3: Theory in context and out* (pp. 315–334).

Rogers, C. S., & Taylor, S. I. (1999, February). The relationship between playfulness and creativity of Japanese preschool children. Paper presented at the annual meeting of The Association for the Study of Play, Santa Fe, New Mexico.

Rogers, C. S., Impara, J. C., Frary, R. B., Harris, T., Meeks, A., Semanic-Lauth, S., & Reynolds, M. R. (1998). Measuring Playfulness: Development of the Child Behaviors Inventory of Playfulness. In G. Chick, A. Aycock, & M. Duncan (Eds.). *Play & culture studies, Vol. 1*, pp. 151–168. Greenwich, CT: Ablex.

Roopnarine, J. L., Johnson, J. E., & Hooper, F. H. (Eds.). (1994). *Children's play in diverse cultures.* Albany: SUNY.

Rothbart, M. K., & Bates, J. E. (1998). Temperament. In W. Damon (Series Ed.) & N. Eisenberg (Vol. Ed.), *Handbook of child psychology: Vol. 3. Social, emotional, and personality development* (5th ed., pp. 105–176). New York: Wiley.

Rubin, K. H., Fein, G. G., & Vandenberg, B. (1983). Play. In E. M. Hetherington (Ed.), P. H. Mussen (Series Ed.), *Handbook of child psychology: Vol. 4. Socialization, personality, and social development* (pp. 693–774). New York: Wiley.

Taylor, S. I., Rogers, C. S., & Kaiser, J. (1999). A comparison of playfulness among American and Japanese preschoolers. In S. Reifel (Ed.), *Play and culture studies, Vol. 2: play contexts revisited* (pp. 143–150). Stamford, CT: Ablex.

Chapter Eight

Playgrounds and Children's Play Supply in 14 Districts of Northeastern Portugal

Beatriz Pereira, Paula Malta, and Hugo Laranjeiro

We begin with some statements focusing on social changes that have important effects on play. Children have fewer opportunities to play outside in the open air. In recent decades, children have lost the liberty to play in the streets. Streets have become dangerous, and the traffic grows every day. Children have fewer opportunities to play at home, in good conditions, in a room with plenty of space. In recent decades, the houses have become smaller. Children have fewer opportunities to play at home with other children. More families are now nuclear (rather than extended) and the number of children is reduced to one or two. Children go to nursery school early in their lives. What are children's opportunities for play? They spend an important part of their spare time watching television (Pereira & Pinto, 1999). Is this what they really would like to do? A study by Pinto (2000) about the daily routine of children and television concluded that children preferred to play outside with friends than watching their favorite show.

Children's and teenagers' spare time is a matter of increasing concern to parents, teachers, and researchers. The use of spare time is important to development in early childhood. For the majority of children, spare time can be the best time in their lives, but for a small minority spare time is used for destroying themselves, others and the environment (Pereira, Neto & Smith, 1997). While some children play, others start smoking, drinking or bullying. "Much of children's play is seen to be physical squabbling, with much low-level physical play involving chasing and fleeing, jumping on backs, and fighting" (Blatchford, 1993).

Looking only at school spare time, we realize children like recess breaks very much (Pereira, 2002; Blatchford, 1994). However, for some of them, it is during recess break that they experience the worst moments at school. This happens to children who have been bullied by their peers (Pereira, 2002).

During recess break children can get injured and, in some cases, spend one or more days at the hospital or at home as a result of unsafe playgrounds. Almost 46% of the school injuries occurred among 10 to 14 year olds, based on 1,558 cases of children between the ages of 0 to 19 years old that were reported to the National Pediatric Trauma Registry (NPTR) between 1988 and 1995 and referred by Children's Safety Network. The ratio of injuries for males vs. females was 3:1, and 49% of the injuries happened within recreational areas.

Falls were the most frequent cause of injury (43%), followed by sports activities (34%) and assaults (10%) (Children's Safety Network, 1997). The leisure spaces available to children do not always fulfill the children's needs. Pereira and Neto (1994, 1997) concluded from a study about children between 3 to 10 years old that more than 50% of children can't play as they would like to. The context can either promote playing or reduce it. Children love exploring the environment; however, when it is poor, it does not enable children to develop motor or social skills. Bronfenbrenner (1979) described social context as a pattern of activities, roles, and interpersonal relations experienced over time by the developing person in a given setting with particular physical and material characteristics. The playground is a social context where children grow up and develop motor skills, socialize, and learn about different topics. It is also important to note that the usage of open air spaces depends on climatic factors, time of the year, distance to the spaces, parental attitudes, social class, available information, and safety of the equipment (Neto, 1997). The importance of the playground is even bigger when we realized that "at least a fifth of the school day is spent in the playground" (Ross & Ryan, 1991).

Hartle and Johnson (1993) compared four types of playgrounds: traditional, contemporary, adventurous and creative. According to Neto, we witness a change of preference from standardized spaces to "unpredictable" spaces that allow the practice of adventure games (skates, roller-skates, bicycles . . .) (Neto, 1997). Frost and Klein (1983) described the equipment of a traditional playground as consisting of climbing bars, seesaws, slides and swings made of metal and located over grass or asphalt.

Neto (1992) shows some concern about the conditions at playgrounds in Portugal. Since young children don't have the autonomy to go to the playground by their own, they need the support of an adult, a relative or someone who takes care of them. It is important to account for the problem of accessibility to the playground by children. As referred by Serrano and Neto (1997), children from rural areas have higher accessibility to streets and playgrounds than children in urban areas. When we talk about the availability of play spaces for young children, we can't forget how to get there. Difficult accessibility is a limitation for playgrounds' daily use by children. Places where children play before going to school and when they return home are the ones located in their residential area, in the streets or in the neighboring park. But these places turn out to be dangerous in our present society (Pereira & Neto, 1999).

The U. S. Consumer Product Safety Commission refers to the importance of the playground's location and the equipment's placement. If there are roads in the vicinity, a barrier surrounding the playground is recommended. Another significant issue is playground supervision. Some authors agree on how supervisors can help promoting safety and developing games, while others defend the importance of free play.

Playgrounds' safety depends on various factors: surface of impact, safety of the fixed and mobile equipment, placement of the equipment, and maintenance. Hudson et al., cited by Mota and Rodrigues (1999), consider that the risk of an accident occurring is minor if the energy absorbency of the surface is high. Tinsworth and Kramer, cited by Mota and Rodrigues, show that more than 50% of the injuries in playgrounds are caused by falls on the surfaces. Thus, the surfaces of playgrounds should be suitable.

In Portugal, legislation only recently addressed children's safety in playgrounds. About 4000 injuries occur per year in playgrounds, and these include only accidents that require medical assistance, as reported under the Decree-Law number 379/97, December 27th. This law sets the safety conditions of playgrounds concerning their location, conception, space organization, equipment, etc. More than a year had passed when we decided to carry out a survey that could describe the characteristics, quality, and safety of playgrounds.

In the last few decades, there has been a growing need to institutionalize children's spare time, due to the difficulties modern parents have in spending time with their children. Thus, parents manage their children's free time by making them participate in activities offered by private or public institutions dedicated to the organization of free time (Neto, 1997). Children who do not have access to institutions where they can spend their free time, called "Free Time Activities", look for playgrounds close to their homes.

GOALS AND METHOD

Portugal is the most western country in Europe. It is bounded by Spain on the North and East and by the Atlantic Ocean on the South and West. It has an area of 91,905 Km^2 and a coastline of 832 km. The population is approximately 10 million people. The sub-region of Alto Trás-os-Montes is a part of the North Region of Portugal. It has over 235,241 inhabitants and an approximate area of 8,136 Km^2. The location of this region in a remote corner of the country and a decline in population has made it one the poorest Portuguese regions. Approximately 20% of children are aged between 0 and 14 years old, according to the National Population Report (INE, 1993). This sub-region has 14 districts. Chaves, the most populous district, has 40,940 inhabitants, contrasting with the smallest with 6,323 (Vimioso).

Goals

The main goal of this research is to describe the playgrounds in the 14 districts of Alto Trás-os-Montes, a region in northern Portugal. We hoped to obtain some ratios of playgrounds per 1000 children and per area that could be used as a base line. It is also our goal to describe how playgrounds look, where they are located, how they are preserved and how safe they are. We also assessed the planning of playgrounds, use, occurrence of accidents, surveillance and criteria regarding the construction of playgrounds, etc.

Sample

Data from the 14 districts in northeastern Portugal (Alto Trás-os-Montes) were collected by means of an interview with the political or technical staffs in Town Halls. In order to know the number of playgrounds per district and some of their characteristics, we had to exclude the ones located in schools that don't allow people outside school to use them; i.e., we only accounted for the ones with public access. Data was analyzed by a computer using the Statistical Package for the Social Sciences (SPSS).

Interviews

The interviews approached the following topics:

a) General description: global location (urban/rural area); year of construction; size.
b) Characteristics of the surface, fence, material of the equipment and support equipment: regarding the playground surface, we asked about the materials used in the main surface and impact surface (dirt, sand, wood, concrete or a synthetic material), whether there was a fence, and what it was made of (bushes, concrete, wire, wood). We also asked what kind of playground equipment was available, and whether it was mainly made of metal, wood or synthetic material.
c) Types of playgrounds and equipment: playgrounds (single or recreation facilities); traditional or new design (repetitive or multiple tasks); equipment (simple or multipurpose); pieces of equipment.

d) Management: we asked who were the owner and the manager in charge of the maintenance.
e) Safety and maintenance: we inquired about the conditions of use and safety.
f) Accessibility and playground usage: we asked who were the most common users. Were they common people, associations, clubs or schools? Were the playgrounds used year round or seasonally, and did children go there every day or only on weekends? How did children get to the playground: by foot, taken by their parents by car or by bus? What was the playground's specific location (residential area, green space, area for sports, commercial area, etc.)?

RESULTS

We registered 67 playgrounds in the region of Alto Trás-os-Montes (Table 8.1). The minimum number of playgrounds by district is one and the maximum is eleven, differing significantly between districts. There is a small correspondence between the number of inhabitants or children and the number of playgrounds. Districts with more inhabitants are not always the ones with more playgrounds. The region of Alto Trás-os-Montes has 0.28 playgrounds per 1000 inhabitants.

Accounting just for children aged between 0–14 years old, there are 1.42 playgrounds for each 1000 children. Although we are aware that the distribution of the playgrounds by area is not the same around the region, it is still significant to realize that the number of playgrounds is 0.08 per 10 km^2. That is, there are 0.17 playgrounds per parish.

Description: Size, Location, and Year of Construction

The percentages presented in our report were adjusted after excluding the missing cases. Regarding size, 69% of the valid cases indicate that public playgrounds have 300 m^2 or less. When we inquired about location, we concluded that there are more playgrounds in urban areas (61.2%) than in rural areas (31.3%) or suburban (7.5%). The medium sized towns we studied have their suburban areas included in the urban area. In those cases, 68.7% of the playgrounds are considered to be in urban areas, despite the fact that the number of rural parishes is far more than the number of urban parishes. The population is nonetheless far more concentrated in urban areas.

Regarding the year of construction, there were 16.4% missing cases. Playgrounds less than ten years old account for 71.4% of cases (Figure 8.1).

Table 8.1 Public Playgrounds' Frequency and Ratio per 1000 Children (0–14 Years Old), 1000 Inhabitants, 10 Km2 and Number of Parish Councils

District	*Number of Public Playgrounds*	*Playgrounds/ 1000 Children*	*Playgrounds/ 1000 Inhabitants*	*Playgrounds 10Km2*	*Playgrounds/ Number of Parishes*
Alfândega da Fé	6	5.06	0.89	0.19	0.30
Boticas	5	3.20	0.63	0.16	0.31
Bragança	3	0.47	0.09	0.03	0.06
Chaves	7	0.85	0.17	0.12	0.14
Macedo Cavaleiros	10	2.49	0.53	0.14	0.26
Miranda do Douro	4	2.86	0.46	0.08	0.25
Mirandela	4	0.76	0.16	0.06	0.11
Mogadouro	11	4.93	0.90	0.15	0.39
Montalegre	3	0.96	0.19	0.04	0.09
Murça	1	0.61	0.14	0.06	0.11
Valpaços	3	0.66	0.13	0.05	0.10
Vila Pouca Aguiar	2	0.51	0.12	0.05	0.13
Vimioso	6	5.10	0.95	0.13	0.43
Vinhais	2	0.89	0.16	0.03	0.06
Total	67	—	—	—	—
Mean ratio	—	1.42	0.28	0.08	0.17

Source: The ratios were calculated based on the 1991 National Population Report (INE, 1993).

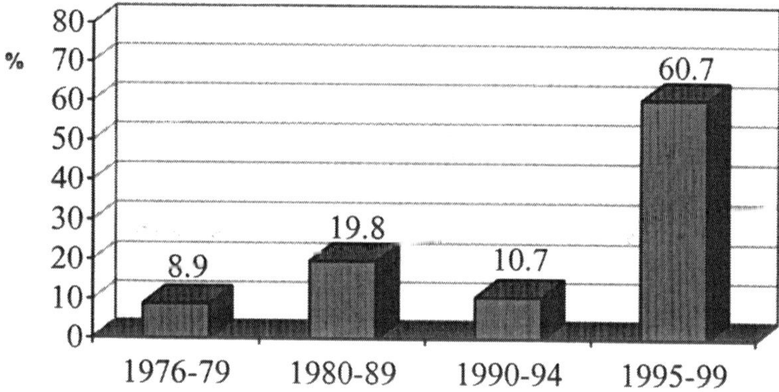

Figure 8.1. Public Playgrounds' Year of Construction.

Characteristics of the Surface, Fence, Material of the Equipment and Support Equipment

The most common surface (55.6%) is sand, followed by dirt mentioned in 23.8% of the total answers. The impact area is mainly covered by sand (70%) (Figure 8.2).

There is a fence in 85.7% of the valid cases and it is generally made of concrete (56.1%). Wire and wood are also common (19.3% each).

Regarding the material of the equipment, it is predominantly made of wood (43.3%) and metal (41.8%). The most frequent support equipment consists of rubbish bins, benches, lamps and rarely a toilet or a grill.

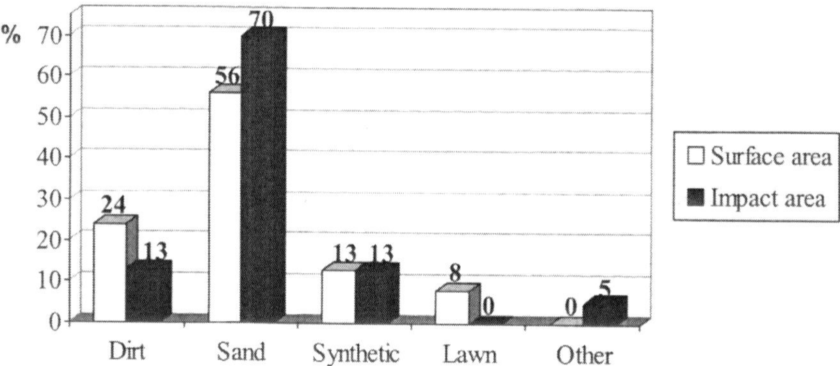

Figure 8.2. Surface and Impact Area of the Studied Public Playgrounds'.

Types of Playgrounds and Equipment

Among the 67 playgrounds reported, 60 are single and 6 are parts of recreational complexes. We define recreation complex as a space where we found at least two of the following units: playground, radical park, courtyard for sports or other. (A "radical park" is one expressly designed to accommodate relatively risky activities, such as roller skating and bicycling.) The most common equipment in our playgrounds is swings, closely followed by slides. Seesaws and merry-go-rounds come next (Table 8.2).

Management

In 59.1% of the cases, the owner of the playgrounds is the Town Hall, while parish councils own 34.8% and other institutions 6.1%. The Town Halls predominantly do the playgrounds' management (70%), whereas Parish Councils assume the responsibility in 23.3% of the playgrounds and others in 6.7% of the cases (Figure 8.3).

Comparing ownership and management, we see that in most of the cases, owner and manager are the same. Town Halls are simultaneously owners and managers in 53.3% of the cases, parish councils are owners and managers in 21.6% of the cases and others are both owners and managers in 6.6% of the cases. In some of the municipalities that we studied, the Town Hall is the manager, but its responsibility doesn't seem clear. Playgrounds encompass education, sports, youth and culture, so there is a problem about who is responsible.

Table 8.2. Existing Equipments in Public Playgrounds.

Type of Equipment	*N*
Swings	60
Slides	48
Seesaws	34
Merry-go-rounds	21
Others	13
Climbing ladders	7
Bridges	4
Suspending ladders	2
Tunnels	1
Climbing walls	0

Note: We collected information on 60 playgrounds (7 missing cases).

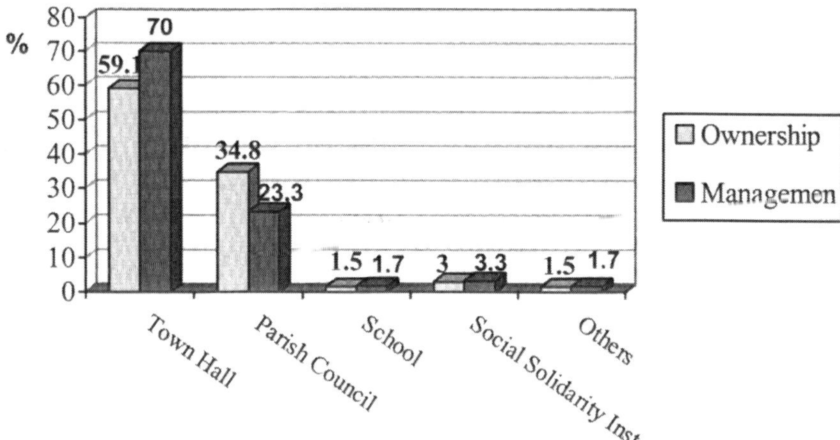

Figure 8.3. Public Playgrounds' Ownership and Management.

Safety and Maintenance

Most of the answers about playgrounds being in good, medium or bad condition indicate that playgrounds are in good condition (66.7%), while 27.3% say that they are in reasonable condition and 5.6% that they are in bad condition. The persons interviewed indicated that playgrounds are safe because they have no reports on injuries. We got answers like "it happens sometimes to children to fall down, but they don't get seriously injured." In this sub-region the playgrounds are permanently open in 93.7% of the cases. Only four of them have a limited schedule. Regarding safety and accessibility, we inquired if the playground was located in an area of intense traffic, little traffic or without traffic. They are located predominantly in areas of little traffic (71.2%), while 9.1% are in areas with intense traffic and 19.7% with no traffic.

Accessibility and Use of the Playgrounds (Who, When, How)

Who Uses the Playgrounds?

Among the public playgrounds we studied, individual children are the ones who use them most during their leisure time (63.6%), while in 27.3% of the cases schools are the major users. In 9.1% of the cases, they are used either by the public or by schools.

When Are the Playgrounds Used?

Most of the playgrounds are used year round (90.6%), while 9.4% have a predominantly seasonal use (20.9% are missing cases). Playgrounds are more often used during the week (85.1%) than during weekends (29.9% are missing cases).

Are Playgrounds Accessible?

The area of location is mainly residential (45.5%) or near schools (28.8%). Green, commercial or sports areas are also common places for this kind of equipment; 80.3% of the answers indicate that children go by foot to the playgrounds.

DISCUSSION

General Description

We have an average of one public playground for every 3,571 inhabitants and for every 704 children up to 14 years of age. Concerning the area, there is one playground for every 125 km^2. We have approximately one playground for 6 parishes. We do not know about any Portuguese or international studies that present these kinds of ratios in order to compare them. This is surprising, but probably could be explained because only in recent years have playgrounds become a concern among politicians, investigators, parents and private associations interested in childhood.

Therefore the number of playgrounds is not as high as could be expected. One of the reasons is the unfamiliarity of the people we interviewed with this issue because it is an under-evaluated subject.

Playgrounds are a recent concern for Town Halls; playgrounds were mostly built in the 1990's. There is a lack of knowledge by the politicians about older playgrounds. In most cases the person interviewed knows mostly about the work done during his tenure in the Town Hall and doesn't have systematic information about playgrounds, contrasting with what happens with spaces for sports. Only a small percentage of the older playgrounds were remodeled. Playgrounds are generally very similar, although in parks and areas for sports they are larger, have more equipment, and are frequented more often by children with adults, usually the family on weekends or holidays.

There are some new playgrounds that belong to private owners, which restrict entry. In the last ten years they opened in shopping centers in several towns. Playgrounds can be found in fast food restaurants, usually in small spaces.

Types of Playgrounds and Equipment

We defined the types of playgrounds according to the design, the characteristics of the equipment, the predominant material and the characteristics of play they offer. The playground could be described as an area of land, often with swings and slides, etc., where children play. A playground can also contain ropes and small structures, e.g. arches, bridges, and tunnels. Traditional playgrounds are small areas with slides, swings, seesaws and merry-go-rounds as described by Frost and Klein in 1983. We can conclude that the playgrounds in this sub-region are traditional. They include three or more pieces of equipment made out of metal and with an impact surface filled with sand. This is a poor and not very interesting environment.

The material of the equipment changed in the last five years from metal to wood or to synthetic material. It is also changing, but slowly, in nursery schools. The most recent playgrounds are equipped with pieces made out of synthetic material or wood. In the region of Alto Trás-os-montes, we did not identify any recreational complexes that included radical parks (areas allowing for high-risk play with skates and bicycles), which means that such parks are as yet poorly distributed.

Management

The major owner of public playgrounds is the Town Hall, which does the management as well. However the management seems very informal; nobody is responsible for the maintenance, which is an issue very often forgotten.

Surface, Safety, and Maintenance

The surface of the playgrounds we studied is generally made out of sand or dirt, while the surface of impact is predominantly sand. In some of the playgrounds, this area is in good condition, but in others, it needs to be repaired. The choice of the material for the surface of impact is important for preventing accidents. The surface of impact is in constant use and there may be holes caused by erosion where water can accumulate.

How do managers get acquainted with the condition of the equipment? This is a problematic question, since most people we interviewed did not know about playgrounds' present condition. It seems councilmen do not want to be considered bad managers, therefore are willing to improve their policies. However when we asked how they knew about the equipment's need for repair, we got answers such as: "The gardeners pass by and tell us if there is any problem" or "It's us when we pass by."

In 1992, Neto demonstrated that playgrounds in Portugal were in bad condition. Now we can see there have been few changes. Playgrounds need periodic maintenance and repair. A team of experts is currently evaluating the conditions of playgrounds according to Decree-Law n. 379/97. A survey is done periodically in order to check if these places are safe for children to play. However, this team doesn't include a play expert.

Managers, parents and teachers agree that the most problematic issues involve daily use, cleaning and other small problems. It is necessary to clean the playgrounds daily, as frequently as the streets are cleaned. It is also urgent that somebody inform the manager when things need to be repaired. Another problem is vandalism. In this case, it is necessary to notify the police. Police should register the occurrence and send an officer to check what happened. The Town Hall has to be informed of the occurrence and promptly send someone to repair the equipment. When this does not happen, the playground is quickly degraded.

Accessibility and Use of thePlaygrounds

Children can frequently go to the playground, because playgrounds in Portugal are predominantly located in residential areas. In our country, playgrounds are made for children up to 10 years old. Children in Portugal often go to the playground alone or with a brother. Only recently have parents started to go along. Children are allowed to be in the playground without the supervision of an adult. However, this freedom of movement is being reduced in towns according to Serrano and Neto (1997). Consequently, the location of the playgrounds seems to be the result of the Portuguese cultural habits of children and parents. This freedom could be a problem for children if an injury occurs; however they usually have the support of the neighbors or other children.

Most children go to the playground by foot, because it is near either their homes or their schools. However, there are leisure parks where the whole family can go for a walk and where a playground is available. The great majority of children use the playground on their own during leisure time. However there are also cases where school pupils are the major users instead of individual children that happen to pass by. When schools are the major users, it means the playground belongs to the school and it is open to the community. We also have playgrounds in other places such as public gardens or parks, leisure parks and near or inside schools, which are important areas for leisure activities but less accessible to younger children, under 10 years old.

CONCLUSIONS

In this study of playgrounds, our primary emphasis is on children and play in a setting that provides challenging risk, but with adequate safety controls. There are significant differences between the districts we studied. There is a range in the number of public playgrounds from 1 to 11 per district. There is a lack of information on playgrounds concerning rules or what to do in case of injuries. There are neither telephones nor first aid facilities. There are few public playgrounds for the number of children, land area and parishes. Instead of being equally distributed, playgrounds are concentrated in the urban areas. The great majority of these playgrounds are located in residential areas, enabling child games on the street and activities based on spontaneity. Very young children could go to the playground on their own since they have autonomy of mobility. Recent changes in society, especially concerning violence, is causing a loss of mobility for children; and they have started to go to the playground with their parents. Therefore, the demand for playgrounds in residential areas may diminish, while the demand for more distant but bigger playgrounds with more variety of equipment, may increase. Councilmen should therefore take into consideration recent changes in people's daily routines while making planning decisions.

The playground surface, specially the surface of impact, must be chosen in accordance with studies on ergonomics, concerning the impact of the human body when a fall occurs. There is much work to be done on this subject. There is a big difference between the equipment built by specific playground manufacturers and improvised equipment, regarding safety and motivation. A playground must be safe, built with safe materials and with an appealing design, without forgetting the importance of a natural environment, where children can play with trees, water, sand, etc.

If the planning of the playground is important, its maintenance is no less. It is not enough to build playgrounds, we must account for their maintenance immediately after their construction.

In conclusion, play and playgrounds are a big challenge for the scientific and educational community. The ratios we calculated may be a source of information for politicians to use in planning playgrounds, calculating the number of playgrounds per 1000 children, determining playground sizes, and deciding upon the actual parishes that should have playgrounds; though there are other aspects which should also be considered.

REFERENCES

Blatchford, P. (1993). *Playtime in the primary school: problems and improvements*. New York, Routledge.

Blatchford, P. (1994). Research on children's school playground behavior in the United Kingdom: A review. In P. Blatchford and S. Sharp (Eds.), *Breaktime and the school: Understanding and changing playground behavior* (pp. 16–35). London and New York, Routledge.

Bronfenbrenner, U. (1979). *The ecology of human development: Experiments by nature and design*. Cambridge, MA: Harvard University Press

Children's Safety Network (1997). *Injuries in the school environment: a resource guide, second edition*, Children's Safety Network National Injury and Violence Prevention Resource Centre.

Decreto-Lei n° 379/97 de 27 de Dezembro (1997). Diário da República—I Série—A, p.6804.

Frost, J. L. & Klein, B. (1983). *Children's play and playgrounds*. Austin, TX: Playscapes International.

Hartle, L. & Johnson, J. E. (1993). Historical and contemporary influences of outdoors play environments. In C. H. Hart (Ed.), *Children on playgrounds* (pp. 14–42). State University of New York, Albany.

Mota, J. & Rodrigues, S. (1999). *Jogo e espaços lúdicos infantis*. Oeiras, Câmara Municipal de Oeiras.

Neto, C. (1992). The present and the future perspectives of the play and playgrounds in Portugal, *Ludens, 12*, 3/3, pp. 83–89.

Neto, C. (ed.) (1997). Tempo e espaço de jogo para a criança: rotinas e mudanças sociais, *Jogo e desenvolvimento da criança*, Lisboa, Edições FMH, UTL, pp. 10–22.

Pereira, B. O. (2002). *Para uma escola sem violência. Estudo e prevenção das práticas agressivas entre crianças*. Lisboa, Fundação Calouste Gulbenkian/Fundação para a Ciència e a Tecnologia.

Pereira, B. O. & Neto, C. (1994). O tempo livre na infância e as práticas lúdicas realizadas e preferidas, *Ludens, 14*(1), 35–41.

Pereira, B. O. & Neto, C. (1997). A infância e as práticas lúdicas: estudo das actividades de tempos livres nas crianças dos 3 aos 10 anos. In M. Pinto and M. J. Sarmento, *As crianças—contextos e identidades*, Braga, Centro de Estudos da Criança—U.M.

Pereira, B. O. & Neto, C. (1999). As crianças, o lazer e os tempos livres. In M. Pinto and M. J. Sarmento, *Saberes sobre as crianças: para uma bibliografia sobre a infância e as crianças em Portugal (1974–1998)*, Braga, Centro de Estudos da Criança—U. M.

Pereira, B. O., Neto, C. & Smith, P. (1997). Os espaços de recreio e a prevenção do 'bullying' na escola, In C. Neto (Ed.), *Jogo e desenvolvimento da criança* (pp. 238–257). Lisboa, Edições FMH, UTL

Pereira, B. O. & Pinto, A. (1999). Dinamizar a escola para prevenir a violência entre pares. *Sonhar VI*, 1, 19–33.

Pinto, M. (2000). *A televisão no quotidiano das crianças*. Porto, Edições Afrontamento.

Ross, C. & Ryan, A. (1991). *"Can I stay in today Miss?": improving the school playground*, Staffordshire, Trentham Books.

Serrano, J. & Neto, C. (1997). As rotinas de vida diária das crianças com idades compreendidas entre os 7 e os 10 anos nos meios rural e urbano. In Neto, C. (Ed.), *Jogo & desenvolvimento da criança*, Lisboa, Edições FMH: Universidade Técnica de Lisboa.

U. S. Consumer Product Safety Commission (s/d) *Handbook for Public Playground Safety*. Washington D. C.

ACKNOWLEDGMENT

This study was supported by the Commission for Coordination of the North Region (CCRN).

Chapter Nine

Playground Safety in Brazil

Francis Wardle

In August 1999, the Second International Playground Safety Conference was held at Pennsylvania State University (Christiansen, 2000). This conference reflected both a growing worldwide concern for playground safety and an ongoing attempt to create a universal safety approach for international playground equipment manufacturing companies. At the conference there were playground safety experts, representatives of playground equipment manufactures, and parks and city officials from around the world. Papers were presented on specific safety issues, including impact absorbent materials, safety policies, and design considerations, by researchers, experts and practitioners from England, USA, Australia, Wales, Taiwan, Canada, China, Japan, Germany and Brazil (Christiansen, 2000).

BACKGROUND INFORMATION

My initial interest in playground safety in Brazil grew out of my participation in a project supported by Partners of the Americas and Rotary International to build a playground in the town of Sete Lagoas, Minas Gerais, Brazil (Finley, 1996). My expectation was to simply design a playground, and then purchase and install the equipment. However, after investigating the available equipment, I discovered that Brazilin playgrounds were unsafe and that I would have to construct my own equipment (Wardle, 1999a). After this initial experience I became interested in the overall issue of playground safety in Brazil. Between 1996 and 2005, I visited Brazil on five different occasions. I was not only interested in the safely of Brazilian playgrounds, but I also wanted to determine to what extent U.S. playground standards and guidelines—specifically the *Handbook for Public Playground Safety* (CPSC, 1997), and *Standards*

Consumer Safety Performance Specifications for Playground Equipment for Public Use (ASTM, 1997)—could be applied in Brazil.

Brazil has no playground safety guidelines. However, with the globalization of U.S. and European playground equipment companies, there is a need for guidelines. There is also growing opposition to these guidelines, as I have discovered in my playground consultation work in the U.S. One of the concerns is that, while they increase the cost of playgrounds, they actually meet fewer of the overall play needs of children; further, that playgrounds using these guideless provide far less of the critically important early childhood outdoor experiences that young children need to have—particularly in the areas of managed risks (Nederland, 2002; Thompson, 2002; Wardle, 2003).

In the U.S., interest concerning playground safety has been driven both by a genuine effort to reduce playground related accidents (recorded in emergency rooms and tabulated by CPSC, 1997) and also by a need to reduce liability costs to manufactures.

PARTICIPANTS

I selected a variety of playgrounds in the state of Minas Gerais and Brasilia, DF, while also examining playgrounds in hotel grounds, country clubs, and the many restaurants scattered along the major highways that cater to traveling families. The major categories of playgrounds I evaluated were city parks, playgrounds in early childhood programs and schools, and playgrounds in country clubs, hotels, apartment complexes and roadside restaurants. The areas selected for the study were: Uberlandia, MG; Belo Horizonte, MG; Diamantina, MG, Brasilia, DF, and Foz do Iguazu in the state of Parana, along with restaurants along the major highways between Belo Horizonte, Diamantina, and Brasilia, DF. The geographic area covered includes three different states and the Federal District of Brasilia.

METHOD

I visited Brazil on five different occasions, from 1996 to 2005, with each visit separated approximately by two years. On each occasion I evaluated playgrounds in the area, including city parks, early childhood programs, schools, restaurants, country clubs and apartment complexes. Specifically, I evaluated four city park playgrounds, 16 schools/early childhood programs serving children, and 20 restaurants, country clubs and apartment complexes. I also interviewed a city park manger, a playground equipment company owner, principals and teachers, and one medical doctor regarding their perception of playground safety in Brazil (Wardle, 1999a: Wardle, 1999b; Wardle, 1999c; Wardle, 2005).

Initially I used the CPSC and ASTM guidelines detailed in their respective publications as my tool to measure safety of playgrounds, along with my own overall knowledge base regarding playground safety in the US (Wardle, 1996–2003). While I wanted to collect data on playground injuries and deaths, the statistics do not seem to be available (Meira, 1996). The manager of the Mangarberias Park, Belo Horizonte also said these statistics are not kept for a variety of reasons (Wardle, 1999). I compared factors such as fall zones, swing measurements, and height recommendations. I also factored in weather-related issues, such as metal slides and shade. Finally, I tried to include cultural factors. For example, Brazil's city park playgrounds are huge and the equipment is much more spread out than in city playgrounds in the US.

RESULTS

Results of observations from my first visit (1996) showed all playground equipment was built either of wood or metal, and, because most playgrounds are constructed by welding metal or bolting wood together, there were many very dangerous protrusions of all sorts. All swing seats were wood or metal; and most pieces of equipment had no fall zones, many built directly on concrete, stone or brick surfaces. Further, linked equipment—with swings, slides, ladders, steps, playhouse and platforms all attached together—was extremely popular, especially for play areas in country clubs, hotels, apartment complexes, and roadside restaurants. Linked equipment, especially when swings are attached, violates many CPSC and ASTM guideless. Finally, in Brazil there appears to be little regard for height limitations of equipment (Wardle, 1999b; 1999c). All of these observations violate one or more of the CSPC and ASTM guileless (1997; 1997). Specific citations were reported after my first study (Wardle, 1999a).

City Parks

The city playgrounds I visited were absolutely huge, with lakes, ponds, expansive walking and riding areas, and huge playgrounds. I evaluated two large city parks in Belo Horizonte, one in Uberlandia, and one in Brasilia. Many of the climbing structures and swings were combined into huge linked structures. Problems observed include equipment that was far too high for the ages of children who use it with some equipment more than 15 feet high, and equipment that encouraged inappropriate and dangerous play—usually running, follow-the-leader-type games, and jumping. Overall, fall zone areas were non-existent, inadequate, too small, under the wrong equipment, and/or totally compacted to render them useless. Almost all equipment was constructed of metal, wood, and rubber tires; slides were wood or metal.

Because of the massive and dense design of some of the equipment, supervision was impossible. Also, if a child were to get into trouble on a piece of equipment, adults could not help, because the entrances and exists to many areas were simply too small for an adult. Much of the equipment is designed in such a way that a falling child would land on metal or concrete play equipment components before hitting the ground. They might also catch their head on monkey bars as they fall. Numerous head entrapments were everywhere. The design and placement of equipment was poor. This results in limiting play to inappropriate activities, scattering equipment in a way that prevents integrating play components, and placing equipment so far away from other equipment that much is not even used. I observed this same phenomenon in the Sarah Kubitschek Municipal Park in Brasilia. It seems that one unforeseen result of the wonderful amount of space Brazil devotes to public park playgrounds is that equipment is often spread out far too much.

In the Sarah Kubitschek Municipal Park in Brasilia, equipment was scattered over a large area of sand-covered fall zones, grass hills, and a lot of trees. Equipment was from the novelty era of the 1950–60s in the U.S. (Johnson, Christie and Wardle, 2005): rockets, space ships, etc. Safety problems with these pieces of equipment included swings that were located in places where passing children could be hit by the hard swing seats; too many seats to a bay, so children hit each other; see-saws that caused children to smash their bare feet (all children and some adults played barefoot); vertical ladders, steps and climbers that had adult spacing and contained head entrapments, multiple crush points and protrusions. Large sand fall zones were provided for several large pieces of equipment, but other pieces of equipment were designed in such as way that falling children would hit other equipment before landing on the absorbent material below. Some climbing equipment had no fall zones. Because of the theme of rockets and space ships, much of the equipment, including slides, far exceeded the CPSC height recommendations (1997).

Mental and Plastic Equipment

In my 2002 visit to Brasilia I inspected a playground equipment store selling new metal equipment. This equipment had many protrusions, entrapments, metal slides (in a tropical climate), and hard, metal pipes. It was the exact same equipment that was popular in early childhood and home-based programs in the U.S. about 20 to 30 years ago, but is apparently very popular in Brazil today. This was quite a surprise to me, as I had assumed the unsafe equipment I observed on my earlier visits was simply playground equipment dumped by U.S. manufactures on the less safety-conscious Brazilian market. But companies in Brazil are actually making and selling this unsafe equipment, with all the same safety problems already mentioned.

Since 2002, I have also observed an increasing number of Little Tikes (Rubbermaid) plastic playgrounds in Brazil, particularly in restaurants, shops, country clubs, and stores that young, middle-class families frequent. Unfortunately, these pieces of equipment were always placed on concrete, tile or brick floors. Further, they were placed very close to walls and barriers, with slides and steps exiting into walls and other pieces of equipment. In a playground I studied in a restaurant in Belo Horizonte, Minas Gerais, the two slides existed less than 12 inches from a wall. Additionally, there was no sense of age-appropriate use. Children ranging in age from one year to 15 years were playing on the equipment, although such equipment is recommended in the U.S. for children age 18 months to 5 years old. There were no signs recommending age limits, safety issues, and supervision requirements.

Finally, since this equipment was used as entertainment for children while parents eat, shop or relax, there was no active supervision of children. In the case of the playground in the restaurant I observed, the parents were eating over 40 feet from the playground and were totally oblivious to what their children were doing (often engaging in very unsafe play). I was part of a group of four families with seven children. This is very different from the active supervisor in the city parks, where middle-class families have maids who very carefully supervise the children.

Child Care/School Playgrounds

Early childhood playgrounds—both private and subsidized—in Brazil are characterized by very small areas (for security reasons, all buildings, child care centers, and schools are protected by high security walls or fences, making space very valuable), often-moveable equipment (to maximize the areas), unsafe equipment, and extremely small or non-existent fall zones. I visited the federal university's Centro de desenvolvimento da crianca, in Belo Horizonte, that has a very large playground with a built-in platform structure with slides and fire poles. Both the slides and fire poles exited onto a brick floor. However, the poles had been blocked off because of too many accidents. When I suggested maybe creating a fall zone, people looked bemused.

Schools suffer from a total absence of funds for the outdoors. Usually they just have a concrete area for playing soccer and volleyball. Even the private schools I visited had little if anything in the way of adequate playgrounds (Wardle, 2005). Resources in Brazilian schools are very limited and reserved for inside. I did visit a very well-equipped federal public school in Uberlandia, but even in this school the playground was very small, inadequate and unsafe.

DISCUSSION

There are many challenges to addressing the issue of playground safety in Brazil. Probably the number one challenge is that few people see a need. As a developing country with extreme issues of poverty, income inequality, crime and land redistribution, etc., playground safety is not viewed as a priority. One reason for this attitude is because there are no statistics to show playground-related deaths and injuries. There is extreme skepticism regarding the seriousness and relevance of playground accidents. According to the manager of Mangabeiras Park in Belo Horizonte, there are no such statistics because parents take full responsibility for caring for their children who have accidents. Some parents take injured children to local hospitals and clinics and some don't, but there are no nationally collected statistics (Wardle, 1999a). Also, this manager said he carries no liability insurance; considerations he uses in purchasing equipment are cost, installation, and maintenance, but not safety.

After examining a series of very dangerous playgrounds and pieces of equipment as part of my research, my host—a surgeon—finally changed from complete indifference to acknowledging the safety issues (Dr Meira, 1996). Others I interviewed only became convinced of the problem when I showed them U.S. accident statistics (CPSC 1997).

Safety Handbook

Brazil does not have a playground safety handbook. And, obviously, the fact that Brazil is a metric country and speaks Portuguese means the American playground guidelines cannot be used in Brazil. This suggests that Brazil may wish to use the Canadian, European or Australian handbooks. However, this would pose an obstacle for American Playground manufacturing companies, which have made some gains in the Brazilian market. Both the *Handbook for Public Playground Safety* (CPSC 1997) and the *Standard Consumer Safety Performance Specifications for Playground Equipment for Public Use*

(ASTM, 1997) use American anthropomorphic measurements. In my studies of Brazilian playgrounds, I soon realized that Brazilian children on the average are much smaller than North American children, due to their genetic background, poor nutrition and health. (Most Brazilian children are the product of a mixture of Portuguese, Black and Indian heritage; according to my host, Dr, Meira, malnutrition is still Brazil's number one health problem)(1996). The result of these realities means that safety standards and guidelines based on American anthropomorphic measurements, such as head entrapments, fall zone sizes, etc., are not applicable for Brazilian playgrounds.

Should Brazil Adopt a U.S. Solution?

The U.S., Canada, and several European nations have well-developed playground guidelines and standards. The U.S. guidelines are articulated in the two books already mentioned, along with their technical counterparts. Both these publications are used extensively by U.S. playground equipment manufactures, playground designers, playground safety inspectors, and local and state childcare licensing officials and regulators. The National Head Start program has also adopted them as the basis for their performance standards for outdoor environments. One question is whether Brazil should adopt these exiting and well-developed guidelines. Participants at the International Playground Safety Conference held at Pennsylvania State University in 1999 expressed a strong belief that developed counties should not impose their playground safety solution on Brazil and that they should be encouraged to develop standards that match their unique culture, needs, resources, and climate (Wardle, 1999b). This view supports a growing position that we must be very careful regarding the potential negative effects of globalization on unique cultures, child rearing practices, and local customs (Johnson, Christie and Wardle, 2005).

As I discovered during one of my visits to Brazil, at least one U.S. company is already aggressively marketing in Brazil, and this trend will only increase. Thus, U.S. playground equipment companies will sell equipment built for the U.S. market (using U.S. safety standards). It would seem that these companies also have an obligation to transfer our overall safety standards to Brazil. Yet my observation of plastic equipment placed unsecured directly on concrete or brick with slide exists less than two feet from walls and pillars suggests this is not being done. Pressure must be placed on international companies to be ethical and responsible members of the world community.

Clearly Brazil needs to look at playground safety, along with the critical issues of poverty, racism, nutrition, crime, education, drugs, employment and medical care. All the major city parks in Brazil have extensive playgrounds contained within their boundaries, so implementing safety standards, at least at the municipal level, would not be difficult. The central question is, to what extent are the U.S. playground safety guidelines—or other standards and guidelines created in developed countries—applicable to Brazil?

Recommendations

Brazil needs to carefully move toward developing national playground safety guidelines. While all existing standards should be used as a baseline, it is critical the unique characteristics of Brazil's people, culture, environment and resources be carefully considered in developing these standards (Ferreira et al, 2005). Since liability concerns are not a consideration, Brazil should focus on standards with safety at their core. Specific areas to consider for these standards include:

- Develop Brazilian-specific anthropomorphic measurements to reflect the age-size relationships of Brazilian children.
- Address the abundance of space and attitudes toward space of the Brazilian culture. This is a tremendous advantage that should be capitalized on.
- Carefully consider the tropical climate. This can have an effect on the need for shade trees, the effects of heavy rain, the destruction of natural materials, and other playground features.
- Include unique cultural aspects in Brazilian playgrounds: the rich history and modern influence of public art and architecture, regional folk games, soccer, salon soccer, beach soccer, volleyball, and other popular pastimes.
- Analyze available and inexpensive resources. Brazil is a country with abundant iron resources, but no natural sources of petroleum (except what they make from agricultural products). This means metal equipment is plentiful, plastic almost nonexistent. Unfortunately, metal is a hard surface that gets very hot; plastic less hard, and does not get hot—although it does fade in the tropical sun. And, despite the international clamor regarding the destruction of the Brazilian rainforests, recyclable wood is plentiful, cheap, and easy to work with and repair. Metal, of course, is quite difficult to repair, and produces very dangerous protrusions.
- Carefully analyze the best fall zone materials. Observations from my studies indicate that sand is almost always preferred. Interestingly, the huge Sarah Kubitsckek Municipal Playground in Brasilia has a shower where the children washed their feet after playing on the playground. No cats were observed on playgrounds during these studies; maybe stray dogs ate them. Cats do not seem to be very popular pets in Brazil, while most middle-class

residents keep dogs as protection from crime. Therefore, it is not clear whether the feces of animals are a problem for fall zone in Brazil as they are in the U.S.

- Understand and include the typical maid service of caring for children in Brazil, although this pattern is slowly changing. Maids have time to take children to the park every day, and stay with them for long periods of time. Also, maids provide careful, individual supervision for one or two children, which means most children on Brazilian playgrounds are carefully supervised, unlike children on U.S. playgrounds, who are either in large supervised groups, or are unsupervised.
- Immediately consider the very dangerous practice of placing equipment directly on concrete, tile and brick, and of placing steps and slide exists too close to obstructions. These are the two most critical safety results I observed. Extreme height would be the third area of concern.

CONCLUSION

As the 1999 Second International Playground Safety Conference at Pennsylvania State University illustrated, there is a growing interest in worldwide playground safety. This is due to concerns about injury and liability, along with a need for consistent safety standards worldwide. These standards are needed as more and more playground companies expand into international markets. Brazil currently has no local or national playground guideless of any kind. Brazil needs to carefully consider her culture, resources, and the role of the playground in their children's lives, to develop standards that match the unique society. Brazil must also respond to the current and future influx of American and European-made equipment into its marketplace with apparently little or no regard for the safety of its children.

REFERENCES

American Society for Testing and Materials. (1997). *Standard consumer safety performance specifications for playground equipment for public use*. Philadelphia, PA: Author.

Ferreira, S., and class. (2005). The Culture of the Cerrado. Presentation given at the Triangulo Mineiro Social Forum, Uberlandia, MG: Federal University at Uberlandia.

Finley, B. (1996). Citizen diplomats. Coloradoans building bridges in Brazil. *Denver Post,* Dec. 16, pp1A, 6A.

Johnson, Christie, and Wardle. (2005). *Play, development, and early education*. Boston. MA: Allyn and Bacon.

Meira, J. (1996). Personal communication (Surgeon). Minas Gerais, Brazil.

Nederland, N. (2002). Personal communication (Migrant Head Start technical assistance specialist).

Thompson, D. (2002). Personal communication (college seminar presentation, Greeley, Colorado).

U. S. Consumer Product Safety Commission (1997). *Handbook for Public Playground Safety.* Washington, DC: U.S. Printing Office.

Wardle, F. (1999a). Building a safe playground in Brazil. In Christiansen (Ed.) *Playground safety 1999: An international conference. Conference proceedings*. State College, Pa: Pennsylvania State University, School of Hotel, Restaurant and Recreation Management.

Wardle, F. (1999b). Building a community playground in Brazil. In Johnson, Christie and Yawkey, T. D. *Play and early childhood development* (pp. 267–268). New York: Longman.

Wardle, F. (1999c). The story of a playground. *Child Care Information Exchanger, 128*, 28–30.

Wardle, F (2003). *Introduction to early childhood education: A multidimensional approach. Boston.* MA: Allyn and Bacon.

Wardle, F. (1996–2003). *Playground safety*. Series of lectures presented at the School of Public Health, University of Northern Colorado, Greeley, Colorado.

Wardle, F. (2005. July). *Francis Wardle's Partner's Trip Report*. Washington, DC: Partners of the Americas, Inc.

ACKNOWLEDGMENT

This research was funded in part by several grants from Partners of the Americas.

Part III

PLAYFULNESS, CREATIVITY, AND SCIENCE

Chapter Ten

Play and Creativity: The Role of the Intersubjective Adult

Deborah W. Tegano and James D. Moran, III

The development of intersubjectivity begins in infancy (Braten, 1998; Trevarthen, 1979) and continues throughout life (Resnick, Levine, & Teasley, 1991). Defined simply, intersubjectivity implies a subjective understanding or an agreement (shared understanding by an individual of two quite different points of view; e.g., simultaneously of both adult and child)) about a shared activity, situation, and/or object (e.g., shared attention, shared definition of a situation or approach to a problem, shared object of an activity) (Matusov, 2001). In this chapter, the concept of intersubjectivity is discussed with regard to practices of early education teachers in developing an awareness of the meaningfulness of play for children within the complexity of early childhood contexts.

We describe how the thoughtful consideration of adult playfulness and creativity may lead teachers to develop an intersubjective perspective in regard to children's play. That is, how might teachers foster a playful disposition with children and accordingly, intersubjectively provide opportunities for children to think creatively and to solve problems (doing so within a daily play-based early childhood curriculum)? According to Bodrova and Leong (2003), teachers' proactive support of mature play is identified as one means to positive learning outcomes for young children. Intersubjective approaches to working with young children, wherein teachers have developed shared understandings with children, encourage teachers to become "play mentors" (Bodrova & Leong, 2003, p.52) who scaffold young children's foundational skills, particularly in the area of creative problem solving. Teachers' awareness of their own playfulness is one component of reflective teacher practice, where playfulness is considered through the lenses of teachers' awareness of their own interactive style, their resistance to evaluation, and their tolerance for ambiguity.

Scholarly studies in the areas of creativity and play began as separate fields of investigations in the late 1960s and have continued to develop toward a significant presence in the field of child development, psychology, and education. However, as scholars examined the meaning of creativity with primates (Vandenberg, 1980) and also with young children (Dansky & Silverman, 1973; Pepler & Ross, 1981), the natural overlap between the study of creativity and play emerged in the literature. This overlap is evidenced in the classic article, "Play, Problem-Solving, and Creativity" by Vandenberg (1980). Researchers in the fields of child development, psychology, and education agree that studying creativity with young children requires a thorough knowledge of the play literature. They also agree that studying children's play leads one into the realm of exploration, discovery, and creativity. Play has a natural outcome for helping to generate ideas, solve problems, and promote critical thinking skills through specific and diverse exploration (Hutt, 1979; Pepler & Ross, 1981) of materials, the environment, and the interactive complexities of the two.

In the same vein, practitioners who worked with young children across the past twenty years watched the pendulum of early childhood educational practices move toward Developmentally Appropriate Practice (DAP) (Bredekamp, 1987; Bredekamp & Copple, 1997). With the National Association for the Education of Young Children's endorsement of DAP, the field of early childhood education embraced play-based early childhood programs as one avenue through which young children develop creative, inquiring minds and construct knowledge about their world. More recently, with increased exposure to Vygotsky's theory (Vygotsky, 1933/78) and to interpretations and applications of his writings (Berk & Winsler, 1995; Crain, 2000; Duncan & Tarulli, 2003; Langford, 2005; Rogoff & Wertsch, 1984; Rogoff, 1990), early childhood educators are more likely to view play and creativity from an intersubjective perspective.

Concurrent with the shift in early childhood teachers' awareness of social constructivist views about appropriate educational practices is the reconceptualization of the teachers' role in promoting play, creativity, and problem solving. In the 1990s, the pendulum again swung from teacher-directed approaches to teacher-facilitator approaches, from direct instruction to prepared environment with little or no instruction, from teacher-as-center of the classroom to teacher-on-the-periphery of the classroom. The "early childhood error," described by Bredekamp and Rosegrant (1992), emerged from the debate on the appropriate roles for early childhood teachers. The "early childhood error" is committed when early childhood educators prepare an appropriate and provocative classroom environment, but do not offer the necessary scaffolding, guidance, and support that is necessary for children to maximize their learning potential (e.g., focused attention, problem-solving, critical thinking). Perhaps the "early childhood error" is committed when teachers do not have the skills necessary to mediate learning for children, even when they have intentionally prepared stimulating environments. These skills develop out of teachers' deepening subjective understandings about play and its role in promoting children's investigations—children as inquirers and problem solvers. In this chapter, we discuss the development of intersubjectivity as the means by which teachers become participant observers *with* the children, actively involved in the classroom, more conscious of when and how to stand back, facilitate, or when to direct children's play.

SOCIOCULTURAL PERSPECTIVES AND THE ROLE OF THE ADULT

Vygotsky described children's learning in terms the use of cultural sign systems determined by children through their social interactions (Vygotsky, 1933/78). Play is thought to be a leading activity (Duncan & Tarulli, 2003) through which children develop shared understandings. Culture is translated to children largely by adults, and thus, educational practices based on Vygotsky's theory include reference to the role of the *adult* in adult-child interactions during play. Thus, an intersubjective adult recognizes that adults' engagement with children during play affects relationships among all participants and these relationships are contextualized within specific cultural situations (e.g., sociodramatic play or participating in a simple board game).

An intersubjective adult, who has developed shared understandings with children about their play, is more likely to be aware of the complexity of children's play. To be intersubjective means to be involved in play, immersed in play, aware of play at an intimate level. An objective observer sees play through the eyes of a trained adult (through the textbook, through predetermined expectations of play, or through the goals and objectives of the curriculum). An intersubjective observer sees children's play through the eyes of the child *and* the adult and seeks to create meaning from the play. An intersubjective adult observes children's play and asks: What is the nature of children's explorations? What questions might the children be asking about the materials? What problems are the children discovering? What are the possible connections that the children are making? From a Vygotskian perspective, the adult seeks to observe the child's zone of proximal development by entering the child's play from an intersubjective perspective, thus helping the child to move to a higher, more complex level of thinking (Vygotsky, 1933/78). These same methods of interacting with children may move children through the processes of creative problem solving.

Concomitant to the field's appreciation for play-based early childhood programming and social constructivist approaches is the increasing use of qualitative research methodologies for studying children's play. Qualitative research techniques are appropriate means to study many complex psychological constructs. Qualitative methods are a natural match for understanding the meanings that children attach to their play, where the very nature of the play is deeply embedded in the context of the play situation. Qualitative research methodologies are also teaching tools. The same scrutiny that a teacher-researcher applies to studying the meaning that children associate with their play may be applied to classroom contexts with informally defined research questions such as, "How might I better understand the meaning of children's conceptualization of play and how might I better promote inquiry-based learning in these contexts?" We propose that from an intersubjective perspective, adults who seek appropriate, noninvasive ways to enter children's play or to observe children's play are more likely to engage in meaningful reflections about the play than those who do not. Adults who recognize the "as if" frame of play (Bateson, 1992) and the intersubjectivity or mutual understanding between child and adult (Goncu, 1993) have an enhanced likelihood of joining children in play in ways that foster children's development, particularly the development of children's creativity and problem solving abilities.

Reitel and Yeatman (1993) remind us that play is a "set of contextually-based transformations, with an ontogeny, history and significance" (p. 352). Qualitative research methodologies make great efforts to define the role of the intersubjective adult, taking the ontogeny and the history of the adult researcher into consideration. Meaningful observation of children's play, whether for the purposes of research, education, or therapy, requires both a respect for the history and context of the play and a healthy introspective examination of what play means to the observer. In one such study, Kontos (1999) observes that teacher engagement in children's play and the quality of those engagements depends on context.

Adult interpretations of play, then, are naturally influenced by the history and contexts of the observer, as well as the history and the contexts of the player(s). That is, not all adults are playful in the same ways or to the same extent. Play in adulthood is qualitatively different than childhood play. Thus, an awareness of one's own qualities of adult playfulness may be an important, though often ignored, aspect for developing an intersubjective capacity. A better understanding of one's own playfulness helps adults to create meaning from children's play, to facilitate and sustain children's play, and thus helps to develop children's creative problem-solving skills.

PLAYFULNESS IN ADULTS

According to Rubin, Fein, & Vandenberg (1983), playfulness is a psychological construct from which the following criteria may be extrapolated for adults. Playful adults: (a) are guided by internal motivation and are oriented toward process; (b) attribute their own meanings to objects or behaviors and are not bound by what they see; (c) focus on pretend and seek freedom from externally imposed rules; and (d) are actively involved. More succinctly, these criteria may be characterized in playful adults as involving three characteristics: open interactive style, resistance to evaluation, and tolerance for ambiguity. These are discussed here with regard to the encouragement of children's creative thinking and problem solving and the influence of the adult in adult-child play interactions. How are adults playful? When are adults truly "players" in adult-child play interactions? How does self-awareness influence the ability to become an intersubjective player and heighten the opportunities for the children to actualize their creative potential?

Interactive Style

Adults differ in the manner or style in which they interact with children (Bloom, 1956; Cassidy, 1989; Graham, Sawyers, & DeBord, 1989; Honig & Wittmer, 1984; Smith & McCabe, 1990; Tizard & Hughes, 1984; Ryu, Tegano, & Moran, 2006). Each of these studies approaches interactive style using a different paradigm to describe adult interaction, though a continuum emerges where adult interactive style is described at either end of the continuum as: (a) cognitively engaging, divergent, open, unstructured or (b) controlling, convergent, closed, structured. To view this as a dichotomy is false, of course, because an adult's interactions move along the continuum as the context of situations change throughout a play activity or session. Yet, taken at their extremes, these descriptions provide guidance for developing an awareness of the impact of adult interactions with children during play. The requisites of play include a focus on process, on active involvement, and a sense that each situation has its own unique meaning and is not bound by rules or evaluation. The requisite play criteria of process, involvement, uniqueness and unboundedness are incongruent with the description of controlling, convergent or structured adults. Bredekamp and Rosegrant's (1992) reference to the "early childhood error" would suggest that teachers become increasingly attuned to interactions that provoke and promote children's thinking, responses deliberately constructed by teachers from their intersubjective knowledge of what learning is relevant and meaningful for children in a particular play context.

For instance, in Ryu et al. (2006) teachers reported different play interaction styles in different contexts. Specifically, preschool teachers reported a belief that their interactive role in pretend play situations was different from their interactive role in manipulative or constructive play (they believed they were less likely to interact in pretend play situations). Similarly, in a second study, kindergarten teachers' play interaction style differed from the play interaction style of preschool teachers where kindergarten teachers were less likely than preschool teachers to participate in children's constructive and manipulative play (Ryu, Tegano, & Moran, 2005). Thus, context significantly influences how teachers interact in children's play. Adults must consider both context and the individual child in considering playful approaches to entering, facilitating, and sustaining children's play.

In addition to context, then, it is adults' awareness of personal characteristics of children that influences interactive style. Good teachers are constantly aware of the unique and complex relationship between the child and the specific context of learning. It is this awareness that nurtures the intersubjective perspective of the teacher and enables the teacher to adapt behaviors that are congruent with a playful environment and in which creative potential is encouraged. An adult participant in play is immersed in play subjectively, and, at the same time, is consciously aware of the influence of interactive style. The recognition of the complexity of being both participant and observer requires suspending judgment and remaining open to new information, as discussed in the next section.

Resistance to Evaluation

One of the criteria of playfulness is freedom from externally imposed rules and thus from the external (and internal) evaluation that results from such rules. Everyone possesses a set of external and internal rules. To keep the natural flow of play going, it is often necessary to suspend these sources of evaluation. When children don a dragon costume they don't stop to evaluate how they feel about it. They just *feel* it and go on. In contrast, adults spend hours dressing, undressing, and redressing for a costume party precisely because the power of evaluation is inhibiting their playful response to dressing-up. Freedom from evaluation is inherent to playful situations. Borich (1993) says that when working with students, adults need not "consult an analytical review" process, but rather rely on an "affective image or sensitivity to [one's] own feeling" (p. 98). Is this not what children do as they play? To borrow from professional development literature, we might say that when we move evaluation aside for a moment, we find our comfort zone and become "playfully serious and seriously playful" (Baden, 1999, p. 49). This should be especially true when we are involved with children. Spontaneity and freedom from evaluation are paramount to playfulness in both children and adults. This is not to say that adults should not be constantly reflecting on how their personality and interactive style influence the quality of their playful interactions with children. It is only to say that to be involved in the flow of play, one must be able to suspend inner judgment and be immersed in the flow of interacting with children. Reflection, by nature of the term, comes later. To reflect is to go back and to examine how freedom from evaluation impacts playful encounters with children.

How can adults be both spontaneous participants in play and also assess the potential for children's creative development? When adults spontaneously participate, children's play becomes an intersubjective activity between the children and the adult (Goncu, 1993). In a mutually constructed play activity children develop shared meaning of which the adult is a part. The adult becomes a player in the true sense. Sandberg and Parmling-Samuelsson's (2005) in-depth interviews of Swedish preschool teachers demonstrate what they call "play willingness" in a statement from one male teacher who truly wanted to spontaneously participate in play:

> I can occasionally participate because I just want to be with the children in play. The other day I just threw myself into the "pillow room." " Now I want to be with you and play a little" and they wanted me to participate. (p. 300)

By trusting one's own playfulness, affective responses flow—laughter, joking, a funny face, or a hug or nudge. This does not mean that the analytical side of the adult has ceased to function. Playful adults become better facilitators of children's creative development precisely because they recognize the potential for problem solving and learning from the child's perspective while immersed in the play scenario. When adults and children are an integral part of the ecology of the play scenario, the potential for inquiry and creative thinking is maximized by the teacher's "inside view" of the situation, in whatever direction the play may head.

Tolerance for Ambiguity

One experiences ambiguity when presented with a set of "unfamiliar, complex, or incongruent cues" (Prosen, 1980, p. 463). Because interactions with children are unpredictable, adults are often in the midst of ambiguity where there is no clear-cut response and no obvious right answer. And, as ambiguous as it seems, there is no accepted level of ambiguity tolerance that is considered optimal for working with children. Because ambiguity tolerance is considered a personality trait, it is not likely to be easily changed in adults, though it certainly can be brought into awareness and become a subject for reflection and dialogue (Prosen, 1980; Tegano, 1990; Tegano, Groves, & Catron, 1999).

In a study using the Myers-Briggs Type Indicator (MBTI), playfulness and ambiguity tolerance were found to be closely related traits in early childhood teachers (Tegano, 1990). Not surprisingly, playful adults were found to be more tolerant of ambiguity. Likewise, an awareness of these traits may be useful to adults as a means for introspective examination of their influence on the creative potential of young children. Tegano, Groves, and Catron (1999) found that a significant number of playful adults tend to see themselves as perceivers on the MBTI (note: perceivers are flexible, adaptable, prefer to keep options open). Similarly, Green and Schaefer (1984) found that teachers who were perceivers on the MBTI preferred preschool materials that were make-believe in nature (materials with open-ended uses), while the judgers preferred academic materials (those more likely to have convergent uses).

An open, flexible, adaptable adult is more likely than others to enter children's play without preconceived outcomes in mind. This adult is more likely to observe, analyze, and reflect on the subjective meaning of play to facilitate children's creative, discovery-based thinking and learning. This description is congruent with the role of the teacher as a facilitator that is inferred in DAP (Bredekamp, 1987; Bredekamp & Copple, 1997) and it is also congruent with the "responsive teacher" that is described by Stremmel and Fu (1993). This adult mutually constructs activities with children, staying open to changing play scenarios and remaining aware of the nuances within the play. The child and the flexible adult share a more collaborative role and there is tolerance for unanticipated paths of learning and a requirement that the adult respect the open-ended nature of learning. This describes the model of play and creative problem solving where adults facilitate children's progress from exploration and discovering problems to generating and experimenting with multiple solutions (Tegano, Moran and Sawyers, 1991; Tegano, Sawyers, & Moran, 1989). For many teachers, however, this is not the preferred style. In a recent study by Ryu (2003), preschool teachers reported more reticence in interacting with children in pretend play than in manipulative or constructive play, perhaps because pretend play is perceived as more open-ended, less goal-directed.

In this open, flexible, adaptable context of play, it may be expected that it will be the intersubjective adult who is better able to join the children in play contexts and co-construct the important questions the children may be formulating, the connections the children may be making, and the theories that the children may be constructing about their world. The teacher is not *just* an observer, but also a *part* of the development of shared understanding through the conscious effort to tolerate the ambiguity that is inherent in play.

AWARENESS AND REFLECTION: KEYS TO THE INTERSUBJECTIVE ADULT

A social constructivist perspective maintains that we co-construct meaning in the continuous dynamic of social encounters against the constantly changing contexts of world, body, others, and time (Berger & Luckman ref., Merleau-Ponty, 1962/86, Pollio & Henley, 1999). In this paradigm, the meaning of a play activity for children transforms itself within each interaction and each context. Adults who study children's play from this perspective, or adults who work with children in classrooms or therapy rooms from a truly "responsive" perspective, are *aware* of their own intersubjective nature. It is not that these adults choose to be in control of their interactive style, their resistance to evaluation, or their tolerance of ambiguity. Rather, it is a willingness to reflect on this awareness that brings adults to the place of entering children's play as a partner.

We cannot expect to "train" adults to work with children through play. Rather, adults *construct* their own meaning of play in their own lives and through the lives of the children in their care (Fosnot, 1989). This dynamic process of constructing meaning from play happens within the complexity of many contexts (the settings, the corporeal body, the interaction with others, and the temporal aspects of a given situation) (Merleau-Ponty, 1926/86). Constructing an understanding of the value of play is not a weekend workshop transformation, though nearly every educational professional has attended one of these workshops. Constructing an understanding of play is a complex process of recognizing the many faces of play and the many contextual frames for play (for children and for adults), keenly observing play (of children and adults), relating these observations to what is known about the nature of play (for children and adults), developing an introspective awareness of personal responses in playful situations, and then working toward integrating this understanding into one's own world view through reflection or some form of dialogue with children or other professionals about the meaning of play. Perhaps the most critical part of this process involves reflection and self-awareness (Bowman, 1989). Experiencing intersubjectivity in children's play is opening oneself up to another level of awareness—one of "knowing." Palmer (1998) talks about the power of being a participant: "We can know reality only by being in community with it ourselves . . . (and if) we are here merely as observers and not participants . . . we would not have the capacity to know" (p. 98).

The "early childhood error" of too much or too little teacher direction may be addressed through teachers' heightened awareness of their own playfulness in determining how they might better become intersubjective participants with children in play. There is no linear path of correcting the "early childhood error." Rather success unfolds from continuous awareness of and reflection on the dynamic processes of play and the many manifestations of playfulness within each classroom, with each group of children, for each individual child, and likewise, for each individual teacher.

We began by stating that the study of children's creativity and the study of children's play have many commonalities. The descriptors of playful adults briefly reviewed here (open-ended interactive style, resistance to evaluation and tolerance of ambiguity) are just as easily found in the literature on creativity. Years ago, a colleague challenged a research program built around creativity with young children: "Creativity is a bit nebulous, don't you think?" The response was clearly, "Of course!" Indeed, it is this nebulous nature of creativity, the ever changing faces of play, and the intersubjective stance of the adult that permit us to continuously construct, de-construct, and co-construct our understanding of its meaning for both children and adults who work with children.

REFERENCES

Baden, C. (1999). The Harvard Management for Lifelong Education Program: Creative approaches to designing a professional development program. *New Directions for Adult and Continuing Education, 81*, 47–55.

Bateson, G. (1976). The theory of play and fantasy. In J. S. Bruner, A. Jolly, & K. Slyva (Eds.), *Play—Its Role in Development and Evolution* (pp. 119–129). NY: Basic Books.

Berger, P. L. & Luckman, T. (1966). *The social construction of reality*. New York: Doubleday.

Berk, L. E., & Winsler, A. (1995). *Scaffolding children's learning: Vygotsky and early childhood education*. Washington, DC: National Association for the Education of Young Children.

Bloom, B.S. (Ed.). (1956). *Taxonomy of education objectives: Cognitive domain*. NY: Longman.

Bodrova, E., & Leong, D. J. (2003). The importance of being playful. *Educational Leadership, 60*(7), 50–53.

Borich, G. D. (1993). *Clearly outstanding*. Boston: Allyn and Bacon.

Bowman, B. T. (1989). Self reflection as an element of professionalism. In F. O. Rust & L. Williams (Eds.), *The Care and Education of Young Children: Expanding Contexts, Sharpening Focus* (pp. 108–115). NY: Teachers College Press.

Braten, S., (Ed.). (1998). *Intersubjective communication and emotion in early ontogeny*. New York: Cambridge University Press.

Bredekamp, S. (Ed.). (1987). *Developmentally appropriate practice in early childhood programs serving children from birth through age 8.* Washington, DC: National Association for the Education of Young Children.

Bredekamp, S., & Copple, C. (Eds.). (1997). *Developmentally appropriate practice in early childhood programs.* Washington, DC: National Association for the Education of Young Children.

Bredekamp, S., & Rosegrant, T. (1992). *Reaching potentials: Appropriate curriculum and assessment for young children*. Washington DC: National Association for the Education of Young Children.

Cain, W. (2000). *Theories of development: Concepts and applications* (4th ed.). New Jersey: Prentice Hall.

Cassidy, (1989). Questioning the young child: Process and function. *Childhood Education, 65,* 146–149.

Dansky, J., & Silverman, I. (1973). Effects of play on associative fluency in preschool-aged children. *Developmental Psychology, 11*, 104.

Duncan, R. M., & Tarulli, D. (2003). Play as the leading activity of the preschool period: Insights from Vygotsky, Leont'ev, and Bakhin. *Early Education and Development, 14*, 271–292.

Fostnot, C. T. (1989). *Enquiring teachers enquiring learners: A constructivist approach for teaching.* NY: Teachers College Press.

Goncu, A. (1993). Development of intersubjectivity in social pretend play. *Human Development, 36,* 185–198.

Graham, B., Sawyers, J., & DeBord, K. B. (1989). Teachers' creativity, playfulness, and style of interaction with children. 41–50.

Green, V. P., & Schaefer, L. (1984). Preschool teachers *Creativity Research Journal, 2,* play materials preferences. *Early Child Development and Care, 14*, 85–92.

Honig, A. S., & Wittmer, D. S. (1984). *Teacher-toddler day care interactions: Where, what, and how*. Paper presented at the International Symposium on Intervention and Stimulation in Infant Development, Jerusalem, Israel. (ERIC Reproduction Service No. ED 252 285)

Hutt, C. (1979). Exploration and play. In B. Sutton-Smith (Ed.), *Play and Learning*. NY: Gardner Press.

Kontos, S. (1999). Preschool teachers' talk, role, and activity setting during free play. *Early Childhood Research Quarterly, 14*, 363–382.

Langford, P. E. (2005). *Vygotsky's developmental and educational psychology*. NY: Psychology Press.

Merleau-Ponty, M. (1962/86). *Phenomenology of perception* (C. Smith, Trans.). New Jersey: The Humanities Press.

Palmer, P. J. (1998). *The courage to teach: Exploring the inner landscape of a teacher's life.* San

Francisco, CA: Jossey-Bass.

Pepler, D. J., & Ross, H. S. (1981). The effects of play on convergent and divergent problem solving. *Child Development, 52*, 1202–10.

Pollio, H. R., Henley, T. (1999). *The Phenomenology of Everyday Life*. Cambridge, UK: Cambridge University Press.

Prosen, S. S. (1980). Ambiguity tolerance. In R. H. Woody (Ed.), *Encyclopedia of Clinical Assessment* (pp.463–472). San Francisco: Jossey-Bass.

Resnick, L. B., Levine, J. M., & Teasley, S. D. (Eds.). (1991). *Perspectives on socially shared cognition*. Washington, D.C.: American Psychological Association.

Reifel, S. & Yeatman, J. (1993). From category to context: Reconsidering classroom play. *Early Childhood Research Quarterly, 8*, 347–367.

Rogoff, B. (1990). *Apprenticeship in thinking: Cognitive development in social context*. New York: Oxford University Press.

Rogoff, B. & Wertsch, J. (1984). *Children's learning in the "zone of proximal development."* San Francisco: Jossey-Bass.

Rubin, K., Fein, G., & Vandenberg, B. (1983). Play. In P. H. Mussen (Series Ed.) & E. M. Hertherington (Vol. Ed.), *Handbook of child psychology: vol. 4. Socialization, personality, and social development* (pp. 693–774). NY: Wiley.

Ryu, M. (2003). *Early childhood teachers' self-reported beliefs and practices about play*. Unpublished master's thesis, The University of Tennessee, Knoxville, TN.

Ryu, M., Tegano, D. W., & Moran, M. J. (2005, April). *Early childhood teachers' beliefs and practices about play: Comparisons across program types and levels.* Poster session presented at the annual meeting of the American Educational Research Association, Montreal, Canada.

Ryu, M., Tegano, D. W., Moran, M. J. (2006). *Teachers' beliefs and practices about play: A context-based analysis.* Manuscript submitted for publication.

Sandberg, A., & Pramling-Samuelsson, I. (2005). An interview study of gender differences in preschool teachers' attitudes toward children's play. *Early Childhood Education Journal, 32(5)*, 297–305.

Smith, M. W., & McCabe, A. (1990). *Socrates versus the drill sergeant: Dimensions of variation in preschool teachers' discourse*. Paper presented at the American Educational Research Association Meeting, April 16–20, Boston, MA.

Stremmel, A. J. & Fu, V. R. (1993). Teaching in the zone of proximal development: Implications for responsive teaching practice. *Child & Youth Care Forum, 22(5),* 337–350.

Tegano, D. W. (1990). The relationship of creativity to playfulness and ambiguity tolerance. *Psychological Reports, 66*, 1047–56.

Tegano, D. W., Groves, M., & Catron, C. E. (1999). Early childhood teachers' playfulness and ambiguity tolerance: Essential elements of encouraging creative potential of children. *Journal of Early Childhood Teacher Education*, 291–300.

Tegano, D. W., Moran, J. D., & Sawyers, J. K. (1991). *Creativity in the early childhood classroom.* Washington, DC: National Education Association.

Tegano, D. W., Sawyers, J. K., & Moran, J. D. (1989). Problem finding and solving in play: The teacher's role. *Childhood Education, 66*, 92–97.

Tizard, B., & Hughes, M. (1984). *Young children learning*. Cambridge, MA: Harvard University Press.

Trevarthen, C. (1979). Communication and cooperation in early infancy: A description of primary intersubjectivity. In M. Bullowa (ed.), *Before Speech: The Beginning of Interpersonal Communication.* Cambridge: Cambridge University Press.

Vandenberg, B. (1980). Play, problem-solving and creativity. In K. H. Rubin (Ed.) , New *Directions for Child Development* (pp.49–68). San Francisco: Jossey-Bass.

Vygotsky, L. S. (1933/78). The role of play in development (M. Lopez-Morillas, trans.). In M. Cole, V. John-Steiner, S. Scribner, & E. Souberman (Eds.), *L. S. Vygotsky: Mind in society*. Cambridge, MA: Harvard University Press.

Chapter Eleven

The Role of Fun, Playfulness, and Creativity in Science: Lessons from Geoscientists

Olga S. Jarrett and Pamela C. Burnley

> Scientific research is a demanding and creative endeavor that has delighted generations of bright minds and has explained seemingly incomprehensible puzzles. . . . One might speak of the curiosity natural to certain minds, a kind of playful engagement with the world. Science, after all, began as an avocation (hobby). (Peters, 1996, p. 187, 31).

The above quotations from a book addressing the scope and nature of modern work in the geosciences raise questions about the role of fun, playfulness and creativity in the development of scientists and in the conduct of science. Are curiosity and creativity learned characteristics? What is the role of informal childhood experiences with play and exploration in developing curiosity and creativity? Does formal schooling enhance or discourage curiosity and creativity? What is the place of fun, playfulness, and creativity in the serious process of scientific investigation and specifically in geoscience research? These are big questions and the answers are not found in one small study. The current study, a limited attempt to think about these questions, is a preliminary investigation into how geology faculty perceive playfulness as a part of their varied backgrounds and as an aspect of their research. Specifically, this study explores (a) their childhood/youth histories of science play, (b) their views on the roles of logic and creativity in hypothesis generation and data examination, and (c) their reflections on the roles of fun and playfulness while engaging in scientific investigations.

Before discussing how fun, playfulness, and creativity might be related to science, some clarification of terms is in order. Play is difficult to define. One approach is to define play as including some, if not all of a list of elements often characteristic of play. One such list of elements (Klugman & Fasoli, 1995) includes: intrinsically motivated, freely chosen, enjoyable, active, and non-literal (i.e. pretend or a conscious distortion of reality). Play can be appropriate or inappropriate (King, 1982, 1986). Fun is usually a subset of play although not all play is enjoyable and not all fun would be considered play. Creativity is originality and freedom, rooted in reality (hallucinations are not considered creative) (Arieti, 1976). Creative thinking is known for its ability to make connections and see patterns and is often associated with intuition, a playful disposition, humor, and breaks from intense concentration [although it does not occur "without previous conscious or unconscious reasoning" (Miller, 2000, p. 332)]. Creative thought often results in great joy and excitement (Csikszentmihalyi, 1996). Fun, playfulness, and creativity share many characteristics.

Although the public image of the scientist may be of a serious individual working in an isolated laboratory, for many eminent scientists, play was an important part of their childhood development, and continued playfulness marked their scientific careers. According to naturalist/sociobiologist E. O. Wilson (1994), a summer playing on the seashore and exploring the creatures he found there sparked his interest in the natural sciences.

The following examples come from the lives of Nobel Prize winners Albert Einstein, Robert Burns Woodward, and Richard Feynman. As a child, Albert Einstein's curiosity about natural phenomena was stimulated by play with a magnetic compass, puzzles, inventing, and model building—stimulation for eventual adult playfulness with phenomena and ideas (Frank, 1947, White & Gribbin, 1994; Rogers & Sluss, 1999). Einstein's famous statement that "imagination is more important than knowledge" indicated the value he placed on playing with ideas. Robert Burns Woodward, organic chemist, set up a basement chemistry lab as a child, engaging his imagination with current issues in chemistry. According to his daughter (Woodward, 1989, p. 248), his lifetime work was playful, carrying over "into mature forms of search and research." Richard Feynman, physicist, recalled the importance of childhood play in his autobiography describing the gadget making and general "piddling around" he did in his home laboratory. As an adult, Feynman (1985, p. 157) reflected that he used to "enjoy doing physics" because he "used to play with it." A conscious decision, "I'm going to play with physics, whenever I want to, without worrying about any importance whatsoever," resulted in the Nobel Prize. The wobble of a plate thrown in the air at a cafeteria led Feynman to play with rotating objects. "The diagrams and the whole business that I got the Nobel Prize for came from that piddling around with the wobbling plate" (p. 158).

According to Csikszentmihalyi (1996) who studied the backgrounds of creative people, E. O. Wilson and cancer researcher George Klein both credited their Boy Scout experiences, especially the ability to follow their own interests, for their careers in science. Brockman (2004) asked 27 eminent scientists to respond to his question: "What happened when you were a kid that led you to pursue a life in science?" Although many different family and situational variables were included in their responses, all shared a curiosity and deep passion for learning and many mentioned childhood experiments and the importance of growing up surrounded by nature. According to Cobb (1977) in a classic book on the ecology of childhood as well as chemist Padilla-Concepcion (2005) writing about youth in the Philippines, the early years are the most important in the development of creative thinking and a joy and sense of wonder about the natural world.

What influence does schooling have on the development of scientists? According to the National Science Education Standards (National Research Council, 1996), science should be taught in schools in such a way that students learn about the nature of science and scientific inquiry through engagement in true inquiry that models how science is actually conducted. Einstein said that education should "evoke the spirit of play in children" (cited in Rogers and Sluss, 1999, p. 11).

However, the school experience of many creative scientists, including Einstein, was not positive. Schools generally do not encourage divergent thinking, but emphasize one correct answer (Loehle, 1990). Previous research by the first author (Jarrett, 1999) indicates that enjoyment of hands-on science in elementary school had an impact on interest in science as an adult and that considering a science activity *fun* motivated preservice teachers' plans to use that activity in the classroom (Jarrett, 1998). Unfortunately, however, most of the preservice teachers surveyed did not enjoy their elementary school science experience, i.e. they could think of no positive science experiences in their own elementary schooling.

In a retrospective study (Palmer, 1999), university students identified "made lessons fun/interesting" as one of the most important attributes of good high school science teaching. Some teachers deliberately try to make science fun, interesting, and exciting (Court, 1993; Beiersdorfer recognized . . ., 1995; Gass, 1998, 2002; Beiersdorfer, 2002; Zembylas, 2004). Beiersdorfer (2002, p. 1), nationally recognized for his excellent science teaching, describes the group projects he assigns in his university classes, some of which involve writing songs and plays. His philosophy is to "create a class environment where they [students] can combine the subject matter of geology or planetary science with their creative spirits." According to Beiersdorfer, "teaching and learning strategies based on engaging a student's creativity allow them to have fun as they learn science. Zoologist Lee Gass (1998, 2002), 2001 CASE Canadian Professor of the Year, describes his work with both high school and university students in ways that make learning creative, safe, and authentic.

However, Beiersdorfer and Gass appear to be unusual rather than typical in deliberately emphasizing fun and creativity. The general lack of mention of the positive influence of formal school experience prior to finding mentors in graduate school (Brockman, 2004; Csikszentmihalyi, 1996) suggests that most formal learning in science is not creative, fun, or engaging. Physician and creativity researcher Edward de Bono (1995, p. 2) claims that schools seldom teach skills of creative hypothesizing and therefore leave creativity to rebels who "can't plan the game and won't play the game."

The role of creative thinking in scientific discovery appears to be well documented (Frank, 1947; Arieti, 1976; Woodward, 1989; Garfield, 1989a; Garfield, 1989b; Loehle, 1990; Csikszentmihalyi, 1996; Kuhn, 1996; Gregory, 1997; Miller, 2000; Padilla-Concepcion, 2005; Doomen & Leuven, n.d.). In his study of creative processes, Arieti (1976) gives examples of leaps of creative thinking as scientists through history made sudden connections or saw patterns; e.g., Newton, the falling apple, and gravity; Galileo, a swinging lamp, and the period of a pendulum; Archimedes, water displacement, and specific gravity; Roentgen, a glowing barium platinocyanide screen, and X rays; and Fleming, the absence of bacteria, and penicillin. Such occurrences, whether or not they are fully authenticated, illustrate the scientists' propensity for playing with ideas, seeing patterns, and making connections. According to Root-Bernstein and Root-Bernstein (2004, p. 138), scientists and artists "use common tools for thinking."

Some writers have tried to identify the scientific processes that involve creativity. Physicist and physiologist Herman Helmholtz identified the cyclical nature of his creative work: "(1) an initial investigation carried on until it is impossible to go further; (2) a period of rest and recovery; and (3) the occurrence of a sudden and unexpected solution" (Arieti, 1976, p. 268). Klahr (2000, p. 19) identified six aspects of the scientific discovery process, some involving the "impenetrable mystery of creativity" and others involving "the best that systematic thought can produce." Doomen and Leuven (n.d.) illustrate the importance of taking time off to relax with the story of the German physicist Max Planck, who worked on a problem for five years, put aside the assumptions he was making, left the problem for a few days and found the solution. Research ecologist Craig Loehle (1990) identified originality/creativity as one of the four requirements for a successful career in science, along with knowledge, technical skill, and communication ability. He says that the most important step in research is choosing a question to investigate after which "put your feet up on the desk and stare out the window. Try to elaborate the idea as much as possible" (p. 248).

What is the relationship between this kind of creativity and playfulness in scientific research? Kuhn (1996) uses play terminology to describe creativity in normal science and in science involving major shifts in thinking. According to Kuhn (1996, p. 52–53) normal science is a "puzzle-solving activity" and discovery commences with the awareness of anomaly; i.e., with the recognition that "nature has somehow violated the paradigm-induced expectations that govern normal science." Kuhn describes major shifts in scientific theories (paradigm shifts) as shifts from "a game played under one set of rules" to the requirement of another set of rules. Biochemist and historian Robert Scott Root-Bernstein identifies several mental qualities that appear to be essential for scientific discovery including "game playing (a willingness to goof around); a facility for cultivating a 'degree of chaos;' . . . and a facility for recognizing patterns" (cited in Garfield, 1989b, p. 316). Theorists on creativity (Arieti, 1976; Csikszentmihalyi, 1996) claim strong links among creativity, play, and playfulness. Three papers that explore the role of playfulness among scientists are: *Playfulness in the biological sciences* (Ganschow with Ganschow, 1998), *Chemists and play* (Kean, 1998), and *Science through play*, by neuropsychologist Richard Gregory (1997). Ganschow and Ganschow (1998), reflecting on Watson and Crick's discovery of the structure of the DNA molecule as well as their own professional experiences, speculate that playfulness among biologists involves the satisfaction of curiosity. They suggest that the scientific process can be categorized into playful and non-playful aspects, with playfulness appropriate and perhaps even necessary at the hypothesis development and inference drawing stages. Part of the playfulness of the latter stage comes from attending conventions and sharing ideas and fun with colleagues. However, between these come the non-playful experimentation/observation phases.

According to Kean (1998), chemists often play with chemistry throughout their careers. She cites a chemist who claims, "I still like to blow things up!" (p. 471). Chemists gain personal satisfaction from figuring out how the world works, attending conferences where there is often a playful sense of community, and seeking out opportunities to share chemistry with children and the general public.

Gregory (1997), drawing on his own research experience and his involvement with hands-on science museums, identified three playful processes of individual and scientific discovery: exploration, explanation, and computation. Since thinking and methods in geology are somewhat different from those of biology and chemistry (Frodeman, 1995; Seddon, 1995; Peters, 1996), a look at creativity and playfulness in the conduct of geoscience research could contribute to the discussion of playfulness in scientific research.

METHOD

The geoscience faculty included in this study were part of a consortium of researchers engaged over a six-year period in a National Science Foundation funded Research Experiences for Undergraduates (REU) summer program. The faculty were from a host research university, a historically black college, a community college, a small state university, and a small private college. Over the six summers, faculty worked with teams of three to five students on four different research projects. Several faculty worked with each team and some faculty worked with more than one team. The research projects were developed out of the interests of the faculty, although students had considerable input affecting projects' evolution each year. Three projects concerned the origin of rocks in various parts of Georgia and involved mineral analysis, examination of fossils, and analysis of fluids trapped in rocks. The fourth project investigated evidence of pollutants in salt marshes. Most projects had field trips for collection of rock specimens with most of the work done in the research university laboratories using sophisticated instruments. Faculty remarked in other surveys conducted during the program (Jarrett & Burnley, 2002) that they enjoyed working together, and those who did not normally have access to good laboratory facilities were particularly grateful for the opportunity to engage in research using state-of-the-art equipment.

The data for this paper were collected from faculty at two times during the program. During the summer of 2000, 11 faculty filled out the Statements about Science Instrument (SASI), a questionnaire on the nature of science and perceptions about scientists, developed by the authors (Burnley, Evans, & Jarrett, 2002). A twelfth professor joined the groups in 2002 and filled out the questionnaire at that time. The following three questions from the SASI, which could relate to playfulness (creativity and intuition), were analyzed in this research:

6. ____ Scientific thinking is logical and linear and does not involve intuition.
   ____ Scientific thinking is a combination of logic and intuition.
   ____ Scientific thinking is primarily intuitive.

7. ____ When developing a research question, logic is more important than creativity.
   ____ When developing a research question, creativity is more important than logic.
   ____ Developing research questions involves only logical thought.
   ____ Developing research questions involves only creativity.

8. ____ When examining data, logic is more important than creativity.
____ When examining data, creativity is more important than logic.
____ Examining data requires only logical thought
____ Examining data requires only creative thought.

On the last day of the 2004 summer program, nine professors completed a questionnaire with the following open-ended questions:

1. What experiences did you have as a child playing with science?
2. Discuss briefly if and when you felt playful in a school and/or university science class or science lab.
3. Were there any times during the program this summer when you felt playful or could describe your experience as fun? Describe.
4. Evaluate the role of playfulness, inspiration, or "ah-ha" feelings you have had while doing research. Give examples.

Responses to the survey questions were analyzed using constant comparative analysis (Glaser & Strauss, 1967) to identify themes. To help establish trustworthiness (Lincoln & Guba, 1985), master's students unrelated to the research also analyzed the responses for themes so that they could be compared and discussed.

RESULTS

Three of the faculty answered the survey questions very briefly, but the other six wrote with great enthusiasm, sometimes continuing their answers on the back of the page. The questions seemed to have prompted memories that they wanted to describe and upon which they enjoyed reflecting.

Questions one and two (above) were analyzed to identify themes in what the professors considered playful in their childhood experiences with science, both informally and in school or in university classes.

Childhood Experiences Playing With Science

The faculty members were particularly enthusiastic in describing childhood play experiences. Responses suggest that "wow" experiences, as well as the ability to explore, made a deep impression on them and perhaps interested them in science. The dominant answers of both men and women involved: (a) outdoor play, in their own yards and neighborhoods and on family vacations; (b) "kitchen chemistry," messing around with household items; and (c) making collections, especially rock and fossil collections. Four professors each mentioned these themes.

In addition, two professors mentioned museum membership and frequent visits, and two discussed the joy of exploring with chemistry sets, microscopes or telescopes. No one mentioned any other "science toys," perhaps because they were not asked specifically about toys. Two other themes emerged, both male-dominated: (a) taking things apart and (b) dangerous or inappropriate play. The latter included fireworks construction, building of "weapons" such as a slingshot, bow and arrow, and pop gun, taking wings off flies, killing worms with too much water, and starting fires. Only one professor mentioned schoolteachers as making science fun or influencing their thinking. For a few, the connection between childhood play and specific professional interests was obvious. A professor studying sedimentology wrote about family vacations collecting fossils. The professor studying ocean and marsh sedimentology wrote:

> Every outdoor experience was observational. We camped or went to a beach with little development, offering us the chance to observe and appreciate the natural world, including, growing horseshoe crab eggs, cutting up fish (for dinner!), and learning about wave motion while swimming, etc.

Times Faculty Felt Playful in a School and/or University Science Class or Science Lab

Two professors said that they were not playful in school. One of these, who had identified many playful experiences with her family said: "I don't recall ever feeling playful in a science class. School was always very serious for me. Work is also generally quite serious and disciplined as well. When I worked with [a specific professor] at [a northeastern] University, I noticed that he had a playful spirit, which I admired and enjoyed. He was very creative and I believe that some of his brilliant creations (he is very highly regarded and is one of the most prolific inventors of diamond anvil cells) came from his playfulness."

The rest gave many examples of fun, joyful, or playful experiences, including doing fieldwork, identification of rocks and minerals, or experimenting with particular phenomena. One said, "The reason I went into geology was the chance to 'play' outside—go on field trips/camping trips and that has continued." Several mentioned fun class activities; e.g., volcano models, Jell-O illustrating rock folding, and making liquid oxygen.

Projects and experiments arising out of their own interests were especially fun, as shown by examples from two professors: "I remember in sixth grade getting to show my class as well as younger elementary classes what was in pond water as well as growing yeast to show them. I really feel like I have played at sciences always." "Science experiments were always 'playful,' in that it was fun to try different things to see what worked. I once tried rubbing alcohol instead of water with plaster of Paris, because I knew it evaporated faster. But of course I learned that the reaction was a chemical one, so alcohol did not work."

The one example of inappropriate play was given by a woman: "In physics class (12th grade) we generated an electrical circuit experiment. Most classmates had linked up light bulbs and bells. We rigged the metal chairs of the row of students in front of us and watched them jump up from their seats as the circuit breaker was closed. It was very amusing but we all got detention for it."

Views on the Roles of Logic and Creativity in Hypothesis Generation and Data Examination

To determine what the faculty believed about the role of creativity and logic in the research process, responses on the three SASI questions were tabulated. On question six concerning scientific thinking, 11 faculty members said that scientific thinking is a combination of logic and intuition. Only one faculty member chose the first answer indicating that no intuition is involved in scientific thought. On question seven on the role of creative versus logical thought in developing hypotheses, 10 faculty members indicated that logic and creativity are both important but that logic is more important than creativity in developing hypotheses. The other two indicated that creativity is more important than logic in this part of the scientific process. For question eight on the roles of creativity and logic when examining data, nine of the faculty said that logic was more important than creativity in data analysis. The other three indicated that examining data required only logical thought.

The Role of Fun and Playfulness While Engaging in Scientific Investigations

Questions three and four related to their faculty research and in particular their research with the summer program. Answers were analyzed to identify elements of play and playfulness in different aspects of research.

Times During the Summer's Program When Faculty Felt Playful or Could Describe the Experience as Fun.

One professor, who did not go into the field, said he did not have any examples of playfulness: "We worked hard. Field work might lend itself to more 'playful' experiences." Actually, most examples from the other professors involved field experiences although others mentioned fun in the lab. Lab experiences that were fun for the faculty included observing items such as dust and hair at 50,000 X magnification under the Scanning Electron Microscope, picking fossils, and identification of minerals in thin section. Faculty found it fun to problem solve with the data, to watch students "get it," successfully fix equipment, or to find meaning in the data and drawing conclusions. Only one professor mentioned the fun of planning with other faculty members, a social/intellectual aspect of the program. One professor identified a variety of aspects that could be considered fun: "The field trip to the GA [Georgia] coast to get the samples. Students always enjoy that aspect of the work. Different tasks can be 'fun' depending on the researcher's perspective. Some people enjoy the challenge of working out problems, same as working on a jig-saw puzzle."

The Role of Playfulness, Inspiration, or "Ah-Ha" Feelings while Doing Research, with Examples.

Seven professors gave examples of fun, inspiration, or "ah-ha" feelings as a part of their career. Some gave specific examples, such as the "ah-ha" feelings involved in getting an identification correct, producing a good graphic, and seeing interrelationships. One discussed the role of recreational experiences such as hiking or scuba diving in arousing curiosity and inspiring a line of inquiry. She gave the following examples: "I was snorkeling and saw some spherical objects congregating at the trough of a rippled area. I did not know what they were but later after I found out what they were, I ended up looking specifically to see where they were and I ended up writing a paper on their relationships (the objects were rhodoliths—calcareous algal nodules). Similarly I have picked up rocks with trace fossils while hiking that have eventually led to papers/presentations on a 'new' or different type of trace."

Starting with the example of analyzing core samples, one professor discussed the role of fun and inspiration in the research process:

> I am forever amazed when I pull a core out of the ground, that I am looking back in time and viewing something no one has ever seen before. I also I like to imagine myself as a detective and so acquire much data/make many observations. I love to "figure it out"—that moment when I synthesize my qualitative and quantitative data and write the story/explanation/history—basically answer my starting question. The process in reaching that understanding is the most fun and potentially the most frustrating. But chasing down papers which you hope support your hypothesis, and which do!! is grand. When I compare my interpretation to others and it works, that's also fun. For this reason writing the paper is fun, until it becomes far too detail oriented, or I am forced to make changes for review/publication. That's often a challenge to get excited about.

Others gave a general philosophy on the general role of fun:

- Research is fun for me. If it wasn't, I most likely would not do it. The excitement of finding new things spurs me on.
- The "ah-ha" moments are what keep us going. Long periods of little progress punctuate with sudden insight and understanding. Suddenly the work is fun again after long periods of drudgery.
- These things [playfulness, inspiration, or 'ah-ha' feelings] maintain interest and motivation.

Although they easily answered the first question about their childhood play, three professors said they had difficulty using the word "play" to describe these enjoyable/fun work situations. One professor who had said that she rarely does things that are not fun and therefore makes things fun, said "I am always serious when collecting data because collecting good data requires concentration. I often giggle and keep it light while working but I still stay focused. I suppose it's a semantic issue with the word play. I wouldn't say I am playing while working but I usually am joyful and coincidentally revel in the process even when concentrating. [Play implies irresponsible action.]" (The brackets are included in the response) Another said "'Play' I think is the wrong word. It implies not being focused, haphazard. But I have had inspirations or 'ah-ha' feelings . . ." The third said, "Playfulness is a hard term for me to apply to what I do unless I think of it in terms of exploration and pattern recognition. Looking at new information and looking for patterns, extracting deeper meaning/paradigms/frameworks is rewarding for me."

DISCUSSION

When discussing their childhood play experiences, the faculty showed similarities to famous scientists discussed in the literature (Wilson, 1994; Brockman, 2004; Feynman, 1985), especially in their mention of playful exploration and experimentation that increased their interest in the natural world. What was unique among these geologists was a tendency to be collectors, especially collectors of rocks and fossils. For many, their interests in the outdoors, e.g. woods and beaches, the tendency to collect, and the engagement in experimentation (kitchen chemistry) had obvious connections to their present field and laboratory work. Interesting was the mention by two quite respectable male professors of unsafe or inappropriate play as children. Such play has not been mentioned in retrospective studies reviewed in this paper. Perhaps scientists do not generally want to admit to such behavior.

Most of the professors gave examples of enjoyable hands-on experiments at school, especially when they could take the initiative or gain recognition for being knowledgeable. Sadly, a few could think of no time when science was fun at school. Fortunately, experiences with family and in informal science settings helped to develop their interest in science. If school science were more generally taught using inquiry methods recommended by the National Science Education Standards (National Research Council, 1996), schools could potentially play a stronger role in interesting students in careers in science and technology. However, the pressure to raise tests scores has promoted more rigid academic approaches to learning (Ziegler and Bishop-Josef, 2004) and has removed much of the fun and inquiry promised in the National Science Education Standards.

In terms of the roles of logic, intuition, and creativity, there was agreement by most of the faculty that scientific thinking involves both intuition and logic and that creativity and logic both play a role in research question development and data analysis. Most felt that logic was more important than creativity, with the minority stating that creativity was more important than logic in the development of a research question and that only logic was needed for data analysis. The findings are in agreement with Granshaw with Granshaw (1998) in that logic and creativity are both important in the generation of research questions. However, Granshaw with Granshaw (1998, p. 458) emphasized more clearly that in the generation of hypotheses "the basis of scientific creativity" can be playful as new ideas are explored. The geologists were in general agreement with Granshaw with Granshaw (1998, p. 458): in examining data, "if the scientist becomes too playful during this period, he or she could diminish the interpretability of the experiment by not attending critically to the design and procedural issues." One suggestion for future research might be to separate "examining data" into its data analyses and data interpretation phases. Data analysis may require more logic and data interpretation may require more creativity.

In discussing the times during the summer when they were having fun or feeling playful and in discussing the role of playfulness, inspiration, or "ah-ha" feelings while doing research, the professors gave examples similar to those found in the literature: the fun of solving problems, seeing patterns, and having sudden insights. Several mentioned the cyclical nature of drudgery and fun in scientific research. Many found their most fun to be in fieldwork, enjoyment of the outdoors that may have drawn them to geology in the first place. One unique story involved constant receptivity to scientific thinking that enabled a professor to notice anomalies while on vacation, leading to research papers. Although readily giving examples about fun experiences and the role of inspiration in research, several professors did not want to use the word *play*. For them play was the opposite of work and involved irresponsible behavior. However, given Klugman & Fasoli's (1995) view that play contains elements of intrinsic motivation, free choice, enjoyment, activity, and non-literality, much of what they described would fit within the definition of *play*.

Returning to the overarching questions at the beginning of this paper, few are answered by the research reported here. The sample of geologists was small; interpretation was drawn from answers to just a few survey questions. However, the pattern seen is similar to that found in studies of eminent scientists in other fields. The role of play experiences inside and outside of formal learning settings appeared to have an important role in the development of productive scientific thinking, both for the scientists reviewed in the literature and for the geologists surveyed in this research. Some of the comments were fascinating and almost demand follow-up with additional questions to learn "the rest of the story." Interviews rather than written answers might be a better method of conducting future research in this area. As the need increases to recruit capable, creative young people into the sciences, more knowledge is needed about the importance of play and creative experimentation in the preparation of scientists and in the lives of scientists.

REFERENCES

Arieti, S. (1976). *Creativity: The magic synthesis*. New York: Basic Books, Inc., Publishers.

Beiersdorfer recognized for making geology playful. (1995, March/April). *Journal of College Science Teaching, 24* (5), 294.

Beiersdorfer, R. E. (2002). Tapping our students' creativity to learn earth and planetary science. *Lunar and Planetary Science, 33*. Retrieved May 31, 2005 from http://www.Lpi.usra.edu/meetings/lpsc2002/pdf/1355.pdf.

Brockman, J. (2004). (Ed.). *Curious minds: How a child becomes a scientist*. New York: Pantheon Books.

Burnley, P. C., Evans W. A, and Jarrett, O. S. (2002) Comparison of Approaches and Instruments for Evaluating a Geological Sciences Research Experiences Program, *Journal of Geoscience Education, 50* (1), 15–24.

Cobb, E. (1977). *The ecology of imagination in childhood*. Dallas: Spring Publications.

Court, D. (1993, May/June). A playful environment in a cooperative physics classroom, *Clearing House*, 66 (5), 295–298.

Csikszentmihalyi, M. (1996). *Creativity: Flow and the psychology of discovery and invention*. New York: HarperCollins Publishers.

de Bono, E. (1995, February). Serious creativity. *R&D Innovator#140, 4*(2). Retrieved May 31, 2005 from http://www.winstonbrill.com/bril001/html/article_index/articles/101–150/article140_body.html.

Doomen, P. & Leuven, K. U. (n.d.) *Creativity in science*. Retrieved May 31, 2005 from http:users.skynet.be/bs661306/peter/doc/hpv00r03-864.htm.

Feynman, R. P. (1985). *"Surely you're joking, Mr. Feynman!" Adventures of a curious character*. New York: Bantam Books.

Frank, P. (1947). *Einstein: His life and times*. New York: Alfred A. Knopf.

Frodeman, R. (1995). Geological reasoning: Geology as an interpretive and historical science. *Geological Society of America Bulletin, 107* (8), 960–968.

Ganschow, R. with Ganschow, L. (1998). Playfulness in the biological sciences In D. P. Fromberg & D. Bergen (Eds.), *Play from birth to twelve and beyond: Contexts, perspectives, and meanings* (pp. 455–460). New York: Garland Publishing.

Garfield, E. (1989a). Creativity and science, Part 1: What makes a person creative? In Essays of an information scientist: Creativity, delayed recognition, and other essays, Vol. 12, p. 296. Retrieved on May 31, 2005 from www.garfield.library.upenn.edu/essays/v12p296y1989.pdf.

Garfield, E. (1989b). Creativity and science, Part 2: The process of scientific discovery. In Essays of an information scientist: Creativity, delayed recognition, and other essays, Vol. 12, p. 314. Retrieved on May 31, 2005 from www.garfield.library.upenn.edu/essays/v12p314y1989.pdf

Gass, L. (1998, July) Teaching for creativity in science: An example. *Center for Development of Teaching and Learning Triannual Newsletter, 2* (2). Retrieved on June 9, 2005 from http://www.cdtl.nus.edu.sg/link/jul1998/practice1.htm.

Gass, L. (2002) An exercise in thinking, writing, and rewriting. Center for Development of Teaching and Learning Brief, National University of Singapore, 5 (4). Retrieved on June 9, 2005 from http://www.cdtl.nus.edu.sg/brief/v5n4/sec4.htm.

Glaser, B. G. & Strauss, A. L. (1967). *Discovery of grounded theory: Strategies for qualitative research*. Hawthorne, NY: Aldine de Gruyter.

Gregory, R. (1997). Science through play. In R. Levinson & J. Thomas, (Eds.), *Science today: Problem or crisis?* (pp. 192–205). New York: Routledge.

Jarrett, O. S. (1998). Playfulness: A motivator in elementary science teacher preparation. *School Science and Mathematics, 98* (4), 181–187.

Jarrett, O. S. (1999). Science interest and confidence among pre-service elementary teachers. *Journal of Elementary Science Education, 11* (1), 49–59.

Jarrett, O. S. & Burnley, P. C. (2002, April). Three years of authentic earth science research: Implications for teaching and learning. Paper presented at the annual meeting of the National Association for Research in Science Teaching, New Orleans.

Kean, E. (1998) Chemists and play. In D. P. Fromberg & D. Bergen (Eds.), *Play from birth to twelve and beyond: Contexts, perspectives, and meanings* (pp. 468–472). New York: Garland Publishing.

King, N. R. (1982). Children's play as a form of resistance in the classroom. *Journal of Education, 164* (4), 320–329.

King, N. R. (1986). When educators study play in schools. *Journal of Curriculum and Supervision, 1* (3), 233–246.

Klahr, D. (2002). *Exploring science: The cognition and development of discovery processes*. Cambridge, MA: The MIT Press.

Klugman, E. & Fasoli, L. (1995). Taking the high road toward a definition of play. In E. Klugman (Ed.). *Play, Policy and Practice* (pp. 195–201). St. Paul, MN: Redleaf Press.

Kuhn, T. S. (1996). *The structure of scientific revolutions, 3rd Edition*. Chicago: The University of Chicago Press.

Lincoln, Y. S. & Guba, E. G. (1985). *Naturalistic inquiry*. Newbury Park, CA: Sage Publications.

Loehle, C. (1990). A guide to increased creativity in research—Inspiration or perspiration? In Essays of an information scientist: Creativity, delayed recognition, and other essays, Vol. 13, p. 242–251. Retrieved on May 31, 2005 from www.garfield.library.upenn.edu/essays/v13p240y1990.pdf.

Miller, A. I. (2000). *Insights of genius: Imagery and creativity in science and art*. Cambridge, MA: The MIT Press.

National Research Council. (1996). *National science education standards*. Washington, DC: National Academy Press.

Padilla-Concepcion, G. (2005). Developing creativity in science among our youth, *Manilla Star*, May 5, 2005. Retrieved May 31, 2005 from http://www.newsflash.org/2004/02/si/si002004.htm.

Palmer, D. (1999). Students' perceptions of high quality science teaching. *Australian Science Teachers Journal*, 45 (3), 41–45.

Peters, E. K. (1996). *No stone unturned: Reasoning about rocks and fossils*. New York: W. H. Freeman and Company.

Rogers, C. S. & Sluss, D. J. (1999). Play and inventiveness: Revisiting Erikson's views on Einstein's playfulness. In S. Reifel (Ed.), *Play & culture studies, Volume 2: Play contexts revisited* (pp. 3–24). Stamford, CT: Ablex Publishing Corporation.

Root-Bernstein, R. & Root-Bernstein, M. (2004). Artistic scientists and scientific artists: The link between polymathy and creativity. In R. J. Sternberg, E. L. Grigorenko, J. L. Singer (Eds.). *Creativity: From potential to realization* (pp. 127–151). Washington, D.C.: American Psychological Association.

Seddon, G. (1996). Thinking like a geologist: The culture of geology, Mawson Lecture 1996. *Australian Journal of Earth Sciences, 43*, 487–495.

White, M. & Gribbin, J. (1994). *Einstein: A life in science*. New York: Dutton.

Wilson, E. O. (1994). *Naturalist*. Washington, DC: Island Press.

Woodward, C. E. (1989). Art and elegance in the synthesis of organic compounds: Robert Burns Woodward. In D. B. Wallace & H. E. Gruber (Eds.). *Creative people at work: Twelve cognitive case studies* (pp. 227–253). New York: Oxford University Press.

Zembylas, M. (2004). Young children's emotional practices while engaged in long-term science investigation. *Journal of Research in Science Teaching, 41* (7), 693–719.

Zigler, E. F. & Bishop-Josef, S. J. (2004). Play under siege: A historical overview. In E. F. Zigler and S. J. Bishop-Josef (Eds.). *Children's play: The roots of reading* (pp. 1–13). Washington, DC: Zero to Three Press.

Part IV

PLAY, COMMUNICATION, AND LITERACY

Chapter Twelve

Storybook Time and Free Play: Playing with Books

Laurelle Phillips

Recent research on ways young children become literate has evolved into an emergent literacy perspective in which reading, writing, listening, and speaking are viewed as interrelated, developing together, and beginning at earlier ages than formal schooling (Tabors, Snow, & Dickinson, 2001). As one aspect of this process, literacy has been incorporated into play in early childhood classrooms (Gillespie, Pelren & Twardosz, 1998; Neuman & Roskos, 1992; Roskos & Neuman, 2001; Rowe, 1994; Schrader, 1989). For young children, play is the medium for learning.

One important responsibility for teachers who work with young children is to encourage children's interest in and exploration of books and reading. The traditional scheduled times in early childhood classrooms for literacy are during storybook reading time and free play. Storybook reading usually consists of reading to a group of children. The National Association for the Education of Young Children (NAEYC) (Bredekamp & Copple, 1997) and the Joint Position Statement of the International Reading Association (IRA) and NAEYC (1998) have advocated reading to young children in small groups. Despite the recent emphasis on early language and literacy development (National Research Council, 2001; IRA/NAEYC, 1998), the resources do not exist to read to each child on a one-to-one basis (Morrow, 2001). In fact, the most common storybook reading context, even for two-year-old children, is the whole or large group (Phillips & Twardosz, 1995).

Free play is a time when young children have a choice of materials to use. Books and literacy materials are usually included in these choices. Reading to children also may influence their choice to read when they have the opportunity. A recent study of three- and four-year-old children by Neuman (1999) found that children who were in the Read Aloud program "wanted to be read to more frequently, to spend more time pretending to read, and to look at books during free play than did their counterparts in the control classrooms (p. 301)." The Read Aloud program flooded the classrooms with books and provided training for the teachers in reading storybooks aloud. One line of investigation that increased the number of books and other literacy materials in all areas of the early childhood classroom for free play found that this led to greater use of literacy materials, including books (Neuman & Roskos, 1992; Schrader, 1989). The presence of adults in the book area and rotation of the book collection also have been found to have positive results encouraging children to use books during free play (Gillespie, Pelren, & Twardosz, 1998).

We do know that children who are read to at an early age in their homes are more interested in books and reading, and it follows that this is also an important part of being in child care. From the literature about reading books in homes, we know that children need to be engaged in the process. Wells (1986) documented the importance of interaction with young children while reading and Heath (1982) investigated the importance of children being engaged in the process of storybook time. In addition to having a book read to them, children need to be active in the process, through interactions and "playing" with literacy materials (Barrentine, 1996; Saracho, 2004; Wells, 1986).

For two-year-old children, the opportunity to hear, use, and interact with books and language during storybook time assumes particular importance because language acquisition is highly dependent on language stimulation (Hart & Risley, 1995; Snow, Tabors & Dickinson, 2001). Two-year-old children need to hear the words read, use words functionally and receive responses from others. Children need patient listening by sensitive and familiar adults because their speech is often difficult to interpret and they need assistance in finding words to express themselves. Two-year-old children vary considerably in their acquisition of and ability to use language (Hart & Risley, 1995; Whitehurst & Fischel, 1994), necessitating individualized attention.

This study was based on social constructivist theory that values the social interaction occurring between adults and children as well as between peers. Vygotskian theory emphasizes interaction between the adult and child, or child and more capable peer, as scaffolding that supports and assists the development of social concepts, such as reading (Brooks & Brooks, 1993). Thus, through reading aloud to the child, asking questions, and soliciting responses, the adult is scaffolding and modeling ways to interact with literature. Through listening to storybooks, interacting with storybooks, and handling storybooks, the child is reviewing, refining, and constructing their own knowledge of the social concepts of literacy. Ideally, storybook reading occurs within "guided" participation (Rogoff, 1998), where the adult adjusts the level of support according to the child's changing abilities, resulting in performance that would be impossible if the child were operating alone.

As the child internalizes the relevant ways of thinking and is able to perform more of the activity independently, the zone shifts and the adult must adjust support (Vygotsky, 1978). From this perspective, the child's active participation is critical for learning and development, as has been demonstrated in a number of studies (Arnold, Lonigan, Whitehurst, & Epstein, 1994; Honig & Shin, 2001; Senehal, Thomas, & Monker, 1995). Thus, the construction of knowledge is accomplished in a play environment through social interaction, where reading in small groups and choosing books during free play is available.

The purpose of this study was to describe the variety of non-verbal ways that two-year-old children participate with books during storybook reading, a topic about which there is little empirical information (Yaden, Rowe, & MacGillivray, 2000). The second purpose was to identify ways two-year-old children use books during free play following storybook reading.

METHODS

Participants and Setting

Participants included 15 children and six teachers from one center. The children were divided between two two-year-old children's classrooms. Classroom One had seven children and Classroom Two had eight children, whose ages ranged from 24 to 35 months at the beginning of the study (mean age = 30.33 months). Two teachers were present in each classroom each day.

Both classrooms had similar daily schedules that consisted of free play, snacks, lunch, naptime, and a structured group time. Both classrooms contained a well-defined book area with pillows for seating, book racks with books displayed, and posters of children and adults reading together. Each classroom had a 30-minute scheduled free play time when each child could choose activities in which to participate. These activities included blocks, art, puzzles, small manipulatives, housekeeping, and books.

Every two weeks, two new sets of books were introduced into the center. Each set contained two books from each one of five predetermined categories. One set of 10 books went into Classroom One and one set of 10 books went into Classroom Two. At the end of the week, the sets were rotated between the classrooms. Each set was composed of five categories as described by Gillespie, Pelren, and Twardosz (1998), and included word or picture identification books (concept books), rhyme or song books, simple narratives, ABC or number books, and predictable books that repeated words or phrases in a pattern. The book titles were selected from the local public library and were identified by the National Library Association as appropriate for very young children (Hooks, 1986; Lipson, 1992). In addition, there were some books defined by the teachers as "favorite" books of the children, and these books remained displayed and available for children's use.

Each day the teachers selected two books from the set to read and discuss with a group of children, so that by the end of the week, each book had been read during storybook reading time. Storybook reading was recorded on videotape for four days each week during the 14 weeks of the study. Following storybook reading, the children were free to choose areas of the classrooms in which to play, with the book area being one of the choices. At least one teacher was present in the book area for at least 10 minutes of free play to read at a child's request.

Measures

Storybook reading sessions were videotaped and transcribed for non-verbal communications. Storybook reading was videotaped three to four times each week for approximately 10 minutes each day for 14 weeks. The videotapes were transcribed and used for analysis. With the assumption that non-verbal participation is an important aspect of communication when studying two-year-old children's interaction with storybooks, all transcripts from this study were reviewed to establish recurring themes using an open coding system. Open coding is "the process of breaking down, examining, comparing, conceptualizing and categorizing data" (Strauss & Corbin, 1990, p. 61), and can be used for theme analysis outside the context of a purely qualitative study. Open coding was undertaken independently by the author and a research assistant who was not involved in the data collection and was unfamiliar with the purpose of the study. Each transcript was examined and all non-verbal participation was underlined and placed on a list with similar behaviors that were then given a conceptual label such as "body movement," "touching book," or "smiling." When a behavior did not seem to fit with others in the list, a new category was created. As the categories emerged, each behavior was reviewed to make sure it belonged in the original category or needed to be moved to another.

After all the data had been categorized, the categories were examined to check for overlaps among them. Some categories were renamed and re-sorted to accommodate new ways of conceptualizing the data. Behaviors were compared within and between categories so that each was conceptualized by one category of non-verbal participation.

The author and a research assistant independently coded the same set of eight transcribed storybook reading sessions into non-verbal categories and gave explanations when interpretations were questionable. Inter-rater reliability for categories of non-verbal participation averaged .96 (range .89–1.00) and was calculated by dividing the number of agreements by the sum of agreements plus disagreements.

Immediately following storybook reading, free play was observed three to four days each week for 30 minutes by trained graduate students. The observation system used a sequence of measures repeated every five minutes throughout free play. This measurement system was designed to record book use behaviors by children in early childhood settings (Reid & Twardosz, 1996; Gillespie, Pelren, & Twardosz, 1998). The sequence began with a brief narrative recording of the classroom activities followed by a PLA-Check in which the observer scanned the room from left to right, counting and recording the number of boys, girls, and teachers present in the classroom, followed by counting and recording the number of boys, girls and teachers involved with books. In the next step of the observation, the observer focused on a child who was using books for five seconds, then recorded the child's code, the name of the book used, and the way in which the book was being used.

After each child and teacher using books had been observed for five seconds, the observer recorded other activities in the classroom that might have an impact on book use until the next five-minute observation period began. This observation sequence was repeated throughout free play. In cases where no one was using books, the observers scanned the room frequently in order to begin a five-second observation immediately if someone began to use books. If no one used books by the end of the five-minute observation period, a new five-minute observation began, starting with a PLA-Check. Types of book use behaviors included:

Reading

Looking at pages silently, vocalizing, or talking about picture to self or to others.

Listening

Listening to another person read or talk about a book or show the pictures. The person may or may not also be looking at the pages, but is clearly attending to the book.

Book Handling

A transitional behavior that includes leafing through the pages of a book faster than is usually used for reading, preparing the book for reading, trying to choose a book, putting a book back on the shelf, and holding a book without reading or looking.

Discussing

This includes asking and answering questions, giving explanations, commenting about the meaning to the text or illustrations, naming and pointing out, reacting to others' comments, or discussing any aspect of the book or related topic.

Not Engaged

This is recorded when a child is in the book area but is not involved in any of the book use behaviors above. For example, the child might be lying down in the book corner.

The researcher simultaneously but independently recorded data with the observers for seven free play sessions distributed across the study. Agreement for book use was determined by comparing the times when both observers agreed it was occurring and ignoring times when neither observer recorded book use. The smaller percentage of book use was then divided by the larger percentage, yielding an average agreement of .99 (range .92–1.00).

Observer and Coder Training

Nine graduate students assisted with the research as observers or coders. Observer training consisted of reading the measurement manual, attending a seminar on the measurement system conducted by the investigator, practicing the measurement system with the investigator using a prepared videotape of group storybook reading, and discussing disagreements in scoring. Training for coders consisted of attending a seminar on the coding categories, practicing coding with a prepared transcription or videotape with the investigator, and discussing disagreements. Periodically, meetings were held during which procedural questions about the behavioral definitions and classroom events were discussed.

RESULTS

Non-verbal communication provided insight into what is important to two-year-old children when they participate in storybook reading. The recurring themes that emerged from the open coding analysis included: (1) behaviors involving the book being read; (2) behaviors involving another person; (3) emotional expression; and (4) extraneous body movements. Behaviors involving the book being read were divided into four subcategories as described below, and behaviors involving another person were subdivided into two categories of teacher and peer interaction. Table 12.1 contains a list of behaviors in each category.

Behaviors Involving Book Being Read

Pretending, or responding with action, occurred when children took on roles from the story, such as pretending to be falling leaves, fierce animals, or a character knocking on a door, honking a horn, or pounding a hammer. In addition, children pretended to eat or drink from the pages when items such as peas, ice cream, or popcorn were represented. Children also responded to the reading with physical movements such as nodding or shaking their heads, or touching their own elbow, chin, or knee when the story involved those body parts. Many of these responses were short episodes that related to a single page in a book.

Handling books actually being read occurred when children held the edges of the books, turned pages, and pointed to the illustrations, which was the most frequent way to handle a book being read. In addition to touching the page, a child might trace the picture of an object on the page with a finger or rub the illustration. Several children held the edge of the book and pulled it open wider in order to see better, and several children turned the pages backward to check on something they had missed that was under discussion. Children also turned the pages forward with or without guidance from the teacher.

In addition to handling books being read, children often held books other than the one being read, perhaps modeling the current teacher behavior. Children would take a book from the bookrack, hold it on their knees, turn the pages, and look at it while the teacher read a different book. In addition, children would reach for the book the teacher had just finished reading and take it from her. It was not clear if children were handling another book because

Table 12.1. Taxonomy of Non-Verbal Behaviors During StoryBook Time

1. Behaviors involving books
   - Ways to pretend/respond
     - growls at the page
     - pretends to eat peas, ice cream, cheese, popcorn, vegetables, etc.
     - blows on a page, as blowing bubbles
     - knocks on door knocker in the book
     - holds hands as if honking a horn
     - pretends to catch a cookie in the air
     - clasps hands together to make a sound like a cricket
     - pretends to pound a hammer
     - puts hands to mouth and pretends to toot a horn
     - pretends to be leaves falling with hand movements
     - raising hand to mouth, pretending to drink
     - clapping hands together as if to catch something
     - holding one hand in front of self like a stop sign
     - pretends to kiss
     - nods/shakes head
     - mouths words read
     - touches/points to own chin, elbow, arm, eye, knee, cheek, face
     - closes both eyes in secession, as if trying to blink
     - sticks out tongue
     - holds doll/toy/object
     - shakes head in time with poetry of the book
     - moves body in time with book/sways with song book
     - jumps up in the air and reaches an arm overhead as if plucking something out of the air
   - Ways to handle book being read
     - pointing to illustration, objects in book
     - glances at picture
     - holds onto edge of the book
     - points to page as counting objects
     - traces the opening of the round log/spots on ladybug
     - turns book back to front
     - turns page of book
     - turns page of book backward
     - rubs finger over the numerals
     - turns two pages at a time
     - touches the page the teacher is trying to turn
     - takes hold of the book edge and pulls it open wider
     - reaches for book edge
     - reaches out and turns page
     - hits book
     - trying to turn the pages of the book to the back
   - Ways to handle book not being read
     - holding another book
     - looking at another book
     - reaches for book teacher just finished reading/takes book from teacher
     - hands book to teacher

gets a book from the book rack
turns pages of book that is across knees and looks at it as teacher reads
gets a book, sits down and holds it
drops book had been holding
turning the book just finished over and over
Ways to get close to book
stands up
leans forward
gets on knees
jumps up
walks to side of book
stands in front of book
looks at book from side
looks at book upside down
moves around another child to get closer to book
walks to the book
scoots

2. Behaviors involving others
sitting/kneeling/standing beside/in front of/on lap/on teacher's knees
touching teacher's shoulder/arm/hair/knee
drops something in teacher's hand
turns head toward teacher
looks up at teacher
watches interaction between teacher and another student
watches and imitates another child
turns toward teacher
moves closer to another child
3. Emotional behaviors
laughs
cries
screams
smiles
4. Extraneous body movements
turns to look at pictures in room
puts hands in lap
pointing to objects in room
rearranges chair and sits down
bounces up and down on the mattress
picks up book on floor
playing with shoe laces
turning somersaults

---

they were not interested in the book being read, or if this was another aspect of holding or playing with toys during reading events.

The fourth behavior related to books being read involved ways to get close to the book or illustration. Children must be close to the book in order to touch or handle it, so they used a variety of movements to get closer. Some movements involved only slight changes of position, such as leaning toward the book or rising up on knees. Others were more obvious or distracting such as standing up, shuffling around another child, jumping up, walking to the side or front of the book, scooting toward the book, or crawling over other children.

Behaviors Involving Others

Interactions with teachers involved ways to be close to the teacher and to touch the teacher as she read. These strategies included touching the teacher's arm, pulling on her shoulder, looking at the teacher for a reaction, and turning toward the teacher. Interaction also involved sitting, kneeling, standing beside or in front of the teacher, and sitting on the teacher's lap. Children would sit as close as the teacher allowed, such as on her legs, lap, and arms, or encircled by the teacher's arms. These non-verbal ways of interacting with the teacher often produced no verbal response from the teacher but rather a physical reaction, such as a glance, nod, or readjustment of the children from an awkward sitting position. Children often touched the teacher as a way of reinforcing what they were verbally expressing.

Non-verbal interactions with other children involved watching others and turning to look at other children. Children also nodded their heads or followed another child's actions and imitated the actions. One observation captured a child putting both hands on another child's face and turning the second child's face toward the book being read, perhaps in an effort to share information or check their understanding. Participation that fit into this category occurred infrequently.

Emotional Expression

Emotions were expressed non-verbally as well as verbally and were fleeting events. They included smiling and expressions of dislike and interest. Although emotional expression occurred throughout the study, the variety was limited, with smiling being the most frequent expression. Children smiled when they saw an illustration that they liked, thought was funny, or was familiar. Storylines also drew smiles from the children.

Extraneous Body Movements

Some non-verbal participation did not appear to relate to the storybook reading, such as turning somersaults while the teacher was reading. Extraneous motions covered movements such as rearranging chairs, playing with

Table 12.2. Average Percentage of Interaction by Non-Verbal Categories

	Classroom One	*Classroom Two*
Behaviors involving books		
Ways to pretend or respond	20.53	17.09
Ways to handle book being read	44.29	40.92
Ways to handle book not being read	4.87	4.10
Ways to get close to book	14.64	20.70
Behaviors involving another person		
Involving the teacher	5.35	3.52
Involving peer	2.39	1.66
Emotional behaviors	3.14	4.00
Extraneous body movements	4.79	8.01

shoelaces, turning to look at pictures on the wall, and bouncing up and down on the mattress in the reading center. It was not clear if children were attending to the story while engaged in these actions, or if they had been distracted from the reading temporarily by objects in the area.

The percentage of non-verbal interactions by categories is presented in Table 12.2. As the table shows, more than 40 percent of the behaviors in both classrooms involved handling the book being read. This includes pointing to and touching the book, which occurred most often in this study. Children wanted to touch the book and to pretend with the book; for example, they would pretend to "grab" something from the pictures to eat or to "knock" on the picture of a door. The need to handle books and pretend resulted in children trying to get close enough to touch the book. The other categories were minor in relationship to these three areas, but important as ways children in this study communicated non-verbally.

PLA-Checks yielded a percentage of children involved in book use at one point in time during each five minutes of free play. These percentages were averaged to obtain a percentage for the day, week, and study. Table 12.3 provides the average percentage of book use per day by categories for each classroom. In Classroom One the average percentage of book use per day was 29 and in Classroom Two the average percentage of book use per day

Table 12.3. Average Percentage of Book Use Behaviors Per Day During Free Play

	R	*L*	*D*	*BH*	*NE*
Classroom One	13.0	44.5	18.5	18.0	6.0
Classroom Two	31.0	31.5	18.0	15.5	4.0

Note: R=Reading, L=Listening, D=Discussing, BH=Book Handling, NE=Not Engaged

was 36. Data on book use behaviors during free play produced a picture of how children used books. Children engaged in all categories of book use throughout the study, with Listening occurring most frequently in both classrooms. In Classroom One, Discussing and Book Handling were tied for second place. In Classroom Two, Reading was a close second to Listening.

DISCUSSION

This study provided the opportunity to examine non-verbal communication during storybook reading time in the lives of two-year-old children in child care. Non-verbal signals are an important communication tool for two-year-old children, useful in understanding the emotions, desires, and thoughts of young children who may not be adapt at verbally expressing themselves.

Similar to Senechal, Thomas, and Monker (1995), who found that three-year-old children who pointed to or labeled pictures had greater increases in vocabulary than non-involved children, this study found that the two-year-old children demonstrated involvement though attempts to touch the book, especially the illustrations. When children were not close enough to physically touch and handle the book, they used many strategies to move closer, such as scooting, walking, crawling, and jumping. The need for young children to touch the book or the illustrations is similar to findings of other emergent literacy researchers (Schrader, 1989) and similar to Phillips and Twardosz's (1995) identification of handling literacy materials as a category of book use for young children. Thus, the opportunity for a child to be close enough to touch the book is a recommendation for storybook reading with two-year-old children.

In addition to videotaping storybook reading, observations of book use during free play contributed knowledge concerning children's desire to use books and enjoyment of books in child care centers. In most two-year-old children's child care classrooms, there are opportunities during the day for free play, or time to choose from a variety of activities in which to participate. Books are often one of these choices. The children in this study were followed during free play to observe how children used books during voluntary book use times. Schrader (1989) speculated that the need to handle literacy materials might be similar to Piaget's stage of exploration in play.

With the growing body of research supporting the value of exploration of literacy materials, classrooms need to freely allow access to books and other literacy materials for explorations without restrictions about keeping books in the book area, or about using books in unconventional ways, except those that might result in books being damaged. Similar to Rowe (1994), children, at several times during this study, carried books to other centers, placed books into other toys for carrying, turned pages of books, and held books for no reason visible to the observer. Therefore, it is recommended that in addition to providing an adult who is accessible to read to children one-on-one or in a small group during free play, time should be provided for children to explore books on their own, especially following storybook reading, when children have the opportunity to continue to participate with the books immediately after hearing them read, and to continue to revisit previously read books.

In an effort to encourage children to voluntarily choose books, several suggestions have been made such as providing a comfortable book area with attractive, age-appropriate books that are rotated at least some of the time (Morrow, 2001). Gillespie, Pelren, and Twardosz (1998) found that rotating books each week and having a teacher present in the book area for part of free play resulted in more children choosing books. It is recommended that book use also be encouraged as play with literacy materials, as this may be necessary for developing concepts of literacy as well as motivation and enjoyment to read.

REFERENCES

Arnold, D. H., Lonigan, D. J., Whitehurst, G. J., & Epstein, J. N. (1994). Accelerating language development through picture book reading: Replication and extension of a videotape training format. *Journal of Educational Psychology, 86*, 235–243.

Barrentine, S.J. (1996). Engaging with reading through interactive read-alouds. *The Reading Teacher, 50*(1), 36–43.

Bredekamp, S., & Copple, C. (Eds.) (1997). *Developmentally appropriate practice in early childhood programs, revised edition*. Washington, DC: National Association for the Education of Young Children.

Brooks, J. G., & Brooks, M. G. (1993). *In search of understanding: The case for constructivist classrooms*. Alexandria, VA: Association for Supervision and Curriculum Development.

Gillespie, C., Pelren, S., & Twardosz, S. (1998). The ecological perspective on the voluntary book use of 2- and 3-year-olds in day care. *Early Education and Development 9*(3), 283–306.

Hart, B., & Risley, T. R. (1995). *Meaningful differences in the everyday experience of young American children*. Baltimore, MD: Paul H. Brookes.

Heath, S. B. (1982). What no bedtime story means: Narrative skills at home and school *Language in Society, 11*, 49–76.

Honig, A., & Shin, M. (2001). Reading aloud with infants and toddlers in child care settings: An observational study. *Early Childhood Education Journal, 28*(3), 193–197.

Hooks, W. H. (Ed.). (1986). *Choosing books for kids: How to choose the right book for the right child at the right time.* NY: Ballantine Books.

International Reading Association/National Association for the Education of Young Children. (1998). *Learning to read and write: Developmentally appropriate practices for young children: A joint position statement*. Washington, DC and Newark, DE: Authors.

Lipson, E. R. (1992). *The New York Times parent's guide to the best books for children*. NY: Random House.

Morrow, L. M. (2001). *Literacy development in the early years: Helping children read and write, 4th ed.* Boston: Allyn and Bacon.

National Research Council (2001). *Eager to learn: Educating our preschoolers*. Committee on Early Childhood Pedagogy. B. T. Bowman, M. S. Donovan, & M. S. Burns (Eds.). Commission on Behavioral and Social Sciences and Education. Washington, DC: National Academy Press.

Neuman, S. B. (1999). Books make a difference: A study of access to literacy. *Reading Research Quarterly 34*(3), 286–311.

Neuman, S. B., & Roskos, K. (1992). Literacy objects as cultural tools: Effects on children's literacy behaviors in play. *Reading Research Quarterly, 27*(3), 202–225.

Phillips, L.B., & Twardosz, S. (1995). *Ecological context and functions of emergent literacy: Two- and three-year-old children in day care*. Paper presented at the 45th Annual National Reading Conference, New Orleans, LA. .

Reid, K. A., & Twardosz, S. (1996). Use of culturally diverse books in daycare. *Early Education and Development, 7*(4), 319–348.

Rogoff, B. (1998). Cognition as a collaborative process. In d. Kuhn & R. S. Siegler (Eds.), *Handbook of child psychology: Vol. 1. Theoretical models of human development, 5th ed.* (pp. 679–744). NY: Wiley.

Roskos, K., & Neuman, S. B. (2001). Environment and its influences for early literacy teaching and learning. In S. B. Neuman & D. K. Dickinson (Eds.), *Handbook of early literacy research* (pp. 281–292). NY: The Guildford Press.

Rowe, D. W. (1994). Learning about literacy and the world: 2-year-olds' and teachers' enactment of a thematic inquiry curriculum. In C. Kinzer & D. J. Lewis (Eds.), *Multidimensional aspects of literacy research, theory, and practice: 43rd Yearbook of the National Reading Conference* (pp. 217–229). Chicago, IL: National Reading Conference.

Saracho, O. N. (2004). Supporting literacy-related play: Roles for teachers of young children. *Early Childhood Education Journal, 31*(3), 171–178.

Schrader, C. T. (1989). Written language use within the context of young children's symbolic play. *Early Childhood Research Quarterly, 4*, 225–244.

Senechal, M., Thomas, E., & Monker, J. (1995). Individual differences in 4-year-old children's acquisition of vocabulary during storybook reading. *Journal of Educational Psychology, 87*(2), 218–229.

Snow, C., Tabors, P., & Dickinson, D. (2001). Language development in the preschool years. In D. Dickinson & P. Tabors (Eds.), *Beginning literacy with language: Young children learning at home and school* (pp. 2–25). Baltimore: Paul H. Brookes.

Strauss, A., & Corbin, J. (1990). *Basics of qualitative research: Grounded theory procedures and techniques*. Newbury Park, CA: Sage Publications.

Tabors, P., Snow, C., & Dickinson, D. (2001). Homes and schools together: Supporting language and literacy development. In D. Dickinson, & P. Tabors (Eds.), *Beginning literacy with language: Young children learning at home and school* (pp. 313–334). Baltimore: Paul H. Brookes.

Vygotsky, L. S. (1978). *Mind in society: The development of higher psychological processes*. Cambridge, MA: Harvard University Press.

Wells, G. (1986). *The meaning makers: Children learning language and using language to learn*. Portsmouth, NJ: Heinemann.

Whitehurst, G. J., & Fischel, J. E. (1994). Practitioner review: Early developmental language delay: What, if anything, should the clinician do about it? *Journal of Child Psychology and Psychiatry, 35,* 613–648.

Yaden, D. B., Rowe, D. W., & MacGillivray, L. (2000). Emergent literacy: A matter (polyphony) of perspectives. In M. L. Kamil, P. B. Mosenthal, P. S. Pearson, & R. Barr (Eds.), *Handbook of reading research, Vol. III*, (pp. 424–454). Mahwah, NJ: Lawrence Erlbaum.

Chapter Thirteen

Effects of Environmental Print Games and Play Props on Young Children's Print Recognition

James Christie, Billie Enz, Myae Han, Jennifer Prior, and Maureen Gerard

Environmental print (EP) refers to print that occurs in real-life contexts (e.g., the word "Pepsi" on a soda can or "McDonald's" on a sign in front of a restaurant). Children begin to recognize EP at a very early age. Research has shown that many three- and four-year-olds can recognize and know the meanings of common product labels, restaurant signs, and street signs (Goodman, 1986; McGee, Lomax, & Head, 1988; Mason, 1980). Even if children do not say the correct word when attempting to read such print, they usually will come up with a related term. For example, when presented with a Pepsi can, the child might say "soda" or "Coke."

Initially, young children attend to the entire visual impact and context of EP—logos, colors, shape and size—rather than just the print (Masonheimer, Drum, & Ehri, 1984). As they grow older, children become able to recognize increasingly "decontextualized" forms of print. Research has revealed a general developmental progression of EP recognition: actual three-dimensional object, two-dimensional color picture of complete logo, stylized "word art" text from logo, text in generic font (Cloer, Aldridge, & Dean, 1981; Kuby, Aldridge, & Snyder, 1994). The ability to recognize isolated words in generic fonts is the usual "gold standard" for word recognition.

Considerable controversy surrounds the role of EP in early literacy development. Several research studies have reported that many children merely read the environment and do not pay attention to the actual print when they recognize EP, casting doubt on EP's contributions to print recognition (Masonheimer, Drum, & Ehri, 1984; Stahl & Murray, 1993). Other researchers have reported that children's responses to EP are influenced by print cues as well as contextual cues, a finding that suggests that EP may help children learn to recognize letters and words (Harste, Burke, & Woodward, 1981: McGee, Lomax, & Head, 1988).

EP's role in literacy education has been rather limited. Schools have traditionally focused on academic forms of print (i.e., alphabet charts, flash cards, textbooks) rather than the practical types of print that one finds outside of school (Hall, 1998). While EP is plentiful in the world outside of school, it is rare in preschool and kindergarten classrooms (Dunn, Beach, & Kontos, 2000). When one does find EP in a classroom, it is usually restricted to a few props in the dramatic play corner (e.g., several empty cereal boxes and other product containers placed in the kitchen area). This absence of EP in classrooms may be caused by teachers' views that EP is not important in early literacy learning, or it may reflect a hesitancy to promote commercial products.

The purpose of this study was to investigate the effects of bringing EP to the forefront in early childhood classrooms. To accomplish this, we developed a set of games and play props that focused children's attention on EP and exposed them to EP with different levels of decontextualization. We decided to use play-related EP materials in order to take advantage of the high level of interest and engagement that play elicits in children (Johnson, Christie, & Wardle, 2005). Next, we located several preschool, pre-kindergarten, and kindergarten classrooms that did not contain any EP. We then infused EP materials into half of these classrooms, and the other half served as control groups. We hypothesized that, by playing with the EP materials, children's recognition of specific EP words and their recognition of alphabet letter in general would both improve.

METHOD

The subjects were 24 students in two preschool classrooms (mean age = 4.5), 25 students in two early kindergarten classrooms (mean age = 5.2), and 32 students in two regular kindergarten classrooms (mean age = 5.6) located in three schools in a suburban school district. The schools served children from lower-middle and middle-income families. One preschool, one early kindergarten, and one kindergarten classroom were randomly assigned to an experimental treatment and the other three classrooms were assigned to a control condition. Prior to the beginning of the study all classrooms were observed to determine the use of EP. None of the classrooms contained EP displays, games, or play props, and EP was not used as an instructional tool by any of the teachers.

Data Collection

Prior to the start of the experiment, children in all six classrooms were individually assessed on two measures:

1. An EP recognition test in which children were asked to identify four levels of increasingly decontextualized EP (see Figure 13.1):
   - Level 1—real object
   - Level 2—color logo with print
   - Level 3—black-and-white stylized print
   - Level 4—black-and-white "generic" print

Level 1 – Real object (i.e., a Pepsi can)

Level 2 – Color logo with print

Level 3 – Black-and-white stylized print

Level 4 – Black-and-white "generic font" print

PEPSI

Figure 13.1. EP Test Levels.

There were ten items: Band-aid, Blockbuster video, Burger King, M&M's, McDonald's, Oreo, Pepsi, Pokemon, stop sign, and Teletubbies. Two points were scored for each correct answer, and one point was awarded if the child gave a response in the same category as the test item (e.g., "soda" for Pepsi). The maximum score was 80: 2 points times 10 items times 4 levels. Testing was suspended if a child missed five items in a row.

2. A letter recognition task in which children are asked to name the letters of the alphabet (in scrambled order). The maximum score was 52: 26 lower-case and 26 upper-case letters.

During the 10-week treatment period, researchers visited each of the experimental and control classrooms three times to determine the extent to which teachers were implementing the treatment conditions described below. The researchers took field notes on the literacy environment in each classroom, ongoing literacy activities and instruction, and how children in the experimental treatments interacted with the EP and responded to the environmental-print-focused instruction. After the experimental condition was implemented for 10 weeks, two pretest assessments were repeated as posttests.

Treatment Conditions

In the three experimental classrooms, materials were added to draw children's attention to a wide variety of EP, including the logos used in the EP recognition test. First, a number of EP puzzles and games were developed and placed in a learning center or table in each classroom:

- matching games—Logos were placed on a large laminated surface along with a Velcro strip on each logo and product names were on small cards with Velcro on the back. The child would attach each name card to the corresponding logo.
- simple shape puzzles—Product logo and product text names were placed on a foam board and then cut apart into interlocking pieces. The child could use both the shape and EP as cues to fit the pieces together.
- cereal box puzzles—The cover of a cereal box was cut into 10 to 15 pieces. Children would work individually or with a partner to put the box cover back together again.
- bingo games—Product logos were placed on a bingo board and the product names were on cards. Children would take turns placing name cards

on the corresponding logos. The first to get three in a row would be the winner.
- memory game—Two sets of 8 logos cards were mixed up and placed in a 4X4 grid. Players took turns, turning over two cards at a time. If the logos on the two cards matched, the player got to keep them.
- flip books—A book was made with two sets of pages, one on top of the other. Logos were placed on the top set of pages, and product names (text) were attached to the bottom pages. Children would turn the top and bottom pages until the name and logo matched.

In addition, theme-related EP was placed in the dramatic play center. For example, if the current play theme was "grocery store," EP such as store signs, shelf labels ("Cereal"), empty product boxes, and employee name tags were added. EP books (file folders containing related sets EP) were placed in the classroom library corner, and EP stationary was placed in the writing center.

New EP activities were introduced every other week throughout the 10-week study. Many of the materials and activities required children to match EP featuring different levels of decontextualization: real object, color logo with print, black-and-white "logo" print, and black-and-white "generic" print. The children played games with EP during large group, small group, and independent activity times. The rest of literacy curriculum and the total amount of time devoted to literacy activity remained the same.

In the control classes, no EP was added to the classroom. The children experienced the regular school literacy curriculum (e.g., storybook reading, phonemic awareness activities, letter recognition activities, etc.), which was very similar to the curriculum in the corresponding experimental classroom.

RESULTS

Table 13.1 reports the means and standard deviations of the pretest and posttest alphabet recognition scores by grade level and treatment, and Table 13.2 reports the same descriptive statistics for the EP test scores. These tables illustrate substantial differences in the pretest scores among the classrooms on both assessments. To compare growth over time, analysis of covariance (ANCOVA) using linear regression (Glass & Hopkins, 1996) was used to statistically control the initial differences in the children's pretest scores. Because all the subjects were from schools matched for SES, issues

Table 13.1. Effects of Environmental Print Games and Play Props.

Means and Standard Deviations of Pretest and Posttest Alphabet Recognition Scores

		Pretest		*Posttest*	
Grade Level	*N*	*Mean*	*SD*	*Mean*	*SD*
Preschool					
Experimental	12	17.0	15.4	20.4	17.4
Control	12	16.0	22.6	18.8	24.2
Pre-Kindergarten					
Experimental	11	45.4	7.5	43.3	11.7
Control	14	24.2	17.6	32.5	14.3
Kindergarten					
Experimental	15	25.8	19.2	39.7	14.2
Control	17	36.2	15.5	41.4	12.2

relating to homogeneity of variance were controlled in advance by the sampling process.

The statistical analysis of the alphabet recognition test results revealed only one significant difference. At the kindergarten level, the experimental group scored significantly higher than the control group (see Table 13.1). The kindergarten control group started the study with a 10-point advantage, but by the end of the study, the kindergarten experimental group had almost caught up with them. It is interesting that there was a reverse pattern at the pre-kindergarten level. Here the experimental started almost 20 points higher, but at the end of the study, the experimental group's lead over the control subjects had been whittled down to about 10 points. However, this difference between the two pre-kindergarten groups was not statistically significant.

The ANCOVA analyses of the EP recognition test data revealed that the experimental group subjects scored higher at all three grade levels, with the advantage being largest at the preschool and kindergarten levels. At the preschool level, the experimental group's total scores ($p < .001$), Level 1 scores ($p < .01$), Level 2 scores ($p < .05$), and Level 3 scores ($p < .01$) were all higher than those of the control group. At the pre-kindergarten level, the experimental group's scores were significantly higher than the control group's scores on the Level 3 part of the test ($p < .05$). At the kindergarten level, significant differences favoring the experimental group were found for total scores ($p < .01$) and Level 3 ($p < .000$). Across the grade levels, the experimental treatment appeared to have its maximum effect on the children's ability to recognize Level 3 EP, the level at which the logo and color cues are removed and only the stylized print remains.

Table 13.2. Effects of Environmental Print Games and Play Props.

		Level 1				Level 2			
		Pretest		Posttest		Pretest		Posttest	
Grade Level	*N*	*Mean*	*SD*	*Mean*	*SD*	*Mean*	*SD*	*Mean*	*SD*
Preschool									
Experimental	12	12.6	1.4	14.1	1.0	11.3	2.9	13.2	2.4
Control	12	11.8	4.4	12.4	2.0	8.9	5.1	10.5	4.2
Pre-Kindergarten									
Experimental	11	13.4	.8	14.4	.8	12.4	4.3	14.4	1.
Control	14	13.8	1.0	13.8	1.0	12.4	2.5	12.3	2.5
Kindergarten									
Experimental	15	12.4	3.0	13.8	2.0	12.0	3.4	13.3	2.6
Control	17	13.2	1.8	13.7	1.1	12.9	2.1	13.1	2.1

DISCUSSION

Our results showed that the EP games and play props were very effective in improving children's recognition of the actual EP that is used in the play materials. The effect was most prominent at Level 3, where the color and logo cues are removed and the child must just focus on the stylized print. This finding suggests that the EP games and props did focus children's attention on the print itself, which has the potential of promoting the recognition of letters and words.

The alphabet recognition test results were not as clear. The EP materials did result in a significant increase in the kindergartners' ability to recognize the letters of the alphabet. However, no difference was found at the preschool level, and the pre-kindergarten control subjects appeared to make more progress than those in the experimental class. However, there may have been a ceiling-effect at the pre-kindergarten level. The experimental class started out the study with a score of 45 (out of a possible 52) and did not have much room to make progress, whereas the control subjects started much lower and had plenty of room to grow.

Our field notes revealed a factor that we did not control: the way in which the teachers interacted with children while they played with EP materials. Each of the three experimental group teachers did this differently. The preschool teacher simply put out the materials and let the children explore them. The pre-kindergarten teacher set up the materials at a center, and an adult aide was always available to assist them while they played the EP games. The kindergarten teacher had a style of interaction that was in the middle—she made the props available and occasionally would interact

Level 3				*Level 4*				*Total*			
Pretest		*Posttest*		*Pretest*		*Posttest*		*Pretest*		*Posttest*	
Mean	*SD*	*Mean*	*SD*	*Mean*	*SD*	*Mean*	*SD*	*Mean*	*SD*	*Mean*	*SD*
3.6	3.3	8.0	5.0	.8	2.0	1.9	3.3	28.3	7.8	37.2	9.2
3.2	3.6	3.9	3.4	.8	2.3	.6	2.3	24.8	12.8	27.5	10.4
9.1	4.4	11.5	4.4	5.1	5.8	6.5	6.1	41.0	12.4	46.7	11.2
5.9	2.1	4.9	2.8	1.9	2.2	1.7	2.3	34.0	6.1	32.7	6.8
6.7	4.0	12.1	4.0	1.7	4.0	5.5	4.8	32.7	11.9	44.7	12.0
8.2	4.6	8.9	5.3	4.6	5.6	5.9	6.2	38.9	12.1	41.7	13.7

with the children while they were engaged with EP games or dramatic play. Of course, the kindergarten children were older and undoubtedly needed less assistance than the younger students in the pre-kindergarten classroom.

It is likely that these differences in teacher behavior may have affected our results. Neuman and Roskos (1993) and Vukelich (1994) both found that when young children played in literacy-enriched settings with a supportive adult, their ability to recognize the EP that was in the setting increased more than when there was no adult support. These researchers refer to Vygotsky's (1978) "zone of proximal development" and suggest the adults may scaffold children's interactions with EP and help children make print-meaning connections that they could not make on their own. Future studies of EP games and activities should control or manipulate this variable.

EP currently receives little attention in most early childhood language arts programs. Results of this study suggest that EP recognition is not merely a marker of children's growing awareness of print, but may also be used as an instructional tool to enhance their print recognition. The EP games and play props appeared to increase children's natural interest in the print that surrounds them in everyday life. The researchers were impressed with the enthusiasm the children demonstrated while engaging in the EP recognition tests and the EP games and play activities. This approach appears to be a developmentally appropriate method for engaging very young children with print. Teachers interested in using EP to promote early literacy will find Prior and Gerard's (2004) book, *Environmental Print Classroom,* to be a useful resource. It contains numerous examples of EP games, instructional activities, and assessment instruments.

REFERENCES

Cloer, T., Aldridge, J., & Dean, R. (1981) Examining different levels of print awareness. *Journal of Language Experience, 4*(1&2), 25–34.

Dunn, L., Beach, S., & Kontos, S. (2000). Supporting literacy in early childhood programs: A challenge for the future. In K. Roskos & J. Christie (Eds.), *Play and literacy in early childhood: Research from multiple perspectives* (pp. 91–105). Mahwah, NJ: Lawrence Erlbaum.

Glass, G., & Hopkins, K. (1996). *Statistical methods in education and psychology* (3rd edition). Boston, Allyn and Bacon.

Goodman, Y. (1986). Children coming to know literacy. In W. H. Teale & E. Sulzby (Eds.). *Emergent literacy: Writing and reading* (pp.1–14). Norwood, NJ: Ablex.

Hall, N. (1999). Real literacy in a school setting: Five-year-olds take on the world. *The Reading Teacher, 52*, 817.

Harste, J., Burke, C., & Woodward, V. (1981). Children, their language and world: Initial encounters with print. In J. Langer & M. Smith-Burke (Eds.), *Bridging the gap: Reader meets author*. Newark, DE: International Reading Association.

Johnson, J., Christie, J., & Wardle, F. (2005). *Play, development, and early education.* New York: Allyn & Bacon.

Kuby, P., Aldridge, J.,& Snyder, S. (1994). Developmental progression of EP recognition in kindergarten children. *Reading Psychology International Quarterly, 15*, 1–9.

McGee, L., Lomax, R., & Head, M. (1988). Young children's written language knowledge: What environmental and functional print reading reveals. *Journal of Reading Behavior, 20*, 99–118.

Mason, J. (1980). When do children begin to read: An exploration of four-year-old children's letter and word reading competencies. *Reading Research Quarterly, 15*, 203–227.

Masonheimer, P., Drum, P.,& Ehri, L. (1984). Does environmental print identification lead children into word reading? *Journal of Reading Behavior, 16*, 257–271.

Neuman, S., & Roskos, K. (1993). Access to print for children of poverty: Differential effects of adult mediation and literacy enriched play settings on environmental print and functional print tasks. *American Educational Research Journal, 30*, 95–122.

Prior, J., & Gerard, M. (2004). *Environmental print classroom: Meaningful connections for learning to read*. Newark, DE: International Reading Association.

Stahl. S., & Murray, B. (1993). Environmental print, phonemic awareness, letter recognition, and word recognition. In D. Leu & C. Kinzer (Eds.). *Examining central issues in literacy research, theory, and practice: Forty-second yearbook of the National Reading Conference* (pp. 227–233). Chicago: National Reading Conference.

Vukelich, C. (1994). Effects of play interventions on young children's reading of environmental print. *Early Childhood Research Quarterly, 9*, 153–170.

Vygotsky, L. (1978). *Mind in society: The development of higher psychological processes*. Cambridge, MA. Harvard University Press.

Chapter Fourteen

Communicative Actions and Language Narratives in Preschoolers' Play with "Talking" and "Non-talking" Rescue Heroes

Doris Bergen

In today's technology-rich world, few human activities have been unaffected by technological devices. Therefore, it is not surprising that the play objects (e.g., toys) of young children have also been changing to incorporate computer chips and other technological aspects. Indeed, most toy stores and toy catalogs now sell technology-enhanced toys as well as the blocks, dolls, and trains of earlier years. Some of these toys elicit only minimal child action, while others directly attempt to affect aspects of the child's play with technology-powered words, sounds, and/or movements. Some request that the child perform certain actions, and the toys even give feedback as to the appropriateness of the child's responses to commands.

Early childhood educators have voiced many opinions about these toys, ranging from praise for their ability to encourage child language and action responses to concern that children's play initiatives will be taken over by the toys (Bergen, 2000). The effects of such toys on children's development are largely speculative, however, because there has been little research on how children play with such toys. Thus, little is known about how the toys may or may not affect the various qualities of child play, including children's communicative actions and language narratives. Possible hypotheses can be drawn from a Gibsonian and a Piagetian perspective. From a Gibsonian perspective (Gibson, 1979/1986; Gibson & Pick, 2000), the affordances of the toys will be likely to influence children's actions. "Affordances" are opportunities for action within a given environment and are specific to individuals. Therefore, the actions that a toy will elicit will vary depending on the "opportunities for action" the toy presents and the physical or perceptual constraints of the children. With a toy that has highly salient qualities (e.g. ability to "talk"), children might repeatedly elicit the toy's actions or imitate the actions or "talk" that the toy encourages. On the other hand, the Piagetian (Piaget, 1962) view that play is an assimilative, not an adaptive (i.e., imitative) process, might lead to a prediction that children will use the cognitive schemes they already possess and incorporate these technology-enhanced toys into their already existing play themes. That is, they might ignore the obvious qualities of the toys and use the toys in ways similar to the ways they typically play. Children's egocentric language narratives and their communication of both procedural knowledge (ability to represent information) and script knowledge (ability to represent figuratively social experience and social values) (Strayer, et al., 1987) would also be evident in their communicative interactions and language narratives.

Realistic toy figures enhanced with computer chips that enable the toy to "talk" when it is activated by the child are popular with both parents and children. Toys of this type include those called "Rescue Heroes" (TM Fisher Price), which replicate fire fighters, police officers, and other pro-social professional roles. These realistic action figures presently come in two versions: ones that "talk" when a button is pushed and ones that do not talk but that have implements that child manipulation can activate. With the cooperation of Fisher Price, Inc., this researcher has studied some aspects of a group of preschool children's play with these toys. The study investigated the percent of time the children spent in exploratory, practice, and pretend play with such toys and how the themes of pretense were affected by the toys' technical features. These results, as well as the differences in play between children who played alone or with an opposite gender peer are reported in detail elsewhere (Bergen, 2004). This paper focuses on the communicative interactions and language narratives that accompanied the children's play. One question of interest was whether the communicative prompts provided by the technology-enhanced figures would influence children's language differentially from the language elicited by the non-talking toys (a Gibsonian view) or whether the assimilative qualities of play would be evident in the actions and language of the children (a Piagetian view), in spite of the salient affordances of the toys.

QUESTIONS OF INTEREST

The overall findings of the study are briefly discussed and then a detailed description of the communicative interactions and language narratives of the children is presented. Answers to the following questions are given:

1. What are some of the major differences in children's play with Rescue Heroes who "talk" and with Rescue Heroes who do not talk?

2. What communicative interactions and language narratives are exhibited by children with the two sets of toys, and how are they exhibited by solitary players and opposite gender peer pairs?
3. What theoretical perspective(s) does the study support–Gibsonian and/or Piagetian?

DESIGN OF THE OVERALL STUDY

The study presented sixty-four children, aged 3½ to 5, (32 M; 32 F) with the toy figures and a set of unit blocks in 2 sessions about 1½–2 weeks apart. All sessions were held at the children's preschools but outside their classrooms. Children from 5 Head Start, 3 private childcare, and 4 university childcare classrooms participated in the study. There was a range of socio-economic levels in the families of the children, with approximately 30% of the children being African-American. The three independent variables in the research condition were randomly assigned, with the same number of children in each condition. These were talking/non-talking toys (T/NT); Rescue Hero video/non-video viewing after 1st session (V/NV); playing alone or with peer of opposite gender (A/P). (Thus, conditions were TNVA, TVA, NTNVA, NTVA, TNVP, TVP, NTNVP, and NTVP.) When parents gave permission for their children to participate in the study, they also completed a questionnaire about their children's play with replica toy figures.

Fisher Price, Inc. provided the toy figures and videos for the study. The three toys used in the study were a male firefighter and a female firefighter (both Euro-American) and a male police officer (African-American) for whom there are talking and non-talking versions. The talking toys had backpacks with buttons and levers that could be pushed to make the toy speak (e.g. they might say "Tornado" or "Do you copy?") while the non-talking toys had backpacks with implements that could be manually activated (i.e., an axe, a water spray, and a handcuff). A small set of unit blocks was also on the table with the toys, in order to support the play and provide an alternate activity choice. A short segment of Rescue Heroes video showing the toys in rescue actions was provided to the children in the video condition. After child agreement, the children were videotaped with a lap-held camera for approximately 20 minutes of playtime. (Children who wished to leave earlier were allowed to do so.)

The mean time for the first session was 17 minutes and for the second session was 16.7 minutes. The videotapes were coded on dimensions of interest; intercoder reliability on amount of time in various types of play averaged

87%, with a range of agreement from 62% to 100%. The coding of language was on the following dimensions: questions, answers, symbolic talk, collaborative talk, control statements, withdraw statements, oblige statements, labeling, and unrelated talk, with agreement between coders of 90%. In addition, the language transcripts were reviewed for evidence of procedural and script knowledge, and for exact repetition of the "talk" phrases of the computer-enhanced toys.

INFORMATION ABOUT PARTICIPANTS FROM PARENT QUESTIONNAIRES

Parents indicated that 24% of the children had Rescue Heroes; 52% had other action figures; and 63% had other pretend replica figures. In 46% of the homes children had watched RH videos or the TV program. Not surprisingly, there were significant differences in the types of toy figures boys and girls had to play with. Parents of boys reported that they had more Rescue Heroes (only one girl had such a toy), $\chi 2 = 14.254$, $p < .001$, and more action figures in general, $\chi 2 = 8.658$, $p < .01$. Parents of girls reported that they had more other pretend figures, $\chi 2 = 24.952$, $p < .001$. Boys were also more likely to have seen Rescue Heroes videos or TV, $\chi 2 = 21.967$, $p < .001$.

GENERAL RESULTS OF THE STUDY

Proportions of Play Type

At Time 1, the mean percentage of time spent in exploratory play (inspecting or activating the toy in various ways) was 13.5%, in practice play (using repeated actions without a pretend theme) 50.4%, and in pretend play 31.1%. The remaining 5% of time was spent disengaged in play (e.g., talking to researcher.) At Time 2 period, exploratory play was only 4.4%, while practice play was 53.9% and pretend play 33.4%, with the remaining time being spent in disengagement. Perhaps the novelty of the toys increased the amount of practice play, which was slightly higher than would typically be expected in children of this age. Pretend play increased slightly during the second time period; however, many pretense episodes were brief in time.

Themes

Children varied in the number of themes they used in the pretend play but at both times the percent of themes that were related to Rescue Heroes was the largest proportion (34/39%). Other theme categories included general violence such as fighting (28/20%) and family or non-rescue helping themes (8/13%). Some children developed themes that were unrelated to the features of the toys or focused primarily on the blocks (22/33%).

Talking/Non-Talking Differences

Overall there were few differences in the children's percentage of total time spent in various types of play with the two types of toys. The T/NT groups showed only a significant difference in one area: At Time 1 the children who had the non-talking toys spent more time in practice play with the toys and blocks together, F (1, 63) = 8.238, $p < .01$. Although there were no significant differences in the amount of time spent in theme play between the two groups, children who played with talking toys were more likely to have a Rescue Hero theme at both the first and second play session, $\chi 2$, 3 = 10.178, $p < .05$; $\chi 2$, 4 = 10.504, $p < .05$. Thus, there appears to have been an effect of the "prompts" provided by the talking toys.

Experience with Rescue Hero Toys/Videos

There were no differences in the amount of time spent in various types of play or in theme play, total number of themes, or number of Rescue Hero themes between children whose parents had reported that the children had previous experiences with Rescue Heroes and those who had not. It appears that the salience of the toy figures, both those with language and sound prompts (talking) or implements prompting actions (non-talking) were sufficient to guide children without prior experience to play rescue themes. Children who saw the video between sessions did not spend a longer time playing at the second time period, nor did they use more Rescue Hero themes in play. However, they did use more relevant words and sounds at Time 2; the video may have encouraged repetition of these stimuli.

Playing Alone or with Peer

Children in the peer condition spend a significantly longer percentage of time playing at both time periods, F (1, 62) = 8.540, $p < .01$; F (1, 62) = 8.692, $p < .01$; less time in exploration at both times, F (1, 62) = 4.089, $p < .05$; F (1, 62) = 10.202, $p < .01$; and more time in practice play with toys, F (1, 62) = 4.679, $p < .05$ and with blocks; F (1, 62) = 5.635, $p < .05$, both at Time 1. They pretended more with toys at Time 1, F (1, 62) = 8.546, $p < .01$, and pretended more with blocks, F (1, 62) = 6.369, $p < .01$ and with toys and blocks, $F\ (1, 62) = 4.823$, $p < .05$ at Time 2. They also showed less disengagement at Time 1, $F\ (1, 62) = 7.724$, $p < .01$. Thus, peer interaction appeared to be a more salient influence on the length and richness of the play than the type of toy that was provided.

Play of Boys and Girls

There were no significant differences in the percentages of time boys and girls spent in practice or pretend play. However, boys spent more time in theme play, $F\ (1, 60) = 274.76$, $p < .05$. This may have been due to the greater number of boys who were familiar with some aspect of Rescue Heroes or to the fact that the "action" appearance and prompts of the toys made them more likely to fit into play themes that boys might use. If the peer pairs had been same gender rather than mixed gender, this difference might have been even greater.

Results Related to Communicative Interactions and Language Narratives

About half of the children made the toys talk by using their own voices (44/45%), and 33% described attributes of the toys ("This one's a girl"), labeled the toys ("the fireman"), or labeled their block structures ("a castle"). While many of the themes were evident in child actions alone, the majority of themes were accompanied by language narrations (for alone-condition children) and language interactions (for peer-condition children). At both time periods most children used relevant language or sounds to accompany their play actions (52/42%). The mean number of communication attempts was similar at both time periods (36/39%), with the percent of language being questions/answers averaging about 14% at both time periods. Symbolic language (having the toys talk; making relevant sounds as implements were used) was a high percent of total language (about 25% over both times).

There were no significant differences in the percentages of questions/answers, symbolic talk, collaborative statements, control statements, withdraw or oblige language, labeling, or unrelated language between the children in the talking and non-talking toy conditions. Each group had similar patterns of language use, as did boys and girls and children who had Rescue Hero experiences at home. However, as would be expected, the children in the peer condition had significantly higher percentages of collaborative, control, and withdraw statements at Time 1 and of collaborative, control, withdraw, oblige, and answering statements at Time 2. (All significant at or below .05). They also talked significantly more overall, with a mean of 57 Time 1 and 64 Time 2 statements, compared to 15 and 14 statements at those times for children who played alone, $F\ (1, 62) = 41.896$, $p < .001$; $F\ (1, 62) = 47.083$, p

<.001. The language of children who played alone was usually symbolic talk, questions/answers to the researcher who was present, or unrelated statements.

EXAMPLES OF REPETITION OF THE STATEMENTS OF TALKING TOYS

As noted earlier, those children who had the talking toys or who saw the videotape more often used the exact words of the toy or those used on the videotape. The types of repetitious talk included these: "Alert! alert! Do you copy?" "Move it!" "May Day! May Day!" The two words used by the toys that were most often repeated were "Fire" and "Tornado." Another favorite word was "Over!" However, one child, a boy, asked, "Why did she (the toy) say 'Over'?" Sometimes children repeated longer sentences or had communication interactions made up of the toys' words. Here are a few examples:

Example A

Girl: This is Wendy Waters. It's Wendy Waters. It's a tornado. It's an emergency.

Example B

Boy: This is Dave (Jake) Justice, over, over. I copy.

Example C

Boy: I'll read you that.

Girl: Over.

Boy: Yes, I copy that.

Girl: Yes, I copy that.

Boy: I copy that too.

A few children also acted out or discussed the video actions, which included the toys flying in an airplane and the rescue of a drowning child:

Example D

Boy: Hey, remember when we watched that movie last time, they (the toys) had nothing on their back (no backpacks). I have to take this one off (the backpack).

Girl: How do you do that?

Boy: What?

Girl: We still need all of our work things. This, remember when they were flying in the airplane?

Boy: Yeah, pretend this is an airplane.

Example E

Boy: He went under the water . . . he drowned . . . mmm (holds breath). This is where tornado water is. I don't wanna go in the tornado water. (No tornado was in video.)

EXAMPLES OF DEMONSTRATIONS OF PROCEDURAL AND PRAGMATIC KNOWLEDGE

There were many evidences of children's knowledge in their language. They described the toys in many ways: "That one's a girl," "These ones put out the fires," "That one makes sounds." "Ah, this one's got a tornado," "This is a fighting girl," "This one's the bad guy and puts everyone in jail." Many children showed procedural knowledge, asking about or explaining how to use the toys: "Buttons! Push this! Push this," "I think this is how they go. No, they all have different bags (backpacks). This still goes on him. Look they all have different bags, don't they," "I can take his helmet off. You can take his helmet off," "That go on here," "Wait, wait! How about we push all the buttons at the same time?"

In peer play, children's knowledge of language pragmatics (appropriate ways to use language) was also evident. For example, children said to other children, "Can I help you?" "You are being mean to me." "Do you want to help me make the castle?" "You can have this and I'll have that." "I'll trade you the son." "Quit calling people stupid!" "She's not sharing." "That's not how you play." "Can you hand over those blocks, please?" Sometimes the toys also talked in pragmatics.

Example F

Boy (toy is talking) She ain't even my friend, are you?

Girl: (toy is talking) No, cause you hurt our feelings.

Boy: Well, I said I'm sorry.

Girl: No you didn't

Boy: Yes, I did

Girl: So you ain't still our friend?

Boy: Yeah, I am . . . (the toy's conversation continues in this vein).

Example G

Boy: [toy is talking] Get out of here. I'm gonna go by myself. Sorry.

Girl: [toy is talking] Stop. I'm on your team, remember? I'm not a stranger. You see? I'm one of your friends.

Boy: Don't tell me. I can do it by myself.

Other procedural and pragmatic knowledge examples are also evident within the script knowledge examples in the following section.

EXAMPLES OF DEMONSTRATIONS OF SCRIPT KNOWLEDGE

Egocentric Speech/Language Narratives

Example H

Male alone, with non-talking toys, RH/general violence themes:

This toy's fun. [To researcher]

[Then the toy begins "talking" along with child narration of action]

Caught him! Whoops! Got him. He fell down. He's dead. Whoopsey! What's that? I caught her. Hey, you get, you get back up here. I got ya, I got her. Look what you did to the building. Stop! There you go! Show you. Argh! Pow! Boom! I got you now. I pull you. Oww, that hurt! You guys are dead. Hahaha [humming] Boom! I'll cut that thing off. Haha. Hey what's wrong with you? Haha, You're dead! . . . What's that handcuff doing on me? Haha. You're still handcuffed on. We need the key, where's the key? Right here? Where's the key? Lock him up. We can't. Lock him up. Lock him up. I locked him. I'm the cops. Thanks. You're welcome.

Example I

Male alone, with talking toys, RH theme [repeating RH words as toy "talks"] Ssshom [flying sounds] . . . Over . . . Oh? Whoa! Look at that falling. I'm coming up. I'm coming up! Tornado. This is Jake Justice [flying sounds]. We're in outer space, outer space. Coming back . . . [later] . . . [gun sounds] This is the pilot. Tornado, over, search again! [gun sounds] Got it! Here's the fire. [flying sounds and gun sounds continue]

Example J

Female alone, with talking toys, RH theme [toy "talks," narration of action interspersed with talk to researcher.] Go rescue a fire. Pow [gun noises]! [To researcher: Can she take her helmet off?] [narration continues] They both fell down. Rescue the fire. Build a house. Pssh [water noises] Okay. Pssh, hold this thing. Hey, pssh. Spray the fire. Pssh, pssh. Rescue Heroes to the rescue. Come on out. [To researcher: I saw this on TV. I was wondering what it did. I like playing with these.] The building's too tall to get the lady. The building's too tall. I can't get you. Come down, come down, come down from there, come down. Someone's in trouble, someone's in trouble, help, help! [To researcher: Do you have any more of these?]

Example K

Female alone, with talking toys, non-RH theme: [Narration of action] I have to build with the big blocks. They have to build a trampoline they can jump on. Hmm . . . oh, I need a square! What's wrong with these things? Duh! Whoa! This is . . . I don't care (boing, boing, boing) I got it . . . 100%. . . . Ow! Don't need this one. Just what I needed! Got it. That looks good? [To researcher: How's the trampoline look?] Oh, I've still got to build the stairs. [First toy climbs up stairs and jumps] Uh-huh, uh-huh, uh-huh! Do-d-do. Yay Wee. Next, Billy the Builder. Look at how high he can go . . . look. Next! Do-do-do-do-do! Do-do-do-do. He can jump even higher. Wanna see? [All three toys are given turns jumping]

Example L

Female alone, with non-talking toys, [Procedural narrative with varied themes.] I need the handcuffs without the boy. OK. Now, oops! I wasn't ready. On your mark, go! Ooh, I almost had it. Oh my god! Ugh! Whoa! That was caught. One more time. Whoa [yells]! Now I'll show you how it's gonna work. We need to move the things back a little so they can be all bigger. There I'll show you how this is. Put everything together this is the stuff that's going to be the TV but this goes here. All this stuff is gonna be the TV . . . This is going to be a hit TV show. And the remote control. I need the remote control. There. That's the remote control. And this thing gonna go on there. And this thing goes here. And this goes here. And that's all! Now I need the handcuff though. Now, ooh-whoa! I'm gonna get it this time. I got something. I got something. I got something! Now all we need is the pulley thing. What happened to the boy? Oh, there it is. Freeze! Put up your hands. Put `em behind your back. Put ``em behind your back . . . [Later] . . . My handcuffs. . . . I know how to do it. Ooh. Oh, shoot. You're gotta handcuff me. Are you ready? Ugh, the handcuff. Hey it got me in jail. But I got the key. . .

Collective Monologues/Brief Collaborative Dialogues

Example M

Male/Female peers, with non-talking toys: [Collective monologue by girl, with occasional communication attempts to peer, not always successful questions/ control statements]

Girl: I'm building something. Oops! Firefighter girl fell down. She keeps falling down. I'll lay her there. You wanna chop it down?

Boy: No answer [he is engaged with police officer, trying to shoot handcuff]

Girl: Can I use that one? [male firefighter]

Boy: Gives it to her with no comment

Girl: [builds with blocks] There it goes up. There. All done. It's tall. It's taller than I am. He caught that boy's leg. [comment on peer's actions] He's got a water spray. She ain't gonna stand up. How do we make her stand up? [Researcher helps]. . . . I'm about to build something else. That goes there, that goes there [7 times]. She's gonna knock it down with her spray. Get up close and knock it down. They're firefighters. I need two of these, two of these like this, and all these. This is going to be something different and cute.[comments on building continue]. . . . These are two steps. This one and this one, they're the same. Only one more. See now they have to go high. They're like stairs . . .

Boy: No comments during this entire time period

Girl: This fire girl look she's got water coming out. But he got chops. She got water. They better sit down. . . .

Boy: I bet I can knock it down. I can.

Girl: Hey, now we need this arm for the slide. They slide down like woo! There. Want me to show you how to work with her? This is how she knocks it down.

Boy: No answer. [He has remained engaged with shooting the handcuff into the air this entire time.]

Example N

Male/female, non-talking toys: [Collective monologue and minimal collaborative dialogue]

Boy: Ow! This is fun. Bet you can't make one of these.

Girl: I bet I can.

Boy: Start like that.

Girl: I'm making something bigger than yours. I'm bigger.

Boy: Cool. He's up there. He's up there and look her gonna knock it down.

Girl: Look at my castle. My man is gonna knock it down.

Boy: My man is gonna knock the girl down. "Help! Somebody! This girl is gonna knock it down." Her can't.

Girl: This boy can't knock it . . .

Boy: Oh! (tower sways, almost falls)

Girl: Whoa, I almost fell. That was cool wasn't it? Knock him down, he's gonna fall.

Collaborative Dialogues

Example O

Male/female, non-talking toys, nonRH theme: [Communication interaction but not theme related]

Boy: That's what you do, Yee, haw! [fighting sounds] Ooh, that's cool. You push right there and it goes–it tries to hit you.

Girl: [giggles as boy tries to hit her toy with implement]

Boy: I gotcha! [fighting sounds] Almost got your head.

Girl: You take this guy and I'll take that one, ok?

Boy: Wait

Girl: You can have this now, ok? You can have this now.

Boy: I had it.

Girl: You can have it now. You can have this now.

Boy: I had it.

Girl: You can have it back.

Boy: I got your leg. I got your leg [toy's leg]. Wait, I got you. Now I have to pull in. All you have to do is do that.

Girl: You can have this now. You can have that now.

Boy: Which one do you want? This one?

Girl: [points and they exchange]

Boy: I like this guy. That's the chopper one. He can save us.

Girl: This is my brother ok? He's a super hero.

Boy: No you're supposed to push with that one. You push it back and he chops. Like that . . . [later]

Girl: This is the home.

Boy: Argh! I almost got him.

Girl: Brother, brother, brother!

Boy: I'll catch that little block. Almost caught that one. Argh!

Girl: Yikes! Knock it over. We'll put these over here and he won't find us.

Boy: I'll knock it down though [fighting sounds]

Girl: He's knocking our home down!

Example P

Male/female, talking toys, elaborated RH theme [Communication interaction that furthers the play theme]

Girl: It's Wendy Waters! It's an emergency! [girl has Wendy Waters]

Boy: Yes! Wait, I have to get my fire thing on. [the backpack]) I have to get this on so I can help you. [boy has Billy Blaze]

Girl: I need you!

Boy: Umm

Girl: Wendy Waters! Hurry up and get here. Hurry!

Boy: I'm coming. I'm coming.

Girl: Hurry, I'm almost dead. Hurry! Hurry!

Boy: I'm coming this time. Brrrr [driving sound]. I'm there. I'll do whatever you want.

[Rescue action takes place]

Boy: I got to go to sleep. [takes off BB backpack]

Girl: I'm going to sleep. [takes Jake Justice]

Boy: No that's my guy!

Girl: No!

Boy: He was at my house. He was at my house. Meet my man going to sleep. [puts two male toys' heads on some blocks] Two pillows–these are my pillows. This is pillows. All work is closed. All the workers got to leave work.

Girl: My pillow?

Boy: Oh, yeah, that's right there until we get up. You have to stay with us too until you sleep.

Example Q

Male/Female, nontalking toys, elaborated RH theme: [Communication interaction that furthers the play theme]

Boy: I'm trying to get you out of there.

Girl: She needs somebody to get her out of here.

Boy: I'm getting her out.

Girl: How can you?

Boy: I'm using this [axe]. Whoa!

Girl: Now I'm locked! Now she's lost, right?

Boy: No, I got her out. [play continues with this theme]

Boy: Now we're trapped. Now we have to get out of here. How do we get out? Oh, use this. You can use my chopper. I'm chopping this off. Here ma'am. Ah! Where's my, ah.

Girl: Is this cool what I'm making? [discussion of who has the most blocks, sharing]

Boy: Ah, I caught you Mr. Robber, I caught you. Now I'm going to pull you right back to me [with handcuff]. Wait. I can call these people anything I want to? Ooh, thank you.

Girl: Me too?

Boy: Ooh, I caught you. Ooh, I caught you Mr. Robber. [toy talking] No one can catch me. Now you can get away Mr. Robber. Now you can get away. Ha, ha, ha.

Girl: You can't get away Mr. Silly.

Boy: No, Mr. Robber. Now I'm done. Stay more in jail. [toy talking] Let me out of here!

Girl: Can't get away, duh. Get out, get out.

Boy: Oh, yeah.

Girl: I'm gonna make a different thing.

Example R

Male/female, talking toys, non-RH theme [Controlling communication attempts; unsuccessful]

Girl: [takes all backpacks off and puts in corner of table behind block "house"] Okay, we're on teams. What do you wanna be? You pick, you pick, you're keeping it. [Boy picks girl toy]. No, that's a girl. Pick one of these boys. [Boy picks boy toy] That's the mom. [pointing to Wendy] You're the son and I'm the dad. [toys talking] Son, let's go home. Go son, I said come on let's go. Son, I tell you go home. Go, son, I said come on let's go. Son, I tell you go home! Mom, come on. No, you came home, you're home. Come on let's go [to son and dad].

Boy: Okay

Girl: Look at me. Mommy and daddy wants to spend time together son. And you need to leave, okay?

Boy: Hey [toy hits other one]

Girl: No, that's not how you play. You can't knock them down, they're your parents. Let's go. Son, son, dad, let's go, let's go.

Boy: [toy hits other ones] Oww!

Girl: Oww, oww, stop it. That's not nice play.

Example S

Male/Female peers, non-talking toys, elaborated RH theme [Controlling communication attempts; partially successful]

Boy: I'm gonna dive. Help me. Somebody help me. Somebody help me [repeated 4 times].

Girl: Why isn't Jake going to help him?

Boy: That isn't going to help him. He needs her to do it. Help him. Help me guys. If you won't do it I'll just drop him in the water.

Girl: I will do it. I wanted to do it.

Boy: What?

Girl: Help him.

Boy: But it's too late. Woo, he's going under water and drownding!

Girl: I helped [her toy makes rescue]. He can float.

Boy: No he can't.

Girl: Yes he can.

Boy: No he can't. Help mmm [drowning noises]. Help me! Help me!

Girl: I got you [her toy makes rescue]

Boy: Woa! Argh! Mmm. Somebody help me. [repeated]

Girl: Oh, no!

Boy: We need help. Help us Mr. Hero. Rescue Hero help, help! We need help. Turn around and help. Turn around and look at me. See my hand [raised for help]

Girl: No.

Boy: Yes.

Girl: We can't help you.

Boy: Why?

Girl: I'm too sick. Wendy is too sick.

Boy: Just help me.

Girl: I gotta stay in my house.

DISCUSSION/CONCLUSIONS

The overall results of this study showed that after an initial exploratory period, most children used both the talking and non-talking toys in similar ways, especially during pretend play. Although the children with technology-enhanced toys were more likely to have a Rescue Hero theme and repeat more phrases and sounds that the toy made, most children used a variety of language narratives. The affordance of the "talking" toys was salient enough so that it engaged most of the children initially; however, it was not so salient that it controlled the total play activity of most children. Their play ranged over a wide set of actions. Whether longer term play with the toys or greater exposure to the videos would elicit greater adherence to the specific themes suggested by the toys (e.g. tornado!) is presently unknown. Surprisingly, children's past experience with Rescue Hero toys was not a major influence in this study. This may be because the affordances of both types of toys were so strongly suggestive of themes related to rescue (e.g. fire and police figures).

The presence of a peer, even though of opposite gender, did increase the time spent in practice and pretend play and increased the variety of pretend actions. The peer's presence increased the length of the overall session and the amount of language expressed by the children. The communicative interactions and language narratives with peers were more varied and complex, and included many examples of assimilation of the toy themes into the past experiential lives of the children. In this sample there were few gender differences, probably because the mixed gender pairs used in the study had an influence on the "typical" themes of play for both genders. Although the language narratives of boys and girls sometimes differed, with each giving different reasons for the toys' actions, many of boys' and girls' actions with the toys were similar.

As the language examples demonstrate, children who played alone exhibited more egocentric language narratives to accompany their play, and many of these had symbolic qualities. These children were not completely egocentric in language, however, but often engaged the researcher in communication interactions. The peer pairs' language corpus ranged from complex and elaborated communication interactions to relatively unsuccessful attempts to collaborate and control the play to primarily parallel play with only brief communication attempts to interact with the peer. There were also instances of communication interactions with the researcher.

Generalization is limited due to the artificial experimental conditions in which the children played and the possible influence of setting variability. However, the case protocols do show that there were many instances of assimilation of the actions into existing play schemes. Also, children brought their existing communication strategies to the new play experience and used their egocentric language narratives to assist in their play.

Although the words of the technology-enhanced toys added a dimension that initially surprised most children in the talking toy condition, they quickly adapted to the actions needed and either incorporated those actions and words in their play or ignored them and used familiar schemes. A surprise in the study was that the non-talking toys had some salient affordances that were also new to most children, and the children in this condition spent focused time adapting their actions in order to be able to activate the various implements (e.g., the handcuff). After practice with these implements, however, they also reacted in assimilative ways to the toys' characteristics, either incorporating them in their communicative play or using language narratives that ignored these features.

The study raises many interesting questions about children's play with technology-enhanced toys that need further exploration. In particular, will the salience of technology-related affordances have direct and long term effects on the types of play children exhibit or will children's own understanding of their experiences result in the assimilation of "strong-affordance" toys to their existing cognitive schemes, communication strategies, and language narratives? Because of the importance of this question and others related to how children's communicative interactions and language narratives may be affected by exposure to "talking" and other types of technology-enhanced toys, other researchers are encouraged to pursue the study of the effects of technology-enhanced toys, using both Gibsonian and Piagetian perspectives.

REFERENCES

Bergen, D. (2004). Preschool children's play with "talking" and "non-talking" Rescue Heroes: Effects of technology-enhanced figures on the types and themes of play. In J. Goldstein, D. Buckingham, & G. Brougere (Eds.) *Toys, games and media.* Erlbaum: Mahwah, NJ.

Bergen, D. (2001). Technology in the classroom: Learning in the robotic world: Active or reactive? *Childhood Education, 77* (4), 249–250.

Gibson, E. J. & Pick, A. D. (2000). *An ecological approach to perceptual learning and development*. New York: Oxford University Press.

Gibson, E. J. (1979/1986). *The ecological approach to visual perception*. Hillsdale, JN: Lawerence Erlbaugh Associates.

Piaget, J. (1962). *Play, dreams, and imitation in childhood*. New York: Norton.

Strayer, F. F. & Moss, E. (1987). *The development of social and representational tactics during early childhood.* Montreal: University of Quebec.

ACKNOWLEDGMENTS

The author thanks Fisher-Price, Inc. who funded the research data-gathering phase, and especially Kathleen Alfano, Director, Fisher-Price Child Research department, for her support and encouragement in making the study possible. Sincere thanks also go to the graduate assistants, Jessica Burnham, Patrick Frato, and Denise Kovacs, who supervised the data collection, coding, and/or transcription phases, and to the undergraduate research assistants, Katie Reinke, Brooke Fox, Rachel Meyer, Mike Keidel, Leslie Smutz, Kristen Olson, Julie Tiermeir, Arron Terrill, Anna Stachel, and Regan Lynch, who participated in data collection, coding, and/or transcription. Without their dedicated assistance, the study could not have been accomplished.

Part V

PLAY ACROSS SPACE AND TIME

Chapter Fifteen

Toy Libraries, Play, and Play Materials

Margie I. Mayfield

Toy libraries are found worldwide and recently seem to be benefiting from increasing interest. For example, the British government recently allocated £6 million for the establishment of 150 new toy libraries for young children in "deprived areas" (Department for Education and Skills, 2001). The Ministry of Education in Scotland added £75,000 to the funding of toy and leisure libraries (Scottish Executive, 2001). In British Columbia, Canada, the Minister of State for Early Childhood Development has expressed interest in establishing toy libraries in public libraries throughout the province (Jang, 2001; Linda Reid, personal communication, October 2001).

Toy libraries are resource centres for children of a variety of ages and their families that provide developmentally appropriate play materials (e.g., toys, games, books, media, etc.), as well as activities and information related to play, learning, and child development (Mayfield, 2001). As Head and Barton (1987) have noted, toy libraries can meet the needs of families in a low key way that is acceptable to parents regardless of their social and economic circumstances, cultural, and ethnic backgrounds. They can provide an informal meeting place where parents can make friends and find support (p. 109).

DEVELOPMENT OF TOY LIBRARIES

Although the first toy library was established in Los Angeles in 1935, it was not until the 1960s that they began in Europe and subsequently spread worldwide. Sweden and England were early leaders in the establishment of toy libraries. In Sweden, toy libraries (called *lekoteks*) originated in 1963 to serve children with special needs and their families, including siblings. The primary focus of Swedish lekoteks has remained children with special needs. Typically, toy libraries for children with special needs have specially designed and modified play materials. These toy libraries are often connected with therapy and rehabilitation programs and may have their own staff designers and makers of adapted play materials.

Toy libraries in England began in the late 1960s and developed in a wide variety of community settings. Although the first one in England targeted children with special needs, rapid growth of more general community-oriented toy libraries followed. Thus, the early English toy libraries had a more diverse clientele than the Swedish ones. These two major models of toy libraries are often referred to as the Swedish model and the English model or the special needs and community models respectively. (Most countries with toy libraries have examples of both models.) However, the distinctions between these two models of toy libraries have been gradually blurring as more special needs toy libraries accommodate the typically developing siblings of children with special needs. Likewise, community toy libraries have increasingly provided play materials for both children and adults with special needs.

In the past two decades, I have visited toy libraries in many countries including Canada, England, Sweden, Australia, Argentina, Denmark, the United States, Venezuela, and Italy. I began formal study and observation of toy libraries with a cross-Canada study. Later I studied toy libraries in England and Sweden (as the originators of the modern toy library) and Australia (because of its many similarities to Canada as well as its innovative delivery models such as using postal buses, helicopters, and commercial airplanes for service to remote and isolated areas). I have also assisted in establishing toy libraries (e.g., in Bangkok) and continue to visit toy libraries whenever possible.

FOSTERING PLAY AND PLAY EDUCATION

Toy libraries are often defined overly simply. For example, a description such as "organizations that lend out toys like libraries lend out books" (Walters, 1998, p. 12) does not reflect the range of goals of toy libraries. While at first glance the obvious goal of toy libraries *is* to lend toys and play materials, they have multiple goals. When I ask directors of toy libraries what the goals are for their toy library, the most frequent responses are typically:

- Provision of toys and play materials
- Promotion of play
- Parent/family/community education about play and play materials

- Provision of a family-focused program not otherwise available in the community
- Provision of social opportunities for families
- Prevention or remediation (Mayfield, 1988; 1993)

These stated goals are congruent with those found in the print materials of these toy libraries, as well as other toy libraries in many countries. In addition, professional organizations, such as the USA Toy Library Association, have been established to promote play, help create toy libraries, and serve as resources for professionals and families (Rettig, 1998). Thus the provision of toys and play materials really serves as a means to a variety of ends rather than being the end itself.

The importance of promoting and educating people about play and especially its value in children's development is a paramount goal for toy libraries. As Misurcova (1986) has noted, the gradual recognition of the role of play in the education of the child combined with the need to create conditions favorable to play has been at the root of the creation of toy libraries. The modern toy library can provide a range of ever expanding and evolving services as illustrated by the extension of toy libraries to serve adults in Britain (adult leisure libraries). Likewise, toy libraries use a variety of strategies to promote play and educate families and the general public, such as brochures, posters, television ads, local newspapers, newsletters, bulletin boards, displays in public buildings, workshops, parent education courses on play, conferences, and book and video lending libraries.

DEVELOPMENT AND USE OF A PLAY MATERIALS TYPOLOGY

A core topic in discussion and research about toy libraries is the types of play materials available. One methodological issue key to researching toy libraries is how to determine accurately what play materials are provided. This problem is compounded in cross-country/cultural research. While some information may be obtained through observation, additional instrumentation is required due to several factors, which prevent all materials in a toy library from being observed at one time (e.g., toys currently checked out by users, toys being cleaned or waiting to be re-shelved, and toys stored behind closed doors).

When I began researching toy libraries, I investigated checklists and toy typologies to systematize the identification of the contents of toy libraries. Yawkey and Toro-Lopez (1985) had observed, "few studies have been conducted on toy categories" (p. 47). As no existing instrumentation was found in the mid-1980s that met my needs, I developed and piloted a descriptive typology for toy libraries. A master list of play materials recommended for toy libraries was made by combining the lists of suggested items from the Canadian Association of Toy Libraries (1981), the American Library Association (Preschool Services, 1981), and Toys 'n' Things (Johnson, 1978). Due to the inconsistency of terminology for some materials and possible confusion from the use of some non-descriptive names and the different names for play materials (even among the English-speaking countries), I decided that a checklist with the names of individual materials grouped by categories would not work. Instead, a card sort activity using pictures of the specific play materials mentioned on the above lists was developed.

Photos or pictures of each play material (e.g., tinkertoys, jump ball, telephone, etc.) or type of material (e.g., bath toys, small cars, etc.) were located in catalogues of toy manufacturers and distributors from North America and Europe. These pictures were then mounted on 5" × 8" (12.7 cm × 20.3 cm) plain white index cards. To assess the content validity, practicality, and usefulness of this typology, eight experts were asked to review the cards to determine if any types of play materials had been omitted. As a result of their comments, a few items were added (e.g., larger wheeled toys). The final typology consisted of 97 cards with one or more pictures of play materials per card (e.g., crib activity centres, nesting toys, puppets, peg boards, lotto games, pull toys, toss games, etc.).

Toy library personnel were asked to sort the picture typology cards into two piles: those that their toy library had and those it did not have. During the process of sorting the cards, most interviewees volunteered information about selection criteria for play materials, the most popular materials, the care and cataloguing of the materials, and other related information. If this information was not volunteered, specific questions were asked upon completion of the card sort. In several toy libraries, personnel actually sorted the cards into three piles: what they had, what they did not have, and what they did not have but would like to have. The cards in the latter pile were then often photocopied for future reference. In a few toy libraries in Sweden and England that had resident play material designers, these individuals further subdivided the third pile into those items that they were interested in designing or adapting for their clientele.

CRITERIA FOR THE SELECTION OF PLAY MATERIALS

Play materials can motivate, stimulate, and promote play. As Misurcova (1986) pointed out, "toys and play are inseparably linked with childhood and adolescence and have proved an effective if informal means of education" (p. 513). Given the variety of play materials available worldwide today, the criteria used by toy library personnel in the selection of play materials are of interest to researchers and others. From the time of my first study, the most frequently mentioned criteria have been relatively consistent across countries and types of toy libraries. These criteria are the following:

- Developmental appropriateness
- Durability
- Safety
- Open-endedness, versatility, flexibility
- Variety; filling in gaps in current collection
- Attractiveness for children
- Cleanable
- Number of pieces (loss is an issue for many toy libraries)
- Cost
- Cultural and ethnic appropriateness for their users
- Popularity among children
- No batteries
- Availability

The exact order of these criteria can and does vary across toy libraries; however, the top five or six are almost the same (although the order may vary). A few criteria are more likely to be associated with specific situations. For example, a community-type toy library is more likely to have concerns about using batteries especially because of the cost than is a special needs toy library where many of their adapted play materials require batteries for operation. Safety, while an essential consideration for all, is a greater concern in North America than in other countries. As one European toy librarian explained, "Liability is a big thing in North America, it is not in Europe."

This listing agrees basically with the general criteria suggested by toy library organizations (e.g., Canadian Association of Toy Libraries, 1986; National Association of Toy and Leisure Libraries, 2000). Although funding is a problem for many toy libraries (see later section), cost does not seem to be a primary criterion in evaluating and selecting play materials. While cost can be a limiting factor in that toy libraries cannot purchase as many materials as they would wish, they do not purchase "inferior" ones because they are less expensive.

FREQUENTLY AVAILABLE PLAY MATERIALS

A logical question deriving from the selection criteria for play materials is which ones are actually selected by toy librarians. From my discussions with toy library personnel and the use of the picture sorting activity, the play materials most frequently available in toy libraries that I have visited are the "classic" play materials such as puzzles, stacking and nesting toys, blocks, books, pull toys, simple board games, small bears, dominoes, farm/airport/animal sets, and small manipulatives such as pegs and beads. The least frequently (i.e., in 33% or less of toy libraries) available play materials tend to be the larger ones (e.g., wall blocks, climbers, and tunnels) and consumables (e.g., paint and plasticene).

In one study, musical toys were reported more frequently in England and Sweden while cassette players and puppets were more frequent in Canada and Australia (Mayfield, 1993). Toys by major manufacturers, such as Fisher-Price, Brio, and Playskool are found worldwide and are well represented in most toy libraries. The global prevalence of these companies may be the reason why "Availability" is a less frequently mentioned selection criterion. Overall, the play materials found in toy libraries tend to be quite similar in my experience. Swiniarski (1991) also noted more similarities than differences among toys found worldwide.

An interesting side note here is that the number of toys in toy libraries I have observed has ranged from approximately 200 in some of the small "toy chest" type toy libraries to more than 6,000. In my experience, the Swedish and Australian toy libraries seemed to be particularly well equipped (approximately 3,000 toys per library). For example in one study (Mayfield, 1993), the Swedish toy library with the fewest number of toys (1,500) still had 650 more than the Canadian toy library with the greatest number (850). It is generally accepted that the toy library with the largest number of toys is the Los Angeles County Toy Loan Program with 35,000 toys, all of which have been donated by volunteers (Björck-Åkesson & Brodin, 1992).

OBSTACLES FOR TOY LIBRARIES

Toy libraries face obstacles in their pursuit of promoting play and providing materials, information, and services for children and families. Over the time I have been observing toy libraries and discussing them with toy library personnel, the biggest obstacles have remained essentially the same. Typically these are (a) funding, (b) lack of sufficient space, (c) under-utilization of the program, and (d) staffing. These have also been reported frequently elsewhere in the literature (e.g., Gentleman, 1983; Hewitt, 1981; National Toy Libraries Association, 1984).

Funding issues are not unique to toy libraries but a current reality for many programs and services for children and families worldwide. Although some federal and provincial/state governments (e.g., in Britain and Canada) have indicated increased funding, lack of funding is a major issue for toy libraries in many countries. Indeed, it is the most frequent reason for not establishing a toy library (Björck-Åkesson & Brodin, 1992). Lack of sufficient funding is related to other problems such as the shortage of staff, space, and play materials as well as insufficient hours of operation. The continuance of current funding provisions is also an issue for many toy libraries. Many toy libraries rely on multiple funding sources and often mix public, private, and charitable funding. While writing grants and reports to several agencies can be time consuming, having multiple funding sources can be advantageous in uncertain financial times.

Two other obstacles are the difficulties of getting certain groups (e.g., single parents, some immigrant groups, and teenage mothers) to use the toy library and under-utilization of the program by other groups. Directors usually attribute under-utilization to lack of awareness about the program. Often, funding limits the type and amount of publicity that can be undertaken. However, toy libraries typically use a variety of means to promote and publicize their programs such as brochures, posters in public places, television spots on community channels, newspaper stories, newsletters, and especially word-of-mouth. A related obstacle is the general public's perceptions or misperceptions of what a toy library is and its purposes. This also can be an obstacle with funding agencies that are not familiar with the concept of a toy library.

In discussions with toy librarians, they often identify the need for more pre-service and in-service training for staff as another potential obstacle. It is not uncommon for people involved in the establishment or operation of toy libraries to have limited or no specific training in toy libraries and thus in-service and professional development opportunities are seen as a need (e.g., Lindberg, Björck-Åkesson, & Brodin, 1988). Although training courses are becoming more available than previously, various options such as short courses, distance education, or correspondence courses could become more accessible as technology develops further and delivery costs are reduced. Professional education also is desirable within organizations administering toy libraries. For example, resistance is sometimes seen among public librarians whose libraries house a toy library. There have been articles in professional publications (e.g., Bears, 1999) on strategies to implement a "no-playthings policy" because playthings distract users from reading books and "whatever helps children develop into lifelong readers, that's the approach to take" (p. 49). The role of play and play materials in children's language and literacy development is an area that seems to need more explanation and promotion.

FUTURE OF TOY LIBRARIES

The characteristics of toy libraries that have enabled their steady, albeit modest, growth over the past four decades bode well for the global future of toy libraries. I think this is due, in great part, to the inherent strengths of toy libraries.

One of the strengths of toy libraries, especially in uncertain times, is their variety and adaptability. Toy libraries can be a part of a larger program (e.g., a family resource centre), be an independent program that stands alone, or share facilities (e.g., with a public school or community recreation centre). The flexibility of toy libraries also can be seen in their locations, which include family resource centres, public libraries, public schools, shopping malls, storefronts, community centres, clinics, treatment centres, churches, government buildings, apartment complexes, and prisons. Many countries use mobile toy library vans in both urban and rural areas. In addition, toy libraries are compatible philosophically and operationally with many other family and community-oriented programs.

Another strength is the toy library's potential for grass roots development. Toy libraries in many countries have been established by one or two individuals who saw needs in their local communities that were not being met by other programs. For example, therapists and parents of children with special needs established early toy libraries in Sweden and a Canadian toy library was begun by a recently retired primary teacher who was motivated to do so by the combination of local needs and an article on toy libraries she had torn out and found when clearing out her classroom. It is not unusual for toy libraries to be started by parents who move to a new community and discover there is no toy library available for themselves and their children. As one parent told me, "I couldn't believe there was no toy library when we moved here and that my neighbours didn't even know what it was. A toy library is so important for families." She started one.

Still another strength of toy libraries is their on-going flexibility to meet local needs. A locally developed toy library can match the needs and wishes of the local community (e.g., days/hours of operation, local languages, location, etc.) and respond to subsequent changing needs. Many toy libraries began as small programs operated by local volunteers or part-time toy librarians. These programs then expanded and evolved into larger, and often more comprehensive, programs as additional needs and funding were identified. An example of this development is that toy libraries were the "foundation program" of many of the current family resource centres in Canada.

Yet another strength is the potential of toy libraries to provide services and facilities for families with young children not otherwise available or accessible in the community. In addition to providing information about play, play materials, and parent education, toy libraries often fill other family needs. For example, one librarian in Toronto told me that different ethnic groups used the toy library on specific afternoons as social gathering places for the mothers and grandmothers because the toy library was one of the few places these women were permitted to go without a male relative.

What toy libraries worldwide do share are the goals, means, and desire to promote play and to provide play materials and other services for children and their families. Toy libraries are a means to encourage play across a diversity of families and communities. They are a testimony to the role and importance of play and play materials in children's development and children's right to the opportunity, means, and support for play.

REFERENCES

Bears, M.K. (1999). Look, Ma! No toys. *School Library Journal, 45*(1), 49.

Björck-Åkesson , E. & Brodin, J.M. (1992). International diversity of toy libraries. *Topics in Early Childhood Special Education, 12*(4), 528–544.

Canadian Association of Toy Libraries (1981). *Toys help*. Toronto: Author.

Canadian Association of Toy Libraries (1986). *Toy libraries: How to start and maintain a toy library in your community*. Toronto: Author.

Department for Education and Skills (2001, February 19). *£6 million to create 150 toy libraries for young children* [Press release]. Retrieved October 19, 2001, from http//www.dfee.gov.uk/pns/DisplayPN.cgi?pn_id=2001_0094.

Gentleman, G. (1983). *Child care family resource centres*. Toronto: Government of Ontario.

Head, J. & Barton, P. (1987). *Toy libraries in the community*. London: Elton.

Hewitt, V.J. (1981). *Toys and games in libraries*. London: Library Association Publishing.

Jang, W. (2001, November 22). Children under 6-years benefit inspire [sic] intellectual development. *Ming Pao* (Richmond, BC), p. A7.

Johnson, E. (1978). *The toy library: A how-to handbook*. St. Paul, MN: Toys 'n' Things Training and Resource Center.

Lindberg, M., Björck-Åkesson , E., & Brodin, J.M. (1988). *Toy libraries in Sweden in 1988*. Paper presented at the First International Conference on Family Support, Stockholm, August 4–10, 1988. (ERIC Document Reproduction Service No. ED 307 765)

Mayfield, M.I. (1988). Toy libraries in Canada: A research study. *Canadian Children, 13*(2), 1–18.

Mayfield, M.I. (1993). Toy libraries: Promoting play, toys, and family support internationally. *Early Child Development and Care, 87*, 1–13.

Mayfield, M.I. (2001). *Early childhood care and education in Canada: Contexts, dimensions, and issues*. Toronto: Prentice Hall.

Misurcova, V. (1986). The toy library—A new phenomenon. *Prospects, 16*(4), 513–520.

National Association of Toy and Leisure Libraries (2000). *Starting out*. London: Author.

National Toy Libraries Association (1984). *Getting going: A guide to setting up and running a toy library.* Potters Bar, Herts., UK: Play Matters.

Preschool Services and Parent education Committee (1981). *Opening doors for preschool children and their parents*. Chicago: American Library Association.

Rettig, M.A. (1998). Guidelines for beginning and maintaining a toy library. *Early Childhood Education Journal, 25*(4), 229–232.

Scottish Executive (2001, May 2). £75,000 boost for toy and leisure libraries [Press release]. Retrieved February 15, 2002, from http://www.scotland.gov.uk/news/2001/05/ se1177.asp

Sutton-Smith, B. (1997). *The ambiguity of play*. Cambridge, MA: Harvard University Press.

Swiniarski,L.B. (1991). Toys: Universals for teaching global education. *Childhood Education, 67*(3), 161–163.

Walters, L.S. (1998, January 16). Kids check out favorite toys—at the library. *Christian Science Monitor, 90*(33), 12.

Yawkey, T.D. & Toro-Lopez, J.A. (1985). Examining descriptive and empirically based typologies of toys for handicapped and non-handicapped children. *Topics in Early Childhood Special Education, 5*(3), 47–58.

Some resource websites on toy libraries are:
http://www.frp.ca—Family Resource Programs Canada
http://usatla.deltacollege.org—USA Toy Library Association
http://www.lekotek.org—National Lekotek Centers (USA)
http://natl.org.uk—National Association of Toy and Leisure Libraries (UK)
http://itla-toylibraries.org—International Toy Libraries Association

Chapter Sixteen

"Hey, No fair": Young Children's Perceptions of Cheating During Play

Robyn M. Holmes, Jennifer M. Valentino-McCarthy, and Susan L. Schmidt

McCabe, Trevino, and Butterfield's (2001) recent review of cheating in academe suggested that these behaviors are not only pervasive but also on the rise in comparison to past decades. Interestingly, the majority of studies that have investigated cheating in school have focused upon college and university level students. Such studies have explored students' perceptions and attitudes toward cheating using national (Wyrobeck & Whitley, 1999) and cross-cultural samples (Lupton & Chapman, 2002; Waugh, Godfrey, Evans, & Craig, 1995); reasons why students cheat (Franklyn-Stokes & Newstead, 1995); sex differences in cheating (Whitley, Nelson & Jones, 1999); individual and contextual factors (DePalmer, Madey, & Bornschein, 1995; McCabe & Trevino, 1997); and cheating in specific academic programs (e.g., Baldwin, Daugherty, Rowley, & Schwarz, 1996; Sierles, Hendrickx, & Circel, 1980) for medical school.

In comparison, fewer studies have investigated children's cheating behaviors in academic settings (Evans & Craig, 1990; Guttmann, 1984; Houser, 1978; Kanfer & Duerfeldt, 1968). For example, Murphy's (1987) work discusses the typical characteristics of the child cheater, parent and teacher vantage points on cheating, the relationship between cheating and moral development.

CHEATING AND MORAL DEVELOPMENT

The literature on the relationship between moral development and cheating behaviors includes theoretical and empirical works. Morality can be defined as the rightness or wrongness of an action and past research suggests that a person's immediate surroundings and culture can influence his or her definition of morals (e.g., Guttmann, 1984; Lobel & Levanon, 1988; Simon, 1991; Waugh, et al., 1995). Such a definition comes in to play during a person's behavioral decision-making process. If a person is strongly socialized to internalize moral values then he or she may be less likely to engage in negative actions such as cheating (Guttmann, 1984). In this instance one's moral values suggest that cheating is not the norm and it is "wrong." However, cheating is dependent upon a variety of factors such as prior personal experiences (Ross & Ross, 1969); cultural ideology (Simon, 1991); and interpretation of the moral dilemma (Gilligan, 1982; Kohlberg, 1984; Peskay, 1977).

For example, Leming (1978) found that when "high moral" children were placed in a low supervision situation, they cheated just as much as the other children. One plausible explanation is that although these children practiced strong moral values, they may have also needed to fulfill a great desire for approval. In addition, some children struggle over whether to "be the best" rather than "trying their best." For example, Lobel and Levanon (1988) found that children with high socioeconomic status and a high need for approval had a tendency to cheat more than other children did. One might suspect that the reason for this behavior is the notion that they *had* to fulfill that need for approval.

The examination of cheating through the lenses of various theoretical frameworks also contributes to our understanding of children's cheating behaviors. Implicit in such investigations is the notion that factors such as parental, societal, religious, and peer influences should be acknowledged in explaining children's moral development (Lerner & Galambos, 1987).

For example, Bandura's (1977) social learning theory suggests that moral development is acquired through both direct and indirect observations of a model. Here the consequences following the behavior determine whether or not the child will spontaneously repeat the behavior. According to this view, a child develops his or her own feelings of right and wrong, as well as the consequences that are associated with the behavior. For example, in the preschool years a child learns to attach leniency or anxiety to punishable behaviors as learned through experiences with parental, teacher, and peer reactions (Festinger, 1957; Ross & Ross, 1969).

Other approaches such as Kohlberg's (1969) cognitive developmental framework suggest that a child's moral thoughts and actions are considered a direct link to his or her own response to negative behaviors. He concludes that even young children have the ability to process various rights, moral obligations, and privileges. Similarly, Guttmann (1984) found that a child's moral behavior and reasoning were directly associated with feelings of guilt and temptation as they related to cheating habits.

Psychoanalytical perspectives have also been employed to explain children's cheating behavior. According to Freud (1938), emphasis can be placed on the direct role of the parent as a primary influence in the formation of the child's conscience. He argued that parents are responsible for the moral standards their children adopt and utilize throughout early childhood in dealing with conflict and judgment. This notion has received support from Woolgar's (2001) findings on moral development. He found that young children's justifications for cheating are a direct result of their moral framework. Finally, Erikson (1966) suggested that a cheater would challenge his or her moral boundaries and cheat to optimize winning. These cheating behaviors emerge in both individual and group level interactions.

CHEATING AND FAIRNESS

A related concept to cheating that deserves discussion is fairness or fair play. This often appears in the sports and moral development literature and is intricately linked to notions of cheating. For example, Covrig's (1996) theoretical work posits a distinction between fairness and fair play. In this work, fairness in a general sense is a culturally sanctioned notion of justice as it applies to everyday face to face encounters. Fair play is more restricted in scope and applies to those interactions that occur during play and formal sport contexts. This construct will be applicable to the current work.

For example, in his discussion on fair play, Covrig (1996) draws upon several explanatory sources. One of those is Piaget's (1951) notion of children's rule use during play. His interpretation of Piaget's work suggests that children modify and manipulate the rules of play for a variety of reasons that include contextual matters and the actors present in the scene. Thus children view fair play as a malleable rather than static construct.

Empirical evidence exists to support this notion. Researchers such as Hughes (1989) have shed light on "gaming," how players manipulate, modify, and employ game rules in specific real life contexts (p. 103). Clearly this construct is important to children during play. Casual observations of such scenes suggest that children identify those players and actions that "violate" the rules of the game (Covrig, 1996, p. 272).

Recently, other researchers such as Bekoff (2001) have explored the evolution of social morality, in particular "behaving fairly" in animal species using the play context (p. 83). Bateson's (1972) construct of "framing" and the notion that players can *metacommunicate* the message *this is play* surface in Bekoff's work, and he suggests that there may be selective pressure to play fairly. His empirical observations of coyotes suggest that cheaters are not selected as play partners. Certainly, researchers are in agreement that play is one context in which individuals (humans and animal species) participate in the socialization process and that learning about a group's rules can be applied to other situational contexts (e.g., Mechling, 1988; Roberts, 1996).

In contrast to studies that have examined cheating in academic and sport settings, very few studies have examined the nature of cheating as it relates to play. Mechling's work (1988) examined the relationship between play, cheating, and creativity. In this work, Mechling (1988) presents several different viewpoints of cheating. Adopting Bateson's (1972) theory of "metacommunication," he focuses upon the game as a "frame" or context in which cheating occurs (p. 347). Thus he views cheating as a contextual action in which one "cuts corners," i.e., breaks or manipulates the rules of a particular frame (p. 347). Other works that peripherally address cheating in play include McCosh's (1976) work on children's humor and Sluckin's (1981) work on the playground as a socializing agent.

The current study explores children's cheating behaviors at play in a kindergarten classroom from an emic perspective. As Mechling (1988) noted, there is a paucity of literature that addresses children's cheating in natural settings and real-life contexts and situations. This work is an attempt to expand our knowledge about cheating in play and draws upon several theoretical frameworks. First, Bateson's "metacommunication" and "framing" influenced the choice of play, i.e., board games. Following Mechling's (1988) logic, games are viewed as a frame in which one can come to understand cheating.

Second, the notion that cheating is contextual draws upon both Batesonian and Vygotskian theories (see also Covrig, 1996 for a related discussion on fairness and fair play). Hence, cheating occurs under certain situations and contexts during which time the players are able to communicate to and with one another about the meaning of the behaviors. Finally, Hughes' (1989) notion of "gaming" is also relevant since the rules by which one cheats are specific to particular contexts and actors present. In this study, we expect to find that children cheat in certain situations and contexts and that these actions are dependent upon a variety of factors that include the actors present, the type of play, and notions of fairness and cheating.

METHOD

Participants

In this sample, there were 12 (3 boys and 9 girls) kindergarten children although two girls departed before the school year ended. Ages ranged from 68 to 80 months with a mean of 72.20 months (SD=4.47months). The class was ethnically diverse. There were five European American children (4 girls, 1 boy), three Chinese American children (2 boys, 1 girl), and one Phillipino (girl), one Korean American (girl), one Japanese (girl), and one Native American (girl) child. The teacher was a European American female who had several years of experience in early childhood education. Consent was granted by the institution's director and the children were treated according to the American Psychological Association's guidelines for ethical codes of conduct (American Psychological Association, 1992).

Stimulus Materials

The children were provided with the following games and playthings from which to choose. Board game selections included "Checkers," "Chess," "Candyland," "Chutes and Ladders," "Snakes and Ladders," "Trouble," and "Operation." In addition, the children used playing cards (regular deck of 52 playing cards) for "War." Other card games such as "Uno," "Scooby Doo," and "Go Fish" were also available. These board and card games were selected because they are deemed developmentally appropriate for this age group. These games have simple rules, are challenging, their outcome is based upon luck, and a sense of fairness is internalized at this age (Rosenfeld, 2005; Van Hoorn, Nourot, Scales, & Alward, 1999). In the early childhood curriculum, board games such as "Chess" (Bankauskas, 2000), "Checkers" (DeVries, et al., 2002), "Chutes and Ladders" (Bjorklund, 2004) and card games such as "Go Fish" (Van Hoorn et al., 1999) have been linked to promoting problem-solving and math and social skills. Finally, the children's teacher was also consulted and many of these games were already part of their classroom's play materials.

Design and Procedure

This study utilized a qualitative design. The primary method of investigation was participant observation and this was supplemented with informal interviewing and teacher perceptions. The fieldwork period began in November 2001 and ended in June 2002 for a total of 32 visits. Typically, visits were one day a week for approximately 1½ hours, although multiple visits in one week and longer observation periods also occurred.

The first author was introduced to the children as "Miss Robyn" and she explained to them that she was "going to watch you play board games and ask you some questions about cheating. If at any time you don't feel like playing or talking with me that's ok. Just tell me so I know you wish to do something else." This stemmed in part from her adult status and the term of address the children use with their teachers. The first author attenuated her adult authority by playing with the children and not administering discipline. Her relationship with the children approximated what Mandell (1988) termed the "friend role" (see also Fine & Sandstrom, 1988; Greig & Taylor, 1999).

For a child researcher, a critical task in successfully achieving this role is the ability to express positive affect without disciplining or controlling the children's behavior (Fine, 1999). To establish a trusting and respectful relationship with the children, the first author played with them during indoor and outdoor playtimes, sat with them during circle time, did schoolwork with them, and did not discipline them. Once the children adjusted to her presence and they were comfortable interacting with her, she asked for requests of games they might like to play.

On each visit, the first author brought no more than two games for the children to play. For example, one day she might have brought "Trouble" and "Candyland." On another occasion, the children could play "War" or "Snakes and Ladders." Usually she asked the children at the end of the visit what games they would like to play next time.

Games were played in the children's classrooms on available tables. Any child who asked to play a particular game was given the opportunity to do so. If the game could not support additional players, these children were slotted to play as soon as the game ended or on the researcher's next visit. The available board games supported a maximum of four players. The exceptions were "Checkers" and "Chess" (two players) and "Operation" (two to six players). Average group size for multiplayer board games was three to four players. "Uno" (two to ten players) and "Scooby Doo" (two to four players) were played most frequently with two players. The card game "War" can support more than four players. The average group size for this game was typically three to four players. Although the children were encouraged to play alone, occasionally the researcher was asked to play and (gladly!) did so.

When observing play, the first author sat either with the children at the playing table or just behind the area in which they were playing. If two games were simultaneously in progress, she adopted a position midway between each playing area so that she could see and hear the activity occurring in both areas. During play, the children conversed informally with her on the topic of cheating. Sample questions included: "How do you feel when someone cheats?" "Is it ever okay to cheat?" "What are some of the ways you can cheat at the game being played?" and "Would you rather cheat against a girl or boy?" All observations and interviews were recorded in the form of field notes. On several occasions the second author had the opportunity to visit with the children, participate in their activities, and record observations as well. After these sessions, the first and second author compared their observational field notes to ensure the reliability of what behaviors constituted cheating during play. Only the first author engaged in informal interviewing with the children.

Coding and Data Analysis

The first author taught the second and third author the coding procedure for the field notes that included observational and interview material. Three coders were employed to ensure reliability. Informal interview questions were the anchor in the coding process. Categorical domains were formed from the children's verbatim responses to these questions and similar responses were subsumed into their respective domains. For example, when asked the question "Why do people cheat at play?," the children's primary response was that "you cheat to win." This repeated response formed the domain 'Cheating to win' and then the children's individual responses such as "you cheat to win" and "I cheat because I want to win." were included in this larger domain. Sometimes, a child's response might include more than one category such as "I know I'm not supposed to cheat (moral issue) but I want to win (cheating to win)." For every response, multiple phrases were coded, placed into their respective categories, and counted separately (see Bernard, 2002; Holmes, 2005).

Observational field notes were coded similarly. First, all examples of the larger domain, *Cheating* were identified. These were then categorized into smaller, inclusive categories such as *cheating to win*, *cheating at school*, and *ways to cheat*. Observations and interview materials were also coded for gender of the participant(s). There were no inter-coder disagreements.

The teacher's perceptions were the third source of data. Observations and children's responses were supported by the teacher's understanding of the children's cheating behaviors. Typically after a visit or several visits, the first author would arrange a time to speak with the teacher when the children were not present, typically after school hours. At this time, the first author would recount her observations and the children's responses to queries on cheating to obtain the teacher's views on the findings. The teacher never directly read the field notes. Rather the first author discussed entries from the field notes with her. This occurred over the fieldwork period. Since she had also been some of the children's preschool teacher, she was believed to be a trusted source regarding the children's behavior patterns.

RESULTS

This section contains the children's responses acquired during informal and unstructured conversations that occurred during free play when they were playing a game. Other play episodes appear as well and these are duly noted.

Why Do (You) People Cheat at Play?

According to these children, people primarily cheat to win. Two girls offered respectively the following explanations. Jane stated, "You cheat to win because it's not fair if you lose all the time, so you can cheat to win." Similarly, Michele added, "Some people want to win and when they can't win fair they cheat. People don't like to lose all the time." The children frequently used the following phrases during play. They were: "I want to win." "Am I winning?" (A question that arose when comparing each other's game piece place on the board); "Yes, I'm winning!" (This exclamation was used by both girls and boys when they were winning a game); and "You're losing, I'm winning." (This was sometimes used as a simple declarative or sometimes employed as power).

Richard further confirmed his classmates' notions and behaviors about cheating, "They want to try to win. Some people cry because they didn't win." Several children (Nicole and Jim) employed similar strategies when losing. If cheating was not effective, they began to cry. I did not see one episode where either of these children were not consoled, told they won, and made to feel better by their classmates.

Observation revealed that the children rarely cheated when they were learning a new game. Helping and cooperating were common among the players. Even those children who were simply watching others play also offered helpful suggestions. Perhaps one cheats when one believes the other players are capable of winning on their own.

Feelings about Cheating

The children were asked, "Do you like it when someone cheats while you're playing?" Not one child reported positive feelings about being the victim of cheating. The children's responses to this query appear in Table 16.1.

Cheating in School

Interestingly, several of the children were puzzled when I asked them about cheating at school. For example, both Jim and Michele responded to this query with, "How do you cheat in school?" These responses were confirmed by the teacher's perceptions and observations. She noted that some

Table 16.1. Children's Reponses to the Query, "Do You Like It When Someone Cheats While You're Playing?"

Sex of Child	*Reponses*
Boys	*Competition:* No, I don't want anyone else to win. I want to win. *Fairness/Logical:* No, because that's not the way you're supposed to play the game.
Girls	*Taken advantage of:* It's like they try and trick you and I don't like being tricked. *Play isn't fun:* When somebody cheats after a while nobody wants to play because it's not fun; It's not that fun. *Play Advantages:* No, because they could block my turn. *Personality:* No, because it's mean. *Feelings:* No, they're mean and it makes you sad. (Kids feel sad and grumpy); No, they hurt my feelings when they cheat on me. Fairness: It's not fair. (2)

Note: Number in parentheses represents the number of children who provided that response.

of the children never cheated at schoolwork although they did not do so for different reasons. She noted that in Michele's case, the decision not to cheat was a moral one; whereas for Jim cheating simply wasn't an option. If he couldn't perform a task he wouldn't complete it. The other two children who never cheated were believed respectively to be a logical thinker and naïve.

In contrast, Jane was able to explain how one cheats at school. She explained, "When you look over at someone's paper and then try to copy it so you can get it right. You don't want to get a bad grade so you copy it." The teacher was also able to confirm this explanation. She noted that the cheating that does occur involves looking at another's paper and noted that five children in the class often did so. However she added that their motivation to cheat differed as well. For example, one female child cheated as a result of parental pressure for good or "perfect" grades; whereas another child cheated for attention. The children's responses to "Why do you cheat in school?" supported this. For example to this query Jane responded, "You cheat to get it right so that it's correct."

Is it Wrong to Cheat in School?

All of the children agreed that cheating in school was wrong. For example, Michele responded, "Cheating is bad. You just shouldn't." Mare added, "Cheating is bad, bad, BAD."

The Consequences of Cheating at School and Play

The children were asked, "What would happen if you cheated in school?" Most acknowledged that cheating had consequences. For example, Jim replied, "Cause you could get in trouble." Michele noted, "You could make your friends mad." Jane expanded upon this, "Yeah, 'cause a friend could get mad at you 'cause they're copying off of you and they're taking what you're thinking. Then the teacher yells at them but it's the other person's fault for looking and copying." To which she added you could get "detention."

The children were asked, "What would happen if you cheated in play?" Michele noted, "It makes people sad. Sometimes we stop because of it." This is related to the strategies the children employed for dealing with cheaters during play. Three emerged from the children's responses and these were confirmed by observation. First, "tell them you can't cheat." This occurred frequently during play. Play would be suspended while the cheater was admonished and then in most cases play would resume.

Second, "call them a cheater." This also occurred during play. The children could easily identity their classmates who cheated often. For example, Jane, Michele, and Mare were playing "Go Fish" when the following conversation arose. Jane to Michele: "Kelly (who was playing with Jim at the next table) always wins 'cause she cheats." Mare to Michele and Jane: "Yeah, she cheats all the time." Michele nodded agreeingly. Third, "Tell the teacher." Frequently the children called their teacher's attention to either the child that was accused of cheating or described the cheating behavior to her for possible resolution. Quite often the children were allowed to resolve their own conflicts on this matter.

Who Do You Cheat Against?

The children were asked whether they would rather cheat against a girl or a boy. Results were somewhat mixed. For example, five girls said they would rather cheat against a boy. Jane noted, "A boy. I like girls better. We're part of the girls club." Mare responded a boy but for different reasons. "A boy because my brother always cheats when we play." The other girls responded a boy "because they're mean." Only one girl reported she would rather cheat against a girl, but no explanation was provided. All boys reported they would rather cheat against a boy because "I just want to cheat."

Fairness and Is It Ever OK to Cheat?/Would You Ever Cheat?

All of the children at one time or another during play used the phrases, "no fair" or "that's not fair" when another child manipulated the rules or cheated.

For example, when Mare was trying to look at Jane's cards during a round of "Go Fish," Jane stated, "You're not supposed to do that (Mare)." To which Kim, the other player in the group added, "Hey that's cheating. That's not fair." In fact, the major reason most children gave for not cheating was related to fairness. However, appeals to fairness also occurred when one child consistently won the game. For example, Kelly was often accused of cheating (almost always warranted) because she won most of the games. Similarly, Jim stated in a game of war with Nicole, "Nic keeps winning. It's not fair."

Interestingly, fairness was also manipulated. For example, in a game of "I Spy" Kelly tricked Jim into selecting a card that would be his target card for a match. When it was not the expected card, he replied, "That's not fair. She tricked me. I get another turn." Kelly agreed and they continued to play. However if he had received the right card, her hint would have been acceptable and he would have kept the match. This ritual occurred numerous times and seemed to be dependent upon the children playing. Both needed to be willing to accept cheating as part of the play.

This supports the children's responses to the query, "When do you cheat?" For example, Nicole stated she cheats "when someone else is cheating." Once a player does cheat, depending upon the players, they will follow suit. For example, when Kelly, Nicole, and Jim were playing cards (all known cheaters), Jim stated, "I gotta peek a couple" and he proceeded to look at his cards. The others players followed suit and no one accused another player of cheating. This behavior was acceptable for this playgroup.

Other examples of attempts to manipulate the rules occurred. For example, Jane and Nicole were playing the card game, "War." A war occurred over aces and Jane lost the ace of spades, her favorite card. She said to Nicole, "I really want that card. That's my favorite card." Nicole replied, "But it's mine." The first author was watching the game and Jane asked her, "Do I have to give it (the card) to her?" She replied, "If you play by the rules, you should give her the card." Jane told Nicole, "I don't want to play anymore." At this point, the game ended because Nicole did not give Jane her card back. If the children involved wish to sustain play, one child typically conceded. Other examples of sustaining play occurred when Jane, Nicole, and Mare were playing war. During a round, Mare said, "I know this isn't how you really play, but we want to keep playing, right?" Players who made statements such as these enjoyed power over their playmates because of the threat of the play ceasing.

Some children also tried diplomatically to further their position in the game. For example when Nicole and Richard were playing "Trouble," she popped the die twice in search of the number of moves she needed. The first author was seated behind the two when Richard approached her to clarify the game rules. He asked, "Are you supposed to pop twice?" The researcher replied, "No, I don't think so." He returned to Nicole with this information who said, "I didn't know you couldn't. Sorry." She smiled sheepishly when he turned to pop the die. Similarly, Kelly was playing "Chutes and Ladders." She asked Michele, "Can I go up the ladder?" Michele replied, "No, you're here." Kelly asked her, "That would be cheating, huh." Requesting to cheat was sometimes a fruitful strategy depending upon the players in the game since some children allowed cheating to occur.

The children also gave definitive answers to the related query, "Is it ever okay to cheat?" (This question was rephrased for some children as "Would you ever cheat?"). All children reported that cheating was not acceptable with the exception of two children. Common responses follow. For example, Jane's response yields clues to the contextual nature of cheating. For her, "It's okay sometimes. Sometimes I cheat because I want to win and when everybody always wins, I want to win too, so I cheat." Similarly, Kelly noted, "Yeah, because when everybody wins and you don't it's not fair. It's okay because you need to win sometimes." Other responses appealed to moral reasons. For example, Wendy noted, ". . . you should tell the teacher cause that's lying and it's not okay to lie." Other children focused upon the consequences of cheating and getting caught. For example, Nicole noted, "It's bad. You could get in trouble." Finally, some children focused upon fairness in their responses. Michele noted, "No, because you see the other person's cards and you know what they have. They win for the wrong reasons."

Ways to Cheat

Although some children never cheated during play, all the children could provide ways to cheat during play which were dependent in part on the game. In Table 16.2 is a list of the ways children revealed one could cheat during play. All were confirmed with observation of play. Interestingly, some children

Table 16.2. Children's Responses to Ways to Cheat During Play

Type of Game	*Ways to Cheat*
Board Games (Trouble, Snakes and Ladders)	Hitting the bubble (encased dice) really hard (G); Rolling or going twice till you get the number you want (G); Going out of turn (B); Moving spaces that don't coincide with your roll (G)
Card Games (I Spy, War, Go Fish)	Peeking (B & G); sneaking (B); Looking through your cards and taking out the ones you want (G); Drawing more than one card (G); Going out of turn (B)

Note: (B) and (G) designate the sex of the child respondent.

cheated subtly while others performed blatant acts of cheating. Observations from both the first and second author confirmed that children tend to cheat when the other player(s) are not attending to the move at hand. For example, when Nicole and the second author were playing "Trouble," Nicole cheated when the second author was distracted. Before the distraction, the second author had three men on the board. After the distraction, only one remained. The second author did not acknowledge she knew the pieces were missing. On her next move, Nicole replied, "I'm still winning."

How Do You Deal With Cheaters?

The children employed several strategies for dealing with cheaters during play and most children consistently used the same strategy. For example, Kim, Richard, Jane, and Michele always acknowledged the cheater and asked him or her to correct or stop the behavior. The cheater would receive comments such as "Hey, you can't do that" or "You're a cheater" and play would continue. Other children like Nicole and Jim often cried when they were accused emphatically about cheating or if they weren't winning.

Cheaters responded to these accusations in diverse yet consistent ways. For example, Jim typically denied the accusation or blamed it on someone else. Other children refused to admit cheating had occurred. During a card game, Jane replied after every accusation, "I didn't peek. You didn't see me peek 'cause I didn't." Other children such as Kelly simply smiled and acknowledged the fact she was cheating. Her attitude was consistently, "Okay you caught me," or "So what?"

Cheating as Power

Players often employed cheating to take control of the play. For example, while playing "Trouble" Kelly moved Joey's piece for him to the space where she wanted it to land. He is a quiet and passive child and did not protest. However in another game when Kelly tried to spin the die and move for Nicole, Nicole stopped her from doing so. "That's my man, you're not supposed to move it. I do." A child's ability to control play was dependent on his or her social status and the status of the other players involved in the game. In this class, every child but one typically controlled their own play.

DISCUSSION

This study's findings support the hypothesis that children cheat in certain situations and contexts. Although alternative explanations for their cheating are possible, these children's decisions to cheat during play were primarily based upon their desire to win, fairness, and whether cheating was deemed appropriate by the playgroup. The children's remarks and observable cheating behaviors clearly suggest that morality, social expectations, and fairness play a major role in the activity of cheating.

With respect to fair play, our findings are consistent with those reported by Covrig (1996). For him, fair play has three major components: *a means to appropriate ends*; *a system of rules*; and *concern for others*. These themes emerge in our findings. For example when the children were asked, "Why do people cheat at play?" a common response was "You cheat to win" or "I want to win." This lends support to the notion that the cheater cheats for the purpose of a favorable outcome. It was apparent that when the cheating strategies failed, most children were inclined to respond by crying and were then, interestingly, consoled by their classmates and told that they had won or were made to feel better.

Pervasive throughout the fieldwork are instances in which the children were caught cheating or breaking the rules. On each of these occasions various reactions from both the cheater(s) as well as the other players were recorded. Our findings support Ross and Ross' (1969) notion that there is a connection between cheating and leniency. He postulates that a child will attach leniency when the rules to an "achievement situation" have been violated or broken. When these children were accused of or caught cheating, the common response was an apology or a form of reasoning to forgo the consequences.

Play, fairness, and cheating appear to be entwined. For example, Bekoff (2001) suggests that children learn the "ground rules" as to what is acceptable during play. He suggests that in order for there to be fair play, a certain understanding must first be acquired. Thereafter, a level of trust and realization can be established as a basis for fair play. Thus playing games serves as a context in which these children learned what is and is not socially acceptable with respect to cheating and other behaviors.

In response to the query "Is it okay to cheat?" some children believed cheating was appropriate in certain situations or contexts. For example, some believed cheating was okay, especially if the child hadn't won in some time. In addition, cheating occurred under *fair* circumstances too (see e.g., Mechling, 1988; Roberts, 1996). Other children approached the query from a moral standpoint. As one child noted, cheating was considered lying and " . . . it's not okay to lie."

Our study suggests that cheating, fair play, and morality have a distinct connection to the domain of play. These children recognize and view cheating as unfair, yet it also has many functions. Some of these functions are seen as unacceptable, while others are deemed situationally permissible. It is also apparent that morality plays a part in a child's decision to cheat as well as the consequences that are attached to the cheating behavior. For example, when children responded to queries about cheating in school, they focused primarily upon the consequences of the behavior. If one cheated in school, one could "get into trouble" and it was "bad." Such consequences did not emerge in play with peers. Given the children's age and cognitive abilities, it seems reasonable to suppose that they had internalized moral values (Rosenfeld, 2005), associated the consequences of their actions with approval or punishment (Kohlberg, 1969; 1984), and considered the context in which these actions occurred (Bekoff, 2001). Finally, we can offer evidence that a child's desire to win is also a reason to cheat (Covrig, 1996).

There were several limitations to the current study. First, although the sample was ethnically diverse it was also small. Thus we are reluctant to extend these findings to a broader sample. Second, the findings relate only to play with board games and cards. Thus some of the behaviors and responses may have been driven in part by the characteristics of the games themselves.

As Mechling (1988) noted, there is a paucity of literature that addresses children's cheating in real-life contexts and natural settings. Future studies may wish to further pursue the relationship between play, cheating, and fairness. It appears that children cheat during play under certain contexts and situations. These themes might be further explored. Finally, it would be interesting to examine the social structure of children's play groups in terms of investigating whether children avoid engaging in play with cheaters or elect to include them in their social units. Such studies may have applied value and help us broaden our understanding of how play functions as a socializing agent.

REFERENCES

American Psychological Association (1992). Ethical principles of psychologists and code of conduct. *American Psychologist, 47,* 1597–1611.

Baldwin, D., Daugherty, S., Rowley, B., & Schwarz, M. (1996). Cheating in medical school: A survey of second-year students at 31 schools. *Academic Medicine, 71,* 267–273.

Bandura, A., (1977). *Advances in experimental social psychology*. Upper Saddle River, NJ: Prentice Hall.

Bankauskas, D. (2000). Teaching chess to young children. *Young Children, 55,* 33–34.

Bateson, G. (1972). *Steps to an ecology of mind*. New York: Ballantine Books.

Bekoff, M. (2001). Social play behavior: Cooperation, fairness, trust, and the evolution of morality. *Journal of Consciousness Studies, 8,* 81–90.

Bernard, H. (2002). *Research methods in anthropology: Qualitative and quantitative approaches (3rd ed)*. Walnut Creek, CA: Altamira Press.

Bjorklund, D. (2004). Young children's arithmetic strategies in social context: How parents contribute to children's strategy development while playing games. *International Journal of Behavioral Development, 28*(4), 347–357.

Covrig, D. (1996). Sport, fair play, and children's conceptions of fairness. *Journal for a Just & Caring Education, 2*, 263–279.

DePalmer, M., Madey, S., & Bornschein, S. (1995). Individual differences and cheating behavior: Guilt and cheating in competitive situations. *Personality and Individual Differences, 18*, 761–769.

DeVries, R., Zan, B., Hildebrandt, C., Edmiaston, R., & Sales, C. (2002). *Developing Constructivist Early Childhood Curriculum: Practical Principles and Activities. Early Childhood Education Series*. Williston, VT: Teachers College Press.

Erikson, K., (1966). *Wayward Puritans; a study in the sociology of deviance.* New York: Wiley.

Evans, E., & Craig, D. (1990). Teacher and student perceptions of academic cheating in middle and senior schools. *Journal of Educational Research, 84,* 44–50.

Festinger, L. (1957). *Theory of Cognitive Dissonance*. Evanston, IL.: Row, Peterson.

Fine, G. (1999). Methodological problems of collecting folklore from children. In B. Sutton-Smith, J. Mechling, T. Johnson & F. McMahon (Eds.), *Children's Folklore: A Source Book* (pp. 121–139). Logan, UT: Utah State University Press.

Fine, G., & Sandstrom, K. (1988). *Knowing children: Participant observation with minors.* (Vol. 15: Qualitative Methods Series). Newbury Park, CA: Sage Publications.

Franklyn-Stokes, A., & Newstead, S. (1995). Undergraduate cheating: Who does what and why? *Studies in Higher Education, 20,* 39–52.

Freud, S. (1938). *A general introduction to psychoanalysis*. (English translation revised ed. By J. Riviere). New York: Garden City Publications.

Gilligan, C. (1982). *In a different voice: Psychological theory and women's development*. Cambridge, MA: Harvard University Press.

Greig, A., & Taylor, J. (1999). *Doing research with children*. Thousand Oaks, CA: Sage Publications.

Guttmann, J. (1984). Cognitive morality and cheating behavior in religious and secular school children. *Journal of Education Research, 77,* 249–254.

Holmes, R.M. (2005). Working to play: College student athletes' conceptions of play and work. In F. McMahon, D. Lytle & B. Sutton-Smith (Eds.). *Play: An interdisciplinary synthesis: Play & Culture Studies, 6* (pp. 209–231). Landham, MD: University Press of America.

Houser, B. (1978, Summer). Cheating among elementary grade level students: An examination. *Journal of Instructional Psychology, 5,* 2–5.

Hughes, L. (1989). Foursquare: A Glossary and "Native" taxonomy of game rules. *Play & Culture, 2,* 103–136.

Kanfer, F., & Duerfeldt, P. (1968). Age, class standing, and commitment as Determinants of cheating in children. *Child Development, 39,* 545–557.

Kohlberg, L., (1969). Stage and Sequence: The cognitive-development approach to socialization. *Handbook of socialization theory and research* (pp. 20). Chicago, Ill: Randy McNally.

Kohlberg, L. (1984). *Essays on moral development (Vol. 2). The psychology of moral development*. San Francisco: Harper & Row.

Leming, J. S. (1978). Cheating behavior, situational influence, and moral development. *Journal of Education Research, 71,* 214–217.

Lerner, R., & Galambos, N. (1987). *Experiencing Adolescents: A Sourcebook for Parents, Teachers, and Teens* (pp. 232–254). New York & London: Teachers College, Columbia University.

Lobel, T. E., & Levanon, I. (1988). Self-esteem, need for approval, and cheating behavior in children. *Journal of Education Research, 80,* 122–123.

Lupton, R., & Chapman, K. (2002). Russian and American college students' attitudes, perceptions and tendencies toward cheating. *Educational Research, 44,* 17–27.

Mandell, N. (1988). The least-adult role in studying children. *Journal of Contemporary Ethnography, 16,* 433–467.

McCabe, D., & Trevino, L. (1997). Individual and contextual influences on academic dishonesty: A multi-campus investigation. *Research in Higher Education, 38,* 279–291.

McCabe, D., Trevino, L., & Butterfield, K. (2001). Cheating in academic institutions: A decade of research. *Ethics & Behavior, 11,* 219–232.

McCosh, S. (1976). *Children's humour: a joke for every occasion*. New York: Granada Publications.

Mechling, J. (1988). On the relation between creativity and cutting corners. In S. Feinstein (Ed.), *Adolescent Psychiatry: developmental and clinical studies* (Annals of the American Society for Adolescent Psychiatry, Vol. 15). (pp. 346–366). Chicago: University of Chicago Press.

Murphy, J. P. (1987). Children and cheating. In A. Thomas & J. Grimes (Eds.), *Children's needs: Psychological perspectives* (pp. 83–87). Washington, DC: The National Association of School Psychologists.

Peskay, J. (1977). Contextual determinants of children's cheating behavior. (Doctoral Dissertation, University of Minnesota, 1977). *Dissertation Abstracts International, 38* (12B), 6124.

Piaget, J. (1951). *Play, dreams and imitation*. (C. Gattegno & F. Hodgson, Trans.). New York: Norton.

Roberts, T. (1996). Cheating in sport: Recent considerations. *Sport Science Review, 5,* 72–86.

Rosenfeld, A. (2005) *The Benefits of Board Games*. Retrieved July 15, 2005 from http://www.scholastic.com/schoolage/kindergarten/development//boardgames.html.

Ross, D., & Ross, S. (1969). Leniency toward cheating in preschool children. *Journal of Education Psychology, 60,* 483–487.

Sierles, F., & Hendrickx, I., & Circel, S. (1980). Cheating in medical school. *Journal of Medical Education, 55,* 145–169.

Simon, R. (1991). *Fair play: Sports, values, and society*. Boulder, CO: Westview Press.

Sluckin, A. (1981). *Growing up in the playground: The social development of children*. London: Routledge & Kegan Paul.

Van Hoorn, J., Nourot, P., Scales, B., & Alward, K. (1999). *Play at the center of the curriculum (2nd ed).* Upper Saddle River, NJ: Prentice Hall, Inc.

Waugh, R.F., Godfrey, J. R., Evans, E. D., & Craig, D. (1995). Measuring students' perceptions about cheating in six countries. *Australian Journal of Psychology, 47,* 73–80.

Whitley, B., Nelson, A., & Jones, C. (1999). Gender differences in cheating attitudes and Classroom cheating behavior: A meta-analysis. *Sex Roles, 41,* 657–680.

Woolgar, M., (2001). Children's play narrative responses to hypothetical dilemmas and their awareness of moral emotions. *British Journal of Developmental Psychology, 19,* 115–128.

Wryobeck, J., & Whitley, B. (1999). Educational value orientation and peer perceptions of cheaters. *Ethics & Behavior, 9,* 231–242.

ACKNOWLEDGMENTS

The first author acknowledges that this work was supported in part by a Grant-in-Aid-for-Creativity from Monmouth University.

The authors wish to thank the children, teacher, director, and learning center for their participation in this project.

Chapter Seventeen

Clinical Approaches to Achieving Positive Environments With Suicidal Aboriginal Adolescents: Play and Culturally Sensitive Considerations

Melanie S. MacNeil

This paper considers the value of creating a positive, playful atmosphere in therapeutic interview settings with Aboriginal youth who have attempted to commit suicide. According to McCrea (2004), the use of humor and caring when interacting with this population of youth offsets difficult life experiences and enhances adaptive coping mechanisms.

The number of suicides in the First Nations population is higher than in non-Aboriginal populations. A First Nations adolescent male aged 10–19 is 5.1 times more likely to die from suicide than a non-Indian adolescent male. In women of the same age group, there are seven times as many suicides among First Nations Canadians (35 per 100,000) than among non-Aboriginal Canadians. For each completed suicide, there are 6–8 attempted suicides among the 8–24 year old males (Ferry, 2000; Health Canada, 2003a; Canadian Institute of Child Health, 2000). The rate of suicide in Canadian Aboriginal youth is 5–6 to 36 times higher than other populations depending on location (Weir & Wallington, 2001). In Northwestern Ontario, there is a rate of 126 deaths per 100,000 and in some areas in the Canadian North, the rate is the highest in the world and is 36 times the national average (Ferry, 2000; Ellroy, 1999; Health Canada, 2003b).

Wide variations in reporting local and regional suicide rates conceal an accurate suicide rate, and current data collection tools are inadequate (Cutcliffe, 2003; MacNeil & Guilmette, 2004). Coultard (1999) contends that under-reporting further conceals an accurate rate. In British Columbia, researchers estimated that 25 % of accidental deaths in Native communities were unreported suicides (Stephenson, 1995; Coultard, 1999; Kirmayer et al., 1993; Chandler & Lalonde, 1998). Chenier (1995) in her mini-review of the Royal Commission on Aboriginal suicide reports similar discrepancies.

Chandler and Lalonde (1998) suggest that reporting differences in youth suicide are related to the degree of cultural continuity that is present in the community. Factors such as self-governance, educational services, land-claim negotiations, and cultural health facilities provided a protective element that translated into lower suicide rates.

There is an urgent need to study attempted adolescent suicide rather than relying on retrospective data collected after the completed act. Suicide is complex and different for Aboriginal youth who have specific risk factors related to social, historical, economic, psychological, and cultural stressors (Chandler, Lalonde, Sokal, & Hallett, 2003). The National Aboriginal Health Organization (NAHO, 2001) and the Institute of Aboriginal People's Health (IAPH, 2002) recognized the need to address cultural, social and emotional issues using research methods that promote health in the individual Aboriginal, the family and community and the use of a playful format that is culturally appropriate for such a serious issue may help to unlock this silent epidemic (MacNeil & Guilmette, 2004). Traditional methods of attempted suicide management are inadequate and non-specific to Aboriginal communities, and individual interventions are limited and do not address the scope of the problem (Niagara District Health Council, 2003b).

The next sections consider historical, socio-economic, psychological, physical, and cultural health risk factors that contribute to high suicide rates among Aboriginal populations and the reasons for playful and culturally sensitive interview strategies used in this research.

HISTORICAL FACTORS

Research indicates that Colonial policies related to residential schools, reserve communities, loss of traditional lands, and erosion of language and cultural traditions have created a loss of cohesion and identity in Aboriginal communities (Coultard 1999; Smye & Browne, 2002; Chandler & Lalonde, 1998). The interview strategies used in this study address these stressors by responding to the education level of respondents, language used, and cultural norms by the use of humorous storytelling. Strategies were based on the premise that play is an important part in the creation of the subject's historical culture, and leads to the importance of differentiating play from non-play (Harris, 1981), the development of a positive playing field is essential. Historically, disadvantaged groups like Aboriginals have dealt with the pain and confusion of different worldviews by joking about their disadvantages (McGhee, 1999).

SOCIO-ECONOMIC FACTORS

A statistical profile on the Health of First Nations in Canada was conducted by Health Canada (2003b). This report indicates conditions such as sewage, poor and polluted water supply, inadequate dwellings, poverty level income, low-level literacy, and inability of Aboriginal adolescents and their families to meet basic needs create a negative living environment. The lack of these basic requirements further impacts First Nations adolescents by creating an environment where they are not able to compete (Smye & Browne, 2002; Kirmayer et al., 1993). The resultant erosion of self-worth and loss of security from these socio-economic disadvantages creates an atmosphere conducive to depression and decreased coping, which may lead to substance abuse, depression, violence, and suicide (Krysinska, 2003). The introduction of play that provides an educational model and also facilitates a sense of fun and joy are necessary for the Aboriginal adolescent. The use of stories, games, and make-believe augment Aboriginal cultural beliefs, can be introduced at any developmental level, and provide a free therapeutic exchange (Lancy, 1976).

PSYCHOLOGICAL FACTORS

Krysinka (2003) postulates that suicidal behavior is precipitated by feelings of loss of significant relationships and employment, and Lynam and Young (2000) indicate that a subsequent loss of dignity translates into feelings of helplessness, despair and loss of meaning. When there is an additional absence of a social role model, a delayed developmental stage, and a lack of historical and cultural safety, the cumulative result may impact emotional, physical and mental health.

In terms of the assessment of mental health in Aboriginal youth, it is important to understand that in the Aboriginal culture, hallucinations may be considered spiritual and not psychotic. Also, the expression of anger may be a desired expression and is not always considered acting out (Chenier, 1995; Cohen, 1999). To provide balance and to make life livable, the use of humor and play plays an essential role in easing the day-to-day burden of a hostile environment (Emmons, 2000). According to Bacon (2001), "it is impossible to write about Native life without humor—that is how people maintain sanity" (p. 1).

To understand psychological factors, interview techniques must facilitate the external environment that Aboriginal youth find themselves in. From previous experiences of sharing information, the respondent may fear involuntary admission to a psychiatric facility. A specific interview strategy to build trust was used to delay questions about the subject's psychological history until later in the interview process. The social and drug history were also discussed later in the interview process so as not to focus on previous negative psychological experiences. Genuine interest and willingness to be involved on the part of the interviewing counselor are prerequisites. Many Aboriginal adolescents have grown up in a pathological environment that provided many examples of psycho-pathology and few examples of fun that the idea of play evokes. According to Eisen's (1987) discussion of coping through play in the holocaust, "children's play constituted a part of the quest for survival" (p. 133).

PHYSICAL HEALTH

Aboriginal youth often find themselves living in areas that are compromised in terms of physical place. An unhealthy external community and housing environment can be responsible for many health problems related to air and water quality and to asbestos and lead contaminants (Bock & Sabin, 1997). To add to unhealthy environmental conditions, self-poisoning, poor nutrition and chronic diseases such as diabetes, obesity, arthrosclerosis and heart disease are high in this at-risk population (Anand et al., 2001). HIV, AIDS and hepatitis are also diseases that are impacting the health of Aboriginal adolescents (Health Canada, 2003a). The practice of risky "play" behaviors such as unprotected sex, sharing of needles, and gun access are important parts in this disease trajectory that require scrutiny (Niagara District Health Council, 2003a, 2003b).

Interview techniques play an important part in addressing these physical health care demands by providing access to resources for assessing and reporting diseases, educational resources, and linkage to Aboriginal health resources. The inclusion within the interview, of resources such as traditional healing, Elder ceremonies, herbs, and music are important play adjuncts that are needed to complement other health care programs and medical interventions. Song and dance are often incorporated into programs and healing circles to promote joy, health and healing in the Aboriginal culture (Chandler & Lalonde, 1998). Such cultural connections help to align youth with support systems and make finding help something positive and fun. According to Lancy, (2002), "children who are malnourished, ill, or physically abused suffer from a sharp drop in play" (p. 57).

CULTURAL HEALTH

Cultural stress creates a loss of confidence in understanding how to live life and make decisions (Ramsden, 1992; Smye & Browne, 2002; Coulthard, 1999). This loss stems from a history of colonization, anti-Indian policies, and individual and institutional discrimination (McConaghy, 1998). Current mental health policies reflect a political, social and cultural suppression of belief systems and a lack of understanding and acceptance of Native spirituality, which affects the creation of appropriate Aboriginal policy. Chandler & Lalonde (1998) discuss the relationship between self-identity as it relates to self-destructive behaviors among First Nations youth who need to be empowered within the context of their own culture. Research reports a relationship between the youth suicide rate and the degree of control that Aboriginal communities have over their own lives (Krysinkska, 2003; Chandler & Lalonde, 1998; Kirmayer et al., 1993; Chenier, 1995). Suicide rates tend to be lower in communities that have governance of and the ability to plan and share in celebrations (Lynman & Young, 2000; Cohen, 1999; Chandler, Lalonde, Sokal, & Hallett, 2003; Niagara District Health Council, 2003b). The addition of a data collection protocol that respects the Aboriginal youth's ability to see his/her situation from a perspective that allows for play may further aid in the promotion of physical and emotional well-being. According to Mestel (1994), events that promote a sharing, hopeful and relaxing effect (such as humor), can affect the physical realm of health by increasing antibodies and decreasing cortisol. Kuiper, Martin, and Olinger (1993) concede that frequent stimulation of the sympathetic system that occurs when laughter is initiated increases overall functioning and enables a healthier response to stress.

PURPOSE

One purpose of this research was to determine how best to create a positive interview experience for Aboriginal youth aged 18–24 who have recently attempted to commit suicide. In the study described below, an Aboriginal Elder counselor conducted interviews with subjects within the context of an environment that fostered dignity and hope in the interviewee. Another purpose of this study was to increase our understanding of this endemic adolescent health problem and further, to lay the groundwork for the development of culturally specific assessment tools that can be used in the development of effective community and individual clinical interventions while collecting data that reflect accurate rates.

METHOD

Subjects

Data were collected from interviews of those individuals who had attempted suicide. A convenience sample of 4 Aboriginal youth was included in this study. These participants were recruited from a relatively homogeneous population of Aboriginals aged 18–24 years.

Setting

The study was performed in a private room, and consent to participate in the study, including audio-video taping of the individual interview, was obtained from the participant by the Aboriginal counselor who conducted the interview. Each study participant was interviewed face-to-face at the crisis center. The interviews took up to one hour. The Aboriginal counselor was trained by the researcher to administer the interviews for this study in accordance with IRB procedures.

Interview Protocol

Semi-structured, face-to-face interviews were conducted by an Aboriginal Elder who counsels at the crisis center. In an informal and relaxed environment that was cultivated by the Elder as conversation rather than questions and answers, youth responses were uninterrupted. The culture of listening was respected and encouraged. A positive environment was created to foster dignity, hope and a sense of play.

Traditional values, rituals and healing ceremonies are imbedded in the interview in order to provide promotion and development of holism, partnership and community involvement. According to Roopnarine and Johnson (1994), by incorporating play that is consistent with the adolescent's culture, health care professionals can learn to deal more "effectively and humanistically" with important differences, and become sensitive to the diversity and variation that exists in cultural groups (p.6).

Informal conversations were initiated by the Elder following a culturally sensitive smudging ceremony in which the adolescent was directly engaged. Smudging is a sacred Aboriginal ceremony where special herbs are burned to provide a cleansing smoke bath to drive out negative energy. This ceremony begins within a framework of Aboriginal history and healing, including the "Eagle-feather" teachings that is reliant upon storytelling and dramatization of experiences (MacNeil & Guilmette, 2004).

Initial questions included in the conversations asked the Aboriginal youth to describe (a) if suicide has ever been contemplated or attempted, (b) if the youth ever accessed the Aboriginal crisis and counseling center before, and (c) if the youth has consented to participate in the study. Further, through the sharing of stories, the Elder and youth determine if sufficient stability has been achieved prior to the counselor interview proceeding. Other questions that had been piloted and refined for conversational discussion within the positive interview environment were explored: general physical habits (such as involvement in physical activities like sport, kick-ball, hopping, and jumping), emotional involvement (including an exploration of participation in drumming ceremonies), healing-circles and story creation, and mental involvement relating to levels of formal education, extra-curricular activities, and memory games. Spiritual health, connected to revelations of activities experienced in sweat lodges, healing circles, and support group networks and perceived life choices relating to alcohol, drugs, weapons, and other youth at-risk involvements are also discussed. Additionally, cultural activities in drama, music, art, potlatch, and dance are explored. The youth and Elder discuss the period prior to the suicide attempt as well as methods of decision making, lifestyle, future plans, world view, and support networks. The subject's place of residence (on or off reserve) and access to youth activities at these locales was also determined.

DATA MANAGEMENT AND ANALYSIS

Interviews were tape recorded, transcribed, and systematically filed according to the identification of themes, and coded accordingly (Polit & Hungler, 1999). A content and thematic analysis was performed to integrate the emerging themes and concepts and to analyze and interpret the qualitative data.

Data collected from this study indicated that a positive interview environment was created that left interviewees with a sense of acceptance and safety. In addition, all subjects interviewed have attended at least one healing circle and continue to visit the Aboriginal Elder for guidance, support and spiritual and emotional counseling. Of the group of subjects interviewed for this pilot study, there have been no known repeat suicide attempts reported, and the subjects reported that they look forward to coming to the center to speak with their Elder. Reports of increased connectivity with their culture have been noted in all cases. A summary and conclusion of the findings will be provided in a research report that provides identifiable characteristics and a description of current experiences of 18–24 year old Aboriginals who have attempted suicide. This synopsis of the results will serve other counselors at the healing center and will inform programming for future counselors in the field of Aboriginal adolescent suicide.

SUMMARY AND CONCLUSIONS

The literature suggests that a suicide intervention protocol designed in a manner that supports caring and provides empowerment and acceptance enhances the spirit at the heart of the Native culture (WHO, 2002; Malus, Kirmayer, & Boothroyd, 1994; Health Canada, 2003b). The hope generated from a positive interaction in the interview environment may then be transmitted to potential suicide victims and aid in the development of strategies that build hope, an important component of mental health (Health and Welfare Canada, 1996; Johnson, 1999; Stout & Kipling, 1999; Tatz, 1999). As Eisen (1987) suggests, attempts to bring normalcy and familiarity to the environment by constructing a sanctuary of culture help to "insulate" adolescents from "a world gone savage" (p. 129). The Institute of Aboriginal People's Health (IAPH) recognizes the need to address cultural, social and emotional issues by using research methods that promote health in the individual Aboriginal, the family and community (IAPH, 2002). The approach described in this study requires training of people doing Aboriginal research to open lines of communication and provide networking among Aboriginal youth, their Elders, and the First Nations communities, particularly in emergency settings, counseling and crisis centers (Tatz, 1999; McConaghy, 1998).

Findings from this study will form the basis for a subsequent quantitative case-control study that will test for differences between Aboriginal youth who attempt suicide and those who do not. With validation of differences, an appropriate and specific suicide risk assessment protocol will be developed and interventions developed and tested. The overall program of research, for which this study was a beginning step, is aimed at trying to develop a risk management system to reduce the suicide rate in Aboriginal youth in Canada.

Future research on Aboriginal health care issues, including gathering of data on attempted suicide, is required using a team approach. The approach in this study will inform future research questions and frame appropriate methodology to collect necessary data. Aboriginal adolescent suicide is different from suicide in other groups and requires a specific assessment within a positive environment that addresses the "nature of Aboriginal suicide by reflecting social factors and community values" (Tatz, 1999, p. 2). This study provides an interview assessment process as the first step in the development of a culturally sensitive, suicide protocol that excludes, "racism, contempt, denigration, and disempowerment [and removes a] mental disorder model" in the assessment process (Tatz, 1999, p. 8). Given the inconsistent nature of the reporting of suicides among Aboriginal youth, more accurate data are needed.

The creation of a positive interview environment and assessment process is proactively aimed at gaining true insight into suicidality from the adolescents' perspective, as well as collecting desperately needed data in a respectful but playful manner.

When data are collected through informal conversations that are initiated by Elders, and that include culturally sensitive ceremonies such as smudging, then Aboriginal adolescents increase engagement in the process of contributing to their own healing. The importance of emphasizing traditional ceremonies that begin within a framework of Aboriginal history is essential (Johnson, 1999). Within Aboriginal lifestyles, healing occurs more collaboratively when cultural stories are used to frame the experiences of youth. "Eagle-feather" teachings represent a dramatization of experiences that provide an ethic of care and respite from the difficult life journeys experienced by these youth.

When an Aboriginal Elder used an informal and relaxed positive environment that cultivated a playful, conversational discussion rather than question and answer inquiries, the youth responses were lively and engaging. Interactions had minimal interruptions, were quite reflective, and represented a culture where active listening supported respect and dignity. Throughout this culturally sensitive process, Aboriginal youth were inclined to be authentic in their discourse including the sharing of critical and often frightening life episodes. Through the sharing of stories, enjoyable and playful activities were also described and supported as relevant in an Aboriginal context. The development of this culturally sensitive suicide assessment within a positive interview environment has empowered the participants described in this study. These revelations shared in informal and playful, engaging discussions have value, and allow youth to maintain dignity as well as a sense of play.

REFERENCES

Anand, S.S., Yusuf, S., Jacobs, R., Davis, A.D., Yi, Q., Gerstein, H., Montague, P.A., Long, E. (2001). Risk factors, atherosclerosis, and cardiovascular disease among Aboriginal people in Canada: The study of health assessment and risk evaluation in Aboriginal peoples [Electronic Version]. *The Lancet, 358*, 1147.

Bacon, K. (2001). An on-line interview with Louise Erdrich. *The Atlantic Unbound*, 1–4. The Atlantic Monthly Source (on-line source).

Bock, K., & Sabin, N. (1997). *The road to immunity: How to survive and thrive in a toxic world*. New York: Pocket Books.

Canadian Institute of Child Health (2000). *The health of Canada's children: A CICH 7Profile*. Ottawa, ON.

Chandler, M.J., Lalonde, C.E., Sokol, B.W., & Hallett, D. (2003). Personal persistence, identity development, and suicide: A study of native and non-native North American adolescents [Electronic Version]. *Monographs of the Society for Research in Child Development, 68*(2) Series No. 273.

Chandler, M.J., & Lalonde, C.E. (1998). Cultural continuity as a hedge against suicide in Canada's First Nations [Electronic Version]. *Transcultural Psychiatry, 35*(2), 193–211.

Chenier, N.M. (1995). Suicide among Aboriginal people: Royal Commission Report. Mini-Review, MR-131E, Retrieved January 7, 2004 from www.parl.gc.ca/information/library/PRBpubs/mr131-e.pdf

Cohen, A. (1999). *The mental health of indigenous peoples: An international overview*. Department of Mental Health, World Health Organization.

Coulthard, G. (1999). *Colonization, Indian policy, suicide, and Aboriginal people.* Retrieved January 7, 2004 from www.ualberta.ca/~pimohte/suicide.html

Cutcliffe, J.R. (2003). Research endeavors into suicide: A need to shift the emphasis [Electronic Version]. *British Journal of Nursing, 12*(2), 92.

Eisen, G. (1987). Coping in adversity: Children's play in the holocaust. In G. A. Fine (Ed.), *Meaningful play, Playful meaning* (pp. 129–141). Champaign, IL: Human Kinetics Publishers.

Ellroy, J. (1999). *Crime wave: reportage and fiction from the underside of L.A.* London, England: Century.

Emmons, S. (2000). *A disarming laughter: The role of humor in tribal cultures: An examination of humor in contemporary Native American literature and art.* University of Oklahoma: Unpublished doctoral dissertation.

Ferry, J. (2000). No easy answer to high native suicide rates [Electronic Version]. *The Lancet* 355, 906.

Harris, J. (1981). Beyond Huizinga: Relationships between play and culture. In A. Cheska (Ed.), *Play as context* (pp. 26–36.). West Point, NY: Leisure Press.

Health Canada (2003a). Acting on what we know: Preventing youth suicide in first nations. Retrieved January 5, 2004 from www.hc-sc.gc.ca/fnihb-dgspni/fnihb/cp/publications/preventing_youth_suicide.htm

Health Canada (2003b). *A statistical profile on the health of first nations in Canada.* Retrieved January 12, 2004 from www.hcsc.gc.ca/fnihb-dgspni/fnihb/sppa/hia/publications/statistical_profile.pdf

Health and Welfare Canada. (1996). *Suicide in Canada: update of the report of the task force on suicide in Canada.* Ottawa, ON: Ministry of National Health and Welfare.

IAPH. (2002). *Institute overview*. Retrieved September 3, 2002 from www.cihr-rsc.gc.ca/institutes/iaph/ about_iaph/iaph_about_institute_e.shtml

Johnson, M. (1999). *Ontario Aboriginal patient advocacy initiative. Medical services.* ON, Canada: Ministry of Health

Kirmayer, L.J., Hayton, B.C., Malus, M., DuFour, R., Jimenez, V., Ternar, Y., Quesney, C., Ferrara, N., Yu, T. (1993). Suicide in Canadian Aboriginal populations: Emerging trends in research and intervention. Retrieved February 5, 2004 from www.library.adelaide.edu.au/guide/med/menthealth/aboriginal.html

Krysinska, K.E. (2003). Loss by suicide: A risk factor for suicidal behavior [Electronic Version]. *Journal of Psychosocial Nursing& Mental Health Services, 41*(7), 34–41.

Kuiper, N., Martin, R., and Olinger, L. (1993). Coping humor, stress, and cognitive appraisals. Canadian Journal of Behavioural Science, 25(1), 81–96.

Lancy, D. (1976). The play behavior of Kpelle children during rapid cultural change. In D. Lancy and A. Tindall (Eds.), *The anthropological study of play: Problem and prospects* (pp. 72–79). Cornwall, NY: Leisure Press.

Lancy, D. (2002). Cultural constraints on children's play. In J. L. Roopnarine (Ed.), *Conceptual, social-cognitive, and contextual issues in the fields of play* (Vol. 4, pp. 53–60). London: Ablex Publishing.

Lynam, J. & Young, R. (2000). Towards the creation of a culturally safe research environment. *Health, 4*(1), 5–23.

MacNeil, M., & Guilmette, A. (2004). Preventing youth suicide: Developing a protocol for early intervention in First Nations communities. *Canadian Journal of Native Studies*, 24(2), 313–325.

Malus, M., Kirmayer, L.J., & Boothroyd, L. (1994). Risk factors for attempted suicide among Inuit youth: A community survey. Culture & Mental Health Research Unit, Report No. 3 retrieved February 5, 2004 from www.library.adelaide.edu.au/guide/med/menthealth/aboriginal.html

McConaghy, C. (1998). Positioned leadership: education and the politics of location in rural and remote post-colonial Australia. In LC Ehrich and J. Knight (Eds). *Leadership in Crisis?: Essays on contemporary Educational Leadership.* Brisbane, Post Pressed.

McCrea, K. (2004). The use of humor and laughter in coping with and reducing stress. In M. Leitner, S. Leitner, and Associates (Eds.), *Leisure enhancement* (pp.241–258). New York: Haworth Press.

McGhee, P. (1999). *Health, healing, and the amuse system*. Dubuque, IA: Kendall-Hunt Publishers.

McKeon, C. (2000). *Suicide in Ireland. A global perspective and a national strategy.* Retrieved November 2, 2000 from www.webireland.ie/aware/suicide.html

Mestel, R. (1994). Let mind talk unto body. *New Scientist*. July, 26–31.

NAHO. (2001). *About the National Aboriginal Health Organization (NAHO).* Retrieved September 3, 2002 from www.naho.ca/english/about_naho.php

Niagara District Health Council (2003a). *Health, healing, and cultural values for Aboriginal communities in Canada. Indian and Inuit health services.* Ottawa, ON: Ministry of Health.

Niagara District Health Council (2003b). *Analysis of suicide deaths and hospitalizations due to suicide attempt for residents of Niagara.* Thorold, ON: Canada.

Polit, D.E., & Hungler, B.P. (1999). *Nursing research methods: Principles and methods*. Philadelphia: Lippincott.

Ramsden, I. (1992). Teaching cultural safety. *New Zealand Nursing Journal, 85*(1), 21–23.

Roopnarine, J., and Johnson, J. (1994). The need to look at play in diverse cultural settings. In J. Roopnarine, J. Johnson, and F. Hooper (Eds.), *Children's play in diverse cultures* (pp. 1–8). Albany, NY: State University of New York Press.

Smye, V. & Browne, A. (2002). 'Cultural safety' and the analysis of health policy affecting Aboriginal people [Electronic Version]. *Nurse Researcher* 9(3), 42–57.

Stephenson, P.H. (1995) *A persistent spirit: Towards understanding Aboriginal health in British Columbia*. Victoria, BC: Western Geographical Press.

Stout, M. & Kipling, G. (1999). *Emerging priorities for the health of First Nations and Inuit children and youth.* Ottawa, ON: Health Canada.

Tatz, C. (1999). Aboriginal suicide is different. A report to the criminology research council. *The Criminal Research Council* 25(7), 25–96.

Weir, E., & Wallington, T. (2001). Suicide: the hidden epidemic. *Canadian Medical Association 165*(5), 634–636.

World Health Organization (2002). World report on Violence and Health. Retrieved February 3, 2004 from www.who.inf/violence_injury_prevention/violence/world_report/wrvheng/en

Chapter Eighteen

Role-Play on Parade: Child, Costume and Ceremonial Exchange at Halloween

Cindy Dell Clark

Each child develops a sense of self in relation to the society in which she lives. This means that social development is a binary process through which the young are simultaneously enculturated within the larger community and its standards of behavior, belief, and knowledge, on the one hand, yet also develop a personal self (identity, personality) replete with unique patterns of feeling, thinking, and behaving (cf. Cole, Cole and Lightfoot, 2005, p. 360). It is misleading that social science disciplinary boundaries bifurcate the developmental process into separate arenas for psyche versus social instantiation. Self is at once a social and personal construct, even in individualist societies such as the United States, where social practices (including social science traditions for studying children individually) serve to convey the culture's shared value of individualism (Kessel and Siegel, 1981). The mutuality and co-constitution between person and culture is not a new idea (e.g. Bronfenbrenner, 1996; Briggs, 1998; Shweder, 1991; Miller & Goodnow, 1995), but one that bears declaration, since it is still common to regard the person as bounded within a border of skin (or a brain and associated nervous system) and to treat sociality as a discrete, separate, externalized factor.

Societies provide pathways and practices through which children become who they are, as persons. Cultural psychologists have referred to such culturally embedded patterns of participation as "selfways" (Markus, Mullaly & Kitayama, 1997; Shweder et. al., 1998). Selfways are means of promoting, attuning and coordinating individual ways of experiencing and organizing the world so as to relate persons to culturally shared meanings and modes. Examples include discursive practices (storytelling, joking, teasing, insult exchange, etc.), rituals, performance, work activities, and other situated activity including play. The study of selfways can uncover the dynamic and ongoing interaction that instantiates members of society as situated selves. Studying selfways reveals the complex, socially situated, vigorous social-and-personal engagement through which selfhood is sustained.

This article provides a glimpse into one such practice in American society: Halloween role-play. Based largely on ethnographic investigation, I will describe and interpret this activity as it constitutes a selfway for young children, considering the perspectives of children (age six and seven) and parents in my account. My observations come from ethnographic research among Philadelphia-area children and families who took part in Halloween during 1999 through 2001 (Clark, 2005). Over that period, I interviewed at home twenty-five six- and seven-year old children (thirteen girls and twelve boys) during the days immediately after Halloween. In addition, I engaged in participant observation at Halloween activities such as community-sponsored pumpkin painting or trick or treat nights at shopping centers). Finally, structured observations of 479 children (of varied ages) were made by trained undergraduates whose homes were visited by Halloween trick or treaters on October 31, 2002; student householders greeted the children, asked their role, and recorded the age and masquerade roles identified by child visitors.

This exploratory study is supportive of the construct of a selfway as an active, engaged, situated social process through which child selves are brought to bear. It is not surprising that Halloween role-play contributes to selfhood, of course, given that mumming and disguise are well known to serve purposes of individual self-integration, as roles are appropriated, tried on and acted out in costume (Firestone, 1978; Marcus, 1993). (I take the word "role" here to mean a constellation of appearance and actions that are enacted by the child, in public display.)

Halloween role-play can also be said to go beyond an act of conscious, straightforward socialization of the young by adults (Clark 2005). First, children actively choose, with fairly wide scope, a pretend role for deployment within Halloween masquerade; each child's agentic choice incorporates unstated social meanings, especially (as I will explain) culturally shared meanings of adult power and gender. Further, children by no means passively copy fixed templates for roles, but creatively, personally assemble and play out a role by appropriating (in a kind of bricolage) culturally available meanings. As a selfway Halloween role-play embodies a complex and flexible matrix of interaction in which children do more than internalize culture, and more than individuate as singular selves, all the while in an atmosphere in which the usual social norms are, even so, placed in suspension.

Before sketching out the basis for these claims, some background on the historic roots and contemporary practice of American Halloween ritual may be helpful.

HISTORIC AND CONTEMPORARY CONTEXT

Halloween traces its roots to the ancient Celtic new year's festival, Samhain (Linton, 1950; Santino, 1983b). Samhain not only marked the yearly transition, but also corresponded to the harvest at the end of October. It was believed that the souls who died during the previous year on Samhain wandered at large (Santino, 1983a). Modern Halloween still incorporates symbols of the harvest (hay bales, corn stalks, scarecrows, etc.), as well as icons of death and visiting apparitions (ghosts, skeletons, gravestones, mummies, vampires and ghouls). Halloween is autumnal, taking place during the demise of agricultural growth, a time in Pennsylvania of days growing shorter and colder and trees defoliating. In turn, Halloween takes on decadent, liminal associations, especially death-related meanings. Early American Puritans condemned Halloween for being opposed to upright values (Rogers, 2002). Over waves of American immigration during the nineteenth century, Halloween was revived, and has since retained its dark, anti-normative, death-related associations. Consistent with Halloween's anti-normative meanings, sects of fundamentalist Christians even today revile Halloween as corruptive (Rogers, 2002).

Halloween is a festival of inversion (cf. Bakhtin, 1994), in which the usual values, priorities or social positions are suspended. At Halloween children are exposed to matters usually considered out of bounds. Things taboo and age inappropriate are made available to the young through decorations (spider webs, bats, skeletons, ghosts, witches, gravestones, mummies, etc.) and gruesome enactments (such as haunted rides, haunted houses, or spooky neighborhood displays). Children who would normally be excluded from attending an actual funeral may find themselves walking past a mock cemetery in the neighborhood, with would-be corpses and ghosts in residence. At a school-sponsored haunted house described by one family, a priest impersonated a murderer. Depravity, albeit in lampooned form, is the order of the day as adults actively intone deadly, degrading, and evil motifs in an atmosphere of liminality (Clark, 2005).

Halloween inverts the relative roles of children and adults, in terms of power relations. Halloween in effect brings about heightened privilege and license in children, through the ritual of trick or treat. They violate rules of stranger avoidance and venture into the neighborhood in costume (often impersonating adult roles), visiting households and speaking the ceremonial threat "trick or treat," which is appeased when the mature resident of the house distributes candy to the children. Adults' associations with candy usually call for control and rationing, since candy is thought to be a cause of childlike loss of control including hyperactivity. The licentiousness of candy is let loose at Halloween, as children treat the amount of candy they receive as a measure of how well the ritual is fulfilled, thereby getting what they want from adults. Adults in recent years inspect candy for possible tampering, but this does not undo children's sense of ritual attainment and privilege from collecting goodies.

Halloween, then, is a time of license for children, in which adulthood can be parodied (through dress-up), and forbidden treats gathered. "Kids rule," on Halloween, a typical mother summarized the turnabout. "It's their night," commented another. Halloween role-play takes place in a context of suspended rank, condoned licentiousness, and child empowerment.

COSTUME CHOICE AND PREPARATION

In keeping with a ritual of symbolic power inversion, parents generally spoke of the preparation of a Halloween role as a process involving a child's creative choice and self-assertion. This sentiment parallels anthropologist Victor Turner's (1969) hypothesis that Halloween is an instance of role reversal, by which children's masking gives them superordinate status. Children told me they felt older and more powerful dressed in Halloween roles. Whether disguised in mature physical beauty (bride, princess and other mature heroines), mock physical power (super hero or sports star), or aggressive dominance (witch, monster, vampire, devil, etc.), children reported that they felt "big" in these roles. Dressed powerfully by virtue of mature beauty, brawn or bravado, children asserted this power when they traveled into the neighborhoods, demanding candy through mock threat ("trick or treat").

Preparing for this time of privilege involves children's active creative choice. Parents reported that they tried to honor the child's selection of role by cooperating in purchasing or constructing a costume, and through assistance with hair, make-up and/or props. Even if they needed to visit several stores to find a particular costume, mothers generally sought to fulfill children's expressed role choice. The appropriateness of children "being themselves" in the act of impersonation was widely given sway by parents.

In the observational data, it was found that variation in costume choice was impressively broad: across 479 observations, there were 233 different roles played by the children observed. Halloween, a shared social ritual in which manufactured costumes are common, paradoxically supports a large degree of individual variation in choices made. Even when children changed their minds or wanted a costume not commercially available, parents in one way or another supported the autonomy of the child in this preference, even (in one case) writing a letter to a costume manufacturer about the need for a particular costume, or (in another case) waiting as long as necessary for an indecisive child to settle on a final choice. Children who wore second-hand costumes formerly belonging to siblings or relatives were generally invited to improvise or combine costumes to create a preferred ensemble.

From the perspective of children aged six to seven, the choice of a costume entails self-readiness to occupy a particular role, to behave and look appropriately. As will be discussed in the next section, Halloween is more than an occasion of dress-up play, since it entails public presentation and display. Costumes are worn to school, in front of family and relatives, and into the community. Public attention is paid to the child's enacted role. "What are you supposed to be?" is a common question explicitly asked by adult householders when the child comes to call Halloween night. Some adults extensively query children's roles, assessing how a child looks, or sometimes engaging the would-be character in mutual pretense.

With a pronounced social stake in successful role-playing, children choose a costume while keeping in mind the requirement that they must publicly enact and pretend the part. In the instance of enacting a frightful role, such as a skeleton, a monstrous being, or the grim reaper, children reported that a degree of courage ("nerve") was a necessary requisite, implying an intimate association was involved with threatening, negative roles. Some children planned to dress as a frightening entity, but "chickened out" before Halloween. Other children postponed the idea of dressing in a frightening costume until future years (when they presumed they would be more "ready"). As Buckingham (1996) has found to be true with horror films, some children protected themselves through the self-regulating act of avoidance of playing a horrifying role.

Those youngsters who dared to be dressed as frightening beings, such as a witch, Frankenstein, or the title character from the movie *Scream*, ironically claimed to be *less* scared while so attired, when trick or treating on Halloween night. This traced to the empowering experience of pretending to be frightening to others. Children seemed delighted in the mock-fearful reactions of adults to their threatening costumed appearance. Children also welcomed the opportunity to imagine and play out appropriate misdeeds, going along with their role. A six-year old dressed as a witch pretended to cast a spell of turning her younger brother into a frog, an animal he disliked. A costumed dragon enjoyed practicing the ability to breathe fire. Masqueraders who carried weapons enthusiastically practiced and played out the use of the weapons. A fearsome role carried with it an opportunity to attain make-believe ascendance, and in the process to gain personal control over what was frightening. In these actions, it is clear that culturally narrated versions of the roles being played were influential on children's behavior; children knew from cultural scripts that a robber carries a gun, that a dragon breathes fire, that a witch casts spells and so on. Nevertheless, children creatively constructed their actions in a role, actively appropriating but not rigidly copying known narrative accounts.

Halloween role-play provides children with a chance to practice personal improvisation of roles, within a public, power-inverting structure. Children become impersonators, not so much by following monolithic cultural scripts, but in ways that each child finds personally approachable. A child's role is a kind of pastiche assembled from a myriad of cultural symbols, structures actions and motifs. Witches, for example, tend to be composites, influenced by numerous sources including fairy tales, movies (Wizard of Oz, Disney, etc.), television, history (Salem trials) and direct experience of one kind or another. Witches can be beautiful, and if they are pretty, are in turn considered to be morally good by six and seven year olds. Witches can also be ugly (green-skinned, old, with warts, etc.) generally connoting a greater degree of immorality and graver danger.

By and large, children chose costumes that symbolized power or ascendance, in keeping with the role reversals of Halloween. Boys generally chose costumes representing dominating characters engaged in offensive struggle, either for the purposes of good or evil. Girls more often chose aesthetic good looks as emblematic of adult power. (These gender-related choices will be discussed later.) In one way or another, the masquerade was generally chosen as a means to symbolic ascendance, although even here there were exceptions. While most children wanted to feel "big" when role-playing, some dressed as diminutive animals, and a few dressed, in counterpoint to the prototypic mature costume, as babies. Children improvised rather than strictly conformed to a fixed template in their choice of a role, and in the way they conceived that role to look and play out. A ghost might be enacted as friendly or scary. A ballerina might simultaneously be a princess. A bride costume might involve horrifying make-up as the bride of Frankenstein. Barbie, the fashion doll, might be enacted as a prom queen, a cheerleader, or a princess. In other words, varied narratives and influences could come into play, assembled through the child's bricolage-like construction of a role as ensemble. Role-play, like language or play in general, involves shared social conventions creatively and dynamically filtered and combined.

ROLE ENACTMENT AND PUBLIC DISPLAY

The importance of enactment to fulfilling the Halloween ritual is encapsulated in a narrative based on the boyhood experience of comedian Jerry Seinfeld (2002). Seinfeld recalls that his Superman costume, despite his expectations, did not live up to his media-influenced hopes.

> Unfortunately these costumes are not exactly the super fit that you are hoping for. You look more like you're wearing Superman's pajamas. It's all loose and flowy, the neckline comes down to about your stomach. You've got that flimsy little ribbon in the back holding it all together. Plus my mother made me wear my winter coat over the costume . . . I don't remember Superman wearing a jacket. I read every comic book. I do not remember him ever once flying with a coat on. . . . So you go out anyway and the mask keeps breaking, the rubber band [on the mask] keeps getting shorter because you need to keep retying it. It's getting tighter and tighter on your face . . . You're trying to breathe through that little hole that gets all sweaty . . . About a half an hour into trick or treating you take that mask off. 'Oh, the heck with it.'" (Seinfeld, 2002: 14–19)

Seinfeld's comic recollection of how roles can come up short underscores that enactment of roles is not a private or interior act. Role enactment takes place publicly, with more than an element of spectacle. The imagined ideal may not perfectly predict the enacted version, just as wedding plans seldom go entirely according to expectation. How the role-play is received by others is germane to fulfilling the ritual.

A salient public context for trying out and performing roles is the school costume parade. (The costume parade is often coupled with a school party, and with a break from studious work routines to eat treats and enjoy amusements.) In the parade, children process around school (perhaps in the school yard or even the surrounding area) dressed in their Halloween costumes. Adults are witness to the school parade, including watchful school administrators, teachers, and visiting parents. In particular cases reported to me, other visitors came; musicians from one neighborhood's local high school serenaded the gathering, and at another school a news crew from the local TV station filmed. The adult role as an appreciative audience was amply noted by young informants, who reportedly "showed off" their fictive selves and were generally praised for the display. If criticisms were spoken—such as the epithet "dead bride" shouted toward one girl dressed in bridal finery during a school parade—the shouter was usually a fellow schoolmate. By contrast, adults were said to be a receptive, supportive audience.

Children generally liked having parents present during the "march" around school, and admitted to disappointment when a parent missed the parade. The Halloween parade, I was told time and again, is fun for children in large part because of providing a chance to see and be seen in costume. This suggests, of course, how important the element of spectacle and role display—a symbolic enactment of ascendancy—is to Halloween ritual. In fact, it was not uncommon for the child to make a visit to a grandparent's or an aunt's house prior to trick or treating, in order to be seen and be praised one further time.

Later, as the dark evening of Halloween descended, these Philadelphia area children went trick or treating, visiting not just known relatives and supporters, but neighbors and strangers. Contributing to the anxiety of the trick or treat visit was the autumnal night gloom and the "scary" decorations. Here the spectacle of impersonation had to be performed after walking through a stranger's yard, often decorated in frightful icons such as bats, spider webs, ghosts, witches, and monsters. Parents, accompanying these six and seven year olds, generally let the children take the lead as they approached the household doorway. Sometimes, parents brought along a flashlight to illuminate the path, or helped to carry a child's props (mock weapons, magic wands, cheerleader pompoms, etc.) between homes. A few parents, in the minority, wore costumes to accompany their children, but most wore ordinary street clothing.

Knocking on the doors of strangers, especially decorated in anti-normative themes, is an inversion of the usual homebound protectiveness practiced towards children in this age group, in recent years. (Indeed, collected treats are presumed by parents to be unsafe until inspected, accentuating the unknown territory traveled.) Yet in this environment, children were expected to assert themselves and to negotiate an exchange (however briefly) with the unfamiliar host. Part of this exchange centered on the impersonating role-play of the child. There were routine conversations about the child's ordinary social identity ("Who are you?" "Is that your brother?") and also talk about the fictive identity encoded in mask and costume ("Who are you supposed to be?" "You look very scary." "Don't you look pretty!") The trick or treater's ordinary identity, and their role-of-disguise, were both ripe for comment, as if to reinforce and endorse the self-relevant nature of the child's masquerade.

Ironically, a costume is exposing as well as concealing, since it puts on display or foregrounds a usually unseen aspect or potential of self, enacted by the child. The revealed aspect may be bravery, or attractiveness, or hostility, or some other facet of being invested in representation-by-clothing. The mother of a boy who turned "knight" for Halloween (a lad who told me it felt better to be a knight than his usual self) felt that the fictional roles of Halloween were arguably more authentic than daily behavior. For she explained, Halloween is a day to let out what is usually held in, to toss aside the usual constraints in favor of free expression. Another mother described Halloween as an "acceptable pretend day," a day when everyone took a "break from normalcy" in order to be more free. Such pretending can stretch one's way of being in the world, in counterpoint (and implicit alternative) to routine personhood. Costume can be therapeutically useful since it encourages the wearer to disrupt familiar patterns and to manipulate sources of anxiety (Coale, 1992). In clinical play therapy, costume serves to encourage children to act out unconscious issues, such as for victims of trauma who act out the part of aggressor, or children engaging in pretend wish fulfillment (Marcus, 1993). Children enjoy role-play that bestows symbolic power. "I have makeup on," one girl said of her Halloween self-portrait, proudly communicating enacted maturity. "The devil's pretty scary so I feel protected by my mask," a boy dressed as the devil explained how he felt standing at a neighbor's doorway. Fantasies of privilege accompanied role-play. A boy with a "digital" wrist imagined using it for fighting. A koala-child climbed from tree to tree, scratching his armpits with animal-like release and freedom. These imagined behaviors were likely off-bounds to the child's conventional social roles, yet were true to each child's personally felt inclinations nevertheless.

Halloween is a time of license and expression. Self, ever enacted through social transactions, on October 31st is given greater range to be altered in appearance and action, giving way to experimentation. Children dressed as superheroes imagined that they flew through the neighborhood. Soldiers and Ninja warriors were powerfully armed for self-protection. Brooms of witches were figured to fly above the fray. The public display of these roles—praised, attended to, and even rewarded with treats—supports the very exploration of selfhood, through the mechanism of masquerade.

GENDERED ASCENDANCE THROUGH ROLE-PLAY

Asked to sum up the experience of Halloween, one six-year old girl, resonating to the holiday's generational inversions, said simply "It's like being big for a day." Mock maturity or ascendance characterized boys and girls alike. Yet this study like others before (Nelson, 2000; Ogletree, Denton & Williams 1993) evidenced a distinctive gender related pattern as to how ascendant roles were instantiated by male versus female children. As can be seen in the Figure 18.1 based on the 2002 observational data, certain sorts of roles were more likely to be adopted by boys, and other sorts for girls.

While no type of costume was exclusively worn by one gender, boys were markedly more likely to dress in roles of power and strength, or of evil or frightening characters. Girls were far more likely to choose roles that aimed to be good looking, to create a pleasing aesthetic impression. Girls were also more likely to play the role of an animal than boys.

It would be tempting to hypothesize that parents dictated these constraining gender roles, despite adult claims to indulge their child's free expression at Halloween. Certainly, parents did exert indirect influence, such as one

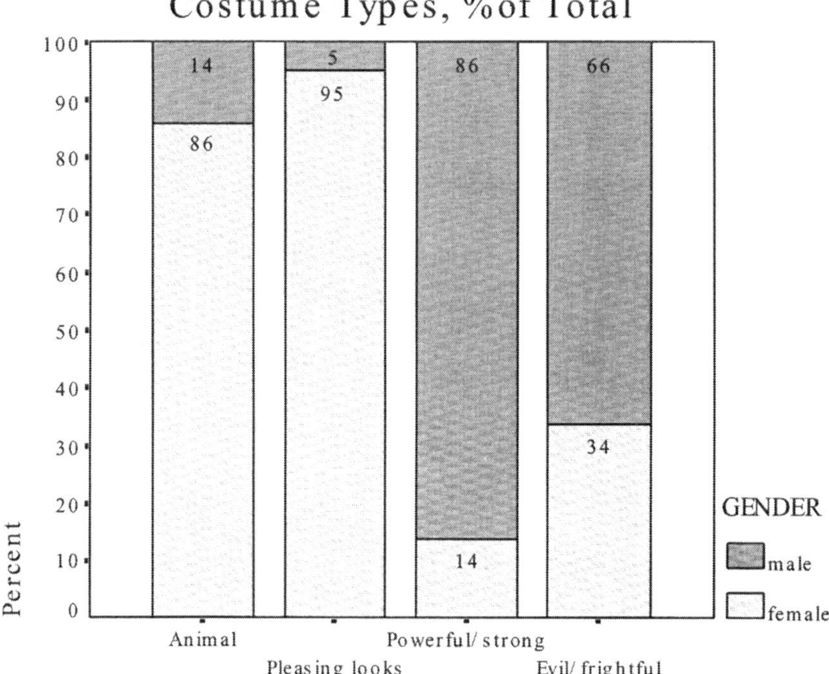

Figure 18.1. Costume Types, Percentage of Total.

mother who acted unimpressed when her daughter wanted to wear a costume with simulated dripping blood. (The child did not wear it.) Yet adults notwithstanding, children themselves gravitated towards particular kinds of adult roles, based on culturally patterned differences in how male and female adults acquire power and ascendance: strength and domineering intimidation is a hegemonic means towards power associated with male adults, whereas allure and attractive looks are relatively more linked as means to power in female adults. Children gravitate towards mature roles of power at Halloween; means to power are gender variable within the social order. Put another way, children aiming to be ascendant were thereby led to practice gender differentiation.

The predisposition of boys towards roles of explicit dominance, whether morally abhorrent or good, seemed to them a way to preemptively induce fear in others. In the words of one boy, "I like to be scary to what scares me." Fearsomeness inoculates against fearfulness, describes this underlying male principle of Halloween roles. This strategy, be feared lest you be scared, is consistent with young male preferences in stories, more generally. Research on the kid-thrilling *Goosebumps* books shows that these fear-raising narratives are primarily read by boys, in line with the hegemonic expectation that masculinity is linked to overcoming fear (Christian-Smith & Erdman, 1997).

Male choices of Halloween roles were also consistent with study of male pretend play, in which the "warrior narrative" is a predominant male theme (Jordan & Cowan, 1995; Thomas, 2003). Within the warrior role, in essence, fragility is masked through dominant aggressive abilities, so called warrior traits. As an example of such a role-play at Halloween, Jake, age seven serves well; he chose as his Halloween role the fictional television hero, Digimon. I met Jake (like other names used here, a pseudonym), a few days after Halloween 2001, and less than two months after the September 11 attacks in nearby New York City, an hour's drive from his home. Jake's older sister (eight years old) had chosen to be a butterfly for Halloween. Jake chose a character whose purpose was to "save the world." Jake decided to be Digimon, a prosocial TV hero, a character he chose after rejecting the role of Pokemon, also a TV character. His mother and he went shopping for the Digimon costume together; Jake was clearly taken with the costume, especially its metallic left arm and wrist, which operates as a cannon in the televised narrative. Jake referred to his portrayed character as a "mega Digimon," high in the hierarchy of power (thanks to his arm's biotechnology).

I asked Jake if I could dress as Digimon for Halloween if I wanted. In reply he warned me that I might fall apart, into pieces, and might get my "brain bashed in" by rivals. His comment discloses that there is inner fragility to even the most powerfully armed character. A costume carries a two-fold capability to expose but also to conceal, to look strong but also to disguise fear (Marcus, 1993). The warrior narrative, whether developed through a biotechnical superiority (arm as weapon), a superpower, or outright ferocity, reflects the masculine imperative to transcend vulnerability.

Only very occasionally did a girl choose an aggressive or dominating role for Halloween. In the 2002 observational data, girls never took superhero roles, for example, although such roles as Spiderman or Batman were among the most common choices for boys. Instead, girls' most prevalent roles were princess or queen, Cinderella, and angel. These roles certainly implied ascendance and yielded a sort of power, but this was ascendance brought through gentility and aesthetic good looks, not through brute domination. Girls occasionally played the part of a witch, an anti-social role (associated with brews and broomsticks, domestic power gone awry) but anti-social roles for boys proliferated in greater variety and number.

Boys chose roles ranging from the movie character Scream, to a gangster or mobster, to the devil, to a dragon, to a vampire, to a ghoul, to a terrorist—all roles which girls never impersonated. Girls' roles were more often morally upright and more often associated with pretty looks: fairies, Snow White and other Disney heroines, cheerleaders, ballerinas, bride, mermaid and other roles trading on pleasant aesthetics. "Looking nice" at Halloween was almost exclusively a feminine prerogative, which also extended to the "cute" animals which a minority of girls chose to portray, such as a ladybug, a bunny, a duck, a cat, dogs of varied breeds, fish or (perhaps a bit more power-connoting) a bumble bee.

Attired to look like media characters—Scarlett O'Hara from *Gone With the Wind*, a "pink lady" from *Grease*, Disney princesses, the fashionable Power Puff girls from cartoons, or an alluring pop singer (Britney Spears)—girls appropriated media-depicted roles in order to impersonate grown up feminine allure. The pretty looks associated with these sorts of characters generally implicated a moral goodness as well as good looks, as if there is an equation of loveliness and good intentions. The "pretty" role, in other words, takes on general moral overtones of social desirability to girls: ugly repels and is bad, beauty attracts and is good.

Hair carefully arranged, frilly costumes, make up and coordinating shoes were all part of the trappings incorporated into costumes of feminine good looks. High heels, tiaras, jewelry and cheerleader pompoms accessorized outfits meant to trade on appearance. Just as boys reflect hegemonic forms of male power in the warrior role, girls' role choices reflect the status quo as well: females appearing in the media generally are dressed more attractively and more alluringly than males (and thereby achieve social impact) (Currie, 1999). Girls preparing for Halloween perceive primping as essential to being placed on a social pedestal, and choose pretty roles because this is a perceived major route to influential feminine impact.

A provocative example of this basis for choice lies in the case of Barbie, the Mattell fashion model doll, whom several female trick or treaters impersonated. As a case study, consider Sara, six years old when I interviewed her a few days after Halloween 2001. Sara chose to dress as Barbie the cheerleader, because her good friend Molly also planned to enact the role of cheerleader for Halloween. The Barbie role came along with the Barbie cheerleader costume that Sara's mother purchased. The costume "had a big B on the front, for Barbie," Sara described. The role of cheerleader, at root an aesthetic role, coincided with the aesthetic focus of the Barbie character. Sara's role was thus doubly representative of "pretty" feminine influence. As cheerleader, she was a sort of mascot for a beauty icon, cheerleading on behalf of Barbie and also impersonating Barbie.

The several girls who pretended to be Barbie, Barbie princess, or Barbie prom queen reveal the well documented reach of Barbie's commercialism (Cunningham, 1993; Handler, 2000; Lord, 1994). Barbie is in some ways a personification of the feminine penchant towards being "dolled up," trading on glamour or appearance (Debouzy, 1996; Rakow, 1999; Rogers, 1999; Steinberg 1997; Urla & Swedland, 1995; Weissman, 1999). Given women's reliance on looks for acceptance, influence and esteem (even at risk of unhealthy bodily proportions), Barbie epitomizes the kind of adult roles which little girls want to claim for a day's mock maturity: cheerleader, princess, date, prom queen, bride, pop singer (Cunningham 1992). In the end, Barbie is a symptom, seen through girls' projecting eyes, of the stake adult women have in gaining or maintaining power as objects of gaze. "Pretty" roles at Halloween, assembled from themes of pretend play (including with Barbie dolls), from media narratives, or from everyday observation reflect a different route to power than for boys.

Girls and boys impersonate adults in different ways on Halloween, but share a proclivity to seek out roles powerful for their gender. The meaning of Halloween roles to children, as representing ascendance, is important to recognize. Halloween is not so much about gender as it is about the power yielded by elders. Yet, since mature power is variant in ways that correlate with gender, so too are Halloween roles.

CONCLUSION

Over the past decade or so, there has been a shift in scholarly notions of what it means to become enculturated or socialized. The earlier, established view that children are passive internalizers in transit towards adulthood has been increasingly jettisoned (Benthall, 1992; Friedl, 2002; Hirshfeld, 2002; Mayall, 2002; Ruark, 2000; Waksler, 1991). Newer models, influenced by the field of children's studies, assume that children actively shape their own socializing process, a process which cannot be understood apart from children's own accounts and agency (e.g. Corsaro, 1997; Corsaro and Miller, 1992; Jenks, 1996; James, Jenks & Prout, 1998; Schwartzman 2001). In the newer, interpretive approach, children are seen to actively shape the form of their own childhoods. The social contextsof children's lives, and the entailed social interactions and practices, are intertwined with and inextricable from children's engagement and meanings.

Halloween role-play provides an intriguing nexus for observing these personal, interpersonal, and sociocultural forces at common juncture. Halloween roles are at once personal and social in how roles are constructed and enacted. The research in this article has only touched the surface of the processes involved, based as it is on post hoc informant reports and limited observation. Yet it is hard to deny that Halloween operates as a "selfway," through which identities are exercised in relationship to culturally shared meanings and modes.

Halloween masquerade plays out a generational inversion by which children ascend to temporary power, on a day when usual social taboos are disregarded and defied. Given this cultural permission, children enjoy the opportunity to carry out the trick or treat exchange and to dress as they wish in the mock attire of adults. Children's masquerade reflects systematic gender variation, in turn reflecting hegemonic adult means to power associated with men versus women.

Children construct roles, assisted by adults, but with a substantial latitude of choice. Gergen (1991) has written that modern selves are "saturated," a pastiche of associations; indeed the assembly of roles at Halloween seems to involve a variegated composite of polyphonic influences, rather than a strict copy of a single template or "master" role. Children actively filter, mix, invert, select, reinterpret, take exception, and redirect in shaping role-play. Witches can be interpreted to be attractive or abhorrent, ghosts can be friends or foe, and a few roles are babyish rather than mature. Roles are dynamic and multi-faceted.

Models of how children participate in selfways such as Halloween need to incorporate concepts that do not give short shrift to either the personal or the cultural. One precedent that might be helpful is *hypertext*, an approach that has influenced fields of literary criticism (Landow, 1992; Mondiano et. al., 2004), family therapy (Boczkowski, 1996) and other disciplines (Edwards, 1994). Hypertext refers to an arrangement of information (common to internet communications) in which there are chunks of informative material and a set of connections leading from one node or chunk to other chunks. In hypertext, a reader or explorer produces their own experience of reading or exploring; each choice of direction leads to an encounter with particular emerging material, such that there are multiple directions through the domain (Conklin, 1987). Hypertext leaves intact the contingent and creative aspects of navigating cultural material (Boczkowski, 1996). The individual does not follow a set path, but determines the order in which information is expressed, as well as which particular bits are included in the trajectory. Ritual role-play, which involves a web of semiotic associations, could possibly be mapped in a hypertext manner. Hypertext has the advantage of allowing for intermediation and collaboration, contingencies, mutability, and multivocality or saturated meanings.

By whatever means or model, Halloween invites us to scrutinize the emergent process by which children become who they are. Individuation and socialization make for a complex brew, in which the child plays an active role, all the while steeped in dynamic and influential social transactions. It is worth gathering new tricks, as researchers, that may lead us to better understand this intricate alchemy.

REFERENCES

Atkinson, J. (2001). Ethnography in the study of children and childhood. In P. Atkinson, A. Coffey, S. Delamont, J. Lofland, & L. Lofland (Eds.), *Handbook of ethnography*, London: Sage.

Bakhtin, M. (1994). Carnival ambivalence. In P. Morris (Ed.), *The Bakhtin reader*. London:Arnold.

Benthall, J. (1992). Child-focused research. *Anthropology Today, 8,* 23–25.

Boczkowski, P. J. (1996). From text to hypertext: Technologies, metaphors, and the social construction of family therapy. *Journal of Systemic Therapies, 15* (4), 59–79.

Briggs, J. (1998). *Inuit morality play: The emotional education of a three-year old*. New Haven: Yale University Press.

Bronfenbrenner, U. (1993). The ecology of cognitive development: Research models and fugitive findings. In R. Woziniak (Ed.), *Development in context: Acting and thinking in specific environments*. 1993.Erlbaum.

Buckingham, D. (1996). *Moving images: Understanding children's emotional responses to television*. Manchester: Manchester University Press.

Christian-Smith, L. K., & Erdman, J. I. (1997). "Mom it's not real!" Children constructing childhood through reading horror fiction. In S. Steinberg & J. Kincheloe (Eds.), *Kinderculture: The corporate construction of childhood* (pp. 129–152). Boulder, CO: Westview Press.

Clark, C. D. (2005). Trick of festival: Children, enculturation and American Halloween. *Ethos, 33* (2), 180–205.

Coale, H. W. (1992). Costume and pretend identities: A constructivist's use of experiences to co-create meanings with clients in therapy. *Journal of Strategic and Systemic Therapies, 11*(1), 45–55.

Cole, M., Cole, S., & Lightfoot, C. (2005). *The development of children*. New York: Worth.

Conklin, J. (1987). Hypertext: An introduction. *Computer, 20*(9), 17–41.

Corsaro, W. A. (1997). *The sociology of childhood* . Thousand Oaks, CA: Pine Forge Press.

Corsaro, W. A. & Miller, P. (1992). *Interpretive approaches to children's socialization*. San Francisco: Jossey-Bass.

Cunningham, K. (1993). Barbie doll culture and the American waistland. *Symbolic Interaction, 16* (1), 79–83.

Currie, D. (1999). *Girl talk: Adolescent magazines and their readers*. Toronto: University of Toronto Press.

Debouzy, M. (1996). The Barbie doll. In J. Dean & J. P. Gabilliet (Eds.) *European readings of American popular culture* (pp.144). Westport, CT: Greenwood Press.

Edwards, P. N. (1994). Hyper text and hypertension: Post-structualist critical theory, social studies of science and software. *Social Studies of Science, 24*, 229–278.

Firestone, M. (1978). Christmas mumming and symbolic interaction. *Ethnos, 6* (2), 92–113.

Friedl, E. (2002). Why are children missing from the anthropology textbooks? *Anthropology News* (May), 19.

Gergen, K. (1991). *The saturated self: Dilemmas of identity in contemporary life*. New York: Basic Books.

Handler, S. (2000). *The body burden, living in the shadow of Barbie*. Cocoa Beach, FL: Blue Note Publications.

Hirschfield, L. (2002). Why don't anthropologists like children? *American Anthropologist, 104*(2), 611–629.

James, A., Jenks, C., & Prout, A. (1998). *Theorizing childhood*. New York: Teachers College Press.

Jenks, C. (1996). *Childhood* (key ideas). London: Routledge.

Jordan, E., & Cowan, A. (1995). Warrior narratives in the kindergarten classroom: Renegotiating the social contract? *Gender and Society, 9*(6), 727–743.

Kashima, Y. (2002). Culture and self: A cultural dynamical analysis. In Y. Kashima, M. Foddy & M. Platow (Eds.), *Self and identity: Personal, social, and symbolic*. Mahwah, NJ: Erlbaum.

Kessel, F. S., & Siegal, A. W. (1981). *The child and other cultural inventions*. New York: Praegar.

Landow, G. P. (1992). *Hypertext: Convergence of contemporary critical theory and technology*. Baltimore, MD: John Hopkins University Press.

Linton, R. (1950). Halloween. *Scientific American, 185* (4), 62–66.

Lord, M. G. (1994). *Forever Barbie: The unauthorized biography of a real doll*. New York: William Morrow.

Marcus, I. (1993). Costume play therapy. In C. Schaeffer & D. Cangelosi (Eds.), *Play therapy*. Northvale, NJ: Jason Aronson.

Markus, H. R., Mullally, P.R., & Kitayma, S. (1997). Selfways: Diversity in modes of cultural participation. In U. Neisser & D.A. Jopling (Eds.), *The conceptual self in context*. Cambridge: Cambridge University Press.

Mayall, B. (2002). *Towards a society for childhood: Thinking from children's lives*. Buckingham: Open University Press.

Miller, P., & Goodnow, J. (1995). Cultural practices: Toward an integration of culture and development. In Goodnow, P. Miller, & R.S. essel (Eds.), *Cultural practices as contexts for development*. San Francisco: Jossey-Bass.

Mondiano, R., Searle, L., & Shillingsburg, P. (2004). *Voicetexthypertext*. Seattle: University of Washington Press.

Nelson, A. (2000). The pink dragon is female: Halloween costumes and gender markers. *Psychology of Women Quarterly, 24,* 137–144.

Ogletree, S., Denton, L., & Williams, S. W. (1993). Age and gender markers in children's Halloween costumes. *Journal of Psychology, 127*, 633–637.

Rakow, L. F., & Rakow, C.S. (1999). Educating Barbie. In S. R. Marrarella & N. O. Pecora (Eds.), *Growing up girls: Popular culture and the construction of identity*. New York: Peter Lang.

Rogers, M. (1999). *Barbie culture*. Thousand Oaks, CA: Sage Publications.

Rogers, N. (2002). *Halloween: From pagan ritual to party night*. New York: Oxford University Press.

Ruark, J. (2000). Seeing children and hearing them, too. *Chronicle of Higher Education* (November, 17), A22.

Santino, J. (1983a). Night of the wandering souls. *Natural History, 92* (42–51).

Santino, J. (1983b). Halloween in America: Contemporary customs and performances. *Western Folklore., 42*(1), 1–20.

Schwartzman, H. (2001). *Children and anthropology: Perspectives for the 21st century*. Westport, CT: Bergin and Garvey.

Seinfeld, J. (2002). *Halloween*. Boston: Little, Brown, & Company.

Shweder, R. A. (1991). Cultural psychology: What is it? In R. A. Shweder (Ed.), *Thinking through cultures: Expeditions into cultural psychology*. Cambridge, MA: Harvard University Press.

Shweder, R. A., Goodnow, J., Hatano, G., LeVine, R. A., Markus, H.R., & Miller, P. (1998). The cultural psychology of development: One mind, many mentalities. In W. Damon (Ed.), Handbook of children psychology (Vol. 1). New York: John Wiley.

Steinberg, S. (1997). The bitch who has everything. In S. Steinberg & Kincheloe (Eds.), Kinderculture: *The corporate construction of childhood.* Boulder, CO: Westview Press.

Thomas, J.B. (2003). *Naked Barbies, warrior Joes, and other forms of visible gender*. Urbana, IL: University of Illinois Press.

Turner, V. (1969). *The ritual process: Structure and anti-structure*. Ithaca: Cornell University Press.

Urla, J., & Swedland, A. (1995*). The anthropometry of Barbie: Unsettling ideals of the feminine body in popular culture*. In J. Terry & J. Urla (Eds.), Deviant bodies. Indianapolis: Indiana University Press.

Waksler, F. C. (1991). *Studying the social worlds of children*: Sociological readings. London: Falmer Press.

Weissman, K. (1999). *Barbie: The icon, the image, the ideal, an analytical interpretation of the Barbie doll in popular culture*. Macquerie Park, Australia: Universal Publishers.

ACKNOWLEDGMENTS

Thanks go to the Rainbow Foundation for Children's Research for funding the ethnographic portion of this research, conducted 1999–2001. I additionally acknowledge Holly Blackford, Wadeeha Henderson, Heather Hess, Valerie Karp, and Trish Russo for assistance in transcribing the interviews. I am grateful also to the students of my Human Development & Family Studies 229 class, who served as observers in the 2002 study. Last but in no way least, I thank my child and adult informants for sharing their time and Halloween experiences.

Epilogue

Contextualizing Play Investigations in the 21st Century

Dorothy Sluss

As we stand at the beginning of a new century, it is intriguing to consider the current state of play scholarship and anticipate the state of play research at the end of this century. After reading the papers presented in this volume, it is clear that the state of play research is varied, interesting, and potentially powerful. Yet, there is much to be done to understand the conundrum of play research. One approach is to contextualize the research presented by placing it within a previously developed framework. This epilogue presents an opportunity to do just this by collectively considering the papers in terms of their contribution to play scholarship.

UNDERSTANDING PLAY RESEARCH

A great deal of research has been completed during the past century on and about play, and much of it has been published in the *Play and Culture* Series. This volume joins six other volumes that focus specifically on interdisciplinary play research. The chapters in this volume provide a sample of research in the early years of the twenty-first century.

One play scholar, Brian Sutton-Smith, suggested that we interpret play in terms of play rhetorics. In his book, *The Ambiguity of Play* (1997), Sutton-Smith described the rhetoric of progress, fate, power, identity, imaginary, self, and frivolity in terms of play. Thomas Henricks uses this approach in Chapter Two, The Promise of Sociology for Play Studies. Examining the sample found in this volume through the lens of play rhetorics provides a picture of play research that is occurring as we enter the twenty-first century.

Play as Progress

The view of play as progress has been and continues to be used by many child specialists, educators, and others to promote a view of play as beneficial for individuals and society at large. In the early part of the century, Susan Isaacs' statement, "play is child's work" (1929) reflected the view that play is a beneficial and necessary part of childhood. This view of play which is sometimes referred to as the play ethos was found in the literature throughout the seventies. Sutton-Smith (1997) states that ". . . so much twentieth-century attention has been given to children's play as a form of progress, . . ."(p. 9). Joe Frost reflects this perspective in the first article in this book, *Genesis and evolution of American play and playgrounds.* He approaches play from a progressive perspective and raises the concern that children are not playing in the same ways or in the same places as in the past. If, indeed, play is an adaptive behavior, then one wonders how, without play-friendly public policy, whether these children will adapt to the increasingly complex challenges of living in tomorrow's world. Frost's concern has been discussed recently in research conducted by medical doctors and published by the American Medical Association (Whitaker & Orzol, 2006) which is very concerned about the lack of physical activity among children which is leading to an epidemic of preventable health issues. If play is beneficial for physical development and the lack of play impedes good health, perhaps the rhetoric of play as progress is appropriate and adaptive.

Two other articles in this volume examined play as progress through investigations of playgrounds. Beatriz Pereira, Paula Malta, and Hugo Laranjerio examined playgrounds in Portugal for their article, *Playgrounds and children's play supply in 14 districts in the northeast of Portugal.* They found a great deal of variability in the quality of playgrounds and the maintenance of the playgrounds. Based on their study, they saw a need for additional residential playgrounds in the area. This study uses the premise that play is progress and the more playgrounds, the better.

The other playground study was conducted by Francis Wardle and viewed play on playgrounds as progress and considered the safety of children who use them in Brazil. In his study, *Play ground safety in Brazil*, Wardle found that, "It is the exact same equipment that was popular in early childhood and home-based programs in the US about 20–30 years ago, but is apparently very popular in Brazil today. This was quite a surprise to me, as I had assumed the unsafe equipment I observed on my earlier visits was simply playground equipment dumped by US manufactures on the less safety-conscious Brazilian market. But companies in Brazil are actually making and selling this unsafe equipment, with all the same safety problems already mentioned"

(p. 308). In his study, he considered the barriers involved in developing standards for playgrounds, given differences in cultures, variations in the size of children, and a metric measuring system. There is an underlying assumption that play is valuable and that safe playgrounds would contribute to the health and development of the children.

Progress and Literacy

Advocates of play as progress have long touted the association between play and literacy. Entire books have linked literacy and play. For example, Zigler, Singer, and Bishop-Josef (2004) wrote *Play: The roots of reading*, which provides research to support play as the bedrock of reading. In addition, Roskos and Christie (2000) wrote *Play and literacy* which uses research to clarify the relationship between play and literacy. Christie and his research team continue this tradition in the article, *Effects of environmental print on young children's print recognition.* They found obvious difference in how teachers use environmental print when they engage children and that it is useful in teaching reading. This study provides evidence for providing high quality teacher education so all teachers will be able to lead and develop literacy through play. In this study the focus is on play as a medium for developing reading skills. The linkage between play and reading, the progress desired, is used to justify play in many classrooms.

In the same vein, but in a different study, play was associated with literacy for toddlers. In her study, *Storybook time and free play: Playing with books,* Laurelle Phillips considered how children play differently after listening to different books being read aloud. Her goal in looking at children's play behaviors related to literacy was to understand how playing with books might stimulate both literacy (progress) and enjoyment. Like Christie's study, this report views literacy as the goal and play as the medium for learning.

Play, Playfulness, Progress, and Science

Literacy is not the only academic area that is frequently linked to play. Science, scientists, and play are frequently liked together. The relationship between play, science, and scientists was examined by Olga S. Jarrett and Pamela Burnley in *The role of fun, playfulness, and creativity in science: Lessons from geoscientists.* They examined the play of people who have scientific dispositions and found that most of the scientists had experienced science as play as a child in informal settings. Given the need for scientists in the world, if play increases the number of scientists, then it value.

In the same way, the disposition of playfulness can advance society if more creative thinkers can provide a greater variety of problem solving possibilities. One study of playfulness was conducted by Satomi Taylor, Cosby Rogers and their research team. In *Playfulness among Swedish and Japanese children: A comparative study,* they look at the playfulness found in children of two different cultures. They found differences between the Swedish and Japanese children at four and six years of age. Unlike what they expected, there were few gender differences in either culture.

The topic of playfulness and creativity was also considered in a study conducted by Deb Tegano and Jim Moran which looked at *Play and creativity: The role of the intersubjective adult.* Their work has powerful implications for teacher educators. Building on the concept that teachers may create the context for play but fail to provide optimal interaction, they discuss the development of the creative individual, the intersubjective adult, and their role in the development of creative thinkers.

Play, Progress, and Toys

Play as progress was considered in a different venue by Margie Mayfield. In her article, *Toy libraries, play, and play materials*, she uses an international perspective to investigate the evolution of toy libraries and their contributions to play. The aim of toy libraries is clearly to stimulate play, which is viewed as a worthwhile goal.

Play, Progress, and Animals

Play as progress is a perspective used with animals as well as humans and was reflected in the work of Peggy O'Neil Wagner in *Playful companions for motherless monkeys.* She found that ". . . for some of the monkeys, bonding took place with non-conspecifics that developed into lasting positive relationships . . . These relationships resembled children and their pets. There were initially endless bouts of chasing, wrestling and slumber parties, but as the animals matured they began longer periods of just hanging out together, as favorite companions tend to do" (p. 85). Those who worked closely with the animals saw the benefits of play among different species of animals. This approach suggests that play is beneficial for animals and their ability to develop skills to adapt to the world.

All these studies have in common a focus on play as beneficial to the organism. There is an underlying assumption that play is good and that materials, toys, play spaces, or companions that contribute to it are equally valuable. This view of play which dominated play research throughout the twentieth century appears to continue to be influential in the twenty-first century.

Play as Fate

Play as fate views play as argon or conflict, chaos or chance, and competition. This type of play was one of the earliest forms of play and is viewed positively when used as games that contribute to educational purposes or seem harmless such as BINGO. In the same vein, this view of play is negative when it is associated with compulsive gambling, card-playing, or unhealthy competition. In the article, *"Hey, no fair:" Young children's perceptions of cheating during play,* Robyn M. Holmes, Jennifer M. Valentino-McCarthy, and Susan L. Schmidt invited children to share their perceptions of cheating. They found that their views of cheating fell into categories defined previously in the literature. Their study adds to the current literature by enhancing our understanding of the views of young children on cheating. Given that lotteries, gambling, and games of chance are very much a part of the American scene, that cheating can lead to aggression and fights (Smith, 1997), and that cheating is one of the situations that often pits country against country, it is encouraging that the volume has a chapter devoted to this topic.

Play as Power

For Sutton-Smith, the rhetoric of power refers to the power of sporting events, athletes, or sporting heroes. For the sake of this analysis, power is expanded to encompass the concept of relationships. The slogan, "power of play" is used by educators, developmentalists, and psychologists to suggest that play itself has power. This view is closely related to the view of play as progress but differs in that it views the relationship involved in play. Thomas Henricks uses a sociologists lens in *The promise of sociology for play studies.* In this article, he examines the role of play using the rhetorics of play to examine the concept and then considers how sociology explains play. He moves from the past to the present and notes that "the social stands beside the personal and the cultural as fundamental contexts for the examination of expressive life" (p. 311). The use of this perspective places the social realm on equal footing with other disciplines in which play is a topic of investigation.

Issues of power are equally evident in an article in the volume by David Kuschner. His article, *Children's play in the journal, Young Children: An analysis of how it is portrayed and why it is valued,* analyzes past studies of play using historical analysis. He examined 30 years of research on play and found that the journal published articles that viewed play as positive, which is a progressive view. At the same time, he discovered a bias that reflected a white, middle-class view of play that closely links play with development.

Power issues were equally evident in a study conducted by James E. Johnson and Pei-Yu Chang. In their study, *Teachers' and parents' attitudes about play and learning in Taiwanese kindergartens,* they found that parents and teachers had different views pertaining to play benefits, and this influenced what occurred in the classroom. The use of a western-influenced view of play or a cultural specific view of play is tied directly to power issues.

To further understand the issues of power related to play, Sue Dockett and Alice Meckley listened to the voices of children. The authors believe that children's voices must be included in research that involves them. In their article, *What young children say about play at school: United States and Australian comparisons*, they noted that teachers can acknowledge and use play in planning and teaching, in classroom organization and interactions with children, all towards promoting equity and increasing teacher involvement in children's play.

Play as Identity

The rhetoric of identity often refers to activities such as festivals, plays, or celebrations that identify and/or advance the group. In this volume, Cindy Dell Clark writes about how children express their identity in *Role play on parade: Child, costume and ceremonial exchange at Halloween.* As children select their costumes, they reflect their view of others and society through their selection of character and choice of costume. Clark encourages the use of hypertext in mapping costume choices and pretend play.

Play as Imaginary

The rhetoric of play as imaginary is usually applied to pretend and imaginative play. This type of play involves abstraction and the substitution of one object or idea for another. In studying children's pretense, Doris Bergen examined language usage during pretend play in *Communicative actions and language narratives in preschoolers' play with "talking" and "non-talking" Rescue Heroes.* She found few differences in the language and pretend play that children used with talking and non-talking action figures. It appears that the child's imagination is sufficient to stimulate play and is unaffected by the communication of the intended recipient.

Play as Self

Play as self focuses on the individual's thoughts and behaviors. One study that considers the role of self was conducted by Melanie S. MacNeil. In her article, *Clinical approaches for achieving positive environments with suicidal Aboriginal adolescents: Play and culturally sensitive considerations*, she considers the impact of a playful context on encouraging more playful, less suicidal environments.

Play as Frivolity

The rhetoric of play as frivolous is typically used to describe activities that are not valuable or beneficial to society but are merely pleasurable or fun. In the past, frivolity was included with fate, power, and identity, but it stands alone in Sutton-Smith's rhetorics.

DISCUSSION AND SUMMARY

The framework created by using the rhetorics of play to examine the chapters in this volume is effective in depicting the rationale for the diversity of research questions examined by the authors. Two areas dominated the framework: play as progress and play as power. Animal scholars and developmental psychologists have long argued the value of play and set the tone for viewing play as progressive. The concept that play is powerful also resonates among play scholars. That these two areas are determinants for play studies in this book is affirming, but creates dissonance. Are we still at a point of needing to justify the study of play so that we must link it to other benefits or attach it to other behaviors that are powerful? The answer is yes. Play as a behavior has not been recognized by scholars or the community at large. In terms of scholarship value, it has not included among the chapters in either the 1998 or in the 2006 editions of the *Handbook of child psychology*. It is not included as a topic in many psychology classes, and TASP is the only group that views play as a major research topic. Not unlike the past century, play is still viewed suspiciously by the education community. Recess is on the decline, and play in kindergarten classrooms must have a learning standard to justify it. Now, more than ever, research must support and establish play as a legitimate activity for animals and humans alike. This volume contributes to this worthy goal.

REFERENCES

American Medical Association (2004). *AMA passes new policies to help fight obesity*. Press release retrieved from American Medical Association internet site at http://ama-assn.org/ama/pub/category/13932.html on June 12, 2006.

Isaacs, S. (1929). *The nursery years*. London: Routledge and Kegan Paul.

Roskos, K., & Christie, J. (2000). *Play and literacy in early childhood.* New Jersey: Lawrence Erlbaum Associates.

Pelligrini, A. D. (1995). *The future of play theory*. Albany: State University of New York Press.

Sluss, D. J. (2005). *Supporting play: Birth to age eight*. New York: Delmar.

Smith, P. (1997). Play, ethology, and education: A personal account. In A. Pelligrini's (Ed.) *The future of play theory*. Albany, NY: State University of New York Press.

Sutton-Smith, B. (1997). *The ambiguity of play.* Cambridge, MA: Harvard University Press.

Whitaker, R. C., & Orzol, S. M. (2006). Obesity among US urban preschool children. *Archives of Pediatrics & Adolescent Medicine 160* (6), 578–584.

Zigler, E. F., Singer, D. G., & Bishop-Josef, S. J. (2004). *Play: The roots of reading*. Washington, DC: Zero to Three Press.

Index

Aboriginals, 277; history of, 278; play examples, 280
Adolescents, 277–88, 312; cultural health, 280; psychological factors, 279; physical health, 280
American play movement, 7
Animal behavior studies, 53
Animal play, 73–86; monkeys and dogs, 81; monkeys and horses, 81; monkeys and sheep, 82; monkeys and cats, 83
Australia, 88

Bandura, A., 261, 273
Bateson, G., 261
Bekoff, 261, 272–73
Books, 205; book handling, 210
Bullying, 89, 108, 147

Canadian Association of Toy Libraries, 252, 253, 257
Ceremonies, 289; costumes, 292; Halloween, 289; historic and contemporary context, 291 (*see also* Halloween); trick or treat, 291
Cheating, 26, 259; and fairness, 261, 268; and moral development, 259; as power, 271; consequences of, 268; in games, 263; in school, 266; reasons for, 266; ways to, 270
Children, 61; Australian, 88–113; Brazilian, 162, 168; Japanese, 135–46, 263, 310; Korean, 62; Portuguese, 147–61; Swedish, 135; Taiwanese, 114-34, 117–18
City parks, 164-65
Culturally diverse, 55, 61–63, 250, 277
Communication, 10, 38, 52; non-verbal, 211; communication interactions, 235
Culture, 164, 168, 178
Creativity, 57, 188; developed in early years, 190
Curriculum, 57, 128, 136, 177, 224, 263

Definitions, 91, 199–200

Erikson, E., 36, 53, 135, 144, 145, 261, 274

Fantasy, 64
First Nations, 277
Friends, 14-15, 33–34, 64, 95, 111
Frost, J., 1–31, 148, 157, 308

Gender, 37, 44, 50, 63, 76, 106, 124, 138–40, 231, 244, 294; choice in role-play, 297, 301; in pretend play, 234

Halloween, 291–306; choice of costume, 293–94, 297, 300; history of Halloween, 291–92; masquerade, 297, 302; rituals, 295. *See also* ceremonies

Handbook for Public Playground Safety (CPSC), 28, 162, 167, 171
Hypertext, 302

Injuries, 19, 21, 30, 148, 149,155, 159, 160, 164, 167; animal, 80
Intersubjectivity, 175–87; awareness and reflections, 183; develops in infancy, 175; teachers, 175

Kindergarten, 93, 118

Language, 57, 103, 117, 205
Laughter, 181, 281, 236, 287
Library, 249–58
Literacy, 56, 66, 88, 105, 156, 203, 205–7, 216, 218–24, 279, 309

National Recreation and Park Association, 30
National Association of Toy and Leisure Libraries, 258
Narratives, 237–38; Egocentric, 237

Piaget, J., 36, 54, 229, 246, 275, 279
Play: adult, 179–84; environment, 64; environmental print, 222–23; evaluating, 180; fighting, 233; free play, 205; impact of testing, 26–27; materials, 249, 251, 263; outdoor, 100; rough and tumble, 78–81; sociocultural perspective, 115, 177, 206
Playfulness, 135–46, 188–204; among Japanese children, 135; among Swedish children, 135; at work, 195; country by age comparison, 143; criteria of, 180; in adults, 179; measures, 136–37; role in sociocultural investigations, 196
Play scenario, 181
Play spaces, 25; Natural, 25, 148, 310
Playground, 3–31, 147–61, 162–74; accessibility and use of, 151–57, 158; adventure playground, 15-17; early American, 3–6; developmental playground, 10–11; equipment, 17–18, 95, 165-66; professional associations, 8–10; rural, 11–14; safety, 18–19, 148–51, 162–63; recommendations for, 169–70; safety handbook for, 167; sand gardens, 6–7; standards, 19; surface of playgrounds, 157–59; types of playgrounds, 151–57
Pretend play, 114; with books, 211
Professional publications, 55

Recess, 89; in Portugal, 147–48
Rhetoric, 33, 34, 307, 311, 313; play as power, 114, 311, 313; play as identity, 312; play as imaginary, 312; play as progress, 34, 308–11
Role-playing, 53, 290, 293

Scaffolding, 176, 206, 306
School, 63, 88, 93, 259, 268, 293–95, 312
Science, 51, 58, 143, 188-204, 304, 309; political, 37, 58; role of creative thinking, 191; social, 289
Scripts, 61, 111, 117, 294
Singer, J., 114, 134, 309, 314
Sports, 100
Social attachment, 54; in monkeys, 73–74, 83
Sociological theories, 3, 32; conflict theory, 39–42; exchange, 45–49; functionalism, 39–42; symbolic interaction, 49–52
Standards for Consumer Safety Performance Specifications for Playground Equipment for Public Use (ASTM), 163
Suicide, 277
Super-hero, 56, 64–69, 93, 295, 293
Sutton-Smith, B., 34–35, 41, 54, 258, 307, 308, 311, 314
Symbolic play, 56–57, 66, 69

Teasing, 34, 289
Toy library, 249–57; first toy library, 249; established in other countries, 250; foster play, 250; materials typology of, 251; obstacles for, 254; selecting materials, 253; U.S. Toy Library Association, 251
Toys, 1, 12, 95, 102, 106, 114–20, 121, 122, 136, 143, 195, 215, 229,

250–52; Korean, 130; rescue heroes, 229; Taiwan, 133; technology-enhanced, 229, 230, 244, 245, 246; with computer chips, 230

U.S. Consumer Product Safety Commission, 149, 161

Views of play, 61, 88; by children, 88–109; by parents, 62, 88, 89; by teachers, 61, 66, 126
Vygotsky, 133, 176, 177, 185, 207

War games, 25, 59
World Health Organization, 286, 288

Contributors

(Authors are listed by alphabetical order. Professional affiliations are listed first followed by individual contact information)

DORIS BERGEN is a Professor in Educational Psychology at Miami University of Ohio where she teaches courses in play, educational psychology, assessment, and early childhood development and serves as director of the Center for Human Development, Learning, and Technology. She has written, edited, and co-edited numerous books, including *Play from birth to twelve and beyond: Contexts, perspectives, and meanings* 2nd ed., (2006), and *Play as a medium for learning and development: A handbook of theory and practice* (1987).
Address: Doris Bergen, 201 McGuffey Hall, Miami University, Oxford, OH 45013
Telephone: (513) 529-6622, Email: bergend@muohio.edu

PAMELA BURNLEY is an Associate Professor in the Department of Geosciences at Georgia State University. Her research specialization is in high-temperature and high-pressure experimental mineral physics and rock deformation. She is also interested in geoscience education, teacher education and incorporating research experiences into the undergraduate curriculum.
Address: Department of Geosciences, P.O. Box 4105, Georgia State University, Atlanta, GA, 30302-4105
Telephone: (404) 463-9551, Email: Burnley@gsu.edu

PEI-YU CHANG is an Assistant Professor of Child Development and Education at Ming-Hsin University of Science and Technology in Taiwan where she teaches courses in early childhood education and play. Her research interests are children's play, arts education, and early childhood programs.

Address: 51-3 Chia-Chin N. Rd., Chu-Bei, Hsinchu County 302, Taiwan
Telephone: (886) 355-84841, Email: pyc@must.edu.tw

JAMES CHRISTIE is a Professor of Curriculum and Instruction at Arizona State University where he teaches courses in language, literacy, and early childhood education. His publications include the co-authored books: *Play, Development, and Early Education; Building a Foundation for Preschool Literacy*; *Teaching Language and Literacy, 2nd edition*; and *Play and Literacy in Early Education*. James is a member of the Early Literacy Development Commission of the International Reading Association.
Address: P.O. Box 871411, Tempe, AZ 85287-1411
Telephone: (480) 965-2314, Email: jchristie@asu.edu

CINDY DELL CLARK is Associate Professor of Human Development and Family Studies at Penn State University and Associate and Fellow of the Rutgers (Camden) Center for Children and Childhood Studies. Her most research addresses the role of imagination in childhood and culture, including in issues of health and illness. In her most recent book, *In Sickness and in Play*, she looks at how children adapt to chronic illness. She has presented and published extensively.
Address: 25 Yearsley Mill Road, Media, PA 19063-5596, Phone: (610) 892-1265, Email: cdc9@psu.edu

SUE DOCKETT is Professor at the Murray School of Education at Charles Sturt University in Australia. She has presented papers and published extensively both in Australia and the United States. She has co-edited several books including, *Programming and Planning in Early Childhood* which is in its fourth edition and *Pedagogy and Play: Bending the Rules*, that focuses extensively on play in group settings.
Address: Murray School of Education, Charles STurt University, P. O. Box 789, Albury, NSW, 2640, AUSTRALIA, Phone: 612-16051-9043,Email: icsu.edu.au.

BILLIE ENZ is the Director of Teacher Education at University College, at Arizona State University. Dr. Enz is a member of the Early Childhood faculty and teaches language and literacy courses. She has authored numerous articles and textbooks in this area. Dr. Enz has also authored several books on new teacher development and mentor training. She is a member of the Commission of Early Childhood Literacy for the International Reading Association, and immediate past president of the Literacy Development in Young Children special interest group. Her most recent grants involve family literacies in different cultures

Address: Mary Lou Fulton College of Education, Division of Curriculum & Instruction, P.O. Box 871011-1711, Phoenix, AZ. 85287-1411, Phone: (480) 965-4284, email: billie.enz@asu.edu.

JOE FROST [Parker Centennial Professor Emeritus, Ed.D.] was a faculty member and administrator at the University of Texas at Austin for 34 years. Dr. Frost has lectured throughout Europe, Asia, and North America. He has authored, co-authored or edited eighteen books and over 100 articles and research reports. His most recent books are: *Play and Child Development*, published by Prentice Hall/Merrill in 2001 (revised 2004) and *The Developmental Benefits of Playgrounds* (2004).
Address: 5517 Courtyard Drive, Austin, Texas 78731
Telephone: (512) 346-5330, Fax: (512) 346-0207, E-mail: jfrost@mail .utexas.edu

MYAE HAN is an Assistant Professor of Individual and Family Studies at the University of Delaware, where she teaches courses in early childhood education and early literacy. Her research interests are children's play and early literacy development. She is currently working on the Delaware Early Reading First project.
Address: University of Delaware, Individual and Family Studies, 111 Alison West, Newark, DE 19716
Telephone: (302) 831-8554, Email: myaehan@udel.edu

THOMAS HENRICKS is a professor of sociology at Elon University in North Carolina. His research interests include anthropology and sociology with a focus on the organization of expressive culture in modern societies. He has published numerous articles and chapters. His most recent book, *Play Reconsidered: Sociological Perspectives on Human Expression*, was published in 2006 by the University of Illinois. He was recently named Distinguished University Professor at Elon University.
Address: 102 Greene, Elon, NC 27244, Phone: (336) 584-0682, Email: henricks@elon.edu

ROBYN M. HOLMES is Professor of Psychology at Monmouth University, West Long Branch, New Jersey. She specializes in child development with a primary interest in children's play and ethnic beliefs and qualitative methods. Current research focuses upon outdoor recess, cheating during play, video game play, and children with special needs. Teaching and research interests include interdisciplinary and cross-cultural approaches.
Address: West Long Branch, New Jersey 07764, Phone: (732) 571-3508, Email: rholmes@monmouth.edu

OLGA JARRETT is Associate Professor in Early Childhood Education at Georgia State University. She has taught courses on play, science education, child development, and research methods and authored numerous articles on recess, play, and science. She served as evaluator for NSF-sponsored Atlanta Consortium for Research in the Earth Sciences (ACRES): Research Experiences for Undergraduates and Science Teachers, 1999-2004.
Address: Department of Early Childhood Education, P.O. Box 3978, Atlanta, GA 30302-3978
Telephone: (404) 651-4509, E-mail: ojarrett@gsu.edu

JAMES JOHNSON is Professor of Early Childhood Education at Pennsylvania State University. His scholarly interests include children's play, early childhood programs, and the educational role of the family. He has authored numerous articles, chapters, and textbooks on early childhood programs including the most recent: *Play, Development, and Early Education* in 2005.
Address: 0012 Physical Plant Building, University Park, PA 16802
Telephone: (814) 865-4731 Email: jej7@psu.edu

DAVID KUSCHNER is an Associate Professor of Early Childhood Education in the College of Education, Criminal Justice, and Human Services at the University of Cincinnati. His research interests include children's play, constructivism, and the history of early childhood education. He has published numerous articles and chapters. His most recent publication is "The dangerously radical concept of free play" which appeared in Volume 11 of *Advances in Early Education and Day Care: Early Education and Care*.
Address: P.O. Box 210105, Cincinnati, OH 45221-0105
Telephone: (513) 556-0493, Email: David.Kuschner@uc.edu

HUGO LARANJERIO graduated with a degree in Sociology from the University of Minho-Portugal. He received his Master's degree in Sociology and Lifestyles at the same university. He has developed his activity mainly as a researcher in the fields of culture and leisure.
Email: hugo@iec.uminho.pt

MELANIE S. MACNEIL is an assistant professor in the Nursing Department at Brock University, Canada. She teaches classes in nursing theory and nursing leadership and is the 2005 recipient of the Faculty of Applied Health Sciences Award for Distinguished Teaching as well as the President of Sigma Theta Tau Honors Society of Nursing (Buffalo Chapter). Her research considers therapeutic approaches to health care with First Nations populations with an emphasis on the use of play and humor in creating positive environments.

Address: St, Catharine's, ON L2T2M7, Canada
Telephone: (905) 641-3660, Email: mmacneil@brocku.ca

MARGIE MAYFIELD is a Professor of Early Childhood Education and Literacy in the Faculty of Education at the University of Victoria, Canada. She has taught courses in early childhood education, language and literacy, and evaluation. Her research interests include comparative early childhood education in Europe, North America, and the Middle East (with an emphasis on Pacific Rim countries), family literacy, family support programs, and community play spaces.
Address: Victoria, BC V8W 3N4, Canada
Telephone: (240) 721-7849, Email: Mayfield@uvic.ca

ALICE MECKLEY is a Professor of Early Childhood Education at Millersville University, Millersville, Pennsylvania. She researches young children's group construction of social play and children's play knowledge. She has studied play in the United States and Australia. Her research centers on play and literacy, constructivist, and early childhood curriculum.
Address: Department of Elementary and Early Childhood Education, Stayer Building, Room 204, Millersville University, Millersville, PA 17551-0302
Telephone: 717-872-3680, Email: alice.meckley@millersville.ca

JAMES D. MORAN III is the Associate Vice Chancellor for Academic and Student Affairs with the Pennsylvania State System of Higher Education. He has over 25 years' experience in higher education as a faculty member at the University of Oklahoma and Virginia Tech, an academic department head at Oklahoma State University in Child and Family Studies and as an academic dean in Human Ecology and Assistant Vice-President of Academic Affairs for the University of Tennessee System. He has published over 65 articles published in refereed journals and was co-author of the NEA publication, *Creativity in Early Childhood Classrooms.*
Address: Pennsylvania State System of Higher Education, Office of the Chancellor, Dixon University Center, 2986 North Second Street, Harrisburg, PA 17110-1201
Telephone: (717) 720-4202, Email: jmoran@passhe.edu

PEGGY O'NEILL-WAGNER began her studies of nonhuman primates as an undergraduate and a graduate student under Dr. Harry Harlow and Stephen J. Suomi at the University of Wisconsin. After thirteen years working with monkeys in laboratory and field settings, she joined Dr. Suomi's NICHD Laboratory of Comparative Ethology staff at the NIH Animal Center in Poolesville,

Maryland in 1984. Since then, she has received numerous awards and acknowledgements for her research and dedication toward developing innovative techniques for enriching the lives of captive primates
Address: P. O. Box 334, Poolesville, MD 20837
Telephone: (301) 496-7037, Email: pow@helix.nih.gov

BEATRIZ PEREIRA is an Associate Professor with Aggregation of Early Childhood Education in the University of Minho-Portugal Institute of Child Studies, Department of Arts and Physical Education. She completed her Ph.D. in Child Studies researching bullying at school and completed her Master's degree about children's play and leisure She also holds a license in Physical Education. She has been Vice-President of the Institute of Child Studies. She has written four books about play, bullying and leisure and has chapters in several books and articles in journals and proceedings of conferences.
Address: Avenida Central no. 100, 4710-229 Braga, Portugal
Telephone: (351) 253601205, Email: beatriz@iec.uminho.pt

LAURELLE B. PHILLIPS is Associate Professor of Early Childhood Education at East Tennessee State University where she teaches courses in language, literacy, and early childhood research. Her research interests include early literacy and language development and children's play. Her article publications include: *Family Fun Day: Making a Difference;* and *Group size and storybook reading; Two year-old children's verbal and non-verbal participation with books.*
Address: ETSU Box 70548, Johnson City, TN 37614-1707
Telephone: (423) 439-7903, Email: phillipl@etsu.ed

JENNIFER PRYOR is an Assistant Professor of Early Childhood at Northern Arizona University where she teaches courses in literacy and early childhood education. Her research interests include early literacy development and parent involvement in education. Her publications include the co-authored books: Environmental Print in the Classroom: Meaningful Connections for Learning to Read; and Parent Involvement in Early Childhood Education :Research into Practice.

Address: 15980 N. Fiesta Blvd. Suite 101, Gilbert, AZ 85233, phone: 480-275-6854, email: JenniferPryor@nav.edu

COSBY STEELE ROGERS is a Professor Emerita in the Department of Human Development at Virginia Tech. Though semi-retired, she teaches a

course on college teaching and supervises doctoral students who teach undergraduate courses at Virginia Tech. She, along with her highly creative architect husband (Bob), lives in Blacksburg, Virginia, but likes to spend time in Arizona as often as possible.
Address: 1602 Shelor Lane, Blacksburg, VA 24261
Telephone: (540) 951-2657, Email: rogersco@vt.edu

SUSAN L. SCHMIDT (M.A. in Psychological Counseling, Monmouth University, 2005) is currently pursuing her licensure to become a Professional Counselor. She is a middle school guidance counselor.

DOROTHY JUSTUS SLUSS is the Associate Dean of Teacher Education and Professional Services in the School of Education at the College of William & Mary in Williamsburg, Virginia, USA. Her research interests include constructivism, early childhood education, teacher education, and play. She has publications in *Young Children, Childhood Education*, and the *Journal of Research in Childhood Education* and has recently published *Supporting Play: Birth to Age Eight.*
Address: Dr. Dorothy Sluss Box 8795, 100 Jones Hall, College of William & Mary, Williamsburg, VA 23187 Telephone: (757) 221-2319, Email: djslus @wm.edu

SATOMI IZUMI TAYLOR is a Professor in the Counseling Educational Psychology and Research Program at the University of Memphis, Tennessee. Her research interests include play, constructivism, and technology in higher education. She conducts research in Japan and America and has presented and published in a variety of venues including the American Research in Education Association.
Address: 100 Ball Hall, Memphis, TN 38152-3570
Phone: (901) 678-5363 Email: sitaylor@memphis.edu

DEBORAH W. TEGANO is an Associate Professor at the University of Tennessee in Knoxville. Her research interests include play; creativity and how adults experience, construct, and apply knowledge about the processes of critical inquiry (problem solving, cycles of inquiry, and visual literacy) and collaboration (communication and team building). She has presented and published in a variety of different venues.
Address: 420 Jessie Harris Building, 1215 W. Cumberland Avenue, Knoxville, TN 37996-1912
Telephone: (865) 974-4538, Email: dwtegano@utk.edu

JENNIFER M. VALENTINO-McCARTHY (M.A. in Psychological Counseling, Monmouth University, 2003) is an Adjunct Professor of Philosophy at the University of Phoenix and currently involved in pharmaceutical research on cardiovascular disease trials.

ANITA VAN BRACKLE earned her B.A. degrees at Radford University and her M.Ed. and Ed.D. from Virginia Tech. She now teaches at Kennesaw State University in Kennesaw, Georgia where she is a Professor in the Department of Elementary and Early Childhood Education. Her research focuses on how math concepts develop and the creation of materials to support that development. She taught for 17 years in public schools and has been working at the university level for 15 years.
Address: Elementary and Early Childhood Education, 1000 Chastain Rd., #0121 Kennesaw Hall Bldg. #1, Room 2302, Kennesaw, GA, 30144-5591

FRANCIS WARDLE has designed playgrounds for Head Start, child care programs, schools, community college child care, churches, and a crèche in Sete Lagoas, Brazil. Dr. Wardle has consulted for Head Start on playground design and safety and was a member of ASTM when the 0-2 playground guidelines were developed. He has written extensively on play and playgrounds and has published *Play, Development and Early Education* (with Johnson and Christie.)
Address: Colorado. 2300 S. Krameria St, Denver, CO 80222
Telephone: (303) 692-9008, Email: Francis@csbchome.org